THE LIFE AND WORK OF JOHN SNETZLER

The Life and Work

of

John Snetzler

Alan Barnes and Martin Renshaw

SCOLAR PRESS

Published by
SCOLAR PRESS
Gower House
Croft Road
Aldershot
Hants GU11 3HR
England

Ashgate Publishing Company
Old Post Road
Brookfield
Vermont 05036
USA

British Library cataloguing-in-publication data:

Barnes, Alan
    The Life and Work of John Snetzler
    i. Title ii. Renshaw, Martin
    786.5

ISBN 0-85967-932-2 (cloth)

Library of Congress cataloguing-in-publication data:

Barnes, Alan.
    The Life and Work of John Snetzler / Alan Barnes and Martin Renshaw
    Includes bibliographical references and index.
    1. Snetzler, John. 1710-1782. 2. Organ-builders – England-Biography.
    3. Organ – construction – England. I. Renshaw, Martin. II. Title.
    ML424.S62B3   1993
    786.5' 19'092 — dc20
    [B] 93-1812 CIP MN

Designed and computer-typeset in Century SchoolBook by Jonathan Foxwood

Printed and bound in Great Britain at The University Press, Cambridge

Contents

Illustrations

Authors' preface and acknowledgements

This book has its origin in research by Alan Barnes, mostly carried out in the later 1970s, for a dissertation for the degree of Doctor of Philosophy at Leicester University. The present book was first conceived as a 'companion' to the pioneering work by David Wickens, *The Instruments of Samuel Green*, published by Macmillan Press in 1987. Dr Barnes's text was then edited by Martin Renshaw for that publisher as one of a proposed series of volumes on the history of the organ in Britain. It has since been twice revised in order to take account of recent research and discoveries, and it has been rearranged for the present publishers.

Alan Barnes wishes to thank the many people, libraries, institutions and other organizations who were involved in his original research; although they are too numerous to mention individually, he thanks them collectively. However, there are some whom he particularly wishes to thank especially for their co-operation, their kindness and their willingness to pass on their varied and considerable knowledge and expertise: D. S. N. Arkley, Dick Barker, Dr James Boeringer, Ralph Bootman, Douglas Brown, Dr John Burgess, John Clare, the Cumbrian Archive Service, the Revd Bernard Edmonds, Randal Henley, Anna Hulbert, Hill, Norman & Beard, Ltd, John Holmes, Father Stephen Holzhauser of the Cistercian abbey of Zwettl, Ronald Jamieson, Kenneth Jones, Eddie Kaiser, Hans Lieb of Schaffhausen, G. S. Lloyd, N. P. Mander, Ltd, Dr Robert Meikle, Austin Niland, Rushworth & Dreaper, Ltd, Dr Joseph Saam, Dr Barbara Schnetzler, Marjorie Schnetzler, John Thompson, Dr Maarten Vente, Jillian White, David Wickens, Michael Wilson, Dr Andrew Wilson-Dickson, and Hans Ulrich Wipf of Schaffhausen.

The authors also wish to thank all the owners of organs named in the text who kindly gave them information about their instruments and those restorers who did the same.

Alan Barnes thanks those who helped with the production of the manuscript of the book in its various stages: Mo Brian, Pauline Fallows, Dorothy Evans and Cynthia Thompson for the many hours of patient typing from a difficult initial script, Jo Johns for reading and correcting it, and his father Sidney Barnes for providing photographs. He also thanks his family, without whose patience and understanding over many years this project would never have been brought to fruition.

Martin Renshaw wishes to express his gratitude to all those who endured further enquiries and to those who communicated new material. In particular, he thanks: David Colthup; Bernard Edmonds; Mr & Mrs Young for access to the Leffler MS; Roy Williamson, Cheltenham; Janet Halton and John McOwat of the Moravian church; Peter Horne, Nottingham; David Wickens for his patience and constant help; James Mackenzie, Michael MacDonald and Sandy Edmonstone for help with Scottish material; Martin Goetze and Dominic Gwynn, who generously shared their research findings and supplied technical drawings; Mrs G. Gimson and Peter Klein for supplying archival photographs; Michael Pendery for his drawing of the organ at Swithland; John Mander and Stephen Bicknell; Kenneth Jones, Ireland; Michael Popkin, Oxford; Richard Barnes, Halifax; Brian Robins; David Hunt and Margaret Phillips; Ingrid Grimes for her meticulous copy-editing; Nigel Farrow and Ellen Keeling of Scolar Press; and all those who are acknowledged in the notes to chapters 3 and 5.

The authors are grateful for permission to use previously published or copyright material from all those noted in the text or are acknowledged in the list of Illustrations, but especially:

Douglas Carrington, Editor of *The Organ*
Lord Lonsdale and the Lowther Family Trustees
The Controller of Her Majesty's Stationery Office and the Public Record Office
Christopher Hogwood
John Ogasapian

The authors apologise for any inadvertent omissions from these acknowledgements; any that are brought to their attention will be rectified in any later edition.

Finally, they would very much like to hear, *via* the publishers, about any material that needs to be corrected, amplified or brought up-to-date. If more Snetzler organs are 'discovered' – four, including an organ of 1742, came to light during the course of and partly as a result of writing this book – we would hope to share the good news in any further edition.

October 1993

Introduction

'He may be considered the first artist who made an organ in this country...'

The present study takes this authoritative claim[1] seriously, and attempts an assessment of John Snetzler the artist–organmaker by investigating his background, training and life, the musical use of his instruments and how they were designed and made. These are not treated as hard and fast categories, hence the title of the book: it is no more productive to try to separate 'life' and 'work' in Snetzler's case than in Handel's. Both were dedicated men who single–mindedly made their way in a culture at first alien but ultimately congenial – and one through which they both spread a wide and lasting influence.

The organ–builder Roger Yates discovered by chance in 1952[2] that Snetzler came from Schaffhausen; when Alan Barnes came to write the thesis on which this book is based, it was in that City that his researches began. Although the written documentation so far discovered is tantalisingly uneven in date and detail, this is not any great disadvantage, as the organs themselves survive as 'documents' in their own right, to be interpreted – as we attempt – in their own biographical and musical contexts.

It will become clear why Snetzler's *church* organs have been lost or radically altered; they were made for a particular musical and ecclesiastical aesthetic which has long ago been generally abandoned. We can only try to imagine what Sir John Sutton was describing when he wrote in 1847, on the very eve of their destruction:

> His instruments are remarkable for the purity of their tone, and the extreme brilliancy of their Chorus stops, which in this respect surpassed any thing that had been heard before in this country, and which have never since been equalled.

But Snetzler's *chamber* organs do remain in quantity, and they represent the full extent of his working life, from the earliest survivals of 1742 to the latest, of 1782. Of course, they have not survived without alteration, and their accurate restoration and authentic use must depend upon as complete a knowledge of his methods and cultural background as possible. This book has been written in the hope – and expectation – that the store of information about his organs, and their appreciation, may be increased, so that Snetzler's life and work may find their proper place in the history of organ–building in Britain.

---

[1] from an MS. probably compiled by William Russell, transcribed *c*1840

[2] TO 134/103

Introductory notes

Pitch notation The system in the diagram uses Helmholtz's, modified somewhat; older styles of notation that occur in (for instance) Leffler and Buckingham are also shown. The Helmholtz system reckons octaves to run from C to B, and this is the standard usage in the abbreviated stop-lists; it should be remembered, though, that older British notations generally assume octaves to run from G to F♯.

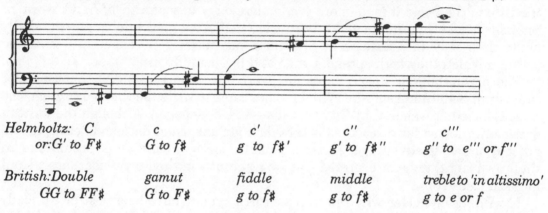

Helmholtz: C	c	c'	c''	c'''
or:G' to F♯	G to f♯	g to f♯'	g' to f♯''	g'' to e''' or f'''

British:Double	gamut	fiddle	middle	treble to 'in altissimo'
GG to FF♯	G to F♯	g to f♯	g to f♯	g to e or f

Italic type This is used to indicate specific pitches according to the Helmholtz notation; note-names are given in roman capitals. Thus, an individual pipe may be referred to by its actual pitch in italics or by a length and the note of the scale it sounds (for example, 5⅓' G) irrespective of the name or the pitch of the key that controls it.

Compass Indications of the compass are noted in actual pitches, for example: *G'–e'''*. This would represent the range covered by the keyboard, soundboard and pipework of either the whole instrument of a one-manual organ or a specified department in a larger organ. The compasses of keyboards on the usual 'long'- or 'short'-octave system which omit some low notes are indicated by specifying the notes between which others are omitted: so that *G', A', C, D–e'''* implies the omission in the 'short-octave' system of the lowest G♯, A♯ and C♯.

A short-compass keyboard (usually the Swell) is specified by its actual compass without special notice, but a short-compass rank within a division is noted using the abbreviation 'sc:' followed by the pitch of the lowest-sounding note in that rank. Where a stop can be drawn in two parts, bass and treble (in Snetzler's mature instruments this usually divides between tenor B and middle C), it is noted as 'b/tr', as in 'Ses[quialtera] b/Cor[net] tr'. [N.B., sc. = *scilicet*]

Documentary sources The most–commonly cited sources are generally referred to by abbreviations thus:

L   Manuscript collection of stop–lists collected by Henry Leffler *c*1800–1819, now in private hands in Norfolk. This collection was extensively transcribed, edited and amplified by Charles Pearce in two books: *Notes on English Organs of the Period 1800–1810* (Vincent Music Publishing, London, 1911) and *Notes on Old London City Churches* (Vincent Music Publishing, London, 1911), but the numbered references in this book are to the pages of the original manuscript.

B   Manuscript notes made by Alexander Buckingham *c*1823–1844; these were edited and extensively transcribed by Leslie Barnard in *The Organ*, issues nos. 205–213 (vol. lii–liv, 1972–4). In order to avoid any errors in transcription from Leslie Barnard's apparently generally very accurate account, the majority of extracts are taken directly from *The Organ*'s letter–press. The articles are referred by the issue and page numbers of *The Organ* thus: xxx/xxx.

S   Manuscript collection of organ stop–lists and notes on heraldry compiled by John Hanson Sperling *c*1850—54; now in the British Library Department of Manuscripts (Loan 79.9). The individual organs are referred to their volume number and page thus: x/xxx.

HR   Edward Hopkins and Edward Rimbault, *The Organ: Its History and Construction* (Cocks, London, 3rd edn 1877, reprinted 1972 by Frits Knuf in Bibliotheca Organologica, no. 4). It is in two separately paginated sections:
          1 (Rimbault:) *New History of the Organ*, and
          2 (Hopkins:) *A Comprehensive Treatise on the Structure and Capabilities of the Organ*.
It is referred to by section and page thus: HR X/xxx.

F   Andrew Freeman's articles: 'John Snetzler and his Organs' in *The Organ*, nos. 53–55 (vol. xiv, 1934–35). The reference is to his numbering of Snetzler's organs in these articles.

W   Michael Wilson, in *The English Chamber Organ* (Cassirer, 1968), described then known Snetzler chamber organs. Reference to his work is by the page number and his numbering of the organs thus: xxx (xx).

In addition, three periodicals are cited frequently, and are abbreviated thus:

TO   *The Organ*, a journal published quarterly from July 1921 to the present; it is cited simply by its issue and page numbers thus: xxx/xxx

BIOSJ   The annual journal of the British Institute of Organ Studies, first published in 1977; it is cited by volume and page numbers thus: xx/xxx

BIOSR   The quarterly *Reporter* published by the British Institute of Organ Studies is cited by volume, number, date and page of issue.

Stop–list abbreviations Only those stops used by Snetzler and his contemporaries are included in this list, together with division names and compass indications. All other stop–names are given in full, as are generic stop–names, such as 'chimney flute' and 'mixture'.

b	bass compass
b/tr	divided–compass stop (bass/treble)
Bdn	'Borduun' (as at King's Lynn, not the later Pedal stop)
Bn	Bassoon
Ch	Choir Organ
Cln	Clarion
Cor	Cornet(t)
Crm	Cremona
Dul	Dulciana
DulPr	Dulciana Principal (also called Celestina)
15	Fifteenth
Fl	Flut(e)
FH	French Horn
Fnt	Furniture or Forniture
GerFl	German Flute
Gt	Great Organ or Full Organ
Hb	Hautboy or Hautbois
m	metal pipework
OD	Open Diapason
Pr	Principal(l)
Sal	Salicional
sc: *x*	short compass: *x* upwards
Ses	Sesquialt[e]ra
SD	Stop[ped] Diapason
Sw	Swell
17	Tierce
tr	treble compass
Tpt	Trumpet(t)
12	Twelfth
VG	Viola di Gamba
VH	Vox Humana or Vox Humane
w	wooden pipework
w/m	wooden bass/metal treble

No apology is made for the use of imperial measurements, feet (') and inches ("), in this book. These British units have not changed since Snetzler's time, and his designs so clearly use them that little can be gained from the anachronistic metric system – even in the calculation of pipe-scaling which, as we explain, was and can still be carried out using simple linear graphs. Anyway, it has reasonably been said that 'the inch is the only true organological unit' – it was also, incidentally, the unit used in the new computer 'program' which type-set this book. Those needing to convert imperial measures to metric could conveniently use a dual-system measuring tape, or should know that 1" = 25·399 mm. and 1' = 304·79 mm.

or (gold) gules (red)

The coat of arms of the Schnetzler family

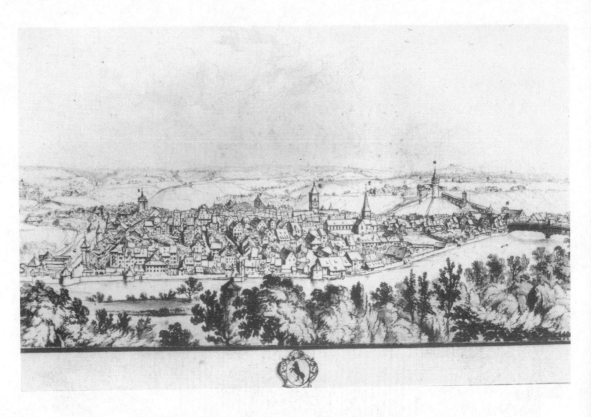

The City of Schaffhausen in the eighteenth century

The place of Snetzler's birth (on the extreme left) is marked with an 'S'

1 His life

DOWNSTREAM of the falls of the Rhine at Schaffhausen, enchantingly described in *Modern Painters* by John Ruskin,[1] the City mills took full advantage of the still-rapid water. In 1710, the tenant ('der Obermüller') of the chief of these on the north bank was Heinrich Schnetzler, and he had followed his father Isaac in that trade. In that year his fifth son was born, and his latinized Christian name was entered on the family's page in the Genealogical Register of the City of Schaffhausen: 'Die Schnetzler: ... Johannes. 1710. 6 Apr. + 1785. 28 Sept.' Another hand has added at the side of this: 'Orgelmacher – 1756 in London'.

The first date given is not Johann Schnetzler's actual date of birth since an entry in the Schaffhausen Baptism Book (now in the Civil Registry Office) shows that the child was in fact baptized on Sunday 6 April 1710, and that the witnesses to the ceremony were Hans Jakob Murbach and Cleophe Stokarin. It is likely that in accordance with Protestant custom, the Schnetzler family would have brought the boy for baptism a few days after his birth.

Johann was born into a typically large petit-bourgeois family which included nine surviving children:

> Margaretha (1693–1766), who married Bernhardin Habicht, a miller, in 1723;
> Isaac (1696–1768), a miller;
> Barbara (1697–?);
> Hans Jakob (1698–?), a saddler who died in Holland;
> Catharina (1700–?);
> Ursula (1701–42), who married Hans Georg Rauschenbach, a baker;
> Hans Heinrich (1703–53), a goldsmith;
> Johann Ulrich (1704–52), a stucco artist and painter;
> Johann (1710–85), the subject of this biography;
> Leonhard (who died a few months after his birth in 1711);
> Leonhard (1714–72), designer and carver of ornaments.

Three of these siblings were to figure particularly in Johann's life. The first was his sister Barbara, who married Benedikt Fischer, a cooper; their youngest son (also named Benedikt) was Schnetzler's chosen heir. He was presumably also his godson, since Johann was present at his christening in 1737. He became a leading official in the City, where he had oversight of all building work, and became an alderman in 1792. Johann's other named heir was 'John Henry' Schnetzler, the son of his older brother, Isaac. (See Appendix 8 for the full text of the Will.) But by far the most important to him was his younger brother, Leonard, who also came to England (he settled in Oxford before 1752), where he designed and carved Snetzler's organ cases and extensively worked for 'the Nobility'.

His older brother, the painter Johann Ulrich, is the only member of the family of whom we have a likeness. How much the brothers physically resembled each other is, naturally, a matter beyond conjecture, but his evident lively and open personality may perhaps be taken as representative of the four youngest 'artistic' brothers.

In common with many other places following the disturbances of the previous century, Schaffhausen – the capital city and the canton of the same name – exported the talent it could not employ. In the Schnetzler family only the eldest son could take over the mill. The other five brothers were not the only citizens to emigrate; others made their mark elsewhere at this time, and they included:

Johann Ulrich Schnetzler

Lorenz Spengler (1720–1807), turner and ivory worker at the Royal Court in Copenhagen, 1782–6;

Johann Jakob Schalch (1723–89), landscape artist in Germany, France, Holland and England (a pupil of Johann Ulrich Schnetzler);

Johann Adam Spengler (1736–90 or –91), a porcelain worker at Hoechst in Germany, and Schoren near Zürich (his son was a modeleur at Derby, England);

Johann Heinrich Hurter (1734–99), a miniaturist at Versailles, and in England and at Düsseldorf;

Johann Jakob Maurer (1737–80), a stucco worker, painter and designer at Amsterdam and Utrecht.

At the age of nineteen, Johann was initiated into his father's Bakers' Guild, when on 29 January 1730, he became a 'Zunftpleger', an approved member and minor functionary, together with eight other young persons. His membership was recorded again on 15 April 1731, with effect until 4 May 1732; this, and the initiation, would presumably be more a 'rite of passage' than a serious commitment to baking.

If by this time Johann had any experience of organ–building (and he could have been apprenticed from the age of twelve), he would most likely have obtained it with or from his cousin Johann Konrad Speisegger (1699–1781). Friedrich Jakob noted that Speisegger took someone from Schaffhausen to help him with work in Zürich; it is possible that this was Johann. If so, he would have worked on the quite substantial and highly ornamented chamber organ built by Speisegger in the Landgut 'Der Schipf ' in Herrliberg near Zürich from 1730 to 1732.[2] There is also a chamber organ in the Allerheiligen Museum (near Schaffhausen's upper mill) made by Speisegger in 1739; it has a number of features in common with Johann's typical chamber organs. If Johann was indeed associated with Speisegger, his apprenticeship could have gone unrecorded; it would have been a 'family' matter, and the usual legal arrangements would not have been needed.

Asides by Burney suggested to later writers[3] that Schnetzler was born in Passau about 1710. Neither Freeman[4] nor Sumner[5] could find any evidence for this, but both seem prepared to accept that he worked on the organs in the cathedral there while it was being built by Johann Ignaz Egedacher of Passau from 1731 to 1733. Burney[6] even goes so far as to say that Schnetzler made some of the front pipes of the large west–end organ, and the Vox Humana and Octave Dulciana in the small organ. He also implied in a letter of 1803[7] that Schnetzler knew of the organs in Vienna, and had worked on the organ at Haarlem (made by Christian Müller from 1735 to 1738) before coming to London; for this last assertion no evidence can now be found.

If Burney's suggestion that Schnetzler worked in Passau[8] was correct, such a move might have been possible after 1730 or 1731 (the Bakers' Guild dates given above), by which time an apprenticeship with Speisegger might have been completed. However, Dr J. Saam[9] has suggested that Schnetzler was apprenticed to Egedacher, of 7 Milchgasse, Passau, from 1732 until 1735 – and further, that he had as fellow apprentices Egedacher's nephew, Rochus, and the sons of Andreas Silbermann. It has not proved possible to verify this suggestion, since the Passau archives contain records of only the master organ–builders of that city, and not their apprentices or journeymen. The library of the Cistercian abbey of Zwettl, eighty kilometres north of Vienna, contains well–preserved records of Egedacher's work there (he built an organ in the church, 1728–31), but a thorough examination of these[10] revealed no evidence of any workmen beyond two named assistants, and no mention of Schnetzler. Neither has there proved to be any written evidence in Vienna that Schnetzler worked with or was apprenticed to Egedacher.

One might have allowed some general credence to Burney's suggestion were it not for a description made in 1838 by Alexander Buckingham of a claviorgan:

> Mifs Tate, Moresby Hall, two miles from Whitehaven, Cumberland – An Organ by Snetzler in 1731 under an Harpsichord by Shudi ... The St. Diapason and Flute is voised with the block sunk instead of the Cap. Inside the Sd Bd is Johanes Schnetzler Organo technus Londini 1731. Whitehaven, 1838. A.B.

This entry from Alexander Buckingham's private notebook was transcribed by Leslie Barnard.[11] The repetition of the date would imply that Buckingham, who was well acquainted with Snetzler's work, was certain that this is what he saw and he (therefore) made no special comment about it. The reported spelling 'Johanes' on Schnetzler's label is similar to the spelling 'Johannes' on the label in the earliest extant organ of 1742 (chapter 3, no. 2), and the description of the way in which the oak pipework is voiced recalls so–called 'German' bevelled blocks and uncut caps, in contrast to the normal eighteenth–century English use of level blocks with chiselled–out caps set a little lower than the blocks. However, there are instances of 'level' pine blocks sometimes being sunk behind their oak facing in order to gain extra capacity in the pipe, and therefore a lower pitch, where height is limited – as in an organ under a harpsichord, so perhaps not too much should be inferred from this detail.

The much more important point is the date, eleven years earlier than any extant organ. This goes against other evidence: first, Schnetzler was apparently in Schaffhausen six years later at his nephew Benedikt Fischer's baptism. Second, his habitual labelling style was *J– S– fecit Londini 17—*, and, third, what does the term 'organo technus', not used in any other organ, imply? There is the possibility that Buckingham misread an actual date of 1737, but even this is five years earlier than any record we otherwise have of Schnetzler's being in London. Unfortunately, all efforts to trace this instrument, vital to the dating of Schnetzler's arrival in London, have so far come to nothing.

There is in fact evidence that Schnetzler was in London for some years before the date (1742) of his earliest-surviving organs. In a letter of July 1743, Lorenz Spengler wrote from London to his family in Schaffhausen to tell them of his compatriots' activities. He included a reference to Schnetzler:

> Mr. Schnetzler the organ maker is not in town, but three English miles from here to take fresh air. He has been sick since Martinsday [i.e., 11 November 1742] and cannot work; since he is so much pressed with work, he does not know how to console his people [clients] ...

The implication of this is that Schnetzler had already obtained some reputation, if not yet a substantial business.

The immediate reasons for his over-work and illness may not be far to seek. The winter of 1740 was long-after remembered for its fierce severity, and storms that year and in 1742 throughout England and over the surrounding seas were among the most destructive recorded (though not as bad as the 'Great Storm' of 1703 chronicled by Defoe) – and they were much more widespread than the 'hurricane' of October 1987. Many lives were lost at sea, and great damage was done to buildings throughout the country, including the destruction of the spire and nave of St Margaret's church, King's Lynn. In London, there was damage to the trees in Hyde Park and to Westminster Abbey and other major buildings. It is quite possible therefore that a sudden demand for the repair of organs was created in circumstances somewhat similar to those following the Great Fire in 1666, and that some of the organs with 'early' dates credited by some nineteenth-century writers to 'Snetzler' (as those in St John's, Smith Square, Westminster, or even perhaps Leominster Priory) were in fact merely repaired by him. The key question, which cannot yet be answered with certainty, is whether Schnetzler came to London because of these circumstances, or was already well-established there as a 'technician'. There are, however, substantial reasons to suppose that the latter was the case.

*

Schnetzler's arrival in London

There were good reasons for a young and industrious Swiss man to make his way to London. It was an extremely active mercantile city, supporting and supported by a rapidly rising national population totalling about 6 million in 1750,[12] which attracted artists and artisans from many countries. Many of these came from Switzerland, from the time of Hans Holbein onwards; not only painters, but also writers, philosophers and musicians. Georg Michael Möser (1706–83) became the first keeper of the Royal Academy of Arts, and after Moser's death, Agostino Carlini of Geneva became Keeper until 1790. The fourth Keeper was Johann Heinrich Füssli (1741–1825); better known here as 'wild' Henry Fuseli, he illustrated the works of Shakespeare and Milton, notoriously drew the female nude, and was a friend of William Blake.

Alexander Trippel

Alexander Trippel (1744–93), who became famous as a sculptor in Rome, came twice to London – in 1754–5 and in 1771–2. A 'distant relative' had invited him, saying that there was a good chance of a good income. This relative may even have been Johann Schnetzler, for in a biography of Johann Ulrich Schnetzler[13] it is said that Trippel began to 'learn the trade of instrument maker with his uncle in London'. He was in fact Schnetzler's great-nephew (the son of Johann's niece), and would have been only ten on his first visit; its brevity suggests that organ-building did not interest him. However, other members of the immigrant community would invariably send back good reports of London's prosperity and culture, and these drew more of their countrymen to see for themselves what London had to offer.

It may reasonably be supposed that Johann and his younger brother Leonard were attracted in this way. It would have been natural for both to have had their early training in Switzerland and then to have joined their compatriots in London as journeymen before setting up their own businesses. Johann could have been particularly attracted by the success of Burkat Tschudi, the harpsichord maker (born in Schwanden, Glarus, in 1702) who had gone to London in 1718 as a joiner and was in business from about 1729 onwards. They were well-acquainted: Snetzler became an executor of his Will, according to a Deed of September 1773. It is also clear that Leonard found his own place in addition to working for his brother, and was apparently well-known as a carver and gilder.[14] His obituary notice in *Jackson's Oxford Journal*, 11 April 1772, ran as follows:

On Wednesday last died, at his Houfe in Gloucester Green, in the Environs of the City, aged near Sixty, Mr. Leonard Snetzler, Defigner and Carver of Ornaments, who had made Oxford his Place of Residence for upwards of Twenty Years – Many Specimens of the Artift's Abilities are to be feen in the Seats of our Nobility in various Parts of England, where he had been employed by the late and prefent Mr. Roberts of this Place.

The situation into which Johann came, as regards organ-making in Britain, was described by Hawkins in 1776,[15] in a passage which follows his history of Harris, Smith and Smith's son-in-law, Christopher Schr(e)ider, in these terms:

Smith's nephews, Gerard and Bernard [here 'Christian' was substituted by Horace Walpole in his copy], worked chiefly in the country, as did one Swarbrick, bred under the elder [i.e., Renatus] Harris, and one Turner of Cambridge; their employment was more in the repairing of old than the building of new organs. About the year 1700, one Jordan, a distiller, who had never been instructed in the business, but had [a] mechanical turn, and was an ingenious man, betook himself to the making of organs, and succeeded beyond expectation. He had a son named Abraham, whom he instructed in the same business; he made the organ for the chapel of the Duke of Chandois at Cannons near Edgware, and many organs for parish churches. Byfield [the 'first'?] and Bridge were two excellent workmen; the former made the [first] organ for Greenwich hospital [*sic* – actually it was made by Abraham Jordan – see p. 11], and the latter that noble instrument in the church of Spitalfields, for which he had only 600l. These are now all dead. In the latter part of their lives, to prevent their underworking each other, there was a coalition between them; so that whoever was the nominal artificer of any instrument, the profits accruing from the making of it were divided among them all.

This account sums up the situation neatly and reasonably accurately, as far as we can tell. Curiously, the only organs that seem likely to have been made by the 'coalition' were those for the two churches of Great Yarmouth, made 1732-4, in the years following the Bridge organ at Christ Church, Spitalfields. For these they received a total of £1400, and perhaps recouped some of the loss made at Spitalfields. It must, however, be stressed that Hawkins does not talk of joint contracts, and his words should not be taken to mean any more than they actually say. Rimbault's comment[16] that the increase in the number of churches built at the beginning of the eighteenth century caused an alarming increase in unskilled organ-builders is not justified by the facts; it seems merely to be his attempt to explain the 'coalition'. But these churches (the churches of the 'Queen Anne's Bounty' from *c*1712 onwards, which provided for the expanding population of London) could have been a factor in suggesting to Schnetzler that London was a place of opportunity.

Whatever the reasons, and whatever the precise date of Schnetzler's arrival in London, he would have readily found a place in the Swiss-German community. If the mid-1730s indeed found him already there, it could hardly have been a more fortuitous time: the Italian opera was on the wane, and – a matter of significance for organs and organ music in Britain for the next hundred years – from March 1735 onwards, Handel introduced organ concertos into his oratorios. He wrote three more in 1736, and John Walsh began to publish them in September 1738 as Handel's opus 4. The organ concerto was thus established as a musical form in its own right in London before anywhere else, and demanded an appropriate instrument.

There is no evidence to suggest that Schnetzler provided Handel with his organs during his earliest years in London (not even for *Messiah* in 1741 or 1742 – see pp. 8–9). Rather, as an immigrant workman, he would more naturally have gravitated towards other immigrant workshops, and perhaps worked as a general instrument maker for Burkat Tschudi or even for Tschudi's master, Hermann Tabel, who was in business until 1738. It is possible that he styled himself 'organo technus' in the 'Schudi' claviorgan for Moresby Hall to imply that, while still in another's 'employ', he was the specialist – the 'technician' – responsible for the organ part. He may also have made other small organs, such as the organ parts of 'organ clocks'. In the established working conditions of the time, it is anachronistic to understand 'employment' in a modern sense outside the strict terms of a 'bound' (and unpaid) apprenticeship. Artisans worked by bartering their time for each other, and only some of these 'rose' to become independent contractors 'employing' others, as needed, by the day (hence the term 'journeymen').

The fact that most of Schnetzler's oldest surviving organs are parts of claviorgans, or small portable organs and small church organs, suggests that he particularly developed his skills in making these types of instruments both before and at the start of his independent career. A letter written in 1762 by Richard Grubb (transcribed in Appendix 4) certainly implies this:

> no one builder at this time gives a finer Tone than Mr. Snetzler, he having
> also much practiced of late in Church as well as small Organs & is allowed
> to be greatly improved and to excell in his way ... I find he now stands as
> high in reputation as any of the Business.

The compasses of his earliest–surviving instruments also seem to be influenced by the harpsichord. An upper termination at f''' in a small organ (whether for house or chapel) was most unusual at the time, but quite common (indeed normal) in harpsichords made by 'foreign' craftsmen. Tabel used this compass from at least 1721 onwards, and the Moresby Hall harpsichord by Schudi of 1731 (or 1737?) apparently likewise; whereas the English harpsichord makers do not appear to have done so until somewhat later (e.g., Hancock, in 1720, has a keyboard to e''', but Crang to f''' not until 1745).

The few instruments that survive cannot be a complete reflection of Schnetzler's collaborative work. We know of the 'Shudi/Schnetzler' claviorgan only through Buckingham's account of it, but Shudi's workshop books mention quite a number of them,[17] and Burney was reported by Rimbault[18] also to have mentioned some examples. Schnetzler was also well-acquainted with the Kirkmans since two of them were granted denization in 1770 on the same warrant as his (see Appendix

6). The 1745 Wemyss claviorgan by 'Jacobus Kirckman' and 'Johan Snetzler' survives (see chapter 3, no. 6); this cannot have been the only example of their joint work.

Organs that are carried around have a limited life: they might be roughly carted in wagons or portered through rubbish-strewn streets, and they were in danger of damage and fire in candle-lit theatres. Nonetheless, it may be significant that the two earliest-dated surviving organs are small, semi-portable instruments, one of which has been consistently linked with an oratorio by Handel – in fact, not 'an oratorio', but '*The* Oratorio'. (For a discussion of the history of this 1742 organ, see chapter 3, no. 4.)

Although there are no documents that link Handel directly with Schnetzler, there would not need to have been any. They lived near to each other for the greater part of their working lives and were both part of the same wave of German-speaking immigration. So did Handel take two organs by Schnetzler with him to Ireland for the series of concerts which included the first performance of *Messiah* on 13 April 1742, as nineteenth-century 'tradition' supposed? Could a visit at this time by Schnetzler himself have been the primary reason for the large number of organs which he made for Irish clients throughout his career, and have been the cause of his illness towards the end of that year? We simply do not know, and against any such speculation must be set various facts. First, that any organs which went to Ireland would have been dated 1741 during their construction, since Handel left London in November 1741 and was playing organ concertos in Dublin before Christmas. Second, Handel reported to Jennens in a letter dated 29 December 1741, among many other things that 'I exert my self on my Organ whit more then usual success'. Handel is known to have ordered organs for himself from Jordan in 1745 and for the Foundling Hospital from or through an apothecary, Dr Justinian Morse of Chipping Barnet, but not from Schnetzler. Third, the proprietors of the 'New Musick-Hall' in Fishamble Street themselves bought an organ from [John] Harris and Byfield of London, and this was installed during the month following Handel's final departure from Ireland in August 1742. Finally, the organ 'specified' by Handel in a letter to Jennens, now in Great Packington church, was built entirely by an English maker, and not by Snetzler (see chapter 5, no. 47).

Unless one makes the unlikely speculation that the two surviving organs of 1742 were taken to Ireland and subsequently altered (both were indeed modified at an early date or during their finishing in the workshop) and then dated at the time of their alteration, then there remains no real case for the old 'pious' supposition of such a direct connection between Schnetzler and *Messiah*. Indeed, the only linkage between the two personalities (and one that is in the mind of an author rather than necessarily in reality) is to be found in *Memoirs of the Life of the late George Frederic Handel* by John Mainwaring, published in 1760. In the course of a discussion of Handel's physical constitution and his love of 'an uncommon portion of food and nourishment' on page 140, Mainwaring comments that 'It would be as unreasonable to confine Handel to the fare and allowance of common men, as to expect that a London merchant should live like a Swiss mechanic'.

'The Charming Brute' – a caricature by Joseph Goupy, 21 March 1754.
Around Handel is his 'nourishment', including a wine barrel,
a goose, oysters, bottles (of porter?) and a 'bill of fare'.

In fact, for the next few years, Schnetzler was to find quite other Germanic clients: the Moravian church.

The Moravians

It would seem that Schnetzler made at least four, and possibly as many as six, organs for Moravian communities: (i/ii) in 1743 and again before or during 1747 for the Fetter Lane chapel, as noted in the Fulneck letters (see chapter 3, no. 5, and Appendix 3); (iii) in 1748 for the Fulneck chapel (chapter 3, no. 9, and Appendix 3); (iv) a bureau organ in 1751 for the Fulneck schoolroom (chapter 3, no. 13); (v) an organ (at present undated) for the 'Unitas Fratrum' at Wyke, near Bradford (chapter 3, no. 113), and possibly (vi) an organ for the Moravian chapel in Bath (chapter 5, no. 25).

These communities were being established in various parts of the country following the re-establishment of the church in 1722 on the estate of Count von Zinzendorf at Herrnhut in Saxony after long disruption by persecution. Their missionary work in the American colonies attracted the attention of John Wesley, who associated himself for a while with the London 'Fetter Lane Society' which had been established by Peter Boehler in 1738. The Moravian Church, which was a continuation of the Bohemian Brethren founded in 1457, regarded itself as an 'ecclesiola' of the Lutheran Church. It stood for a simple and unworldly form of communitarian Christianity characterized by self-improvement and dignified worship – and it was often contrasted with the later more 'enthusiastic' Methodist activities. No doubt this was because, as E. P. Thompson remarked,[19] the Moravians 'never became fully naturalized in England in the eighteenth century ... the societies remained dependent upon German preachers and administrators'.

It would be logical for Schnetzler to gravitate towards this Germanic church, since (like Handel) he pursued as far as he could an independent path. He seems never to have fully become an 'Establishment' figure, but more naturally made connections with Unitarians (for instance, with the Strutt family of Derbyshire) and with the Calvinists (almost certainly the dominant religious influence in Schaffhausen) and other forms of dissent, including freemasonry. It may well be that from his arrival in London he had been a member of the Calvinist church in the Savoy to which he gave an organ. As this church met in river-front rooms of the partly demolished Savoy Palace (originally built as a castle in the thirteenth century), alongside churches for Dutch, High German (Moravian) and Lutheran immigrants as well as those for other dissenters and Quakers, such connections would not be difficult to cultivate; they are implicit and explicit in the Fulneck letters.

Dr John Speller[20] has pointed out the predilection for 'sweet' and quiet tone colours in Moravian organs; again, therefore, Schnetzler's mid-south continental cultural background and his experience with small-scale work would have been suitable and congenial to Moravian musicians in a way that the bolder work of the contemporary native builders was not. The establishment of Moravian communities in Yorkshire and Lancashire and in the West Country, and the long-standing strength of the Calvinists in the northern counties and the Unitarians in the midland manufacturing cities, helps to explain the geographical distribution of his instruments.

'John Snetzler': building a business in London

It would seem that after about 1748 to 1750, 'Snetzler' (as he thenceforth usually styled himself) was able to plan a regular flow of work. Even so, when he was finally 'successful' (when he made the organ for King's Lynn, 1753–4), Snetzler was already more than middle-aged according to the life-expectancy of the time. He had by then been in London for at least seventeen years or possibly for as long as twenty-three years, depending on one's interpretation of the reported Moresby

Hall date. As he had probably been working independently for at least thirteen years, this turning-point had not been reached quickly.

Panoramic views of London published by the Buck brothers in 1749 (some of which decorate the title pages of this book) show an expanding but still quite compact city. Its most westerly buildings were on the Millbank; the thirty-year old St John's, Smith Square, was their parish church. The second crossing of the Thames (Westminster Bridge, designed by Charles Labelye, a Swiss engineer) was about to be completed after twelve years' work. There were practically no buildings of consequence on the opposite bank of the Thames except for those in Southwark, next to the southern end of the old London Bridge. There were still houses and shops on the bridge, but these were soon to be demolished. Ships were unloaded in front of the Custom House near the Tower; when the goods were cleared, smaller boats took them to the multitudinous wharfs and jetties all along the Thames. The river was crowded with boats, ferries and craft of all kinds when this traffic was not interrupted by severe frosts and frost-fairs, one of the most elaborate of which was held on the Thames in the cold winter of 1739–40.

The population of London was increasing very quickly; during the eighteenth century it doubled in size from a base of about half a million people, living in mainly medieval timber-framed houses, to a million who lived in new buildings of brick and stone. It has been calculated[21] that there were about 100,000 journeymen and artisans of all kinds in London by the early years of the nineteenth century. These were not rough tradesmen of the village kind, but skilled workmen: jewellers, cabinet-makers, printers, clockmakers – each with systems of apprenticeships, internal customs and gradations, by which men could rise to be élite master-artisans who considered themselves to be the social equals of other 'professionals'.

This large pool of labour and skill could be drawn upon by anyone fortunate or thrifty enough to be able to put up the money to rent workshops and men. As organs were not paid for in instalments but in lump sums, generally after completion (credit, often lengthy, was expected and given in all aspects of 'trade'), the accumulation of the necessary capital would be a prolonged task. It seems that it took Snetzler at least ten years to achieve it; his initial difficulties are summed up in telling phrases in his letters to Fulneck (see chapter 3, no. 9) about his needing to fund the construction of an organ from the proceeds of one just completed. However, Handel's career pointed the way: he made and lost more than one 'fortune', but he died free of debt and full of esteem.

A glimpse of the way in which an order for an organ might have been obtained at this time has been afforded through the researches of Lady Susi Jeans.[22] The General Court, and later the Directors, of the Greenwich Hospital asked for proposals for a new organ from three builders. Their minutes record that on 7 December 1748:

> Mr Abram. Jordan, Mr. John Schnetzler [*sic*] and Mr. Thos. Griffin deliver'd in Proposals for making an Organ for the New Chapel; The Board took the same into Consideration and there appearing to be but a Trifling Difference with regard to the Price; The Directors thought it most proper

& safe to agree with Mr. Jordan on the foot of his Proposal, Vizt. 400 Guineas with a Mahogany Case, or 300 Guineas without the Case, he being a Person of Known Experience and Reputation in his Profession; & ordered that the Secretary do acquaint him therewith.

Abraham Jordan's organ was not completed, tested and paid for until 12 June 1751, after many delays – though the organist had been appointed over a year before. It was destroyed in the fire of 2 January 1779 and replaced in 1789 by the present Samuel Green instrument.

Snetzler's appearance among these other builders does not imply that he had already any great reputation; the Board may have advertised for tenders. The implication that Jordan was the maker with the greatest 'Reputation' is a perfectly reasonable one in the circumstances, although he was perhaps in ill–health himself at this time. He eventually resigned from the care of the organ because of a 'Parlytick Disorder', according to the Directors' minutes of a meeting on 15 May 1754 attended by his foreman, John Sedgwick.

Charles Burney and King's Lynn

It was the organ made for the partly–rebuilt parish church of King's Lynn that finally took Snetzler from being the maker of 'small Organs' to the fully established and reputable maker of large church instruments. The building of the organ seems largely to have come about by means of the formidable personality of Charles Burney. He was born in Shrewsbury in 1726 and educated there and in Chester, and was taken in 1744 to London by Dr Arne as an articled pupil. There he was introduced to an extensive circle of musical acquaintances which evidently included Handel and Snetzler. He was appointed organist at the church of St Dionis Backchurch (City of London) in October 1749, but overwork and fear of ill–health led him to accept the post of organist at Lynn in early 1752.

He related the story of how he was able to obtain a new organ in his *General History*:[23]

> Harris's organ, after its rejection at the Temple, was part of it erected at St. Andrew's, Holborn, and part of it in the cathedral of Christ-church, Dublin; but about thirty years ago, Byfield having been sent for to repair the latter, he prevailed on the chapter to have a new instrument, taking the old organ in exchange, as part of payment. Soon after, having had an application from the corporation of Lynn Regis, in Norfolk, to build them a new organ for St. Margaret's church, he wished very much to persuade them to purchase the instrument made by Harris, which had been a second time excommunicated; but being already in possession of an old organ, they determined to have a new one; and, by the author of this book, employed Snetzler to construct one, which he did very much to his own credit and their satisfaction.

He adds, in another footnote:[24]

Snetzler, by the instrument he made for Lynn Regis, gave such a specimen of his abilities that he was soon called to almost every quarter of the kingdom.

It was no small achievement for both Burney and Snetzler to have had built a new organ of their design in the face of Byfield's reputation and the fame of the Harris organ (despite its losing the Temple 'battle'), and when Burney was relatively young and the middle-aged Snetzler's capability to build sizeable instruments was as yet unproven. Indeed, there is more than a hint of self-satisfaction in Burney's account. The account[25] of the matter given by Sir John Hawkins (1719–89), writing in 1776 (thirteen years before Burney's History, which in other matters elaborated upon Hawkins's text), by contrast gives slighter notice to Snetzler, and praises the old Harris organ:

> Harris's organ was afterwards purchased for the cathedral of Christ Church at Dublin, and set up there; but about twenty years ago Mr. Byfield was sent for from England to repair it, which he objected to, and prevailed on the chapter to have a new one made by himself, he allowing for the old one in exchange. When he had got it he would have treated with the parishioners of Lynn in Norfolk for the sale of it; but they disdaining the offer of a second-hand instrument, refused to purchase it, and employed Snetzler to build them a new one, for which they paid him 700l. Byfield dying, his widow sold Harris's organ to the parish of Wolverhampton for 500l. and there it remains to this day. One of two eminent masters now living, who were requested by the churchwardens of Wolverhampton to give their opinions of this instrument, declares it to be the best modern organ he ever touched.

It is quite evident that the employment of Snetzler was controversial, but Burney was not exaggerating when he implied that this instrument made Snetzler's 'name'. It was as a result of this organ, opened on Sunday 17 March 1754, and those that quickly followed, that someone could write in the genealogical book in Schaffhausen: 'Orgelmacher – 1756 in London'.

House and workshops

By 1751, Snetzler lived on the Oxford road in the parish of St Marylebone, in a house previously occupied by Isabella Westley. It was quite a new house, for it does not appear on Roade's map of 1731 when the road was still called the Tyburn Road. Following the development of the Grosvenor estate, the road's name became descriptive of its ultimate destination: where the Marble Arch now stands, on the site of the Tyburn gallows, the country road to Oxford began. Later the road became 'Oxford Street', when the area to the west of the Edgware road was built up. In 1771 the houses along it were numbered, and Snetzler's became no. 22.[26] He stayed at this address until 1781, when the rate books show that the occupants were John Thompson and Richard King.

His workshops were very nearby, in Soho, in an area whose character had not changed much until recent years – De Quincy remarked sardonically last century that there were 'more prostitutes than horses in Oxford Street parish'. In his Deposition relating to the organ for Halifax parish church (see chapter 3, no. 67), Snetzler describes his 'Shop or Warehouse' as being in Dean Street near Oxford Road. The epithet 'warehouse' implies a large building where finished organs could

be erected and then packed; there were no doubt other places where the smaller work was carried on – quite possibly including his own house.

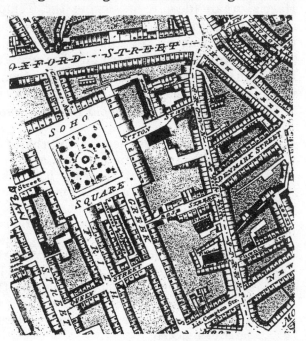

Late eighteenth–century Soho

If Henry Bevington, upon starting his own business in 1794, in fact took over what had been one of Snetzler's premises behind no. 10 Rose Street (now Manette Street) on the other (south–east) side of Soho Square from Dean Street, it would seem that Snetzler's eventual considerable turnover of work necessitated a number of premises for the workmen as well as the 'warehouse' for those parts that were completed or bought in from the many sub–contractors who would have been involved in the supply of iron– and brass–work, cases and perhaps metal pipes.

Once he was thus established, and the music–loving George III was on the throne (from 1760), Snetzler's future was assured. His reputation had reached the colonies, too; a vestryman of Trinity church, New York, Goldsbrow Banyar, wrote to the parish's London agent, 17 August 1761, that 'Mr. Snetzlaar ... is the most eminent Builder, and ... full of Business' The next year, the agent, Richard Grubb, was able to confirm this: 'he now stands as high in reputation as any of the Business'. Again, in 1767, when securing an organ for the church of St Michael in 'Charles Town' (Charleston), John Nutt, the London agent for the colony of South Carolina, was able to assure his clients that 'Mr Snetzler' was 'now the most considerable [i.e., most active] and the most reputable organ builder in England'.

From this time forward, Snetzler's life is written mostly in his instruments, the and the development of his business must therefore be traced in chapter 3.

Denization

On 12 April 1770, a warrant for a Bill of Denization of 'John Snetzler of Oxford Road in the Parish of St. Mary Le Bone in the County of Middlesex Organ Builder' and others (including Abraham Kirkman and Jacob Kirkman 'the Younger') was signed 'By His Majesty's Command'. This granted Snetzler the 'Rights Privileges & Immunities as other Free Denizens', and included in these rights were those of voting and full citizenship. This last right presumably allowed Snetzler to form some sort of business partnership with James Jones; it is recorded in various sources after this date, as at Hereford cathedral (1772), and St Mary's church, Huntingdon (1774). Jones is also mentioned in correspondence with the churchwardens of Holy Trinity, Hull, who wrote as late as 1783 to 'desire Messrs. Snetzler & Jones to examine the organ, and make an estimate of the charge of effectually repairing the same'.

There is a full transcript of the Denization warrant in Appendix 6.

Jezler's letters

Some small glimpses of the Schnetzler family are to be found in a series of letters, originals and copies of which are preserved in the Schaffhausen Stadtbibliothek, written by Christoph Jezler as he travelled in England and Holland in 1771 and 1772. The first reference is apparently to John Snetzler, and would appear to date from the latter part of 1771 or early 1772; it includes the following paragraph:

> With Herr Schnetzler, [I] also once saw the so–called New Pantheon in Oxford Street, which is a very big hall with beautiful galleries, which it is intended soon to [open?]. It is high, and gets most of its air from above, through windows in the ceiling. There are many columns in it, of carved marble, which is yellow, has an attractive appearance, and is beautifully polished, which a German from Saxony has done.

This description of the Pantheon is indeed strongly reminiscent of the work by the same team at Kedleston. (See also chapter 3, no. 41b.)

The second brief mention, in a letter written 27 April 1772 from Amsterdam to Jakob Peyer in Schaffhausen, is apparently a reference to another part of the Schnetzler family, a 'Herr Schnetzler' who might be identified with Hans Jakob, Johann's older brother, who is known to have been a saddler and to have died in Holland. A third reference is contained in a letter written 9 (?) November 1772, perhaps in Amsterdam, to Mr Meyer, a partner ('associé') in Messrs. Kuft (?) & Meyer of London. It concludes with this passage:

> I am heartily glad that you are keeping well, most esteemed Sir. May the Almighty send you an uninterrupted continuance. I shall be glad too, if Herr Peyr [*sic*], Herr Mihr, Herr Schnetzler, Herr d'Antoniers and Herr Schirs are keeping well. Please commend me to these gentlemen.

'These gentlemen' are clearly all part of the immigrant community; one wonders if they were in any direct way concerned with Snetzler's business activities, and if perhaps 'Herr Peyr' was in fact the David Peyerimhoff who was one of Johann's executors.

Retirement

James Jones was an executor of Snetzler's Will, which is dated 18 October 1784. The Will notes Snetzler as 'at present residing in Bentinck Street in the Parish of Saint James Westminster', in which street (at no. 14)[27] he had been living since March 1784.

He stayed there until October 1784. The Will was proved on 20 October 1785 by James Jones and David Peyerimhoff, when Snetzler was described as 'formerly of the Parish of St. Marylebone but late of the Canton of Schaffhausen'.[28] The Schaffhausen Parish Register notes Snetzler's death on 28 September 1785. Since the Register apparently normally notes the place of death if not in Schaffhausen, it must be presumed that he died there and that the Will was drawn up in preparation for his final departure thither. 'Final' because it now appears that the three-year gap between his leaving Oxford Street in 1781 and his living for a while in Bentinck Street is to be explained by a prolonged visit to Switzerland; it was this absence that caused Burney's and Sutton's remarks discussed below.

The latest year in which Snetzler is known to have worked in Britain is 1781 – at St George's chapel, Windsor, and St Anne's church, Belfast – and as this coincides with his moving from Oxford Road, it would seem to be the year of his retirement from direct day-to-day involvement in organ building in this country. The Eton College accounts (see chapter 3, no. 14) show payments to him for maintenance of the chapel organ until 1784, the year of the Will, so he must still then have been at least nominally in business.

The rather strange story, apparently emanating from Burney and picked up by John Sutton (and, in turn, Rimbault) that Snetzler 'saved sufficient money to return and settle in his native country' (which Burney thought was Passau), but later missed 'London porter and English fare ... so he came back to London, where he died', seems to be one of Burney's 'biographical anecdotes' designed to 'engage attention' and to be 'more trivial than tiresome'.[29] Nonetheless, it has (tiresomely) misled later writers into believing that Snetzler returned to London and died there. More recent writers, not having found his place of death, have imagined his burial at sea.[30] Actually, Burney was himself in London at the time, among other engagements writing his *General History*, to which publication both John Snetzler and Samuel Green were subscribers,[31] and he was surely aware of Snetzler's movements. Presumably the main point of his story was to indicate that Snetzler was notorious for his liking of porter, a strong dark beer. But it appears now that Snetzler definitely left England in 1781 and even made (at least) one more organ, which has only very recently 'surfaced' in Switzerland. A full description of it will be found in chapter 3, no. 104. It is a very small instrument, but its three stops ('Gedeckt' and Flute of oak and pine, and a Dulciana) are those that perfectly epitomize Snetzler's life-long predelictions. Perhaps he made it for himself? It is dated on a label which reads '*Johannes Schnetzler 1782*'.

Like Handel, Snetzler did not marry. He was therefore free to go about the country finishing organs and attending their opening concerts, but he could not start a 'dynasty'. His legacy was less direct, but some insight into what he left to organ–building is provided in a letter[32] dated 20 January 1787 from Charles Burney to Thomas Jefferson, written not very long after Snetzler's death:

> As to the Question you ask concerning the propensity of organs made in England or France? I can only answer that as far as I have seen, heard or examined, the mechanism of the English is infinitely superior as well as the tone of the solo stops, given the org. builder here, is a very ingenious & experimental man, & not only makes dayly discoveries & improvements himself, but readily adopts those that may be made or recommended to him by others. Pour la forme & ornaments The Fr. will doubtless beat us, mais, pour le fond, I think we always had, and still have it all to nothing against the rest of Europe. We are notorious for want of invention yet give us but a principle to work on, & we are sure of leaving an invention better than we find it.

Snetzler's part in creating these 'superior' organs was crucial; his ability to organize their production in quantity was entirely new. Aside from the plain evidence of his surviving work, and the prices he was able to obtain for his instruments, we have no other well–informed contemporary assessment of his milieu than this.

Rimbault[33] is wildly uncertain of the actual date of Snetzler's death. Certainly, 1784 was a gala year, and it may be that Snetzler's final departure was unnoticed. In May of that year, wrongly supposed to be the centenary of Handel's birth, the first great Handel Commemoration was held in Westminster Abbey and at the Pantheon. If Snetzler returned for this and to draw up his Will, such a personal act of homage would have seemed entirely appropriate. Although his organ in the Pantheon was used for some of the Commemoration concerts, the 'new order' was indicated clearly in the use in the abbey of an organ by 'the ingenious Mr. Samuel Green'. He may well have murmered a 'Nunc Dimittis' as he greeted the prime movers of the Commemoration[34] – all of them his clients – and prepared to return to his roots.

Successors

There may lie a deep irony in the employment of Green at the Westminster Abbey Commemoration concerts; this also may not have gone unnoticed by Snetzler. Superficially, the circumstances seem to imply that his own immediate successors were not capable of carrying out such work, but in fact the connection between Snetzler and Green may have already been made. David Wickens[35] has proposed that evidence of Green's style of pipework suggests that he may have worked with Snetzler from about 1761 to 1768, the years between his apprenticeship with Pyke and his working with the younger Byfield. In this respect perhaps, as in many other matters, Green was Snetzler's foremost heir – to Royal patronage, to a wide circle of clients throughout England, Wales and Ireland, and in America, and to an organized method of working that distinguished both men from previous builders.

Burney's description of a 'very ingenious & experimental man' in fact fits Green perfectly.

Marks on pipes in the organ at Rotherham (1777) are not by Snetzler but by a hand similar to those made on the pipework in the Ohrmann & (John) Nutt organ made for Macclesfield Old Church (1803). It was indeed said (in a reference to an incident c1781)[36] that they had 'formerly worked for Messrs. Snetzler and Jones, organ builders in Stephen Street, Tottenham-court-road' (Jones's address). Others say that Ohrmann had been foreman to Snetzler (and Jones). It would seem that the retirement of a builder as busy as Snetzler, because he would have sub-contracted work to others, inevitably meant that parts of his remaining business fell into various hands. Precisely whose these might have been is now difficult for us to distinguish, as several 'firms', beside Green's, seem to be involved:

James Jones rented a house and paid rates for a workshop at 9 Stephen Street by 1776; he could have made parts here for Snetzler and for his own instruments, which are recorded c1774 and in 1780 (see chapter 5, p. 265). Whether Jones was actually a legal partner of Snetzler is not absolutely certain, but their relationship was, as we have seen, close enough for this to have been assumed to have been the case by various clients and later commentators. Jones moved from Stephen Street at about the time that Snetzler made his Will in 1784. He evidently retired in 1786, having carried on the major part of the business from the time of Snetzler's apparent withdrawal in 1781. He was present when Snetzler's Will was proved in October 1785; nothing further is known of him.

'Nutt & Co., organ builders, 16 Denmark Street, Soho' are recorded in 1790 in Wakefield's *Directory*. This seems to be the firm of John Nutt, the agent in London for the colony of South Carolina (see chapter 3, no. 77), since he also appears in Holden's *Triennial Directory* for 1805–7 as 'John Nutt' at 13 Tottenham Court Road, New Road, the same address as 'Ohrman & Nutt' in the 1802 *Annual Directory*. 'Ohmon & Nutt' tuned the 1790 Green organ at Heaton Hall in 1796–7,[37] and Ohrmann & Nutt are apparently first mentioned in a directory in 1799.[38] If Ohrmann continued to work first with Jones and then independently, maintaining Snetzler's organs (as at Lightcliffe, see chapter 3, no. 94) and then entered into an arrangement with John Nutt, this would perhaps explain the gap in our knowledge of Ohrmann's work after Snetzler had finally retired to Switzerland until Jones's own retirement.

It is just possible that Samuel Green took over 'the connection and good will' and carried out much of the actual maintenance work until his death in 1796, and that Ohrmann worked for him and for his widow Sarah in some capacity. (Hence the work at Heaton Hall, perhaps.) There is, however, no direct evidence for this; he was not, apparently, Green's foreman.[39] At any rate, Ohrmann earned himself a reputation as 'a most industrious Swede';[40] he and Nutt are known to have made an organ now in New Zealand and the organ for Macclesfield, Old Church (1803).[41] 'Ohrmann & Co.'[42] were contracted to change the pitch of the organ in St Paul's cathedral in 1803, and it was during this work that Ohrmann caught a chill. He died from the effects of this later that year, and in his Will he left his tools, stock and £5 in cash 'to his late partner John Nutt' and Nutt's daughters, and stated that there were two organs then being built or repaired. John Nutt died in 1804 (having already placed his order for his listing in Holden's *Trienniel Directory*), and, as with Jones, any 'succession' seems to end there.

It was another builder who seems ultimately to have been in a position to 'carry on' the work. This was *Thomas Elliot*, whose earliest surviving work is dated 1790, and who was first recorded in 1791 at Wharton's Court in Holborn[43] and then at 10 Sutton Street (now Sutton Row), Soho Square in 1794.[44] Again, his ante- cedents are not precisely known, though the 1790 organ contains metal pipes identical in style with those normally made by Hugh Russell of Theobald's Road, Holborn. His background (like Russell's) seems to have been at least as much musical as commercial, though a connection of some kind with Nutt has been posited.[45] He is known to have sung bass at the 1784 Handel Commemoration at Westminster Abbey, and elsewhere. He may have been an organist, too, as one of the subscribers to William Russell's first set of Voluntaries (1804) was a 'Mr. Elliott, Organist of Curzon Chapel'.

Upon John Nutt's decease in 1804, it seems that Elliot moved next door to Ann Corbitt (née Nutt) in Tottenham Court. It was from 12 Tottenham Court, New Road, that Elliot ran his business, first employing Alexander Buckingham (his foreman from about 1806 until about 1818) and then William Hill (working from 1815), as well as George Corbitt (who worked until 1835) and others. Buckingham was a fervent admirer of Snetzler[46] and worked on a considerable number of his organs; his interest in them strongly suggests that a major part of the Snetzler business had passed to Elliot indirectly through John and Ann Nutt. Hill's own early training is not known; he married Thomas's daughter, Mary, and eventually took over the business fully at Elliot's death in 1832.

Henry Bevington is said[47] to have been apprenticed to Ohrmann at 8 Rose Street, Soho, and to have set up his own business in 1794, later (after Ohrmann's death in 1803?) moving to that address. The firm he founded continued until *c*1939 in various addresses in the vicinity, making a large number of organs of all sizes which were scaled and voiced along conservative lines. *George Holdich*, later an associate (of some sort) of Henry Bevington, worked on a number of Snetzler's organs during the middle of the nineteenth century.

John Lincoln and his son *Henry Cephas Lincoln*, who made at least two organs with casework designed in a style which was until recently frequently mistaken for the Snetzlers', also worked on a number of Snetzler organs.

Other craftsmen who were actually associated with Snetzler, and whose work has consequently also been confused with his, include in particular the two northern organ builders, Thomas Haxby and John Donaldson. That *Thomas Haxby* knew Snetzler is documented:[48] during the dispute over the organ at Halifax (see chapter 3, no. 67), Haxby was called to witness before an ecclesiastical court at York that Snetzler's signature on the Deposition made before Samuel Bonner in London was authentic. Haxby's own Deposition in the case includes this passage: 'he knows Mr. John Snetzler an Organ Builder who does or did live in Oxford Road in Middlesex and has often seen him write and has received Letters from him'. This passage may indicate either that he learned some organ-building from Snetzler – he could have first met him in 1755, when Snetzler installed the organ in the York Assembly Rooms – or that he used pipework from Snetzler in his organs (see chapter 5).

A notebook in the York Public Library[49] contains the assertion that *John Donaldson* was in the employ of Snetzler. This cannot be proved, although as the earliest-surviving organ made by Donaldson is dated 1780, at about the time that Snetzler 'retired', it is a real possibility. Some of his organs have been taken for Snetzler's, and he worked on at least two organs formerly made or repaired by the older builder. Donaldson moved to York about 1790, four years before Haxby's death; like him, he made and repaired other keyboard instruments (see chapter 5).

Brice Seede and his son *Richard Seede* made organs in the West Country *c*1752–1823. Richard Seede would have known the Snetzler organ(s) at Lulworth Castle in Dorset (see chapter 3, no. 24), and he included what seems to be a Snetzler rank (whose pipes are marked 'Flut') in his organ in the Roman Catholic Chapel there in 1785.[50] His most completely preserved organ (apparently dated 1783, and now in Pamber Priory, Basingstoke) contains some features – a shifting movement with double sliders, 'grooved' basses, a Dulciana, a treble compass to f''' in a chamber organ – consistent with a knowledge of Snetzler's work not shared even by some of the Seedes' contemporaries in London, though the organ is not generally as sophisticated as are Samuel Green's typical instruments.[51]

*

Endnotes

1. *Modern Painters I*, Part 2, section 5, chapter 2.

2. Illustrated in the 'Feestbundel' for Maarten Vente, *Visitatio Organorum*, ed. Albert Dunning, (Frits Knuf, Buren, 1980), vol. II, p. 368.

3. Especially Edward Rimbault in HR1, p. 147.

4. F (TO 53/54).

5. William Sumner, 'John Snetzler and his First English Organs' (TO 131/105).

6. Charles Burney, *The Present State of Music* (London, 1773), vol. 1, p. 78.

7. Letter of January 1803, reprinted in *The Musical Times*, September 1904.

8. Also in Burney, *Present State*, vol. 1, p. 78.

9. Dr J. Saam, in correspondence with Alan Barnes, 28 September 1976.

10. Searched by Alan Barnes.

11. B (TO 205/4).

12. Paul Johnson, *The Offshore Islanders* (Weidenfeld & Nicolson, 1972), p. 270.

13. 'Johann Ulrich Schnetzler, Maler und Stukkateur', from *Schaffhauser Biographien des 18. und 19. Jahrhunderts*, Schaffhauser Beitrage zur Geschichte, vol. 33 (Thayngen, 1956).

14. In the same edition of the *Oxford Journal*, there appears a notice from the 'present' Mr Roberts 'Stucco-Plafterer', who '... begs leave to acquaint the Nobility and Gentry, that the Carving and Gilding Bufinefs in all its Branches is performed by him as heretofore, in the neweft Tafte. – He thinks this publick Notice the more requifite on Account of Mr. Snetzler's Death, who by many was fuppofed to be the only Person in Oxford who executed thefe Branches of Bufinefs'.

15. John Hawkins, *A General History of the Science and Practice of Music* (London, 1776), Book XV, chapter CXLV, p. 692 fn.

16. HR1, p. 145.

17. Raymond Russell, *The Harpsichord and Clavichord* (Faber and Faber, 1959), p. 83, mentions this but cannot find the Burney reference.

18. Russell, loc. cit.

19. E. P. Thompson, *The Making of the English Working Class* (Penguin, 1980), p. 51.

20. *The Tracker* (Journal of the Organ Historical Society), vol. 3, no. 5, p. 19.

21. Dorothy George's figure, quoted in Thompson, op. cit., p. 260.

22. Susi Jeans, 'An Organ by Abraham Jordan, Junior, at the Old Chapel at Greenwich Hospital', (TO 182/68).

23. Charles Burney, *A General History of Music* (London, 1776–89; repr. Dover Publications, 1957 in two volumes), vol. II, p. 345.

24. Burney, op. cit., vol. II, p. 347 – he notes also: 'At present Green, an Englishman and an excellent mechanic, is deservedly in possession of the public favour'.

25. John Hawkins, op. cit., p. 695.

26. A photograph, taken by Bernard Edmonds in 1955 and reproduced in BIOSJ 13/60, shows that Snetzler's house was a typical three-storey Georgian brick building (probably with an attic) standing on the corner of Hanway Street, near St Giles Circus, and practically opposite Charles Street, the northern entrance to Soho Square.

27. Also illustrated by Bernard Edmonds, BIOSJ 13/64; the street was later renamed Livonia Street, and the house was demolished in 1955.

28. The wording is as given by Bernard Edmonds in 'Rose Yard' (BIOSJ 13/66).

29. As Burney put in in the Preface to his *General History*, completed in 1789.

30. As in Cecil Clutton's historical part of *The British Organ* (Batsford, 1963), p. 89; in the second edition (Eyre Methuen, 1982), p. 79.

31. Percy Scholes, *The Great Dr Burney* (Oxford, 1948) vol. I, p. 295.

32. Quoted in Russell, op. cit., p. 181.

33. HR1, p. 148.

34. Joah Bates, Sir Watkin Williams Wynn and Viscount Fitzwilliam; see Richard Luckett, *Handel's Messiah: a Celebration* (Gollancz, 1992), p. 196.

35. David Wickens, *The Instruments of Samuel Green* (Macmillan, 1987), p. 62.

36. Quoted by Bernard Edmonds and Nicholas Plumley in 'Thomas Elliot, Organ-builder', BIOSJ 12/57.

37. Information kindly communicated by David Wickens.

38. Edmonds and Plumley, loc. cit. (BIOSJ 12/57).

39. According to a note in a manuscript account, lodged with the British Organ archive since 1986, of the Walker organ which superseded Snetzler's in Armagh Cathedral (1765; see chapter 3, no. 68). This erroneously suggests that it was built by Green, and notes that 'Mr Wright, his [Green's] Foreman told me he attended the putting up'. Perhaps Green later moved the organ within the cathedral; it is of course possible that Mr Wright worked for Snetzler before working for Green.

40. Andrew Freeman, 'The Organs of St. Paul's Cathedral' (TO 5/6). He mentions that, 'with W. Nutt', Ohrmann took the organ to pieces, cleaned it and lowered its pitch by a semitone, all at a cost of £264. 12s.

41. David Wickens, op. cit., p. 167.

42. BIOSJ 12/58.

43. Lyndesay Langwill and Noel Boston, *Church and Chamber Barrel-Organs* (1st ed., Edinburgh, 1967), p. 54.

44. In *Doane's Directory* for 1794, quoted by Langwill and Boston, loc. cit.

45. BIOSJ 12/58.

46. A letter from 'Musicus' (Thomas Woolley, who twice aspired to become the organist of St Mary's; see chapter 3, no. 90), to the *Nottingham Journal* in 1839, pasted into Buckingham's Notebook (TO 213/47–8), includes this passage: 'Mr. Buckingham entertains the highest opinion – almost amounting to reverence – of Snetzler's organs, which has operated powerfully on his mind, to do himself the greatest credit in modernising the work of so renowned a builder'.

47. The assertion was made by Langwill and Boston, op. cit., pp. 49–50.

48. Borthwick Institute, Chancery, ref. CP.1.1449; quoted by David Haxby and John Malden, 'Thomas Haxby of York (1729–1796)', BIOSJ 7/59–76.

49. Quoted by Bernard Edmonds in 'Yorkshire Organ Builders: the Earlier Years', BIOSJ 9/48.

50. See BIOSJ 11/12 concerning the 'Flut'.

51. A general survey of the work of the Seedes is given by Christopher Kent in BIOSJ 5/83–97; see also BIOSJ 11/6–25 and 100–104.

2 His designs

I General background and musical use

1 Background

The eighteenth-century British organ, despite the efforts of immigrant or foreign-trained builders since the Restoration in 1660, remained at heart a simple concept. For its liturgical role and for musical purposes it required only three elements – a good chorus, some accompanimental stops and a few colouristic sounds. A sense of Classical 'good taste' required that the organs should be contained in decently-designed cases and be tonally unprovoking. Usually though, the reasonable, Classical ideal of economy of means was not distinguished from a desire to economize on resources, and the Harris 'dynasty' in particular seems to have waged a constant but generally unsuccessful battle against the cool, paternalistic hand of unenthusiastic conservatism.

Handel's music had awoken interest in the organ as a concerto instrument, but reverence for his music was not likely to be the cause of wild tonal experiments – rather, the scene was set for someone who could improve upon the existing structures in matters of detail rather than grand design. Just as the lasting importance of Bernard Smith may ultimately have been in his raising of the social and architectural status of the organ maker, so the influence of Snetzler may have lain in the more mundane but vitally important matters of attending to detail, of producing a large output of work by organizing a business effectively, and of meeting a surge in demand for a species of organ (the chamber organ) at a time when London was the trading centre of the 'Western' world. These factors – a straightforward 'product', a conservative market and a growing economy – led to an organ-type of considerable sophistication which was unmatched anywhere else for technical polish and practical flair. Snetzler, the careful, small-scale craftsman from a background of artisan-businessmen, seems to have found himself in the right place at the right time.

The opinion of his fellow organ makers is not known; that he was kept out of the City of London by the restrictive practices of the guilds' rules is certain – he did not make a single organ for a City church, though he knew at least one City Mayor. However, above all his competitors he had the benefit of the wider patronage of the Court and all the smaller country 'courts' of the aristocracy. It is hard to go behind the 'tradesman's' language of the few letters that survive from Snetzler's maturity – more must lie in uncatalogued archives in country houses – to see how he viewed his clients or they him. His eccentricities, at any rate, were tolerated with the same uncondescending amusement as those of Handel or the Royal family.

2 *Musical use*

There is no detailed account of the musical use of the organ that is exactly contemporary with Snetzler's working life (apart from some asides in two letters to the *Gentleman's Magazine* by William Hayes in 1765 and William Ludlam in 1772, transcribed in Appendices 5 and 7), but it is clear from John Marsh's description of the characteristic British organ in 1791 that little had changed by then. Marsh was a solicitor by profession, but a keen and well-acquainted musician by inclination; he was brought up in London, and later lived in and near Canterbury, where he was a leading light in musical circles. In 1787, he moved to Chichester and he became an assistant organist at the cathedral. Here the organ was still the Renatus Harris instrument of 1677, with a small Swell added by Knight in 1778. Marsh left lengthy notes and diaries of his extensive musical experiences.[1] In 1824, Buckingham[2] described two organs that he owned.

Throughout the Preface to his *Eighteen voluntaries ... chiefly intended for the use of young practicioners ...* (transcribed in Appendix 9), Marsh is at pains to suggest that the organist's role in service-playing is that of a restrained accompanist, and that he should not play so loudly or extrovertly as to detract from the words of the liturgy or the solemnity of the occasion. We need to remember that he is referring to church organs of small to moderate size which, stop for stop, were not as loud as the majority of those of the next hundred years. It is clear from John Sutton's later verbal assaults upon 'Music Mills' (in 1847) that the larger early-Victorian organ fostered a more assertive style of playing, using the Swell (coupled) and more frequent changes of stops. This in its turn engendered the more overt quasi-operatic style of choral singing – more emotional, less blended, using vibrato – that still can be heard, two centuries and a cultural world away from the ideals of Marsh:

> In the first place he [the organist] should totally divest himself of the idea of setting down merely to entertain, or exhibit his Skill to an audience, as at a Concert; instead of which it would be much more to his credit to make Style the object of his ambition, rather than Execution [brilliant finger-work], considering at the same time the solemnity of the service, of which Voluntary playing forms, if not an essential, yet an ornamental part ... many ... are apt to be too ambitious of being distinguished above the Voices, thereby making the Organ a Principal instead of an Accompaniment ... I ... caution ... performers against being led away by their ideas into a rapid hurry-scurry style of playing, which is neither proper for the Organ or the Church. In order to make the audience feel, they must have time so to do, which cannot be the case in a quick succession of fleeting passages, which make no impression, but leave the mind in the same (if not a worse) state than it found it in.

Even Marsh's remarks on the Tierce and Larigot ('put in by Organ-Builders, merely to make a shew of Stops to draw') seem to have been motivated more by a sense of what was fitting to the organ's liturgical role than by a distaste for these stops *per se*. His strictures somewhat echo those of Ludlam, and were repeated by

Blewitt,[3] and his entire *Preface* is required reading for all who seek to understand the church–musical aesthetic of the second half of the eighteenth century.

These various 'authorities' did not feel it was necessary to prescribe what sort of tone the organ should produce, as long as it suited the building and was regular and blending. They did not indulge in 'tone-tasting', although they clearly had their favourites among the builders.

Snetzler's organs seem to have been 'spirited, brilliant, charming, cheerful and well blended' – and were so described by those who knew them at first hand – but it has to be recalled that the buildings in which they were heard were frequently in an acoustical condition that differed from their present state. Victorian 'restorations' removed box–pews, galleries and much other post–medieval clutter from churches (before introducing neo–medieval clutter such as pewing, screens and choir–stalls) but in the process they also frequently changed a lively acoustic into a dead one. Many medieval churches' rafters were 'ceiled' in lath–and–plaster work during the sixteenth and seventeenth centuries in order to imitate to some extent the wide and flat 'auditory' ceilings of contemporary Classical churches. Indeed, St Martin's church, Leicester, was 'ceiled' expressly in order to improve the acoustics of the building at the time of the installation of Snetzler's organ in 1774 (see chapter 3, no. 87). In the process, a measure of thermal insulation and a bonus of musical benefits accrued. With such ceilings, the sound of an organ standing on a west or east gallery was dispersed rapidly and efficiently throughout the main body of the building (the chancel being used only for part of the infrequent communion services), and its tonal output did not need to be loud so much as bright and carrying, or 'vocal'.

Since the pitch of organs was usually the same as that of woodwind instruments, one might wonder if these (for instance, the serpent or bassoon, hautboys or clarionets) might have been admitted in a general way as well as for special occasions into the organ galleries, and so helped the organ to accompany the congregation. In fact there is little evidence for this, and we must accept that these organs of moderate size were felt to be completely adequate in an age which knew no sound louder than an organ except a clap of thunder, and which could describe a Block Flute stop as 'clear, sweet and piercing', and coupled pedals as having 'a most solemn and awful effect' (see Appendix 7).

II The church and larger house organs

1 Early tonal designs

It is clear from the correspondence concerning Snetzler's organ for Fulneck, near Pudsey, Leeds, that although he is proposing an organ for an immigrant-led community, the type of instrument Snetzler suggested was in fact a compromise between the organs he and the Moravian leaders were familiar with in southern Germany and the prevailing British style. The compromise here involved the addition of string-toned stops and the 'lieblich' registers typical of organs for 'pietistic' churches in continental Europe and North America to a tonal design with typical British compasses and chorus structure.

A unison 'Viola di Gamba' which shared the bass of the wooden Open Diapason – probably both of these were thought of as 'lieblich' stops – was added to the otherwise almost conventional Great. The best employment of a Salicional stop, which Snetzler initially describes as having 'a sound like a Violoncello', was the cause of much discussion in the letters. It may eventually have become part of the 'interior' Swell, with an Open Diapason, Principal and 'Cornetin' (a small-scale and/or two-rank Cornet), but this is not certain. It seems from the letters that Snetzler uses the names 'Salicional' and 'Viola di Gamba' almost interchangeably; the ranks may have been cylindrical in construction, or even possibly small-scale conical, as in contemporary Thuringian organs.[4] No ranks of either name or marking survive.

The Great chorus was based on the wooden Open Diapason, a wooden Stopped Diapason, a Principal (in the front, like a 'Prestant'), an 'Octave' (Fifteenth), and a divided Sesquialtera/Cornet of three to four ranks. This last was probably arranged as in other early organs, with three ranks in the bass, and four in the treble, so that the Cornet could be accompanied on the undivided Stopped Diapason – not, it should be said, necessarily for Cornet voluntaries, but primarily for the 'giving out' and leading of hymn-tunes.

The pre-contract version of the Great stop-list includes a short-compass Open Diapason of metal in addition to the wooden one; evidently there was perceived to be a need to bolster the treble or melodic line (probably when the Cornet was employed), and this need is as likely to have been created by an unforced voicing style (on a lower wind-pressure than a Trumpet would require, he implies) as by the modest size of the chapel. If the organ, as finally made, contained the contracted-for Salicional in the Swell, then very possibly the short-compass Open Diapason was actually installed on the Great. Alternatively, a Twelfth (originally proposed, but not in the contract) might have been substituted, as this stop appears in virtually every other Great chorus Snetzler made, including that on the organ apparently made the year before (1747) for the Qualified Church in Edinburgh (see chapter 3, no. 7).

2 String-toned stops in later organs

The exact nature of the early 'Salicional' and 'Viola di Gamba' cannot now be determined; they could well have been versions of his later Dulcianas, but stronger in tone, and (probably) more slow-speaking even if they were somewhat larger in scale. If their wind-pressure is increased, the voicing of Snetzler's Principal pipes quickly becomes somewhat 'forced' and 'acid' because of their low mouths and wide flues, so it is easy to understand how he might have voiced a Viola with a low mouth and a fender (as used on the Dulcianas) and produced a broad, bright and 'stringy' tone from such a pipe. Indeed, unless the winding of Snetzler's typical pipes is carefully controlled at their tips, their tone can readily become over-assertive (as Buckingham also noted at William Strutt's house; see chapter 3, no. 107b) and over-bright. It is possible (as noted in chapter 4, p. 258) that

Snetzler found by experience that 'bright' string stops were thought by British organists to be unnecessary in organs which anyway contained a 'Cremona' (reed) rank and that he accordingly discontinued their use.

After Fulneck, we have no further evidence for the use of small–scaled ranks until the building of the organs for King's Lynn (1754–5) and Chesterfield (1756), and they do not appear in chamber organs until after 1755. The Choir manual of the King's Lynn organ contained a Dulciana of metal, evidently of a complete compass, *G', A'–e'''*, but no Open Diapason, unlike the Harris organ at St Dionis, Backchurch, which may have been to some extent its model (see Appendix 1). The Dulciana at Lynn is clearly thought of as a suitable accompanimental stop, more useful than an Open Diapason. In this Burney was well ahead of his time, for this use of a Dulciana instead of an Open Diapason in a church organ was not revived until towards the end of the century.

The King's Lynn organ also employed a Dulciana on the Swell; this too was ahead of its time, as not until 1786 did Green use his version of the stop in a Swell. These Lynn Dulcianas appear to be the first of their kind; they may share certain characteristics of the earlier 'Salicional' and 'Viola di Gamba', but the change of name must indicate the invention or introduction of a 'new' stop. The two ranks still at Lynn are made with a slight outward taper (about 10 per cent), and the mouths throughout the rank are eared and fendered in a way that Snetzler was to use for his later cylindrical dulcianas.

There has been much discussion over the origin of the term 'dulciana', but the name may simply have been imported as one that suited the pre–existing English taste for punning descriptions which were conflations of various elements – in this case, 'dolce' or 'dulcis', 'Dulcinea' and 'dolcan' – so that it was re–coined to name the cantabile stops at Lynn. The use of fenders by Snetzler suggests that he viewed the stops as quiet strings, cousins of the 'viola douce' and 'salizional' of the southern German organ; they were therefore not originally of the firmer 'echo open diapason' style of Green's dulcianas.

The Chesterfield organ again had a Dulciana 'all through of metal' on the Choir manual, according to Buckingham (see chapter 3, no. 31), and a Dulciana in the Swell. The Hillington organ (1756) also has a Dulciana in the Swell. Whether the Hackney/Poole organ (1757) originally contained a Choir Dulciana it is not now possible to say, but the small German Calvinist organ (?1757) contained one descending to 4' C, and the St George's, Hanover Square, organ (1761) one on the Choir to gamut G. After Chesterfield, Snetzler in fact generally used Open Diapasons instead of Dulcianas in his church organs, presumably thinking (or discovering by experience) that Dulcianas were too quiet to be effective in large buildings. So the larger church organs of the 1760s and 1770s – for New York, Ludlow, Halifax, Beverley, Leicester, Nottingham, and elsewhere – did not originally contain dulcianas. Only the smaller organs for smaller buildings, such as those for Peterhouse Chapel and Richmond/Wilton, do contain them – but in the Choir/Swell division. It was left to Green to popularize this stop in a church organ; Snetzler appears ultimately to have been content to retain it for chamber organs only, perhaps because his fendered Dulcianas were susceptible to the dust and débris that collects on the open soundboards of church organs.

How the organist used the early Dulcianas is not absolutely clear. By the end of the century, the Green type of Dulciana could be used on its own, but the fendered stop needs the help of a Stopped Diapason so that it can speak promptly. The lack of an Open Diapason in the Choir divisions of Lynn and Chesterfield suggests that the Dulciana might have been seen as a colour to be added to the Stopped Diapason to produce a combination equivalent in power, if not in quality of tone, to the more usual combined Open and Stopped Diapasons. Snetzler's Dulciana and Stopped Diapason combination is not, however, equally restful or sombre in quality, and it may not have found general favour until the Dulciana had been softened – at which point it would indeed have been useful only in chamber organs.

John Speller[5] suggests that since Alexander Cumming introduced a Celestina stop (a Dulciana Principal of Metal, as Buckingham calls it in his notes) into the Earl of Lonsdale's organ, for which Snetzler made the pipework (apparently in the mid-1770s; see chapter 3, no. 97), this stop could have been 'originated' by Snetzler. However, he did not employ it elsewhere, except on the Choir manual at Durham Cathedral (1766; see chapter 3, no. 71) and in the organ (?1769) for Miss Bristoe (chapter 3, no. 106). It occurs in a number of (later) organs by Green.

3 Choruses and mixtures

Chorus work on the church organs followed established convention. Its structure was built upon the metal Open Diapason, Principal and Fifteenth, the scaling of which was appropriate to the size of building. In Snetzler's work, each of these ranks was of the same scaling, and it appears that the Twelfth also followed this pattern. The compound stops also followed suit, except that if there was only one of these, the Cornet part of it was of slightly larger scale. The normal composition for a three to four rank Sesquialtera/Cornet, in the absence of a separate short-compass Cornet, was 17–19–22 in the bass, and 8–12–15–17 in the treble. Such a stop would have a dual role as a chorus mixture and as a solo Cornet, but these two functions are not completely compatible.

Therefore, wherever possible, Snetzler provided a separate solo Cornet of five ranks, scaled about two pipes larger than the equivalent pipes in the main chorus, from middle C upwards (1–8–12–15–17). It was designed to be useful for solos and for a British type of 'Grand Jeu' with the Trumpet and Clarion reed stops. Indeed, there is evidence that in some organs (for example, at Leicester, 1774) a Clarion was taken only as far up as tenor B (*b*); the implication of this must be that the Cornet 'took over' for the upper part of the compass where the Clarion would be more likely to go out of tune and where it is inherently weak.

On the very largest organs, a separate tierce (of the same scaling as the chorus, it appears) was provided; this would give the organist another kind of Cornet of full compass, more brightly voiced than the treble Cornet, and stronger than the Cornet treble of the Sesquialtera. Much has been made of an all-too-evident

British love of the tierce–mixture, but such a Classical ensemble tuned in meantone temperament is indeed just as Isaac Nicholl described his 1781 organ: 'of exquisite beauty, fulness, and richness of tone. The full organ blended to absolute perfection, forming one grand 8ft. tone'. (See chapter 3, no. 102.)

Where a separate Cornet was provided, the chorus mixture was labelled simply 'Sesquialtra'. The evidence in the organs at Cobham Hall (1778) and the parish church of Ludlow (1764) is that this full–compass mixture did not crudely 'jump' at the tenor B/middle C division of the Sesquialtera/Cornet divided mixture, but that an intermediate step was provided thus:

$$G'\ 17\text{--}19\text{--}22\ /\ g\sharp\ 15\text{--}17\text{--}19\ /\ g\sharp'\ 12\text{--}15\text{--}17$$

Hopkins and Rimbault[6] give the four–rank Sesquialtera at Nottingham (1777) as:

$$G'\ 15\text{--}17\text{--}19\text{--}22\ /\ g\sharp\ 12\text{--}15\text{--}17\text{--}19\ /\ g\sharp'\ 8\text{--}12\text{--}15\text{--}17$$

but its original composition may have been more complex than this; recent investigation of the surviving pipework of this organ suggests that the Sesquialtera may have 'broken' at least four times, once in each octave above tenor C, with a resulting composition in the extreme treble of, possibly, 1–3–5–8. How much later builders, including Buckingham, may have contributed to this unexpected arrangement is not yet clear.

The very largest organs contained an additional mixture called a 'Furniture' (marked 'Forn' on the pipes at Ickham, Kent; see chapter 3, no. 108) of three ranks which complemented the Sesquialtera. The Halifax scheme (1766) was as follows:[7]

	Sesquialtera	Furniture
G'	15–17–19–22	22–26–29
c	15–17–19–22	15–19–22
c'	8–12–15–17	15–19–22
g'	8–12–15–17	8–12–15
c'''	1—8–12–15	8–12–15

In this instance, the tierce (the 17th) drops out altogether in the treble. Note how the two mixtures are arranged so that their breaks are staggered. The function of the Furniture is to 'furnish' or fill out the chorus; it is not a 'sharp' mixture, but it is scaled in the same way as the whole chorus.

Evidence from the original pipework obtained by David Wickens[8] concerning the mixtures at Ludlow (1764) indicates a slightly different arrangement where there are three ranks in the Sesquialtera:

	Sesquialtera	Furniture
G'	17–19–22	22–26–29
c	17–19–22	15–19–22
c'	15–17–19	15–19–22
g'	15–17–19	8–12–15
c'''	15–17–17	8–12–15

It will be seen that the Furniture appears to have been deliberately designed as a non-tierce mixture. Whether it was used separately from the Sesquialtra might be doubted, since organ-tutors (both Marsh and Blewitt) imply that it was added to the rest of the chorus only when a particularly strong sound was required.

4 Cornets

The entirely separate short-compass stop of five ranks (unison, octave, twelfth, fifteenth and seventeenth) was not strictly part of the chorus. It was slightly larger in scale and was voiced to produce an homogeneous colour, bolder but slightly 'smoother' in tone than the normal chorus. It was not, however, so completely different in timbre from the main chorus that it could not be added to it. (It was not at all as smooth as a French *Grand Cornet*, for instance.) As Hopkins pointed out a century later:[9]

> The Cornet is a very useful stop for a large organ to contain ... The Cornet was originally used for giving out the melody of a chorale upon, and hence was usually only a Treble stop in English instruments ... not having any "breaks" itself, it covers up those in the other Compound stops very effectively.

Unfortunately, the use of the word 'Cornet' to name the treble part of a mixture (when that was in fact merely a quasi-Cornet of three or four ranks) and at the same time the five-rank, short-compass solo stop means that the sources for the stop-lists in Chapters 3 and 5 are not always clear about which is meant. If, for instance, a source simply has 'Sesquialtra (three ranks) and Cornet (four ranks)' that is more likely to mean a single, divided, mixture than two separate stops – but one cannot always tell for certain unless the numbers of pipes in the stops are calculated. Sperling tries to distinguish the solo Cornet from a mixture by calling it a 'Mounted Cornet', and this is a useful distinction, but there is no actual evidence that Snetzler's Cornets were ever 'mounted' on a block fed by conveyances from a front slider of the Great soundboard – there appears to be no surviving large Great soundboard. A swell-box over the Great would anyway reduce the available height, and therefore the effectiveness, of any such 'mounting'.

Nor is there any evidence that the high-Swell chorus including the Cornet mixture (usually of three ranks, 12–15–17) was voiced to be used instead of a 'solo' Great Cornet. It was considered only as an echo to it, as Marsh observed:

> The CORNET in the Swell shou'd, I think, never be used as such, it being necessarily so very inferior to the great Cornet...

The Great Cornet at Cobham was placed at the rear of the Great soundboards, between the 'Sesquialtra' (a full-compass mixture) and the Trumpet. This may have been a frequent arrangement, though Green's Cornets were placed, at varying levels, just behind the open diapasons at the front of the Great soundboards.

5 Various chorus structures

Usually, the context makes the original specification of the chorus clear. A small one- or two-manual organ would contain a chorus of Open Diapason, Stopped Diapason, Principal, Twelfth and/or Flute, Fifteenth, divided Sesquialtera and Cornet, and an optional Trumpet. In a larger organ the Flute would have been placed on the Choir soundboard, and omitted from the Great, which would therefore have a chorus of Open Diapason, Stopped Diapason, Principal, Twelfth, Fifteenth, Sesquialtera throughout, Trumpet and Cornet (of five ranks), to which could be added a Clarion (possibly in the bass only, as noted above) and a separate Tierce.

The largest schemes would increase the foundation tone at the same time as amplifying the mixtures: two Open Diapasons, Stopped Diapason, Principal, Twelfth, Fifteenth, Tierce, Sesquialtera throughout, Furniture throughout, Trumpet, Clarion and Cornet. As there were no inter-manual couplers, this Great chorus (referred to as 'the organ' in some sources and as the 'Full organ' in others, and thus indicated in published music) had to do all the work of accompanying large congregations on its own. The means by which this was achieved is set out in chapter 4.

6 Wooden pipework: diapasons and flutes

The wooden Open Diapason in the contract for the organ at Fulneck, the report by Buckingham of beautifully made wooden pipes in the very early Moresby Hall claviorgan, and the survival of pipes made from oak, pine and pear in the 1742 organ belonging to Alan Cuckston (see chapter 3, no. 3) and in other early organs (as well as the very latest, of 1782, no. 104), suggest Snetzler's special interest in wooden pipework. Indeed, such ranks have purely practical advantages – their basses can be mitred (as Snetzler points out in the Fulneck correspondence) and they are more easily transported – but the persistence of short-compass wooden Open Diapasons in the earlier chamber organs seems to hint at a predilection for these ranks. In the bureau organs and most chamber organs, the Stopped Diapasons and Flutes were made of wood throughout their compass. In church organs, however, where metal chimney flutes would stay better in tune with the other metal stops in the varying church temperatures, these were used instead for trebles above the 2' C pipe (actual length 1') in each rank, as Buckingham notes at Chesterfield (chapter 3, no. 31), apparently with some surprise. In the Swell, metal pipes were used down to the lowest note of the compass (generally 'fiddle G') for the sake of tonal consistency and tuning stability.

The presence of the Stopped Diapason in the 'chorus' schemes above may seem strange to us now, but it is clear that this stop was then regarded as the essential foundation stop to which were added the Open Diapasons and the upperwork, or just the Flute, on both Great and Choir. Only in later part of the century, when the Dulciana had come to be regarded as a 'solo' stop (then so-called to mean an uncombined stop, not the modern powerful stop), the Stopped Diapason would be shut off momentarily.

The Stopped Diapasons and Flutes in Snetzler's organs (as in those of his contemporaries) were thought of as 'paired': identical in scaling and construction, whether made of wood throughout or with wooden basses and metal chimney flute trebles. Chimney flutes were used for church organs, not only because they are less susceptible than small wooden pipes to pitch–derangement from climatic changes and dust, but also because they produce a somewhat more solid, carrying tone. There is no great difference in their overall cost; they do not have moveable canisters, so they have to be 'cut down' in the final processes of tuning and voicing like the other metal pipework, and then their tops soldered.

In some organs at least (Swithland, 1765, is one; see chapter 3, no. 66), the Flute was taken no lower than 'tenor C' (*c*): that is, to its lowest metal pipe. This shows clearly that it was intended to partner the Stopped Diapason, whose 'quinty' bass would cover the 'break' into two stops. In fact, if the Flute were to be carried down to the lowest note (as was done elsewhere, according to those sources which meticulously describe the Flute as 'thro''), care would have to be taken to make the bass of the Flute rather less 'quinty' than its equivalent in the Stopped Diapason tenor octave. The British taste was for 'plump' quick-speaking and bright-toned but well-controlled wooden stopped basses – analogues of the 'big' basses of the Kirkman harpsichords – and they carry well in a large building, but they can be rather uncomfortable when heard at close quarters, or when used to accompany a solo voice.

At Ludlow the basses of the Great Stopped Diapasons are larger in scale than their equivalents in the Choir, although of the same scale from middle C upwards; but the voicing of the two trebles would also be varied both in power and quality – just as the otherwise identically–made members of the choruses would be subtly distinguished from each other according to their places in the tonal scheme. Unaltered organs suggest that Snetzler's normal practice was to voice and regulate the Flute only slightly more brightly, pipe for pipe, than the Stopped Diapason.

The 'German Flute' in the King's Lynn organ is an harmonic chimney flute: that is, one made about three times its usual length and pierced with a substantial hole at its mid–body node. (A similar stop reappears from time to time in later builders' stop-lists; it was 're-invented' by William Thynne as a 'Zauberflöte' in the latter part of the nineteenth century.) It was presumably employed as a 'solo' stop, voiced to imitate the transverse flute (then usually called the 'German Flute'), as a contrast to the wooden Stopped Diapason trebles whose sound is more akin to the recorder (the 'English Flute').

7 Reed stops

Almost nothing survives of these. We can only note the existence of a Great Trumpet at Rotherham (now on a Choir soundboard and revoiced with later shallots and tongues), unaltered or restorable Hautboys at Kedleston (1766), Cobham (1778) and, possibly, Theddingworth (1763), and the complete lack of any surviving Bassoons, Cremonas, Vox Humanas or Clarions.

As with the Cornets, the exact disposition of these last four stops is not always clear in the sources. The sole surviving eighteenth–century Bassoon is in Green's

1792 organ now at St Thomas's church, Salisbury. This may be similar to the Snetzler stop: it is a small-scaled Trumpet. The Bassoon stop was often used as the Choir reed, and it presumably created the effect of a 'small-scale Great' when used with the Choir Open Diapason, Stopped Diapason, Principal and Fifteenth 'chorus'. (Only in the large organ for Beverley Minster did the Choir manual contain a mixture as well.) Choir organs made by later builders frequently included a reed stop made with a Bassoon bass and a Cremona treble (usually from *g*), whether so described or not in the sources. It is possible that some of the Snetzler stop-list sources should be interpreted thus, and such an arrangement was clearly stated at Halifax. In other instances, the Bassoon is used as a 'Choir bass' to the Swell reeds; the seemingly odd compass of the Choir Bassoon at King's Lynn (which Leffler describes as 'up to G above mid. C ... 36 [pipes]') may be a forerunner of this.

Most sources make it clear that where there is a Bassoon (and Cremona), then the Choir Vox Humana is a completely separate rank of full compass. It would seem that the Vox Humana drops out of Snetzler's stop-lists from about 1770, and this is probably symptomatic of a general decline in interest and demand for this time-consuming (and therefore expensive) stop, which cost an extra £26. 5s. at Halifax, at least half as much again as any other Choir organ stop. Specific directions for the use of the Bassoon or Vox Humana are anyway relatively uncommon in published music, as Robin Langley has pointed out.[10]

The beaked shallots of the Great Trumpet at Newby Hall are of the same kind as those of the Hautboys at Kedleston and Cobham, and those used by British builders until at least the mid-1820s. The surviving Hautboys are directly imitative of their contemporary woodwind hautboys: plangent and tinged with a hint of the open-air shawm.

Marsh, though writing near the end of the eighteenth century, makes a number of observations relevant at any period:

> The [reed] Stops are the most liable of any to get out of tune, (particularly the Clario[n], Vox Humane, and Cremona) of which [fact] the Performer should be aware, when he fixes upon his Voluntary, especially in the Country, where the Organs are in general very much neglected. [And where, evidently, the organists did not tune the reeds.]
>
> The TRUMPET...when it does not render the Organ too powerful for the Voices, always improves as well as increases the Chorus, as by being in unison with the Diapasons, it strengthens the foundation, and thereby qualifies the 3rds and 5ths in the Sesquialtera, &c. by rendering them less prominent. – This Mixture [by which he means 'combination of stops'] should however only be used to accompany Voices in Cathedrals, in the Chorusses of Verse Services or Anthems (which should be very full in order to make the greater Contrast to the Verse) and in Gloria Patrias, Hallelujahs, &c. where the drowning of the words is of no great consequence; and in Parish Churches, only for a single Verse or two by way of contrast; or where the Congregation and Church are very large; or where some Score of Charity Children add their voices to the Chorus, when the

deep and powerful Bass of the Trumpet serves to qualify the shrillness of the Children's Voices; ...

The CLARION ... or Octave Trumpet, which also where the Church and Congregation are very large, improves the Chorus [*sc.* of stops] by rendering it more brilliant. This Stop however must never be used but in addition to all the foregoing [stops of the chorus], the force of which altogether, will be too great to accompany Voices even in Gloria Patrias, &c. except on particular festivals or times when the Church is much crowded, or the Voices exceedingly numerous, for which purpose it should be reserved.

9 The sound of the church organs

Descriptions of the organs made by Snetzler noted by his contemporaries and by those who knew his organs at first hand will be found at various places in this book, but these are necessarily generalized. Only one person appears to have tried to describe the tone quality of various organ stops, but since he has popularly but erroneously been supposed (then and now) to be mad, too little notice has been taken of him. The poet Christopher Smart was a friend of Charles Burney, and a passage from *Jubilate Agno* (written about 1759 to 1763), shows that he too appreciated the organ. His poet's ear picked up the timbres of the various stops, and he tried to imitate them onomatopoeically ('by rhimes') thus:[11]

> For the spiritual musick is as follows.
> For there is the thunder-stop, which is the voice of God direct.
> For the rest of the stops are by their rhimes.
> For the trumpet rhimes are sound bound, soar more and the like.
> For the Shawm rhimes are lawn fawn moon boon and the like.
> For the harp rhimes are sing ring string & the like.
> For the cymbal rhimes are bell well toll soul and the like.
> For the flute rhimes are tooth youth suit mute & the like.
> For the dulcimer rhimes are grace place beat heat & the like.
> For the Clarinet rhimes are clean seen and the like.
> For the Bassoon rhimes are pass, class and the like. God be gracious to
> Baumgarden.[12]
> For the dulcimer are rather van fan & the like and grace place &c are of
> the bassoon.
> For beat heat, weep peep &c are of the pipe.
> For every word has its marrow in the English tongue for order and for
> delight.

It seems likely that Smart's initial idea was to imitate the common organ stops and he extrapolated this to include other sounds, but in fact dulcimers and harps did occasionally appear in eighteenth-century organs. The 'cymbal' here does seem to mean a high-pitched mixture: Burney (who often used semi-Gallic terms) may have so named the 'Furniture' stop. The 'descriptions' of the reed stops are particularly interesting – the more so since so few of this date have survived in Britain. They are certainly very evocative of their contemporary French equivalents. Vowel sounds in the descriptive words should approximate to those used now by a native Derbyshire or Yorkshire speaker; southern English pronunciation has changed greatly in two hundred years.

Since Karl Friedrich Baumgarten, who settled in London *c*1758 and died there in 1824, was the organist at the Lutheran Chapel in the Savoy (and this was Snetzler's major London instrument), it is even possible that Smart was, in part, describing that organ (see chapter 3, no. 37). It included a Bassoon on the Choir organ, and perhaps this very stop made such a strong impression upon Smart that he associated its sound with a memory of kindness received from Baumgarten. He may also have heard a Thunder stop here, too; there is no (other) record of it, and one wonders if it was included in Snetzler's organs elsewhere.

Smart's interest in musical instruments was not a merely casual one, nor confined to the organ. In *Jubilate Agno* there are several references to contemporary issues, including the best material for harpsichord wire (Smart is on the side of 'gold', i.e., brass), and choice of temperament (fragment B2, line 364: 'there is no musick in flats & sharps which are not in God's natural key'). He also specifically mentions the Arnes, father and son, and his friend, Arne's pupil (fragment D, line 196):

> Let Arne, house of Arne rejoice with The Jay of Bengal. God be gracious to
> Arne and his wife [,] to Michael [,] & Charles Burney.

III The house organs

1 Claviorgans

The known contents of the claviorgans are:

?1731 or ?1737, Moresby Hall: (*C–f '''*): SD, Dul (sc: *c'*), Fl, 15, Ses II (b/tr)

The Stopped Diapason and Flute of 'Wainscott', with sunk blocks 'Under an Harpsichord by Shudi' and labelled 'Johanes Schnetzler Organo technus Londini 1731', according to Buckingham.

1745, Earl of Wemyss: (*G', A'–f '''*): SD, OD (sc: *c'*), Fl, 15, Ses II

The harpsichord nameboard reads 'Jacobus Kirkman fecit Londini', and it is labelled 'Johan Snetzler fecit Londini 1745'. This form '... fecit Londini ...' was used by 'Hermanus' Tabel and 'Jacobus' Kirkman, but English makers, and the later Kirkmans, generally appear to have used the form '... Londini fecit'.

The link between Shudi and Snetzler has already been mentioned; he was bequeathed by Shudi the ring given to him by Frederick the Great.[13] It is also recorded[14] that 'an organized double keyed harpsichord by Shudi' was sold by the Duke of Leeds at Christie's on 11 June 1800 to one 'Smith'.

The restricted height under the harpsichord led naturally to the use of a short-compass open unison stop such as the Dulciana and Open Diapason respectively noted above. The Stopped Diapason, Flute, Fifteenth and Sesquialtera chorus would have added a 'reedy' intensity to the sound of the harpsichord – the quint-partials of the two wooden flutes and the tierce of the Sesquialtera would have helped to make the sound of the strings and pipes combine – but the two 'choirs' would mostly have been used antiphonally. There seems to be little evidence that claviorgans were used as 'continuo' instruments (the difficulty of keeping the two sections in tune under concert conditions suggests that they were not); it is more likely that the organ tone was envisaged as a coloration or prolongation of that of the harpsichord.

2 Bureau organs

The tonal scheme was much the same as that in the harpsichord-organs, but the compass was limited by the available space. The schemes recorded are:

[1742	Yale (*C–d'''*, *e'''*):	SD, Fl, 15, Ses (b/tr)/Cor (tr); to which was later added an OD (sc: *c'*)]
1751	Johnson (*C, D–e'''*):	SD, Fl, 15, 19 (originally II)
1752	New Haven (*C, D–e'''*):	SD, Fl, 15, 'Ses b'/ 'Cor tr'
1754	Mersham (*C, D–e'''*):	SD, Fl, ?OD (sc:), ?Pr (sc:)
1763	Schaffhausen (*C, D–e'''*):	SD, Fl, 15, Ses b/Cor tr
1764	Dolmetsch (*C, D–e'''*):	SD, Fl, 15, Ses b/Cor tr
(und.)	King's College (*C, D–e'''*):	SD, Fl, 15, II (b/tr)

In those instances where the composition of the mixture is recorded, it is of two ranks:

C 19–22/*c'* 12–17 [i.e., it is a sort of Sesquialtra/Cornet]

This type of organ is eminently suitable for continuo use, as it could relatively easily be carried around and retuned as necessary. The most-used stops, the Stopped Diapason and Flute, would need to be tuned frequently, and this is perfectly possible with two stopped wooden ranks. The Fifteenth and mixture would be used to support a chorus of singers or for specially bold effects. Modern 'box' organs with three or four stops, a common sight on present-day concert platforms, are the lineal descendants of these instruments.

The four-stop organ belonging to Miss Bristoe (chapter 3, no. 106), would appear from its stop-list to have been designed from the outset as an especially quiet house organ, if this is in fact its original disposition. Its tonal scheme is similar to those specified for small house organs until at least the 1860s.

3 Chamber organs

The tonal and mechanical designs of these instruments are closely interwoven; see chapter 4 for a detailed discussion. They generally follow the pattern of a chorus based on an all-wood Stopped Diapason which is supplemented in the smaller organs by a *c'* (2')-compass wooden Open Diapason or in the larger by a *c* (4')-compass metal Open Diapason. To these are added a Principal of metal, a wooden Flute, and metal Twelfth, Fifteenth and Sesquialtera/Cornet mixture. After 1755, a Dulciana, usually to *c* (4' pipe), and from time to time, a short-compass reed: an unenclosed Cremona or an enclosed Hautboy were included.

IV Casework

1 Church organs: introduction

The external design of organs is functional to a large degree, because it is intimately related to the disposition of the internal mechanisms and pipework. This point needs to be restated if only because British organs went through, and to some extent are still going through, a lengthy period when this relationship was abandoned.

Within the Classical tradition, the organ case is also effectively related to the size of the building by being large enough to contain the amount of pipework (and therefore its associated mechanisms) deemed necessary to furnish the musical output required. As, obviously, a large building, seating many persons, must require a large organ, and so on, various stop-lists have been suggested for varying situations by the major authorities – by Dom Bédos and many others. The organ is placed as advantageously as possible in the building, usually on a gallery. In a British church, this gallery might be either at the west end of the nave, or (in a large building) at the junction of nave and chancel. The size, proportions and detailing of the gallery and case are adjusted to suit the overall architectural environment. Designers of organs in Flanders, Holland, German-speaking countries, France and Britain would naturally have thought along these lines and produced an organ whose tonal and visual designs were integrated. The organ-builder, acting as both maker and designer, would then have produced an instrument 'organically' related in all its parts; only when his two functions were artificially divided by the intervention of an architect-designer (as at St Paul's Cathedral in the early years of the eighteenth century, and more and more frequently elsewhere towards the end of the century) would this integration be threatened. Such intervention is perhaps not unreasonable – the cost of a case was quite typically up to a quarter of the whole cost of an organ – but what it led to was often both architecturally and musically second-best.

With the single exception of that at Hillsborough, Ulster (chapter 3, no. 86), there is no church organ case by Snetzler still placed on a gallery specially designed for it. Badly-sited organs have been quite 'normal' for the past 150 years, so it takes quite an effort of aural and visual imagination fully to understand his organs in their original circumstances.

Leonard and John Snetzler's 'personal' style of casework design consisted of particular decorative elements – groupings and proportionings of pipe displays and details of mouldings. Despite John Sutton's assertion[15] in 1847 that 'After the time of Schmidt and Harris, Organ Cafes became plainer and meaner every year, and the old form was entirely deferted', the Snetzlers' cases were fine pieces in their own right, and neither plain nor meanly detailed. It should be remembered that though Sutton was writing a tract against the destruction of old organs, he did not see that the design of the typical seventeenth- and eighteenth-century organ case was essentially compounded of Classical elements (derived from the proportions and constituents of Greek and Roman architecture), but viewed it rather with a neo-medieval, Pre-Raphaelite eye:

> Snetzler, Green and others, in the middle [*sic*] of the last century, enclofed their Organs in Cafes as much like a square box as possible, the fide being quite as broad as the front, and the tryptic-like form, which was kept up by Schmidt by making the front overhang on each fide, was difcontinued.

In fact, the overhang (an element more Gothic than Classical in origin) was not a feature of all seventeenth century cases, and even less so of the early eighteenth century, for the simple reason that whereas in Smith's 'overhanging' organs the bellows were placed behind the organ, or to one side, in later organs the bellows and their operators were incorporated in the case. In the scaled engraving of the organ that Renatus Harris made in 1710 for Salisbury Cathedral, published in 1745, it is specifically mentioned that 'The Organ Blower, as well as the Bellows which are very Large have Room in the Body of ye Case'. This was the largest organ in Britain when it was built; clearly, any adequate blowing system would require as capacious a floor area as the case would allow, and so in a number of later moderate to large organs the overhang was eliminated and the case sides were extended backwards.

The small organ at Finedon (1717, by Christopher Schreider, a son-in-law of Smith) is one of the last made by that 'dynasty' with a case with overhanging sides, but Snetzler's cases at King's Lynn, Ludlow and Swithland certainly incorporated them. The first two were large and wide cases on galleries (western and eastern respectively) apparently sufficiently deep to allow the bellows to be placed behind the organs, and the last was so small that its six stops could be winded in a chamber organ manner.

Swithland's case is a 'Gothick' one, made in 1765, and is the oldest of the surviving four made by Snetzler in this style. This case, the double-fronted case for Beverley Minster (1769), and those for Hillsborough (1773) and Rotherham (1777), are essentially Classical in proportion but with Gothic detailing. The last two are the same as his 'normal' double-storeyed cases, but with adjustments to the style of the toe-boards of the flats, the tower brackets, and the panelling. Instead of Rococo flourishes, the ornaments on the tower cornices are 'openwork' spires.

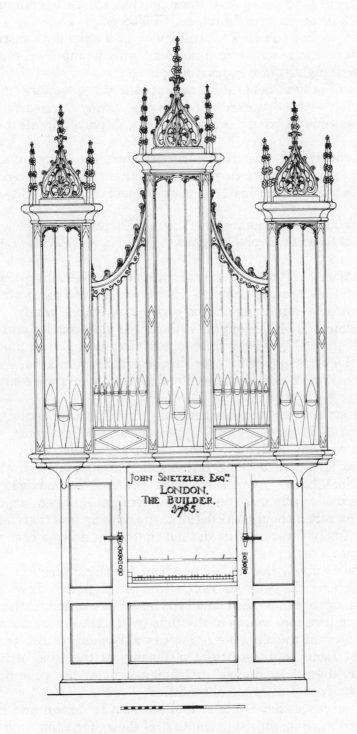

JOHN SNETZLER ESQ^R.
LONDON.
THE BUILDER.
1765.

The organ at Swithland as originally made

Details of the Swithland organ case were matched by the panelling of its gallery front (see p. 134), as in the church at Hillsborough, an early Gothic–revival ensemble. At Beverley, the organ formed part of a splendid construction which comprised a stone choir–screen or 'pulpitum' with wrought–iron gates, the tall organ case and draught–reducing curtains.

In fact it was the next generation that produced the 'gothick' designs that so displeased Sutton – those tricked out with the 'barley fugar ornaments we see about Chriftmas time in pastry cooks' windows, difplayed in all their glory on a twelfth cake'.

It has been suggested[16] that Batty Langley started a school of architecture in Soho, and that his pupils were carpenters; whether this influenced the Snetzlers is not known, but the title of his 1742 book suggests the possibility:

> Gothic Architecture, Improved by Rules and Proportions, in many Grand
> Designs of Columns, Doors, Windows ... Temples, and Pavilions etc.

The great majority of Snetzler's cases contain Rococo detailing of a kind familiar to both John and his brother Leonard the carver, as well as to other immigrant artisans. The earliest–surviving church organ case, in the chapel of the Fulneck Moravian settlement (1748), is of pine with carved pipe–shades and other wooden ornaments of high quality whose style is reminiscent of Rococo plasterwork. The implication of the correspondence over this organ (chapter 3, no. 9 and Appendix 3) is that the case was made at Fulneck and its ornaments were supplied from or *via* London.

The Rococo style later became generally familiar in London following the publication from 1754 onwards of Chippendale's *The Gentleman and Cabinet-Maker's Director*. As Michael Wilson remarks,[17] this work 'ensured that Rococo–inspired furniture became fashionable throughout the whole country'. Whereas Snetzler's house organ cases were executed in mahogany, the church organ cases were normally made in the clear straight–grained, usually imported, oak called 'wainscott'; although the detail of the carving was therefore necessarily somewhat less finely finished, this did not matter in a large case whose details were viewed from a distance.

There is a particularly Rococo feeling about the florid crestings of the flats in the Lynn case, and the way in which they engage the three towers. More restrained crestings are to be seen on all the larger cases, and all these include the characteristic sinuous toe–boards of the flats (with criss–cross cartouches) of the kind also employed in the chamber organ cases. Without doubt, the case as well as the organ at Lynn was the height of fashion at the time of its design and building. It was then a 'landmark' instrument, but at the time of writing it is visually and tonally in a disgraceful condition.

The two Choir cases that Snetzler had occasion to design and make are also distinctly Rococo in style, although the first of these (for Eton College, 1751) is a companion to the robustly 'Roman' Classical case made in 1700 for the Bernard Smith organ. These cases survive at Hawkesyard Priory (chapter 3, no. 14), where

Rococo carving at Fulneck and King's Lynn

41

the various elements of the Choir case are rather jumbled and disparted, evidently because the main case was set too low in 1899. Its original arrangement seems to have been similar to that made c1760 for Chester Cathedral, and which is now at Valletta Cathedral, Malta (chapter 3, no. 46). This was also an organ worked on by Smith, though the main case may have been made originally by Pease and Frye in 1665. The present main case would appear to have been considerably altered (possibly in the nineteenth century), and is now in a style that matches the Choir case.

Both of these Choir cases are small; they contain soundboards with three and four stops respectively. The fronts of each case consist of two towers flanking three flats, the central flat having its own bracket.

2 Form and function in the church organ cases

Snetzler's cases are designed differently from those of other builders for functional reasons as well as because of the whims of fashion.

The simplest church organ is practically no different from the developed chamber organ, and consists of wind–raising apparatus in the lower part of the case, key and stop actions above this, and a soundboard and pipework above them. Its case is only as deep as the soundboard, as at Swithland (see p. 39). The addition of a second keyboard with its own mechanisms and pipework affected the disposition of the casework in one of four ways, depending upon where the pipes might be placed. First, the additional soundboard might be behind the player within a small but complete 'Choir' case. Second, a small soundboard might be put in the space below the first set of pipes, and behind the music desk, in a small, closed 'Echo' box. Third, when this 'Echo' was later developed into a 'Swell' of longer compass, the Swell was mounted on a frame over the Great pipework; the case would then have to be taller, at least in the centre of the front, to mask the swell–box. The fourth arrangement, apparently first exploited by Snetzler in the organ for King's Lynn, and subsequently used elsewhere, was to combine the Choir and Swell on one soundboard placed behind the Great pipework, the case being deepened in consequence. Thus changes to the tonal design and the spatial disposition of the pipework are reflected in changes made to the outward appearance of the instruments.

The earliest church organ of which we have reasonably detailed knowledge is that made for the Moravians at Fulneck in 1748. This contained a Great of about nine stops with a compass from *G'* upwards, including a Principal of metal throughout, to 6' G. The contract stipulates a case with a total of 'five towers' (that is, three actual towers and two intervening flats), with fine ornaments and carving. The carving was to be gilded, and the (existing) softwood panels were to be painted – though we do not know what sort of painting was first applied; was it 'grained' as was, and is, the 1765 Swithland case? The front pipes were to be polished, not gilded. (The contrast between 'silver' polished pipes and gold ornaments was once thought by British connoisseurs to be a solecism, as it is in heraldry, hence the 'normal' indigenous preference for gilded front pipes.) The Open Diapason was to be of wood, so it would not be used in the front display. The contract confirms what we would expect: that the 6' Principal pipes would be used to form the front towers.

The organ also contained a small 'Swell' of four stops. A letter dated 16 January 1748, written before the contract was drawn up, notes that insufficient headroom would necessitate the mitring of the longest pipes of the Open Diapason on the Great (these would be about 12' long, and the Fulneck chapel gallery ceiling is only 10' 10" from the floor), and that the depth of the gallery, only 7', left little room for tuner or organist – at 1' 6" each – as well as only 4' for the organ. The Swell soundboard would have to be above or below that of the Great; the depth of the gallery would not allow it to be behind. The letter sets out the alternatives:

> I do not know how a swell could be provided except with a separate keyboard almost below it [that is, with the pipes just above and behind the keyboards, under the Great soundboard]. The pipes could be placed above in a small box in the middle of the organ with about four stops, viz. 1. Diapason, 2. Solicional, 3. Cornet, 4. Trumpet.

Since its compass was from middle C upwards only this Swell, as thus described, might have been winded from rear or intercalated grooves on the Great soundboard (the latter as in the two–manual 1756 organ at Hillington; see chapter 3, no. 33). But since the front of the casework is at its lowest in the centre, it seems more likely that the Swell was set below the Great soundboard. Snetzler implies that this is so in a letter of 9 April 1748, where he says that a proposed Hautboy in the Swell would be difficult to get at and to tune, and suggests a 'Cornetin' instead. Other organs of the period, by British makers, were made in this way[18] (as was probably the Echo in the Eton College organ as Smith left it), and surviving evidence from these is that the Swell was played from the lower of the two keyboards.[19] The evidence further implies that the Swell/Echo was set back (and down) behind the key action to the Great, and not as in a 'brustwerk'.[20]

The next–dated case of which we have definite knowledge is that made for King's Lynn in 1753–4. It will be observed that the upper front of this large case also consists of three towers, the shortest of which is in the centre. Here there are also the wide intervening flats of a form that was to become characteristic of Snetzler's 'frontispieces', with much exuberant carving presumably done (and designed?) by Leonard Snetzler. There are three manuals: a large Great, a Choir and a Swell. The presence of a Swell would normally require that the central tower was high enough to screen the swell–box and its mechanism, but in this organ the Choir and the Swell were, it seems, originally combined on shared or adjacent soundboards behind the Great pipework, so that three basses of the Choir ranks – Stopped Diapason, Dulciana and Flute – could be readily 'borrowed' to form basses to the short-compass 'tenor F' Swell ranks. One wonders if this was a development of the 'borrowed' stops on the Backchurch organ (see Appendix 1); did Burney suggest it? Did later comments about the numbers of half-stops imply not criticism so much as some puzzlement as to how these stops were to be used?

The two large towers and the wide flats in the upper casework at Lynn would have been essential for the accommodation of the bass pipes of the 'long octaves'

Great keyboard. These are the pipes 8' long and under (from the Open Diapason) which are played from the low C, C♯, D (and higher) keys, and those 6' and under (from the Principal rank); their accommodation in the case-front naturally determined its size, and to some extent its configuration.

By contrast, the part of the case for St Paul's church, Sheffield (1755) which survives (altered and painted) at Wingerworth church, Derbyshire, seems to be a first version, but with only single-storey flats, of a type that was to become Snetzler's 'standard' frontispiece for his larger church organs. This is the earliest of the Snetzler organs for which we have Alexander Buckingham's knowledgeable comments; he noted that it was contained

> In a Wainscott Case 18 ft, high, 10ft. 5½ in. wide, 7ft. 10in. deep ... In 1810 it was thoroughly repaired with considerable Additions by J. Lincoln at the expense of the Seatholders. It appears in 1810 it was made long octaves with new sets of keys the Pedals added also the Trumpet and St. Diapason in the Swell...

These remarks imply an organ originally made with only the *G', A', C, D, D♯* pipes required by the bass of the 'short-octave' manual compass. It was not necessary to accommodate the large A♯, B and C♯ pipes in the case towers, which therefore were not so bold as those at King's Lynn, but were designed with the longest pipes in the centre tower. A drawing of the case when it was still in St Paul's church (see chapter 3, no. 21) shows that the largest front pipe was in fact about 8' in speaking length. This is confirmed by Buckingham; he states that even after the 1830 work 'The Open Diapason [goes] to CC of metal' and that there were 'St. Diapason and metal helpers' for 'the four lowest Notes'. Although the Open Diapason basses are in the central tower, the *C♯* was not included among them (see concerning Whitehaven below). This would have simplified the disposition of the front pipes; the *C♯* remained a Stopped Diapason with a 'helper' even when the compass was modified by Lincoln to 'long octaves'.

The casework of the Sheffield organ was 7' 10" deep in order to accommodate the Choir organ. The Chesterfield organ of 1756 had a similar case-front and a had a depth, recorded by Buckingham in 1823, of 7'. At Whitehaven, St Nicholas, (1755) the casework was 3' 9" deep, according to Buckingham's account of 1824, but this organ was then of two manuals only; there was no Choir organ, and the stop-list of the Swell implies that Blyth may have made or altered this in 1797. Buckingham also notes the case as being of 'Wainscott' and '18ft. high, 10ft. 6ins. wide'. This height would imply a Swell over the Great soundboard. He goes on: 'Two diagonal bellows ... Open to CC of metal, the GG AA BB ♮♮ CC♯ [again because of the arrangement of the front pipe-towers] is Stop Diapason with a metal helper'. This case does not survive, so its form can only be estimated from the details Buckingham recorded.

A comparison of the Sheffield and Chesterfield case-fronts with the case made for the German Lutheran Chapel of the Savoy (*c*1757 or later), another three-manual organ, will reveal an essential difference: the space taken up at Sheffield by two large scrolls over the flats is given over to a second storey of pipes.

Case made for St Paul's church, Sheffield

A photograph (see p. 56) of the Savoy organ (destroyed in 1940) shows that it was only a double panel deep. This would imply a depth of about 5' for an organ of the same tonal size as Sheffield's organ whose case, according to Buckingham, was half as deep again. Even if the Lincolns had deepened the Sheffield case for some reason (and no pedal pipes were added in 1810, which might have occasioned this), the two–storied casework at the Savoy suggests that the Swell was now definitely placed over the Great, and that the second storey of pipes was added to mask the swell–box and its associated shutter mechanisms.

Another detail which would indicate a 'high Swell' should be noticed: an horizontal panel over the 'console' opening. One can clearly be seen in the old photograph of the Ludlow organ, chapter 3, no. 63; it provides access for adjustment to the lower ends of trackers which at this point are connected to backfalls bringing the action forward over the music desk, and which continue vertically to the high Swell placed over the Great pipework.

In the organs of Snetzler's maturity, and when the various schemes had become systematized, the frontispieces of the larger church organs became standardized to the 'Savoy' pattern, even where there was a combined Choir/Swell soundboard:

1762	New York Trinity Church	3-manual
1764	Cambridge (USA), Christ Church	3-manual
1764	Ludlow	3-manual
1764	Cambridge, Peterhouse Chapel	3-manual (Choir/Swell)
1766	Halifax	3-manual
1767	Charleston	3-manual
1770	Drogheda	3-manual (Choir/Swell)
1772	Andover	3-manual (Choir/Swell)
1773	Hillsborough	3-manual, Gothic case
1775	Bath, Margaret Street	3-manual
1777	Rotherham	3-manual, Gothic case
1777	Nottingham	3-manual, double front

Other large organ cases were designed specially for their locations, as at Beverley Minster (1767–9), a 3-manual 'double-front' organ. The original layout of this organ is not now clear, though a good deal of the casework and pipework survives. The Wyatt-designed casework at Burton-on-Trent (1771) seems never to have been related functionally to its contents, and (as we have noted) this lack of relationship pointed to future designs.

3 The casework of house organs

Apart from claviorgans, the first organs made by Snetzler were either small semi-portable organs or 'bureau' organs, or were house organs whose designs were apparently derived from them. They have their continental counterparts – the small 'cabinet organ' in German-speaking countries of the kind made by Speisegger, and those made in Holland by Müller and his contemporaries. Similar small house organs, with a compact arrangement of pipework, a feeder and reservoir wind supply and a simple 'pin' key action, were still being made in Switzerland as 'Toggenburger' organs in the early nineteenth century.

The painted organ of 1742 (now at Yale) shows some affinity with the Speisegger organs in its decoration, but this is unique; there was by then no general market in Britain for painted furniture. Mahogany, first used in quantity at Cannons (1713–20), was subsequently imported into London in bulk and, though at first expensive, its dominance in fashionable furniture making by the late 1730s was complete. Most mahogany was then of the heavy 'Spanish' kind; the lighter 'Honduras' logs arrived later in the century. The 1742 Cuckston organ's case appears originally to have had a finish entirely of mahogany, using both solid timber and characteristically applied veneer.

At about the same time as Snetzler arrived in London, the Chippendales arrived there from Yorkshire. As we saw on p. 40, Thomas Chippendale's *Director* (1754 and later) established the Rococo style. Though this was pioneered in the 1740s by Italian plasterers, it did not become the dominant fashion until well into the 1750s. Snetzler's case for the Picton Castle chamber organ was therefore 'advanced' in 1750: it anticipated the height of this fashion by some years. The general design of its pipe-array and ornamentation remained a standard pattern for most of his career, no doubt because its style neatly hit a compromise between sober post-Palladian designs and wilder flights of fancy, both of which were to be exemplified in the *Director*. Even the craze later in the 1750s for 'Chinese' ornamentation found a gentle reflection in the glazed dust-doors of some of Snetzler's chamber organs.

The characteristic 'standard' or 'normal' case-front of Snetzler's chamber instruments consist of a three-part centre with gilt dummy metal or wood front pipes. Their tips are housed in a sinuous toe-board that rises towards the centre so that music books might be accommodated on a small ledge or music desk above the keyboard without the likelihood of damage to the gilding of the front pipes. Over the centre flat is an arch and a boldly carved festoon hangs from its 'keystone'. The pipes in the side flats are engrailed with further carving. Between the flats are strong mullions which, together with the outer mullions, support a cornice which runs along the front and sides of the case. A 'broken' pediment with, generally, a plinth in its centre, is fixed upon the cornice. The whole composition is a strong one, and there is a sense of depth which is created by the vanishing-points of the toe-board and the pipe-shade carving; it almost seems a deliberate, though faint, harking back to the Dallam 'perspective' case-fronts, but in a Rococo guise. Whatever its antecedents might be, it is a masterly conception.

The organ in Picton Castle   *The organ at Birmingham University*

None of the designs Snetzler employed was in fact taken from the *Director*; instead, they seem to have been usually the result of collaboration between John and Leonard and their workshop associates. By contrast, the case of the 'anonymous' organ for Polebarn House, Trowbridge, whose design was taken from the 1762 edition,[21] was quite non-functional. One suspects that this design would generally have been rejected by the practical organ builder as too fanciful for most situations or tastes.

A decade after the Picton design was promulgated, a second type was developed, apparently in response to an enlargement of the tonal resources of the organ which necessitated a taller instrument. Although the earlier 'standard' design was capable of enlargement (it was at its largest in the organ for the Boston Concert Hall, 1762), it would seem that designs made by Robert Adam, probably for the large barrel organ at Luton Park (or Hoo) *c*1762, suggested another style of case altogether. One of his designs shows a pedimented case with caryatids and a large central ellipse garlanded with a wreath. Although there are no front pipes on this drawing, it was but a short step from this to the first positively-dated (1764) 'wreathed-oval' case, now in Westminster Abbey. It would seem that about half a dozen of these cases were made. That now at Wynnstay (see chapter 3, no. 88) is a more elaborate version which also includes the caryatids; it is a pity that it cannot yet be precisely dated.

The organ case for the Earl of Bute, designed by Robert Adam

Some aspects of the design of the 1760 chamber organ now at Eton College are also significant; much of its ornamentation is similar to that of the organ (1755) made for the York Assembly Rooms, now at Sculthorpe, but its oval is not 'wreathed'. It was an even simpler version of this 'simple oval' design that Green was to use from 1777 onwards. His small chamber organ, dated 1778, for Cobham Hall (now in Hastingleigh church, Kent)[22] was in this respect a contrast with Snetzler's 'wreathed-oval' case for the large organ in the Music Room there which is also dated 1778.

Apart from these two 'oval' designs, there is the organ made for the Smith–Rylands in 1759 (chapter 3, no. 42). This seems to be a special design for its original (music room?) location; mechanically it is identical to the 1760 Eton chamber organ.

The organ at Eton College

The organ at 'Hatchlands'

The remaining house organs are larger special commissions. Where possible, they are described and illustrated in detail in their respective places in chapter 3:

1755–6	Lulworth Castle – an organ costing £196, which implies a sizeable instrument; no details have survived (chapter 3, no. 24).
1756	The Duke of Bedford; a large Rococo case, now at Hillington church, Norfolk, elaborated from the standard chamber organ type (no. 33).
1759	Nathaniel Curzon, at Kedleston or London (no. 41a); moved to the Pantheon (no. 41b) c1771–2; no details survive, although designs for it in its proposed location survive.
	The present organ at Kedleston, installed 1765–6, is described in chapter 3, at no. 69; it has a case made on the spot after a design by Robert Adam.
1762	The Earl of Bute at Luton Park – see above and chapter 3, no. 98.
1766	The Earl Fitzwilliam at Richmond (no. 70). As this organ has a stop–list similar to that at Cobham Hall, it might have had a similar case, but no details of it survive.
1778	The Earl of Darnley at Cobham Hall (no. 99). The organ is in a chamber, so it has no visible cladding other than the front, which is a version of the 'wreathed oval' type, enlarged in rather the same way that Green later 'stretched' his standard style of case for the large chamber organ at Attingham Park.[23]
17??	An undated organ, moved to William Strutt's house in 1813 (no. 107b), tonally similar to that supplied c1755 to the Earl of Scarborough (no. 28). It seems to have been a church organ, but it may possibly have been made for a music room.

4 The construction of church and chamber organ cases

We can see from the Fulneck letters that the cost of transport was then a considerable item in the overall cost of the organ. It is true that Snetzler had been pressed to a fairly low price by Mr Schlicht; he had even agreed that the cost of transport would be included, as well as that of the case. It is therefore not surprising that Snetzler decided to make or have made the main parts of the case made (by local joiners, presumably) 'on the spot', along with the bellows, in order to reduce his expenditure on packing cases, cartage costs, and the road tolls from London to Leeds.

Once Snetzler was fully established and able to command relatively high prices for his organs, and carriage costs in addition, only the problem of packing and transporting the cases remained. There is no evidence of the cases of the larger organs from King's Lynn onwards (whose transport from London cost an additional 5 per cent of the contract price) being made anywhere but in the 'shops' in London. This is in contrast to the cases of Green's largest organs, which were (at Lichfield, for instance) made locally and at extra cost. Green was to rationalize the making of his chamber organ cases into an easily demountable system, and the church organ cases of moderate size which he designed were similarly constructed, but Snetzler's cases were made of larger elements.

It is now almost impossible to say whether his church organ cases were made with integral frames in order to support the soundboards and actions, or whether the larger organs' actions were supported internally on separate frames. John Holmes's description of the organ formerly at Durrow, Eire (see chapter 3, no. 10) suggests that there were frames in smaller organs at least. All the larger church organs have been radically rebuilt mechanically and the vital evidence has disappeared. The documentary evidence that Snetzler brought 'the organ' with him to Fulneck is inconclusive on this point; it is more likely that he brought the necessary parts for assembly within a locally made case designed to include supports for the mechanisms and that this case was ornamented with carvings brought from London.

Vestiges of marks on the inside of the casework at Swithland (1765) suggest that horizontal members of the internal structure were indeed supported on vertical posts glued directly to the case panels, and the positioning of holes for the stop-traces through the frames of the panels adjacent to the keyboard here and in other organs suggests that there was no completely independent inner framework of the kind used by Green. The Cobham Hall Snetzler organ (1778) is supported on a frame, but as there is no casework other than the front this, like the 1771 Newby Hall organ presumed to have been made by Haxby (which is also in a recess and for which the case was also made separately), may be rather a response to a particular situation than evidence of a general mode of construction. Another organ with an unusual case, made in 1759 apparently for a particular location, is that now at 'Hatchlands'. Here, for no obvious reason, the organ's main structure and the casework are entirely separate: even the stays for the larger pipes are supported by frames attached to the organ's main frame rather than on the inner sides of the casework, although the stop-traces are arranged to pass through holes in the bases of the two large pilasters which frame the case-front. This last detail suggests that the specially designed cases were also made in London.

The cases of the chamber organs are generally made with solid sides of softwood veneered with mahogany, or with solid mahogany panels, as at Merevale (chapter 3, no. 93). However, this construction is not obvious because applied mouldings along the sides continue the front impost and other mouldings. The sides are supported on a solid glued-together plinth or base which covers the complete ground-area of the organ and which contains the feeder and reservoir. At the front of this there are hinged double panels at kneeboard level. There is another pair of panels each side of the keyboard, and above the unstructural impost are the panels into which are placed the pipes of the 'flats'. The back usually comprises two or four plain softwood panels. The cornice, like the plinth, is a complete horizontal frame; it binds the various elements of the upper case together and usually supports a pediment.

In the later and larger chamber organs, there is a moulding (bolder than the impost) which runs across the front of the organ just below the keyboard and along the sides. This characteristic makes it possible for one to see that the organ is composed of three layers from the ground upwards: wind system, key and stop actions, soundboard and pipes. The purpose of a horizontal panel under the 'oval' is to give access to the face-board of the soundboard. Even more clearly than the church organ cases, therefore, the external form of the chamber organs illustrates their internal arrangement.

5 Other casework details

Various ornamental and practical features are illustrated here:

Pediment and pipe-shade carving: Blickling church

'Hatchlands': construction of pediment

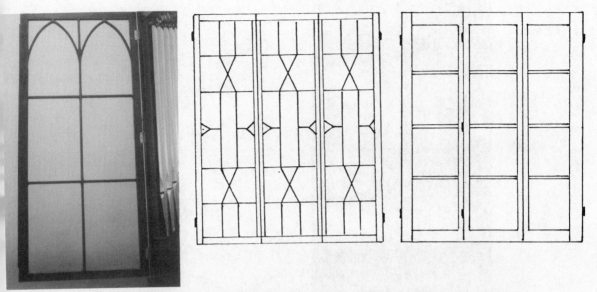

Glazed doors: 'gothic' (Birmingham University), 'Chinese' (Wesley's Chapel, Bristol) and plain (Somerset)

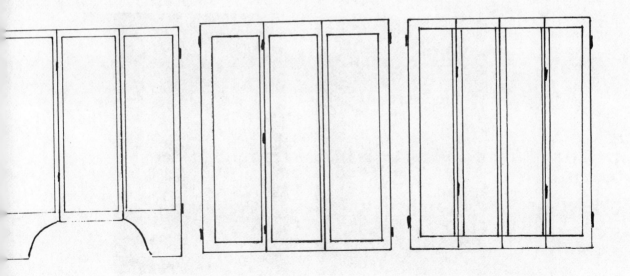

Wooden doors: three-fold (Lodge Canongate and Clare College) and four-fold (St Andrew-by-the-Wardrobe)

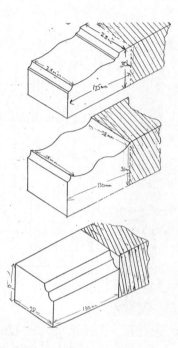

Key cheeks: the carved cheeks at Hillington and various other shapes
(top to bottom: South Dennis / Blickling, Eton College and Sculthorpe)

Casework veneer: 1742 'Cuckston' organ
Note the contrast in styles between the lowest (left) and highest (right)
panels (original) and the later (?early nineteenth century) middle panel

Endnotes

1. His full–length memoirs (in thirty–seven volumes) are in the Huntington Library, California, U.S.A. (MS HM 54457, vols 1–37); there is a shorter version in Cambridge University Library (MS. Add. 77576), and four volumes, one of autobiography and three of 'Recollections' (apparently summaries of the 'Huntington' volumes) are in the Library of the Royal College of Organists, London: Sowerbutts Collection (see the *RCO Journal*, number one: 1993, p. 27 ff.).

2. TO 207/105–6.

3. A general introduction to Blewitt's treatise is given by Philip Sawyer, 'A Neglected Late 18th Century Organ Treatise' (BIOSJ 10/76).

4. See Lynn Edwards, 'The Thuringian Organ 1702–1720', *The Organ Yearbook 1991*, pp. 129–30.

5. In *The Tracker*, vol. 35, no. 2, 1991. Admirers of Cervantes (and Robert Louis Stevenson) may notice a subliminal connection between 'dulciana' and 'celestina'; one wonders if this conjunction of names was deliberately conceived in the eighteenth–century mind.

6. HR2, p. 276.

7. Ibid., p. 277.

8. Published in Richard Francis and Peter Klein, *The Organs and Organists of Ludlow Parish Church*, (Ludlow, 1982), p. 61, and in a private communication in which he notes that rank I of the Sesquialtera is marked 'tierce', rank II '19th' to b♮" then '17th' to the top note, and rank III '22nd' to b♮" then '15th' to the top note.

9. HR2, p. 275.

10. Robin Langley, ed., *Early English Organ Music* (Novello, 1988), vol. 5, p. 58.

11. Christopher Smart, *Jubilate Agno*, ed. W. H. Bond (Hart–Davis, 1954), fragment B2, ll. 584–97.

12. K. F. Baumgarten was born in Lübeck c1740. Apart from playing the organ at the German Lutheran church, he was successively leader of the orchestras at the Haymarket, Dublin and Covent Garden Theatres, and a composer of theatre and church music. He was a subscriber to William Russell's first set of *Voluntaries* (1804).

13. D. H. Boalch, *Makers of the Harpsichord and Clavichord 1440–1840* (London, 1974), p. 168.

14. Ibid., p. 158.

15. Sir John Sutton, *A Short Account of Organs Built in England* (London, published anonymously, 1847; reprinted Positif Press, Oxford, 1979), p. 98.

16. Nicholas Plumley, 'The Englishness of the English Organ Case' (BIOSJ 4/18, fn. 7).

17. Michael Wilson, *The English Country House and its Furnishings* (Batsford, 1977), p. 89.

18. Buckingham (TO 206/55) mentions the original Swell in the organ at Grantham parish church, built by Harris and Byfield in 1735, which he describes as 'situated behind the desk board'.

19. As was originally the situation in the organ, formerly ascribed to Snetzler, installed in Leatherhead parish church in 1843; see chapter 5, p. 269.

20. As is shown in the section, drawn 1784, of the organ case at Norwich Cathedral, BIOSJ 14/44.

21. This case is illustrated in Michael Wilson, *The English Chamber Organ*, plate 34, and (in colour) on the front cover of Peter Williams's edition of Handel's *Organ Concertos, Op. 7* (O.U.P., 1988).

22. David Wickens, *The Instruments of Samuel Green* (Macmillan, 1987), p. 113.

23. Ibid., Plate 16.

The organ in St Mary-le-Savoy Lutheran Church

3 His work

THIS CHAPTER arranges Snetzler's work as far as possible chronologically. Each organ is headed with its original location or – if moved – its present (June 1993) or last-known location. The abbreviated references below each location are to those sources cited fully in the Introductory notes (see p. xiii). Bibliographical references at the end of each entry are indicated by figures in square brackets in the text.

1 Whitehaven, Moresby Hall, Miss Tate
(1731)

B 213/45

The only source which documents this claviorgan by Shudi and Schnetzler is its description by Alexander Buckingham in 1838:

> Mifs Tate, Moresby Hall, two miles from Whitehaven, Cumberland—An Organ by Snetzler in 1731 under an Harpsichord by Shudi. The Compafs CC to F in alt. Contain St. Diapason, Flute, Dulciana treble to m/C, Fifteenth, Sexqualtra bafs 2 ranks and Cornet treble 2 ranks. The Sound Board is well made very good work the St. Diapason and Flute pipes are Wood of Wainscott and are as well or better Made than I ever seen any before. The metal pipes are in a bad Condition. The St. Diapason and Flute is voised with the block sunk instead of the Cap. The Cap is a straight piece of wood fair or a little above the top of the block. Inside the Sd Bd is Johanes Schnetzler Organo technus Londini 1731. Whitehaven, 1838. A.B.

The presence of the Dulciana treble in what is a stop-list otherwise typical of a 'bureau' organ is unexpected, and in the 1742 organ (no. 3) this is in effect replaced by an Open Diapason. In fact, it would not actually have been labelled 'Dulciana' as the organ was presumably controlled by unlabelled brass knobs as in the Wemyss claviorgan (no. 6), nor would 'Sexqualtra bafs' be a Snetzler appellation, but perhaps an Open Diapason seemed to Buckingham to be of small scale. In this apparently earlier organ, the rank's compass was to middle C, and in the 1742 organ the Open Diapason started at middle C♯. This is perhaps a more significant anomaly because the musical impetus for a change from this older 'break point' to a tenor B/middle C break has previously been thought to have been manifest later than the early 1740s. One wonders, too, if the harpsichord's lowest note was also 'CC'.

Both harpsichord and organ have so far proved elusive. Shudi's earliest extant harpsichord is dated 1729, and the present whereabouts of this instrument is therefore of interest equally to historians of harpsichord and organ.

However one might read the date given by Buckingham (see chapter 1, p. 4), his account pushes back the likely year of Snetzler's arrival in London; it helps to make some sense of the comment that he was overworked in the latter part of 1742, and goes some way to explain why there are persistent rumours connecting his organs with the first performances of *Messiah*.

2 Kilmore (?), County Armagh, Revd R. Johnston (1742 or earlier)

The organ referred to in Thomas Drew's letter [1] as belonging to the Revd Richard Johnston (no. 4), and previously to the architect Francis Johnston (1761–1829) [2] and – before about 1800 – to Lord Ely of Rathfarnham Castle, Dublin ('who had it direct from Handel'), has been searched for by Sumner [3] without success. It might have come to the mainland, and one wonders if Drew's suggestion of contacting the then 'vicar of Romsey Abbey' (a mistake, it is suggested, for Waltham Abbey?) over its whereabouts in 1899 was followed up by his correspondent, T. W. Browne.

Lord Ely had enclosed the organ in an 'elaborate case of mahogany carved with allegorical figures', according to Drew. A photograph of this case (not suitable for publication) shows an elaborately moulded wide but shallow casework with 'french'-mouthed front dummies arranged 7–9–15–9–7. It contained fewer stops than Drew's own instrument (the Yale organ, no. 4), with a 'rounder and fuller tone...meant for orchestral business' and with 'one little black–keyed manual'. It was reported to have been labelled *Johannes Schnetzler Londini* and dated 1742, though if Handel had indeed brought it to Dublin with him one would have expected it to have been dated 1741 for reasons which are discussed under the heading of no. 4.

It has been reported [4] that the organ was sold in 1920 to a buyer in Denmark, but the organ has not yet been traced in that country, or elsewhere.

[1] February 1899 (Bodleian Library, MS. Eng. lett. c. 130, fols. 146–51).
[2] Dictionary of National Biography, vol. 30, p. 61.
[3] TO 153/37.
[4] *via* Alan Cuckston, who also kindly made a copy of the photograph available.

3 Ripon, North Yorkshire, Alan Cuckston (1742)

The organ is labelled *Johannes Schnetzler fecit Londini 1742*. The completely Germanic form of Snetzler's name and the middle C♯ lower termination of the Open Diapason and Cornet suggest that this organ was made before the 'Yale' organ dated the same year (no. 4).

The keyboard, of blackwood naturals (unusually, with arcaded fronts) and ivory-plated sharps, operates a pin action to pallets in the grid directly beneath. There are four horizontal iron rollers, concealed in the treble by a wide key-cheek (duplicated in the bass for symmetry). The single–rise wedge–reservoir and feeder are accessible by two doors, and there are arrangements for pedals for blowing (apparently modified later) and for operating a 'shifting movement' (not restored at the time of writing) of two wide sliders which cut off wind to the Fifteenth and the compound stops. The vertically arranged stop–action may originally have been operated by plain pear-wood levers moved horizontally; later engraved stop-knobs have been inserted into the remains of these. The stop–list, as it finally left the workshop, appears to have been:

(*G'*, *A'-f '''*): OD (sc: *c♯'*), SD, Fl, 15, Cor II (sc: *c♯'*) 12–17, Ses III/II (bass and treble not divided, but breaking at middle C♯) 19–22–(26)/8–15

The originally intended stoplist would appear to have been:

SD, Pr, Fl, ?15, Cor II tr, Ses III/II

but this seems to have been altered during or shortly after construction. Some of the present Fifteenth bass pipes are marked 'p'.

At a later date, possibly coinciding with alterations to the casework, the third rank of the Sesquialtra bass was suppressed, and the tierce of the Cornet was suppressed from middle b♮ upwards, the oak rackboard being neatly spliced to conceal these alterations from the top view.

The final workshop stop–list might at first sight appear to be consistent with the organ's origin being a portable 'chest' organ. However, the original parts of the casework shows that the organ first stood to a total height of about 7' 3", and in fact the six longest Stopped Diapason pipes were originally mitred to this height. The case is 4' 6" wide by 1' 10" deep; the organ was and is in fact a small chamber organ at which the player sat.

The Stopped Diapason and Flute pipes are made of wood throughout. In the bass they are of Scot's pine with oak fittings (with unmoulded caps), but the 12"-long pipes and smaller have front planks made from pear. The pipes 6" and smaller have sides and backs made of fine oak, apparently 'Danzig' or Baltic oak.

Mechanically, the organ remains as first made, including its original pallet and grid leatherings, and brass action 'pins', pallet guides and springs. Only the casework has been altered, probably during the first part of the nineteenth century, to its present form by means of the insertion of a new mid-panel, an impost rail and a 'Gothick' front. The detailing of the surviving original casework is interesting not only for the way in which the veneers are applied, but also for its very early use of solid and veneered mahogany.

The upper part of the case has been modified in more recent times and the cornice (whether original or 'Gothick') has been lost, together with the later central pipe–flat of gilded 'flat–backs'. It is not now possible to deduce what sort of upper front the organ might have had – perhaps a pair of doors, concealing a painted representation of front pipes?

Research currently being carried out may reveal more of the history of this fortunate survival. It was 'discovered' in an Edinburgh attic in 1940, when such places were being cleared out for fear of inendiary bombs, by the father of the organ's previous owner, J. Bennet McNeill. One would very much like to know why a 'long octaves' compass, and one that extended as far as f''', was employed here, in contrast to the e''' compass of many subsequent organs, large and small, and why in this organ (uniquely in Snetzler's work) the divided ranks break between middle C and middle C♯.

Exploratory restoration work by Martin Renshaw of the wooden pipework and the Fifteenth re-established what appear to be the original wind-pressure (2" water-gauge), and pitch (A = 423Hz at 55 degrees Fahrenheit, in meantone temperament). The other surviving pipework was reconstituted by Dominic Gwynn and Martin Goetze (with new pipes by Derek Jones) in the late summer of 1993.

4 Yale University, Harford (U. S. A.), Belle Skinner Collection (1742)

The soundboard is labelled: *John: Schnetzler fecit Londini 1742*.[1] The lower part of the organ, which has two iron carrying handles, is apparently of mahogany veneered on softwood. Strictly speaking, it is a portable 'chest' organ, not a 'bureau' organ, and some features of its internal disposition are reminiscent of seventeenth-century 'English' organs.

In its first state, the organ's compass and stop-list were:

$(C-d''', e'''$ [sic]): Diapaison [i.e., Stopped Diapason], Flauta [i.e., Flute], 'Fiffteenth', Sesquialtra II [b], Sesquialtra II [tr], Cornet II [tr]

At a later date, an 'Op. Diapason' was added [sc: from c', not $c♯'$ as in the other 1742 organ, no. 3] at the back of the soundboard, and the lower case (veneered in mahogany) and a new upper case were painted with floriate patterns in green, deep pink and gold. The stops are operated by vertical wooden levers in horizontal keyboard cheeks.

There is a persistent tradition that this organ was used by Handel for the first performance of *Messiah* in Dublin, 13 April 1742. In fact Handel had left London at the beginning of November 1741, had passed through Chester (where Burney saw him for the first time, and where Handel tried to rehearse parts of *Messiah*), and arrived in Dublin on 18 November. His concert on 23 December included 'a Concerto on the Organ' ('whit more then usual success [sic]', he reported to Jennens on the 29th). The concert was repeated on 13 January 1742, and 'several concertos on the Organ' were played on the 20th (see letter below). Before the first performance of *Messiah*, there were some further concerts at which there were also 'some Concertoes on the Organ, by Mr. Handell'. After more concerts, including 'Messiah with Concertos on the organ' (John Faulkner's *Dublin Journal*, 29 May 1742) [2], and a visit to the failing Dean Swift, Handel left Dublin in August 1742. He did not perform again that year; *Messiah* was eventually first performed in London 'With a Concerto on the Organ' in March 1743.[3] The oratorio finally achieved success only in 1750 and in succeeding years when it was performed in the new Chapel of the Foundling Hospital.

It is therefore not possible to associate the surviving 1742 organs with Handel's concerts in Dublin. In fact, Thomas Drew (in the letter quoted below) does not make any so direct a connection. He records that his organ, now at Yale, was made for Archbishop Robinson of Armagh, who he assumes to have been connected with Handel as one of his patrons. He instead associates the (missing) Johnston organ (no. 2) specifically with Handel when he writes that 'Lord Ely ... had it direct from Handel', and that it 'is undoubtedly one used by Handel ... in Dublin when producing the Messiah'.

A new organ, made by Harris & Byfield, was in fact set up in Dublin in September 1742; as the following extract from the *Dublin Journal*, transcribed by Sumner, [4] noted:

> Saturday, September 18th to Tuesday, 21st, 1742.
> The organ in the New Music Room in Fishamble Street being about up, the Committee are desired to meet next Wednesday evening to settle the Music for the ensuing Winter.
>   Signed by Order.   William Neale. Treasurer.

The Yale organ case, following cleaning and restoration by Anna Hulbert

In the Bodleian Library, Oxford, there is a letter [5], written by Sir Thomas Drew in February 1899 and addressed to T. W. Browne, E[sq.], which includes the following:

> The Organ which I failed to arouse local interest in 25 years ago, & might then have been bought for £100, is undoubtedly one used by Handel during his sojourn in Dublin when producing the <u>Messiah</u>. It will be found to bear the same inscription as my small instrument <u>Johannes Schnetzler Londini</u> & I doubt not the same date 1742. It is now at Kilmore Co Armagh, in possession of the Rev. Richard Johnston aged 84. He has three or four sons. I do not [know] where the organ may go to at his decease – If I were opening any communication about it, I should choose, of the Johnstons, one who is I think the Vicar of Romsey Abbey, Hants. [this may be a mistake for Waltham Abbey, Herts.] & takes some interest about Organs.
>
> I know the unbroken history of the instrument since the beginning of the Century. Francis Johnston, Architect, who was a noteable collector of pictures & curios, bought it from Lord Ely of Rathfarnham Castle Dublin, 1800–10 – Johnston died about 1827. I saw it at a last Sale of his effects in 1872 at his house in Eccles St Dublin. It had I believe lain there locked and untouched for 40 years. It was then in good condition. ([The next two sentences crossed out:] It might have been been [*sic*] bought for any bid. It interested no one but myself.)
>
> Lord Ely, who had it direct from Handel, had glorified it by enclosing it in an elaborate case of mahogany carved with allegorical figures. Within is the plain small instrument having no connexion with its 'Shrine'. Its few stops, & its rounder & fuller tone when compared with my little organ, led me to think it was intended for orchestral business, & not a mere toy – my little instrument has, in comparison, more stops & its characteristic a pretty affectation of grand tone in miniature which used to delight my friend Sir Robert Stewart.
>
> Handel produced Acis & Galatea [actually, [6] *L'Allegro*] at the Music Hall Fishamble St Dublin Jan. 13th 1741–2 'with several concertos on the Organ & other Instruments'.
>
> The large number of Schnetzler's organs throughout Ireland – 1740–50 – is traceable to the introduction & influence of Handel on the musical Gentry of Ireland; the history of whose enthusiasm for him in connexion with the production of the <u>Messiah</u> you are no doubt acquainted with – I have met with them in my business visits up & down. They have always interested me as a memory & savour of Handel & inspired a feeling of regret that I could find no sentiment of regard for them among Choirs, local organists, parsons or Churchwardens & but the iconoclastic contempt of jobbing new organ–builders. I have seen a number broken up & might have rescued some victims for a £5 note if I could but have housed them.
>
> I saw Schnetzler's finest Irish organ built for Armagh Cathedral, burnt at Belfast about 1849 & heard it a few hours before. It was built for primate Robinson of Armagh 1765. My little Chamber instrument was the original property of primate Robinson, who may be assumed, as a noteable musical patron, to have had acquaintance with Handel & possibly his advice. So it pleases to fancy that it may have once Known the hand of the

Master.

My little Schnetzler is enclosed in a plain case once decorated with gilding but 3ft 8in & 2ft 3in & standing 5 1/2 feet high. Its stops are

> Diapason
> Flauta
> An unamed [*sic*] & curious harmonic stop possibly defective
> Op. Diapason
> Fifteenth
> Cornet
> Sesquialter

It has of course one little black-keyed manual (as in the Johnston organ). It is blown by the foot & seems to me to have a certain amount of expression of swell by the direct action of the foot on the small bellows, at least from the sympathetic foot of one who can "humour" the bellows.

Still a number of Schnetzler organs must survive in Ireland through the poverty or indifference or ignorance of those who have them. To my amateur sense all seem to have the same marked character – the sweet mellow & satisfying diapasons, & the intentional <u>nasal</u> or violin tone of the metal stops which is in my fancy an echo of the Handel orchestra.

Years ago I tried to obtain for a Mr Ellis [7] from such organs, an ascertained musical pitch of Handel's period. Those I had immediate access to I found had known the modern tuner, & I had not time to pursue the subject. It is to be found though I feel sure.

There is a Schnetzler at St Peter's Drogheda; & I have requisitioned the organist to play it for me when I visited it. It has been added to, but, owing to poverty, not much improved. It is not valued there, & played by a poor organist with contempt for its antiquated & not up-to-date imbecility. It may not be much of an Organ, but has specially struck me as a typical one with an echo from the orchestral tone of the Handel Era.

My connection with the three Cathedrals of Christchurch & St Patricks Dublin & Armagh as architect, & my freedom of records forces me into a certain interest with such bye subjects as this; & a sole musical gift of a good & sensitive musical ear make the whole organ subject a bye-enjoyment, not in communication with anyone else. I am pleased to open it up with a musician. If there is any more information you care for I shall be pleased indeed to continue correspondence.

I had noted your part in the production of Handel's original score [;] I wish we could hear it here –

> Yours faithfully,
> Thomas Drew.

From this it appears that of the two small organs he mentions, the first, which he claims to have been used for *Messiah* in Dublin, belonged in his time to the Johnston family at Kilmore, Co. Armagh, and previously to Francis Johnston, Lord Ely and perhaps Handel (no. 2 in this chapter). He notes that 'it will be found to bear the same inscription as my small instrument <u>Johannes Schnetzler Londini</u> & I doubt not the same date 1742'. This is, of course, the same inscription as the

Cuckston organ's (apart from the omission of the word 'fecit'), but it appears that the organ contained fewer stops than either the Yale organ or the Cuckston organ and that it bore no relationship to its later elaborate encasing.

The other small organ was his own, and he mentions the stops, which nearly coincide with the Yale University organ as given above. The 'unamed & curious harmonic stop possibly defective' seems to be part of the Sesquialtera. The Yale organ's size (42½" by 27¾" by 65" high) coincides with Thomas Drew's description given above. The case following its cleaning by Anna Hulbert certainly now resembles another sort of 'shrine': two upper doors open to reveal a triple facade of pipes painted on canvas. It is strange that Drew does not mention this, but merely describes the organ as having a 'plain case, once decorated with gilding' which is an odd description unless the later varnishing removed by Anna Hulbert was then already completely opaque.

It seems that the organ was purchased from Sir Thornley Stokes of Dublin for the Karl Freund collection in the United States before going to Yale. The organ was worked on by John Challis in 1935; he added tuning slides, and noted that the pitch was nearly a semitone lower than modern pitch, and the wind–pressure was under 1½" ('37 mm'), which seems rather low. The organ was conserved by N. P. Mander Ltd. of London in 1984; missing pipes from the Cornet and Sesquialtera were installed. There is a 'machine' or 'shifting movement' pedal, working against a (restored) wooden spring which momentarily takes off the upperwork. In his post–restoration report, John Mander noted that the soundboard grid was made in the German fashion, with fillets top and bottom between the bars; the lower surface is covered with parchment, and the upper with leather (under the sliders).

[1] See photograph of the label, Appendix 2 and BIOSJ 9/47.
[2] H. C. Robbins Landon, *Handel and His World* (Weidenfeld & Nicolson, London 1984), p. 189.
[3] Christopher Hogwood, *Handel* (Thames and Hudson, 1984), pp. 171–80.
[4] TO 153/37.
[5] MS. Eng. lett. c. 130, fols. 146–51.
[6] Landon, op. cit., p. 179.
[7] Alexander J. Ellis; his researches into the history of musical pitch were published in full (with further work by Arthur Mendel) by Frits Knuf, Buren, Holland (1968).

5 London, Fetter Lane, Moravian Chapel
(1743)

The return of John Wesley from America in 1738 marked a turning–point in his religious life; he met the Moravian pastor Peter Boehler, who convinced him of the gospel of justification by faith alone. Wesley found himself excluded from London churches, and founded a religious society which eventually met in Fetter Lane; this was in effect the first Methodist group. Later in the year he visited the Moravian settlement of Herrnhut 'where he found piety and industry, an attitude of surrender to faith. The good life was untrammelled by dogma' [1] and 'on his return he preached his new theme of conscious salvation all over London and in the vicinity of Oxford. He devoted much energy to the embryonic Methodism of the Fetter Lane Society, which now numbered thirty-two members'.

Whitefield, looking for someone to 'methodize' a religious campaign in England, asked John Wesley to take his place in Bristol, where his energy indeed succeeded (see no. 51). Meanwhile, the Moravians in the Fetter Lane Society broke with the Wesleys in July 1740; the Wesleyans went to settle in the old 'Foundery' at Moorfields (whence the 'Foundery Collection' of hymns was to emerge – including one tune called 'Savannah or Hernnhut' still sung today), and the Moravians formed a London Moravian Congregation on 10 November 1742.

An organ was built by Snetzler in 1743 and placed on the west gallery of the chapel in Fetter Lane. During repairs to the building in 1747 it was stored in 'Brother Bowes's hall' for safe-keeping. (Bowes was a Yorkshireman chiefly employed in dealing in clocks.) From the Fulneck correspondence we know that it was a two-manual organ with a high-pitched Sesquialtera bass, a short-compass Swell, and a case of similar size to that made for the "higher German Chapel" (see no. 8). Beyond that, there is considerable confusion.

According to Janet Halton, the Librarian at Moravian Church House, London, the organ made in 1743 was rebuilt in 1796, 1841 and 1898. The stop-list given in 1889 was:

> Great: OD (w), OD (m), SD (b & tr), Dul, Pr, Fl, 12. 15, Ses IV, Posaune
> Swell: OD, SD, Gamba, Dolce, Pr, 15, Hb
> Pedal: OD, Bdn
> 5 couplers, 3 composition pedals

The organ was sold on 19 December 1919 for £90.

It was stated in Hopkins & Rimbault [2] that G. P. England made an organ for Fetter Lane in 1790, which may be an error for the 1796 date given above. The only stop-list for this organ of 1790 or 1796 notes only one manual (OD, SD, Dul, Pr, 12, 15, according to Boeringer [3]), but as this does not include the Swell noted in the Fulneck correspondence, it cannot be complete. It would be more likely that G. P. England *re*made the Snetzler organ in a new case, perhaps because the original case (of softwood, like that at Fulneck?) was damaged by worm, or was too small for a Swell in a high position. A drawing made at Fetter Lane in 1907 shows a case in a style which suggests that it was either substantially remade or was completely renewed in 1796, presumably with new front pipes.

The organ, following work in 1841 by J. W. Walker which cost £178 and was completed by 14 November under the eye of Peter Latrobe, was described in the London Diary (of the Church) as containing in it 'the best parts of the old organ together with some new stops, bellows, machinery etc.'

Walker's shop-books [4] show that they 'moved' an organ into the Chapel in 1841 which Sperling, apparently erroneously, records [5] as:

Charter House Chapel

> Old organ by Snetzler removed 18–– to Moravian Chapel Fetter Lane and enlarged by Walker. Great GG to F. Swell to tenor F, pedals 1 1/2 8ves.
> [Gt:] OD, SD, Clarabella [tr or replacing Cornet?], Pr, Fl, 15, Ses III, Tpt
> [Sw:] OD, SD, Pr, Hb

If it were not for the existence of a Swell four–slider soundboard of (originally) 37 notes (so an *f–f '''* compass would be possible) apparently labelled *John Snetzler fecit Londini 1743*, the date of the organ originally made for Fetter Lane (though the date on the label is not absolutely distinct), Sperling's claim that an organ came from the Charterhouse might be sustained. It would seem either that he has confused the organ with another, or that (as at Leatherhead in the same year, whose second–hand organ was claimed to be by Snetzler – see chapter 5, no. 5) the confusion was Walker's.

The organ was apparently enlarged by Walker in 1855 (to the stop–list of 1889 given above?), and then rebuilt in 1898. At this time, the Swell soundboard, already extended, was removed from the organ by Alfred Hunter and given in 1900 to G. W. Hole of Sculthorpe, Norfolk. The Church Diary records that the organ was re–opened on the 8 May 1898, and that on the 18th there was a social tea and an organ recital by 'J. Hunter and his wife'. The Swell soundboard is now in the store of N. P. Mander Ltd in London, and Stephen Bicknell has confirmed its compass, number of sliders and apparent date.

When it was sold in 1919, the organ from Fetter Lane found its way to Yoxford in Suffolk, but only the (?1796) case and front pipes were used there to clothe an organ of 1870.

[1] J. Pudney, *John Wesley and his World* (Thames and Hudson, 1978), p. 60.
[2] HR I/108; III/155.
[3] James Boeringer, *Organa Britannica*, vol. XX, p. XX.
[4] J. W. Walker, *Shop–books*, 7.220 (10 November 1841).
[5] S I/217.

6 Edinburgh, Earl of Wemyss
(Kirckman and Snetzler, dated 1745)

This claviorgan has been in the possession of the family since its construction. The nameboard is inscribed *Jacobus Kirckman fecit Londini* and the organ is labelled *Johan Snetzler fecit Londini 1745*. Although 'Johannes Schnetzler' had become 'John Snetzler' in 1743 (see no. 5), it would seem that he – like Kir[c]kman – reverted partially to his Germanic name when he was working collaboratively (as also in the Moresby Hall claviorgan, no. 1).

The case is of figured walnut with sycamore marquetry; the organ occupies the whole space under the harpsichord, and is about 30" in height. The two–manual harpsichord controls 2 x 8' and 1 x 4' registers on the lower keyboard, and a lute and 8' dogleg on the upper keyboard. The organ is played from the lower keyboard, to which it can be coupled by means of two small brass knobs below and to left and right of the lower keyboard. These bring to the 'on' position a register containing the vertical stickers of the organ's pin–action. The upper end of the stickers are engaged by blocks on the underside of the lower keyboard's levers.

The stops of the organ are controlled by brass knobs similar to those for the harpsichord; three at the bass end of the lower keyboard (Open Diapason, Stopped Diapason, Flute) and two at the treble end (Fifteenth, mixture) – these are let into the end–blocks. The Open Diapason goes from middle C up, and the mixture is composed of 19th and 22nd ranks in the bass, and 12th and 15th in the treble, from c'' [?] upwards. It appears that the organ's compass is G', A'–f''', whereas the keyboards' compass is F', G'–f'''. The high f''' should be noted; it was normal for Snetzler's church and larger chamber organs to ascend only to e''', but the early chamber organs (not bureau organs) were frequently of this higher compass, perhaps to match the normal range of the harpsichords with which they might be played. So were his later house organs of shorter compass differently viewed: as solo small–scale 'church' organs?

There are three foot levers: (a) for the shifting movement which takes off the Fifteenth and mixture, (b) for the winding of the bellows and reservoir, with an alternative position to the right of the instrument, and (c) a pedal to open a 'swell' panel (about 18¾" by 26¾") below the treble cheek of the harpsichord.

The larger wooden pipes are conveyed off to horizontal racks beyond the organ's soundboard, under the tail of the harpsichord. The instrument is illustrated in the *Early Keyboard Instruments* off–print of the *New Grove Dictionary of Music and Musicians* (Macmillan, 1989), p. 187.

7 Glasgow University, Music School
(1747)

Snetzler made a one–manual organ for the Qualified (that is, Episcopal) Chapel, Carrubers' Close, Edinburgh in 1747. It seems to have had this stop–list:[1]

(?G', A'–e'''): OD, SD, Pr, 12, 15, Ses III and Cor IV [combined?]

In 1774, the organ was sold to the Qualified Chapel in Glasgow; it was moved thither in 1775, but apparently not used until 1777. A Swell of five stops was added by John Donaldson of Newcastle in 1788; the organ was sold to the Unitarian Church in Glasgow in 1812, and installed there by Robert Mirrlees. The congregation moved to a new church in St Vincent Street, Glasgow, and the organ was rebuilt with entirely new mechanisms by Henry Bevington in his Soho workshops – not far, probably, from where it was first made – in 1853–6. Bevington played for the opening of the organ in the church himself. The casework, a Tuscan temple in style and shape, dates from this period. It was moved from its gallery in about 1887 and slightly enlarged.

Nothing much more was done to the organ until it was renovated by James MacKenzie in 1959, and partially tonally restored by him in 1974–6. Upon the closure of the church, he moved it to the Concert Hall of the University in 1985.

Parts of the original Open Diapason, Stopped Diapason (bass), Principal, Twelfth and Fifteenth remain, the metal of which he reports to be pitted with dross from its original casting.

[1] The date of 1747 and history of the organ are taken from D. Kerr Jamieson, *The Snetzler Organ at Glasgow Unitarian Church* (pamphlet, 1976).

8 London, German High Chapel in the Savoy
(first organ, 1748 or before)

The only evidence for this organ is the reference to it in a letter from Snetzler dated 16 January 1748 to Fulneck: 'As you require a front with towers, I have had this drawing made of our organ in the higher German Chapel, and will send it over. This is about the size of the available space [at Fulneck].' The implication is that the first organ was of similar size to that made for Fulneck, (see no. 9).

The later organ, eventually moved to the new church in Cleveland Street and destroyed in the Second World War, was considerably larger (see no. 37).

9 Fulneck, Yorkshire, Moravian Chapel
(1748)

The Moravian community in London evidently recommended Snetzler to the leaders of another congregation which was building a new chapel from 1746 onwards as the centre-piece of a long terrace of community buildings in the hills to the west of Leeds. (They had previously hoped to establish their community at Lightcliffe, near Halifax, about twelve miles away.) In the series of nine letters in German (transcribed and translated in full in Appendix 3) which are still preserved in the church office archives at 'Fulneck' (so named after Fulnek in Moravia), Schnetzler's correspondent was Mr Schlicht. Schnetzler wrote to him on 16 December 1747 as follows, in translation:

> Most honoured Sir,
> I take the liberty of troubling you with this present letter because I hear that the worthy congregation in your place is thinking of having an organ set up in your chapel ... my best performance can be expected, with good and inexpensive work.

Schnetzler suggests that he should come to see the chapel to discuss the building's size and the strength of the organ required. He would not charge for this visit, but regard it 'as a pleasure trip'. It is not clear whether or not he went to Fulneck at this time. Probably not; it seems that the chapel was still under construction, as he refers to a drawing which apparently shows the dimensions of the area for the organ. Various suggestions seem also to have been made regarding the stop-list, but Schnetzler is worried that the space available was insufficient:

the gallery is hardly [large] enough for this, because space also has to be allowed for coming round behind the organ: at least 1 1/2 feet to allow for this, and then at least 1 1/2 feet in front of the keyboard for the organist to play, so that for the depth of the organ not more than 3 feet is left over. To this there should be [added] at least 4 feet for all these stops, so that at least 7 feet is required in depth of the gallery, and because there is not enough [height?], many of the biggest pipes have to be mitred.

The present gallery in the chapel at Fulneck is elegantly cantilevered forward, perhaps to accommodate a later pedalboard, but as the present and original depth of it (at the sides of the middle section) is indeed only 7 feet, it may be that the extra space was in fact made for Schnetzler. The height from gallery floor to ceiling is 10' 10", and the case was made to fit this precisely.

There was also a misunderstanding about the payment for the organ, which Schnetzler hastens to correct:

you notified me that half the money would be paid as cash down, and the rest a certain time later. I supposed that this would be 2 or 3 months, while you took it to be 12 months. It was a big misunderstanding on my part ... In any contract it would ... be very difficult for me to set back the payment so long while I have only made a start and must help myself, with a completed article, to undertake yet another.

This last sentence has previously been interpreted as meaning that Schnetzler was new to the trade ('I have only made a start'), but in his convoluted German – our present translators suggest that he had been in England long enough to forget some of his native grammar and spelling – he seems rather to be saying that he needs payment from one organ to fund the start of another one. This, as all organ-builders know, is not at all the same thing.

Schnetzler also suggests a suitable stoplist:

1. Open Diapason of wood throughout   } with a double slider
2. Stop Diapason of wood   } by which the[se] 4
3. Principal in front metal   } Registers remain as they
4. Open Diap. half–[compass] metal   } are, but the other 5 can
5. Twelfth metal   be pulled on and off
6. Fifteenth metal
7. Sesquialtera in [the] bass metal } separated, as ordered
8. Cornet in [the] Discant metal   }
9. Solicional of metal; has a sound like a Violoncello. It has the same pitch
    as an Open Diapason, which is very pleasant.

I do not know how a Swell could be fitted in other than with a [short–compass] keyboard which goes halfway through, and the pipes in a small box just above it and in the middle of the organ with perhaps 4 stops, such as 1. Diap. 2. Solicional 3. Cornet 4 Trumpet.

As you require a case–front with towers, I have had this drawing made of our organ in the higher German Chapel, and will send it over. This is about the size of the available space.

The lowest price for making such an organ will be £150, and without a swell £125. If it is made with the reeds you ordered it will come to £160 without the swell.

If necessary, such work can be completed in a period of 4 months for delivery ... P. S. I have seen in various places in Germany that where the church has not been high enough they have made it [the ceiling] some 3 feet higher where the organ was to stand, which has not looked bad.

Although there is now a cavity into the roof space at Fulneck, this last expedient appears to have been adopted by later builders to accommodate a large swell-box, and not by Schnetzler. The correspondents continued to discuss the financing of the organ, and on 4 February, Schnetzler wrote:

I want in addition to do this, because you consider the construction will cost so much: I shall take all the expenses upon myself, and build and set up the organ for you at my own expense, if in return the last half of the money, instead of being paid in 6 months, could be paid in 3 months.

There also appears to have been considerable discussion about the stop-list, and some confusion; a contract in German was drawn up and signed in London on 15 February 1748 in these terms:

Herr Johann Schnetzler, organ builder in London, promises to the community in Fulneck, near Pudsey in Yorkshire, to make an organ with the following stops etc.

1. Stopped Diapason of wood from Contra G to highest e, i.e. 58 [sic] pipes.
2. Open Diapason, of wood – just the same [compass]
3. Viola di Gamba, of metal, the last octave in the bass taken from the Open Diapason.
4. Salicional of metal, from middle C up to the highest E.
5. Principal – of metal – 58 pipes.
6. Octav – of metal – 58 ditto.
7. Cornet – of metal 3 or 4 ranks.
8. Sesquialtera of metal. N.B. one Octave deeper than the one in Fetter Lane.
9. Trumpet right through [will] thus also [have] 58 pipes.

In this organ a Swell will be made with the following 4 stops.

1. Open Diapason of wood, from middle C up to highest E.
2. Open Diapason of metal – just the same.
3. Principal 8 feet; of metal, also the same.
4. Cornet 3 or 4 ranks of metal, id.

The two manuals on the organ and the Swell will be well inlaid with beautiful black wood, and the semitones [*sic*] with well-laid ivory, and made of such length as the one[s] in Fetter Lane.

Wood and metal of the best quality shall be used for the pipes, and each shall speak clearly.

The front of this work will be made with five towers [*sic*; actually three towers and two flats] and provided with attractive ornaments and carvings. The carvings or foliage, and the cornices, in the places where very appropriate, shall be beautifully gilded, but the case etc. shall be beautifully painted.

The pipes of the Principal in the front shall also not be gilded, but quite white and beautifully polished.

Each of the loud stops will be made with a double slider, to which there is a pedal underneath, which is pushed to the side [and] so that either on pulling or release no sound or change in the playing may be observed [i.e., a silently-acting shifting-movement which can be locked on (?) without interruption to the music].

The whole organ shall be properly provided with wind, and the pallets protected [*sic*; presumably meaning that the grid will be covered with leather also, as in the 1742 Cuckston organ] so as to make sure that there is no so-called 'howling' in the organ. However, the touch is to be easy and regular.

The temperament shall so far as ever possible be installed in such a way that all notes [*sic*: meaning, keys?] can be played.

In short, everything shall be done with all diligence, durability and beauty.

For this work which Joh. Schnetzler promises to deliver in 4 months, the said community shall pay him One hundred and forty pounds sterling, half thereof when the organ is delivered and installed on the site ready for use, and it has been found to be proved and in accordance with the Contract, and the other half one quarter of a year later.

However, all expenses of carriage from London, and so on, to the place where the organ is to be installed, shall be included in this £140.

I hereby testify with my signature by my own hand that I agree to this.
Charles Metcalfe, Director
John Snetzler [*sic*], Organ Maker
Wm Bell, aforesaid [*sic*] fully-authorised engineer
Given at London, the 15th day of February 1747/8
Paul John Brockmer, as witness.

The contract is also sealed.

The implication of the paragraph about the temperament is that it will be equal; this, the small internal Swell, and the polished front pipes are Germanic traits. The Fetter Lane organ (no. 5), of which we otherwise know only much later details and from here only about the style of its keyboards, may well have been similar to this organ both in its casework and stoplist. (If so, the Swell soundboard dated 1743 might have been placed internally; it would be a unique survival.)

A letter from Mr Schlicht seems to have arrived just before the signing of the contract. A reply to this was made 18 February in which some changes to the

Swell stops are proposed:

> As you want the Salicional out of the Swell in the [Great] organ (which I would rather have in the Swell, because it has a proper and agreeable tone with the Swell), the Principal in the Swell must be 4 feet tone, because Open Diapason is of metal and Principal 8 feet tone, the same. The Open Diapason is nothing other than an 8–foot Principal, so it would not be so well to have 3 Open Diapasons in the Swell ... for the sake of the Trumpet the organ must have sharper [heavier] wind than is required for a pleasant effect in the subtle stops.

'Pleasant', 'agreeable' and 'subtle' are typical 'pietistic' mid–European adjectives, when applied to organ tone, as previously mentioned (chapter 1, p. 10).

Mr Slicht replied to this letter on 21 February 1748 in the only letter to Schnetzler kept in the Fulneck archives. It was presumably preserved there because in effect it became part of the contract. He proposed further changes to the stop–list:

Pudsey, 21 February 1747/8

Most honoured Herr Schnetzler,

We are equally satisfied that the Trumpet is left out, it has only come in because there were a lot of them [meaning: because they are conventional?]. The arrangement is then the following, and is to remain accordingly:

1. Open Diapason of wood, as you can set the pipes so [i.e., mitre them]
2. Stopped Diapason, of wood, as you stated.
3. Open Diapason of metal, half through.
4. Salicional, metal, right through as far as it will go.
5. Viola Di Gamba, metal, half through.
6. A pretty Flute, right through.
7. Principal, metal.
8. Cornet, 4 Ranks   } an octave lower than usual
   Sesquialtera, 3 Ranks   }
9. Twelfth.
10. Fifteenth.

To the Swell there come:
1. Open Diapason OF METAL.
2. Salicional of metal.
3. Hautboix, really pretty.

We shall seldom need the Cornet in the Swell. It is therefore easy to leave them [*sic*] out, and I think these 3 registers will sound really charming together, or 2 and 2, because I am also of the opinion that wooden pipes are not much use in the Swell, so we want to make the Open Diapason of metal, as stated.

And that would be an admirable disposition of a small organ, and just as

I should like to have it. I also believe that you yourself will find nothing to find fault with.

You can thus at present only hold Herr Benzien to the Contract, to make an NB that the Registers are chosen as I have stated them, or this letter can repay [?] it. The rest remains as already stated in the Contract.

I think you are fairly convinced that you have no harm to expect of us. We deal honourably and without falsehood, and promise ourselves the like from you, especially I who am from my heart

Herr Schnetzler,

    Your sincere friend and servant,

    C. F. L. Schlicht.

We must assume that this became the final stop-list, one shot through with a desire for 'pretty' and charming sounds in the pietistic manner, although Schnetzler tried to change it yet again. In the next-dated letter, 9 April, Schnetzler wrote in reply to a suggestion that the case should be made at Fulneck:

> You instructed me in one [a letter] that you wrote to me, that you have good cabinet-makers on the spot. I find on thinking it over many times, that it would be much better if the organ case could be made there, because otherwise, if I made it here, it would have to be unusually large and would thus involve me in very great expense both for the crates and for carriage charges ... I should like to do everything relating to the organ here in London, apart from the organ case and the bellows which amount to a heavy weight and can be made on the spot as well as they can here. I expect to have my work finished here at the end of the month of May. Then, on my arrival in Yorkshire, orders can be given for the organ case, and as long as work is in progress on this I can get the bellows ready at the same time, which cannot take much more than 14 days ...
>
> ...in the Swell there are only to be these 3 stops: Open Diapason, Salicional and Hautbois, which are three equally-sounding [i.e., unison] voices, and so do not have the desired effect for a Swell. I therefore think it is better to make two other stops instead of the Hautbois, such as a Principal and a Cornetin, which is an extremely pleasant stop. I have this week the honour of having Herr Benzien and Herr Brokmer on my premises, and had just such an organ there, in which there was this stop, which pleased both of them very much. Herr Brokmer also thinks that it would certainly be better, besides the trouble there will be about tuning because it will not [be possible] to come to the Swell so conveniently.

This leaves the exact composition of the Swell as delivered rather uncertain. One wonders also what organ Schnetzler was making in April 1748 that had such a Swell or 'Cornetin'? (Was it no. 11 in this chapter?)

Two final letters in November and December 1748 concern details of the case decoration, and Schnetzler asks in November: 'If anything can be heard of to my advantage, I beg you not to forget me'. There are a couple of problems to be sorted out in December:

> I ... am sorry that the ornament is not liked. I had flattered myself that in this place it would show exceedingly well ... I am very glad that the organ is doing so well ... The letter that I received from Mr Mitcalve some time ago has disquieted me considerably, particularly when I reckoned by the number of the pipes in the contract and counted them on a keyboard which I had not done previously, because only the compass of Double GG to high E was already enough, and G sharp is never thought of.

Evidently, Mr Mitcalve (the organist?) had counted the notes in the contract and on the organ keyboard, and found a discrepancy of one – which was indeed Snetzler's fault. The absence of the low G♯, typical of English organs tuned in meantone temperament (where a root-position chord of G♯/A♭ is just the one with the tuning 'wolf '), makes one wonder if the organ was in fact tuned in a temperament that allowed for the 'playing of all keys'.

The only parts of the organ to survive successive rebuildings in 1855, 1929 and 1982 (when some smaller front pipes were removed in favour of near-copies in spotted metal) are the case – extended and several times over-painted – and the pipes in the towers. These were originally speaking pipes, and since they do not appear to be marked with any particular pitch names, they may well also have been made 'on the spot' along with the bellows and the case. Their original soldering is none too clean, but they are made of an alloy with a high proportion of tin and were evidently highly polished at some time, though now they are sprayed with 'gold' paint. Six old pipes with sunken blocks in the German manner are to be found in the pedal Bourdon rank, but it is not certain that they are original. There is also a solitary Flute pipe (a 3"-long C, stopped, of pine with an oak cap) in the vestry archive, which is typical of Snetzler's work, but which seems likely to have come from another organ, possibly the Schoolroom bureau organ (no. 13), since it has a very short foot that plugged directly into a soundboard, and is small in scale.

The carvings of the pipe-shades and the tower brackets, originally gilded, are of high quality, and very assured.

10 London, Dr J. R. Mirrey
(organ dated 1748, now part of a claviorgan)

The organ, now part of a claviorgan with a Crang harpsichord of 1745, was originally a complete church or chamber organ of about six stops. It was discovered, derelict, in the Roman Catholic church at Durrow, Eire, and purchased from there by John Holmes in 1954. The case, of three towers and two flats, was being used as a vestibule to a gallery to which doors in its sides gave access. Parts of the organ, including metal and wooden pipes, the soundboard with Snetzler's label, the wedge-reservoir and parts of the keyboard and action were 'dumped' in the belfry behind.

John Holmes described the organ thus in 1985:

The organ was so built as to use the case as a building frame. The soundboard is mainly of oak. The reservoir and its feeder are both of the diagonal type, and have pine or redwood frames and top and bottom boards. When acquired, they were leathered with a strong brown leather more typical of forge bellows work than organ work.

All wood pipes had short conical feet of oak ... These fitted into coned-out holes in the top-boards and there were no rackboards. The larger bass pipes had oak clips to hold them upright. trebles from about the 3" pipe up were of oak with caps [*sic*, but presumably meaning fronts] of a finely grained wood, like pearwood. All metal pipes were plain metal, very thin, lightly nicked and with quite small footholes ...

The stop knobs were located at each end of the keyboard and were of square section lignum vitae or ebony, with very small turned 'pulls'. Presumably, stop names were given on paper or leather labels alongside each knob.

Both compound stops had, according to the soundboard borings, one rank for their lowest 28 notes, and thereafter two ranks for the remaining 28 notes. The stop names are, in all cases, deduced from surviving pipes. There was insufficient pipework to identify the composition of the two compound stops. The stop knobs for the 4ft Principal, and the two 8fts were at the bass end, and the rest at the treble end. All wood pipes had their blocks and feet made from either a single piece of oak, or from two pieces joined vertical and parallel with the flue, so as to make up enough thickness, but none had separate feet fitted. As far as I can recall, most if not all wood pipes were lightly nicked on the block only, not on the caps.

The soundboard extended out beneath the keyboard, and the pallets are opened by a brass pin in turn pushed down by depressing a key above it. The keys had little leather pads on their underside where they engaged with the rounded tops of the pins. The pallet springs were the usual leg type but of hard brass. Only a few keys survived. The naturals were of ebony with nicely rounded edges, and the sharps were likewise but with ivory strips on top. The action of the few keys that remained was, after cleaning and repair, very crisp and absolutely silent.

Inside the windchest, some strips of parchment with writing in Latin were glued to the underside of the bars. Because the strips were no more than 1" to 2" wide, it was impossible to deduce exactly what was written.

The slides were bedded on white sheepskin glued to the upperboards, i.e., above the slides, and there is no scoring at all. The upperboards, slides, table, cheeks and some other small parts were of oak and the rest of straight-grained pine.

The organ had apparently been dismantled in 1926; its original stop-list appears to have been:

(*G'*, *A'–e'''*): OD (sc: *c'*), SD, Pr, Fl, 15, Ses III, Cor II (sc: *c'*)

The similarity of this with the 'Cuckston' organ of 1742 (no. 3), apart from the *c'* start of the short-compass ranks, will be noted. There was a shifting movement; the keyboard was in the usual style, with a 'pin' action, as described above.

The 1748 casework from Durrow

John Holmes attempted to restore the organ with help and advice from Roger Yates and Noel Mander, but the task proving too time-consuming, he was persuaded to sell it to Michael Thomas, who in 1962 amalgamated the soundboard and pipework with a Crang claviorgan, the original organ part of which had been discarded in 1953. [1]

The claviorgan was purchased by Dr Rodger Mirrey in 1965. The fate of the case is unfortunately not known; it is notably 'normal English' in design except for its carvings and the 'double' kneeboard.

[1] Raymond Russell, *The Harpsichord and Clavichord* (Faber and Faber, 1959), p. 83.

11 Finchley, Middlesex, St Mary's church (1749)

L 110; S I/72; HR 2; F 3

Two stop-lists relating to an organ at this church are extant. The earlier (in Leffler and 'Organographia') gives the following:

> Great (*G', A', C, D–d'''*): OD thro', SD, Pr, Fl, 12, 15, Sesq IV thro'
> Swell (*g–d'''*): OD, 'Dulciano' [Leffler], Pr, Cor II, Tpt [this not in Leffler]

The date of 1749 is Rimbault's. The later stop-list (in Sperling's notebooks), perhaps reflecting changes made in 1817 or later, gives:

> Great (*G', A'–f '''*): OD 'to CC', SD, Pr, Fl, 12, 15, Sex b/tr III,
>   Cln b/Tpt tr
> Swell (*g–f '''*): OD, SD, Pr, Cor III, Tpt

Sperling mentions that the organ was 'presented' in 1817; as Leffler's account could just possibly have been written as late as this (it is on page 110 in his manuscript, and written when the organist was Mr J[nr?] Whitaker) it might have then come from elsewhere. However, a Mr Whitaker was 'Organist of St. Bartholomew the Great [in the City; [1]] Finchley, Middlesex, and Woburn Chapel', according to the list of subscribers to William Russell's (first) set of *Voluntaries* (1804), so the organ may rather have been rebuilt in 1817, perhaps by Hugh and Timothy Russell. It was replaced later in the nineteenth century, and its successor was destroyed in the Second World War.

[1] Donovan Dawe, *Organists of the City of London 1666–1850* (Dawe, 1983), p. 155.

*

12 Haverfordwest, Picton Castle
(1750)

F 6; W 111 (25)

The organ is labelled *John Snetzler fecit Londini 1750*. It is encased in mahogany, and is probably the earliest extant example of its style of design. The casework consists of three compartments of pipes (arranged 6–10–6) on a curved toe-board which rises towards the centre. The pipe-shade carving is in low relief with a central pendentive like a petalled flower; all this work is considerably plainer than the post–1755 versions of the design. The key action is a pin-action with the pallets directly under the keys on an elongation of the soundboard grid, as in the 1742 Cuckston organ. The naturals of the keyboard are of blackwood and the sharps are of ivory–capped stained pear. The stop-list comprises:

(G', A'–f '''): OD, SD, Pr, Fl, 15, Ses b/Cor tr

A shifting movement takes off all except the Open Diapason and Stopped Diapason. Winding is by pedal or hand pump. The organ was restored 1961–2 by N. P. Mander, Ltd. At this time, a later swell-box was removed, the front pipes were regilded and the case was refurbished, and 88 missing pipes in the mixture replaced. The organ is placed on a (specially-made?) gallery in the contemporary Hall of the Castle; it is illustrated in chapter 2, p. 47.

13 Edinburgh, Sir Ronald Johnson
(1751)

This bureau organ, the earliest surviving example, is labelled *John Snetzler fecit Londini 1751*. The present owner bought it in 1947 from Mr A. F. Mordaunt-Smith, then aged about 75, who had been a pupil at the Moravian School in Fulneck. He had acquired the organ from the Moravians in the 1890s. Moravian officials say that the organ stood for a number of years in the Prayer Room there. It now has these stops:

(C', D'–e'''): SD, Fl, 15, Larigot b/Larigot tr

The divided Larigot replaced a 2' Flute bass and 4' Principal treble when the organ was overhauled by N.P. Mander Ltd in 1965. An electric blower was added then. The keyboard, of blackwood with ivory-capped sharps, operates a pin-action.
Sir Ronald Johnson described other features thus, in a letter:

> The pipes placed at the front are the divided stop, with the levers nearest the front ... the stops on the left are: Stopped Diapason (nearest the desk), Flute, Larigot Bass. On the right there is a Fifteenth and Larigot Treble. Each stop has two rows of pipes, but the bottom five pipes of the Stopped

Diapason are trunked [conveyed] off. The trunk stands vertically on the left
side of the back of the organ and the five pipes are horizontal and mitred,
so that their stoppers face outwards at the right–hand side.

It is probable that the divided stop was originally a divided two–rank mixture, as
in the other bureau organs. It has not been established if the C Flute pipe still at
Fulneck (see no. 9) is missing from this organ.

Sir Ronald Johnson's bureau organ
note the splayed sticker action, and the contra–disposed feeder and (empty)
reservoir

*

14 Rugeley, Staffordshire, Hawkesyard Priory chapel (1750–51)

L 186; S II/17; F7

The cases and some of the mechanism and pipework of this organ had their origin in the chapel of Eton College, Buckinghamshire, where 'Father' Smith made an organ in 1700–01. It stood on a gallery, part of the way along the building, and its case was presumably double–fronted. It apparently comprised two manuals, Great and short–compass (*c'*) Echo.

In 1751, according to Andrew Freeman (who seems to have had access to a document 'probably in the builder's handwriting', now unavailable), Snetzler made 'Proposals for a very thorough rebuilding at a cost of £400. The work was to include new keys of increased compass, a new and separate case for the choir organ, two new open diapasons for the fronts, the conversion of the echo into the swell, and many other things. It is interesting to note that the word is written *choir* and not *chair* – the earliest authentic instance of the use of that word in this connection I have yet met with.'

As there are the remains of a Rococo Choir case at Hawkesyard, and as by *c*1810 there was a three–stop Choir organ, it is presumed that Snetzler provided this, together with any necessary remaking of the console and key- and stop-actions. Payments for maintenance of the organ were made to him regularly from 1751 onwards, in which year he was paid £5. 7s. 6d. for 'looking to the organ this year'. In the 1770s, the work was described as 'cleaning the organ', and payments were made to him every year up to and including 1784.

Leffler's manuscript gives the stoplist (under "Eton College") during the 1810s as:

Organ built by Father Schmidt. Three rows of Keys short 8ves GG to C.
Echo (over the keys) from C down to Mid C.

[Great]		[Choir]		[Echo]	
Open Diap	50	Stop Diap	50	Open Diap	25
Stop Diap	50	Principal	50	Principal	25
Principal	50	Flute	50	Cornet 2 rk	50
Flute	50		---	Trumpt	25
Twelfth	50		150		---
Fifteenth	50		---		125
Sexqa 3 ranks	150				150
Trumpet	50				575
Cornet to C♯ 3 rk	75				---
	---				856
	575				===

The Echo was not necessarily enclosed in a box, but it was almost certainly set behind the two original keyboards and music desk.

The Smith organ was rebuilt in 1841 by John Gray (possibly using only one of the original two case-fronts); the surviving G'–f ''' 59-note soundboards at Hawkesyard appear to have been made by him, as well as the front pipes of the main (upper) case. In 1841, the majority of the pipes were taken to Bishopstone in Herefordshire in an organ rebuilt there by Gray under the direction of Vincent Novello. The Snetzler Choir Stop Diapason and Flute ranks were apparently included in this pipework; that organ was dispersed in the 1940s.

The Smith and Snetzler cases, the work by Gray and the surviving earlier material were removed from Eton in 1852; they were purchased by Josiah Spode and installed by Holdich on a landing of the staircase in his home, Hawkesyard Park. The Choir organ case seems then either to have been stored or used as a chamber organ front, but it might have gone to Bradfield, Essex, for a time (see chapter 5, no. 16).

Following Spode's death, the organ was rebuilt by Hill in the new chapel of the Dominican Priory in the Park in 1899, and the Choir case was disjointedly placed below the surviving Smith front, 'fixed by the [building] contractors', according to Hill's estimate of that time. There do not appear to be any obviously Snetzler pipes among the extraordinary collection of pipework of all dates in the organ, unless the front pipes of the Choir case (part of the 1750 Principal) are his, but there are some pipes of the 'Green' type, similar to Snetzler's 'middle period' work, in various ranks on the main Great soundboard.

In 1988, the Dominicans moved away from the Priory, which has now been modified into a retirement home. The chapel and its furnishings are protected from alteration in the conditions of the sale to the present owners, and the organ awaits a full 'archaeological' survey.

Snetzler Choir case at Hawkesyard Priory

15 New Haven, Connecticut (U. S. A.), private owner (1752)

W 109 (20)

This is a bureau organ, labelled and dated 1752. Its internal construction has the same features as the other bureau organs and it has a mahogany case with brass carrying handles. The keyboard is original, but the key action has been modified. The stop–list comprises:

(*C, D–e'''*): SD, Fl, 15, Ses b II, Cor tr II

In the centre, where the two lower panels meet, there is a slot for the winding pedal. To the left of this is another slot for the shifting movement.

    The original owner of the organ is not known; at some time it was acquired by J. A. Fuller Maitland (of *The Times*), and later by Canon Wallis of Lichfield, Staffordshire. Upon the sale of Canon Wallis's effects in 1957, the organ was purchased by the present owner. It was renovated by N. P. Mander Ltd., and fitted with an electric blower. The Revd B. B. Edmonds has suggested that this organ may be the same as that owned by W. MacPherson, a musician in Edinburgh, and/or the same as that apparently owned by the Aberdeen Musical Society – the stop–lists of both organs have been given as 'Diapason, Flute, Mixture, Cornet'. Farmer [1] quotes the cost of a bureau organ purchased for the Aberdeen Society and dated 1752 as £46; it would seem that this may well be the same instrument.

[1] Henry Farmer, *The History of Music in Scotland* (Hinrichsen, 1947), p. 277.

16 King's Lynn, Norfolk, St Margaret's Church (1753–4)

L 143; S II/188; HR 4; F 8

Throughout medieval times, Lynn was a flourishing port which traded raw materials for finished goods directly with the Hanseatic ports. Its 'mother' parish church of St Margaret possessed an organ by William Beton, probably made in the early sixteenth century. This was sold in 1565; the proceeds were used for church repairs at a time when organs were in disfavour with protestant tendencies. Another organ was erected 1676–7; the Faculty for this was granted by the Bishop of Norwich on 17 August 1677. As it was evidently maintained by Thomas Thamar, he presumably installed it.

    In 1741 the church was badly damaged by the fall of the western spire during the severe gales of that year, and the organ no doubt suffered both from the storms and the consequent complete rebuilding of the nave. Charles Burney became organist in January 1752, and immmediately set about procuring a better instrument. The churchwardens, apparently on Burney's advice, contacted Snetzler for an estimate of a sale price for their old organ, and the cost of any repair needed to maximize its value. He valued the organ at one hundred pounds, but his opinion was that there was no point in spending further money on it, saying to the Churchwardens, Burney reported: 'If they would lay out another hundred pounds upon it, perhaps it would then be worth fifty.' [1] He was right, for it took a further thirteen years before it was finally sold by auction (31 March 1766) – for £33.

Despite the possibility of another second–hand organ from Dublin (see pp. 12–13), the town Corporation decided to purchase a new instrument from Snetzler at a cost of £700, having on 12 October 1752 'agreed that the old organ erected in 1676 was then old and removed from a College in Cambridge ... [and] is so much decayed in its several parts as to be rendered useless.'

A Faculty was granted 'to take down and sell the old organ and erect new one in west end' on 8 December 1753. By this time the new organ was completed in Snetzler's workshop, and it was transported from London to Lynn in that same month by Mr Bidwell at a cost of £36. 19s. It weighed 164 cwt. 26 lb.

King's Lynn organ: view from south choir aisle

The organ's opening was recorded in the London *Evening Post* for 28 March 1754:

> Last Sunday [actually 17 March] the new Organ at King's Lynn, Norfolk, erected in St. Margaret's Church by Mr. John Snetzler of Oxford road, was opened by Mr. Burney, and gave the utmost satisfaction, being for Sweetness of Tone and Variety of Stops, universally esteemed one of the finest Instruments in England.

Percy Scholes [2] suggested that this puff may have had its origin in a display of the organ by leading London organists in the workshops before its transport to Lynn.

Leffler's manuscript account of the organ is as follows:

> Lynn, Norfolk
> Organ built in 1754 by 'Joannes Schnetzler' [sic: he seems to be mis-quoting the painted inscription 'JOHANNES SNETZLER Londini Fecit 1754' over the console] has three complete setts of keys long octaves from GG to E; Swell down to F, repair'd by Lincoln in 1796 & again in 1816 –

Great		Choir		Swell	
Bourdon to CC	53	Dulciana of Metal		Open Diap	36
Open Diap	57	all thro'	57	Stop Diap	36
Stop Diap	57	Stop Diap	57	Dulciana	36
Principal	57	Principal	57	German flute	
Twelfth	57	Flute	57	to Mid C	29
Fifteenth	57	Fifteenth	57	Cornet 4 rks	144
Tierce	57	Bafsoon up to G		Trumpet	36
Sexqa 4 ranks the		above Mid C	36	French Horn	36
largest rank is 15th	228	Vox Hume	57	Hautboy	36

Furniture 3 rks	171		378		----
Trumpet	57		----		389
Clarion	57				378
Cornet to C					1053
5 ranks	145				----
	----	Organist Mr Taylor			1820
	1053				----

> The old organ was given by
> John Turner in 1679
> The Trumpet has been taken out
> of the Swell & the Stop nailed up.

The Bourdon is a double
 Diapason of Metal; except the
 lowest CC & CC♯.
The Bafs of the Choir Flute, Stop Diap & Dulciana form a Bafs to the Swell and are made
 to draw separate for that Purpose; the Organ therefore appears to contain 30 stops tho'
 really 27.

This account appears from the manuscript to have been written between the 1796 and 1816 work; the words '& again in 1816' seem to have been added. Later authorities, notably Hopkins and Rimbault, give conflicting accounts, but Leffler's gives the impression of having been derived from an inspection made on the spot, either personally or by his close friend William Russell, who had been in Norfolk in September 1812 to reopen the organ at Yarmouth Parish Church after repairs by G. P. England.

The Great Bourdon was a novelty; Burney [3] called it a 'borduun' and described it as 'a metal stop ... an octave below the Open Diapason ... [which] has the effect of a double bass in the chorus'. Leffler seems to imply that it was of [Open] Diapason construction. The German Flute was evidently a harmonic chimney flute at octave pitch, [4] and the French Horn was, according to Burney, 'a louder and coarser sort of Hautboy'. [5]

The use of Choir stops to provide a bass to the Swell strongly suggests the likelihood that Choir and Swell soundboard(s) were placed behind the Great; the effect of this on the design of the front casework is discussed in chapter 2, at p. 48. The original depth of the casework appears to have been 7'; it is 13' wide on the ground, and 15' wide above the corbelled waist/impost. The front pipes are arranged 5–11–5–11–5. A label reading *John Snetzler fecit Londini 1753* was removed from one of the original soundboards when they were replaced in 1895.

Minor repairs were carried out by John Lincoln in 1795, Henry Lincoln in 1816, and more extensive work was done by Joseph Hart of Redgrave, Suffolk, 1826–7.[6] In 1852, Holdich added some pedal pipes. 'For some time', according to the current church guide, the organ 'had been under the chancel arch, entirely separating the chancel from the nave'. It was moved to the north chancel aisle by Hill in 1870 and thenafter to a loft in the north transept, at which time a Holdich Principal on the Great was removed in favour of a Horn Diapason by Norman & Beard, who also restored the two Dulcianas, the pipes of which had been stored 'under the bellows'. The organ was rebuilt 1894–5 by Wordsworth of Leeds, retaining thirteen of the original stops, including the two Dulcianas.

The construction of the Dulciana has given rise to much speculation, but it can be confirmed that it was and is as described by Roberts:[7] 'of dolcan form throughout, with wide mouths and ears continued round and across [sic] the mouth, which acted as a beard or bridle'. In fact, the 'beards' are fenders; the ears are carried across the lower lip of every pipe as a flat plate.

The approximate scales given by Roberts were confirmed by more recent investigation by Dick Barker. Both Dulciana ranks are of the same scaling; there are now 53 pipes from *C* to *e'''* in the Choir Dulciana, marked 'Choir', and 35 from *f* to *e'''* in the Swell Dulciana, marked 'Swel'. (See chapter 4, p. 249, for details of their scaling.) There are three sets of marks on the pipes: Snetzler's own characteristic marks, a later mark (possibly 1895) and an inked mark of uncertain date. All the marks are of the same note, so although the pipes have been cut to a higher pitch and fitted with tuning slides, the pipes still speak from the same nominal keys as originally.

The organ was rebuilt in 1962 by Rushworth & Dreaper, and still contains parts of eleven original stops; other old pipework is in storage.

[1] Charles Burney, *A General History of Music* (1776–9, repr. Dover, 1957), vol. II, p. 345.
[2] Percy Scholes, *The Great Dr. Burney* (Oxford University Press, 1948), vol. I, p. 79.
[3] Burney, loc. cit.
[4] James Wedgwood, *Dictionary of Organ Stops* (Vincent, London, 2nd edn., 1907), p. 186; see also chapter 4, p. 250, for further discussion of this rank.
[5] Burney, letter of Jan. 1803 to Callcott (repr. in *The Musical Times*, Sept. 1904).
[6] information about Hart's work was kindly communicated by Peter Bumstead.
[7] W. A. Roberts, 'Snetzler and the First Dulciana in England' (TO 26/81).

17 'Mersham-le-Hatch', Ashford, Kent (1754)

W 110 (22)

The organ is labelled *John Snetzler fecit Londini 1754*; the paper label has been removed from the soundboard and put in a small frame over the present keyboard. It was formerly owned by Captain Lane of Snaresbrook, Essex, who presented it to the Caldecott Community's chapel, then in East London. For the duration of the Second World War, the organ was taken by the Revd Gordon Paget to his rectory at Hedenham, Norfolk. [1] It was then brought to the Community's school, newly re-established at Mersham in the Robert Adam house begun in 1762 for Sir Wyndham Knatchbull Wyndham, eldest son of a friend of Handel. [2] It is placed in the former entrance hall of the house, now used as a conference room.

The organ's present upper structure with its wooden dummy pipes, a keyboard of the style used in square pianos, an extra reservoir above the pipework, pedals with harmonium reeds, a swell-box, and other mechanical parts in harmonium maker's style, have been added to what seems to have been a mahogany-cased bureau organ. The original small soundboard, made for four ranks (some divided), some lower parts of the case including the knee-board (inlaid with three box-wood 'gothic' arches), the feeder and wedge-reservoir and parts of the key and stop actions remain, together with 51 unaltered pine Stopped Diapasons and one pine Flute pipe. The original stop-list may have been:

(*C, D–e'''*): SD b/tr (from *c*). OD (sc: *g*), Pr tr (sc: *c*, bass from Fl), Fl

but as the lack of a Fifteenth and a mixture indicates, this would not have been typical. Only a complete dismantling of the soundboard, which retains its original pallets and their markings and leathering, might reveal the original layout and stop-list. The wind-seal at the entry of the action into the soundboard is a lead strip (now leathered, as it may have been originally, to prevent noise from the stickers) through which the angled sticker pins pass to the upper surfaces of the pallets.

[1] Gordon Paget, 'The Snetzler Organ in Norwich Cathedral' (TO 147/133).
[2] 'Sir Windham Knatchbull' is mentioned in a letter by Handel to Jennens, quoted in
H. C. Robbins Landon, *Handel and His World* (Weidenfeld & Nicolson, 1984), p. 178.

18 Dublin, St Stephen's church
(1754?)

This organ was apparently intended for the chapel of the Rotunda Hospital in
Dublin, but was placed instead in the Rotunda Rooms. It was later moved to the
house of Lord Mornington in Upper Merrion Street, and subsequently to St
Stephen's church.

Some original front pipes survive in the case which, if the date is correct, is the
first of the type with double–storeyed flats. This design was, however, not used in
the Sheffield organ of the following year, so the date is suspect. The case is large
enough, and evidently designed for, an organ with Great and Swell of normal
church stop–list.

19 Organ labelled '*John Snetzler fecit Londini 1754*'

Bernard Edmonds, in private notes, records an organ with this label, slightly
enlarged and modernized, in a cinema (the Belsize Palace) in Kilburn, London, in
1903. It was rebuilt with new actions by Brindley & Foster of Sheffield in 1927 for
installation in the Blackpool Picture Palace, Lancashire.

No further details are known.

20 Norwich, Norfolk, the cathedral
(1754? or 1748)

This much–travelled chamber organ was, according to a previous owner (Mrs
Braithwaite) made for the Duke of Bedford. Its history subsequently has frequently
been confused with the larger organ now at Hillington, Norfolk, which was made
for the Duke in 1756 (no. 33). Indeed, even the date may have been confused with
it, as the Revd B. B. Edmonds has a 'tracing' of a label apparently in this organ
which reads '1748'; if this is correct, then this organ and not that at Picton Castle
(no. 12) is the earliest of its style of case design.

Elliston [1] quotes Mrs. Braithwaite as saying that the organ she owned was
stored for fifty years after leaving the residence of the Duke and before being
installed at the church at Woburn Sands.

What actually happened during those years has been discovered by Roy
Williamson in the Gray & Davison archives at the British Organ Archive. In their
Volume 1, p. 27 (April 1822), the firm noted that the organ (previously stored) was
repaired, packed, transported to Gloucester and installed in a house (called 'The
Spa' in the books, but in fact in the Spa area of the city, in Spa Road) of Alex

Maitland. In Volume 8a, p. 303 (22 May 1866), the organ, now belonging to the Revd Dr Maitland of Gloucester, was recorded as being taken down and stored in Gray & Davison's factory. On 18 September 1868, the organ was noted as being repaired, its fronts gilded, and being transported to Woburn Sands and erected. The latter entries are under the account of a Robert Steven of Leckhampton, near Cheltenham.

It was sold from Woburn Sands to Canon Hopkins of Ely in about 1880 (through the intervention of the cathedral organist there, Dr Chipp), and the organ builder Monk removed the Sesquialtera and Cornet (later to reappear in Canon Dickson's chamber organ) in favour of a Dulciana, and added a small slide-in pedalboard of 18 notes, *C'–F*. Mrs Braithwaite subsequently acquired the organ, and installed it in her house (Acton Place) at Long Melford, Suffolk.

In 1910, the organ was placed in the mission church of St Catherine, Long Melford, where Elliston saw it and recorded details of it for his book (see chapter 4, p. 253). It was sold to the Revd Gordon Paget for £30, and he moved it to Hedenham Rectory. In 1947, the organ was presented by him to Norwich Cathedral. The organ has been twice renovated since, by W. Boggis and by Storr Brothers.

The stop-list is now:

(*G', A'–f '''*): OD (w, sc: *c*), SD, Dul [1880], Pr, Fl, 15 [? not original]

Elliston recorded the windpressure as '2¼" bare', and the pitch then as 'just above C = 517.3 fork.'

The casework is of the 'normal' standard broken-pedimented type (see above); the [re-]gilded metal front dummy pipes, arranged 7–10–7, are original.

Gordon Paget [2] recorded that

> the dulciana is modern and the fifteenth seems to be a replacement. When ... particulars were all taken down by the late Mr. Thomas Elliston of Sudbury, whose book *Organs and Tuning* should be in the library of every organ-lover, the name of the builder was not apparent, but an address label of Messrs. Hill & Son was found inside the organ which stated that 'This house was founded by John Snetzler about 1755, who was succeeded in 1780 by his foreman Ohrmann', and ... Mrs. Braithwaite the former owner could vouch for having seen Snetzler's name inside.

Elliston's 'particulars' (see p. 253) confirm Snetzler as the maker of this organ; the 'light-coloured hardwood fronts' he noted are in fact of pear, as in the 1742 Cuckston organ (no. 3) and in the organ from Durrow (no. 10).

[1] Thomas Elliston, *Organs and Tuning* (3rd edn., London, 1924), pp. 586–70.
[2] Gordon Paget, 'The Snetzler Organ in Norwich Cathedral' (TO 147/133).

21 Wingerworth, Derbyshire, All Saints' church (1755)

B 212/121; S III/59; HR 5; F 9

Part of the case and some pipework from the organ made for the 1720–1748 Classical church of St Paul, Sheffield, have survived two moves and much rebuilding.

Buckingham recorded these details in 1830:

St. Paul's, Sheffield—An Organ with 3 sets of Keys the Great and Choir organ from GG long octaves to E in alt, the Swell from G to E in alt, a set of 12 Pedals from GG to G.

GREAT ORGAN		CHOIR ORGAN		SWELL ORGAN	
Op. Diapason	61	St. Diapason	57	Op. Diapason	34
St. Diapason	57	Principal	57	St. Diapason	34
Principal	57	Flute	57	Cornet 4R	136
Twelfth	57	Fifteenth	57	Trumpet	34
Fifteenth	57			Hautboy	34
Sexqualtera bafs 4R	112		228		
Cornet 4R	116		———		272
Trumpet	57			Choir	228
	———			Great	574
	574				———
	———			Total	1074

Mr. Thos. Frith Organist. The Open Diapason to CC of Metal the four lowest Notes is a St. Diapason and metal helpers. There is two Diagonal bellows and a Coupla Stop to draw the Pedals on the Great Organ. In a Wainscott Case 18ft. high, 10ft. 5½in. wide, 7ft. 10in. deep. There is a Copper plate screwed on the Desk board over the keys on which is engraved—This Organ Built by J. Snetzler was Erected in 1755 by the Subscription of the Seatholders and others. In 1810 it was thoroughly repaired with considerable Additions by J. Lincoln at the expense of the Seatholders. It appears in 1810 it was made long octaves with new sets of keys the Pedals added also the Trumpet and St. Diapason in the Swell. In 1827 it was Cleand a few of the Metal pipes repaired and the Pedals to act on the Great and Choir keys by Henry Lincoln for which he Charged and received £75 10s., worth about 45. Sheffield, 14 September 1830. A.B.

The stop-list itself appears not to have been changed by the Lincolns, except for the addition of the Stopped Diapason and the Trumpet in the Swell. (As at Lynn, there is no Principal, hence the four-rank Cornet, 8–12–15–17.) It is possible that the Swell was originally played from the Choir keys. If so, this may be the first organ in which this system was used; it would be a logical development of the 'choir basses' idea at King's Lynn.

A local organ-builder, Francis Jones, substituted a Dulciana for the Choir Fifteenth in 1839, among other work. The whole organ was replaced, except for the case and (evidently) some pipework, by Brindley & Foster in 1872. The organ was removed to a new St Paul's church at Arbourthorne in 1939 by Cedric Arnold. When this church closed, the organ was rebuilt in Wingerworth church by J. Poyser of Derby. There is thought to be original Stopped Diapason and Principal pipework on the Great soundboard, and an original Open Diapason (perhaps that formerly on the Great) in the Swell-box.

Only the upper front parts of the case survive, painted turquoise. It is of the single–storey King's Lynn type with Rococo carving but it has a high central tower (see p. 45). This drawing of St Paul's church (adapted from *The Building News* of 16 June 1911 by Peter Horne) shows the organ in a high west gallery with the side extensions to the original case still to be seen at Wingerworth.

In Sheffield, this relatively modest organ spoke from a position close to the flat ceiling into a building with seats for 1,400 people.

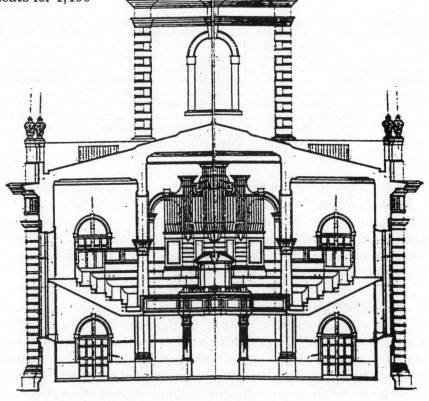

St Paul's church, Sheffield

22 Leith, Scotland, unknown location
(?1755)

There is a reference in the Minute Book in September 1754 of the Canongate Lodge, Edinburgh, to a proposed organ:

> Mr Snetzlear further said that he expected to be in this place about the month of July next year to put up one organ for a meeting place in Leith.

However, since the Canongate organ was not delivered until 1757 (see no. 32) it may be doubted that the Leith organ arrived in 1755. Nothing further is known of it.

23 Lowgate, Hull, St Mary's church
(1755)

S III/57; HR 3; F 10

That organs were made for Sheffield and Hull in the year after the Lynn organ may seem to argue that Burney was right in asserting that Snetzler 'was soon called to almost every quarter of the kingdom'. Indeed, the two organs appear to have been identical. Snetzler must by now have brought together a team of workmen, as his subsequent workshop production rapidly increased. In fact the Hull organ had been ordered much earlier, at a vestry meeting on 29 July 1751, when provision was also made for the stipend of an organist (at £25 per annum) by raising the pew rents. The upper termination of the keyboard compass at d''' is to be noted: this may be a matter of provincial conservatism or merely indicative of the early date. (We do not definitely know the original compass of the Sheffield organ.)

The organ was not altered until about 1820; in July of that year (evidently after the alteration) the stop–list had become:

> Great: (G' [?short octave]–d'''): OD, SD, Pr, 12, 15, Ses II [?b]/Cor II [?tr], Tpt
> Choir: (G' [?short octave]–d'''): SD, Pr, Fl, 15
> Swell: (g–d'''): OD, Pr, Hb
> Swell to Great coupler.

The organ was 'improved' and pedals added at this period, and it would seem from the above that the Great mixture was then reduced from three ranks to two, and (by analogy with the Sheffield organ) that a Swell Cornet had been reduced to its Principal (–8) rank only. The coupler is not original, by the same analogy. As at Sheffield, it is possible that the Swell and Choir were played originally from the same keyboard. The keyboards are reported to have been of blackwood, with ivory–capped sharps.

The organ was repaired in 1838 and enlarged in 1849. In 1856, its compass was extended by Forster & Andrews, and it was moved, with the loss of the case, by the same firm to a new south aisle in 1863. The organ was entirely replaced by a new Brindley & Foster organ in 1904.

24 Lulworth Castle, Dorset, Edward Weld (1755–6)

Snetzler provided an organ, or possibly two organs, for the Weld family. In a letter dated 2 July 1753 [1], Edward Weld wrote to his brother Simeon in London to ask him to 'bespeak an Organ not exceeding 80 guineas'. Later in the year he wrote again to his brother about the organ. On 30 May 1755, Snetzler was paid 'part of 80 guins for an organ', so it may either have been definitely ordered or even completed by then. The latter would at first sight seem the more likely, but the very next year Edward noted that on 22 January (1756) 'Mr Snetzler came to set up ye Organ and went ye 24'. It appears that he was paid a total of £193. 18s. 7d. for this organ in advance, and two guineas upon its completion on 24 January.

Since there is no note of an earlier delivery of an organ, it is likely that the first thoughts grew into a larger organ (80 guineas would have bought a normal chamber organ), or that an additional organ (for a chapel within the castle?) was obtained. If so, two or three days would hardly be sufficient for final voicing adjustments and tuning, let alone putting it (or them) up, unless most of this work had already been done in the workshops and Snetzler came only to carry out the finishing touches after the organ had been erected by an associate or a local man.

Twenty years later, Thomas Weld employed the Seedes who installed an organ of their own making in 1777, at a cost of £204.14s. Modifications were made to it or another organ at a cost of about £82 in 1779. One of these Seede organs seems to have been used as a basis for the organ erected in the new chapel in the grounds of the castle by Richard Seede in 1785.

The castle was burnt out in 1929, but the chapel and its (now restored) organ survive. One enigma remains – there is a rank of pipes in the chapel organ marked 'Flut' in a manner characteristic of Snetzler, among the Seede pipework. Other Seede organs show traits that could be traced to their makers' knowledge of Snetzler organs; did they first become acquainted with them at Lulworth?

[1] Dr John Rowntree kindly supplied details of the documentation of the Lulworth organs.

25 Sculthorpe, Norfolk, St Mary and All Saints' church (1755)

HR 19; F 74; W 111 (27)

A chamber organ with an oak case based on the 'normal' standard type, but much elaborated with carvings of musical trophies and other decorations, was made for the Assembly Rooms at York, and labelled *John Snetzler fecit Londini 1755*. It was moved to Sculthorpe in Norfolk in 1860 (was the Sutton family involved in this?) when the present nave was built. The texts painted on the case, and its present colour scheme, were added at this time.

The stop-list is as follows:

(G', A'–e'''): OD, SD, Pr, Fl, Ses (b/tr) III (now II) [*sic*: there is no separate 15]

The keyboard is of blackwood with ivory-capped sharps. The ebony stop-knobs are labelled with nineteenth-century labels; there are traces of earlier (original?) labels under the Victorian paintwork.

There are five small toe-pedals apparently intended to be permanently coupled to the keyboard, but they are not original, and are at present not working. They are contained within a softwood plinth added under the original oak skirting, as can clearly be seen from the rear of the organ. The later plinth appears to be part of a general reconstruction (also in 1860?) to include a double-rise compensated horizontal reservoir as a substitute for an original wind system and the addition of a swell-louvre front. This latter has caused the upper sides of the casework to be extended forward, somewhat crudely.

The organ was renovated and fitted with an electric blower in 1950 by N. P. Mander Ltd; at that time it was found that 'York' was scribed on the C pipe of the Open Diapason. The case is 6' 1" wide by 2' 10" deep by 14' 2" high overall.

The organ in Sculthorpe church   *The organ in Clare College*

26 Cambridge, Clare College
(1755)

F 25; W 106 (12)

This chamber organ is thought to be labelled 1755, but Andrew Freeman notes a chamber organ he dates 1756 as one formerly in Shaw House, Newbury. It was sold in 1906 to J. A. Fuller Maitland of Kensington, London, and moved there by Frederick Rothwell of Harrow. It was moved again to Borwick Hall, Carnforth, Lancashire, in 1920. Fuller Maitland, an editor of early English keyboard music, also owned at one time the 1752 bureau organ now in New Haven, Connecticut, U. S. A. (no. 15), and other members of the family of that name owned the chamber organ now in Norwich Cathedral (no. 20).

The organ was acquired by Margaret Royds of Heysham, Lancashire in 1939; she presented it immediately to the mission church of St James in Heysham. The reservoir was repaired and fitted with an electric blower in 1955. In 1970, the church decided that

> By reason of its nature as a chamber organ it is more suited to recitals
> than to the accompaniment of a choir and congregation in church ... so it
> is being offered for sale in the hope that it will find a sympathetic owner
> and at the same time raise enough money to enable us to buy a worthy
> successor for the new church shortly to be built.

The organ was extensively advertised, and was bought by Bernard Bibby in 1970 and in recent years moved to Cambridge.

Its mahogany casework is of the 'normal' chamber organ type, with folding glazed doors, and it has the following stop-list:

(*G', A'–f '''*): OD, SD (b/tr), Dul, Fl (b/tr), 15, Ses b III/Cor tr III, Hb (in a swell)

The stop-names are engraved on small metal plates inlaid into the casework; the organ stands about 6' wide by 3' deep by 8' 9" high.

A shifting movement momentarily cancels the Principal, Fifteenth, 'Sesquialtra' and 'Cornett' ranks. The pedal for this is to the left of that for the sliding-shutter swell for the Hautboy. The keyboard is of blackwood with 'skunk-tail' sharps (blackwood with a central fillet of ivory), and is the earliest-dated surviving example of its kind made by Snetzler.

27 Arlecdon, Cumberland, St Michael's church
(1755)

B 207/176–7; S II/50; HR 21; F 16

This two-manual church organ was made for St Nicholas church (or chapel)

Whitehaven, Cumberland. Its early history is related by Alexander Buckingham:

St. Nicholas Church, Whitehaven, Cumberland—An Organ with two sets of keys the Great Organ from GG long octaves to E in alt, the Swell Organ from G below middle C to E in alt. A piano movement that leaves the Diapasons Principal and Flute.

GREAT ORGAN						SWELL ORGAN				
Open Diapason	...	...	...	62		Open Diapason	...	...	...	34
Stop Diapason	...	...	...	57		Dulciana	...	...	...	34
Principal	...	...	...	57		Principal	...	...	...	34
Flute ...	...	...	...	57		Hautboy	...	...	...	34
Twelfth	...	...	...	57						
Fifteenth	...	...	...	57						136
Sesqualtra bafs 3R	...	...	...	84		Great Organ	...	...	...	633
Cornet treble 5R	...	...	...	145						
Trumpet bafs and treble	...	...	57			Total	...	...	...	769
				633						

Mr. Howgill, Organist. Mrs. Curtis in 1825. The Open Diapason to CC of metal, the GG AA BB ♮ CC ♯ is a Stop Diapason with a metal helper. The Great Principal is by Donaldson of York. He was employed to do something to the organ when he robbed it of the original principal and was afterwards made to put in another. The Trumpet is not the original, neither can I say by whom it was altered. I think added by Donaldson or Blyth. The whole of the organ has been ill-used by persons who have pretended to tune it, etc. There are two diagonal bellows. The Case is Wainscott 18 ft. high, 10 ft. 6 ins. wide, 3 ft. 9 ins. deep. Made by Snetzler in 1755. The Bellows was made new horizontal with double feeders by A. Buckingham in 1825. Blyth's bill for repairing in 1797 was £52 10s. 0d. Snetzler had for the Organ £231 16s. 0d. The Freight was £26 17s. 5d. Whitehaven 1 October, 1824.

Caine [1] quotes a fulsome tribute to the organ's maker:

The organ in St Nicholas' Chapel, Whitehaven, was built by that ingenious artist Snetzler, whose high character is universally known from the many noble monuments which he has left of consummate skill in his profession. It was opened in the year 1756.

His (later) stop-list agrees with Buckingham's, but includes a four-stop Choir (not in Sperling), consisting of Open Diapason, Stopped Diapason, Principal and Flute ranks. As the cost of a good one-manual organ was given in 1772 by Ludlam as about £240, the organ cannot originally have been larger than a two-manual instrument. Sperling notes an intermediate state, with a four-rank Sesquialtera bass, a total of 820 pipes and two and a half octaves of German pedals. He reports that it was 'A remarkably good organ all through'.

Nonetheless, the organ gave way to a new Harrison organ (of equally great fame until its destruction by fire in 1971), installed 1902–4. The Snetzler organ was advertised in the November 1901 issue of *Musical Opinion* and purchased by Arlecdon in 1904. It was removed thither and rebuilt by Harrison in 1905.

[1] C. Caine, *Churches of the Whitehaven Rural Deanery* (Whitehaven, 1913), pp. 112–113.

28 Handsworth, Sheffield, St Mary's church
(1755 or 1775)

B 213/45

The organ was made for the Earl of Scarborough at Sandbeck Hall (where Green was to make a large chamber organ in 1790), but was moved to Handsworth 1830–1, apparently by Parkyn of York. He changed the organ in various ways which are not altogether clear from Buckingham's account of 1834:

Handsworth Church near Sheffield—An Organ with two sets of Keys the Compafs from GG long octaves to E in alt, Sweil from G to E and Shifting Movement.

GREAT ORGAN		SWELL ORGAN	
Op. Diapason to gamut G	58	Op. Diapason	34
St. Diapason bafs and treble	58	St. Diapason	34
Principal	58	Principal	34
Flute bafs and treble	58	Hautboy	34
Dulciana treble from m/C	30		——
Twelfth	58		136
Fifteenth	58	Great Organ	408
Trumpet treble m/C	30		——
	——		Total 546
	408		

The Open Diapason to G, the lower octave communicated to the St. Diapason with helpers. The Bellows horizontal, in a deal Case 13ft. 2in. high, 9ft. 3in. wide, 4ft. 8in. deep. This Organ was made by Snetzler but the Swell, New Horizontal bellows and two new set of keys and what he calls Cleaning and tuning and repairing by Parkyn of York for 39 pounds but the whole of it is badly done and I venture to say he spoilt the Organ. The Hautboy in the Swell was taken out of the Great Organ. Handsworth, 24 September 1834.

The deal case seems unlikely for a house organ; was it placed in a chapel? Did Parkyn install the Dulciana instead of the Hautboy (perhaps previously in a small swell–box?) which he moved to the Swell organ? Or did he enclose a Choir in a swell–box? (£39 would be too little for moving the organ and supplying a completely new Swell, bellows, keyboards, etc.)

The organ was moved in about 1869, and was rebuilt by Keates of Sheffield in 1889, when the case was discarded. It was moved and rebuilt again by Keates in 1933 or 1934 and repaired c1944.

In 1989 the organ was replaced by a new instrument installed by Principal Pipe Organs. The Great Stopped Diapason is reported by them to be by Snetzler; the caps on this rank do not have a moulding on them – a fact which may imply an earlier rather than a later date.

29 Birmingham University, Barber Institute
(1755 or 1756)

F 11; W 101 (2)

A chamber organ of the usual type, with glazed doors and a mahogany case, possibly made at the same time as that now in Cambridge (no. 26).

Its early history is not known, but it was acquired by Noel Mander in 1958 from Henry Poyser, organ-builder of Chester, together with the information that Poyser's father had bought it from a chemist's shop, and that it had previously been in Buckingham House, London. The last assertion is not mentioned by Freeman, who gives this stop-list:

(*G', A'–f '''*): 'Dulciama'[*sic*], SD, Pr, Fl, 15, Ses b II/'Cornet' tr II

The absence of an Open Diapason will be noted, unless the 'Dulciama' is in fact a softened Open Diapason. The stop names may well not be original – Snetzler habitually spelt the treble mixture 'Cornett' – and they are engraved on brass plates let into the console woodwork. However, they were apparently already in place when Freeman saw the Birmingham organ at Poyser's workshop, and the Cambridge organ's stop-names are similarly displayed.

The keyboard is unusual in that it has ivory naturals and blackwood sharps, and is the earliest-dated one of this kind. This is again, as is the keyboard of the organ at Cambridge (no. 26), a divergence from Snetzler's normal keyboard style. As the 1760 organ now at Eton College, also associated with Buckingham House (no. 44) shares this feature – and intervening ones, for example, the 1759 chamber organ at 'Hatchlands' (no. 42) do not – it may be that there is some truth in the story that the organ had royal associations. The stop-knobs are of ebony. A shelf behind the broken pediment of the case now supports a crown from the former organ case in what is now Newcastle Cathedral.

A shifting movement takes off the Principal, Fifteenth and mixture; there is also a pedal for blowing as well as a (later?) hand-pump. The organ was renovated and fitted with an electric blower by N. P. Mander Ltd in 1958, and was further renovated in 1978.

The organ is illustrated in chapter 2, p. 47.

30 Doncaster, Yorkshire, St George's church (1756)

B 206/51; F 13

Hopkins and Rimbault (1, p. 136) note that:

> The celebrated Snetzler was employed upon the instrument in 1758, as appears by the following receipt: – 'April 26, 1756. Received of Mr. Francis Caley, church-warden, the sum of Twenty pounds for Repairing and Tuneing the Organ, by me, John Snetzler'.

Buckingham, who moved the organ in 1823, was apparently unaware of this, so the work cannot have been signed *in situ*. The church was totally destroyed by fire in 1853.

31 Chesterfield, Derbyshire, St Mary and All Saints' church (1756)

B 206/54; S II/73; HR 1; F 12

According to Sumner [1], a label framed and fixed to the 1922 console read *John Snetzler, Londini, Fecit 1756*, but the organ was thought by Rimbault to have been made as early as 1741. Did Snetzler in fact carry out repairs to a previous organ after storm damage that year? Sumner also quoted Ford's *History of Chesterfield*:

> In the year 1755 a fine organ was contracted for of £500 value to be made by Mr. Schnetzler of London, Organ maker; and the said organ and a new gallery at the West end of the Parish Church of Chesterfield (appropriated by a Faculty from the Court of Lichfield towards the support and main-tenance of an Organist well qualified to perform the Service of the Church) were erected in the said Church by the voluntary contributions of some Noblemen and Gentlemen who had estates in the said parish, together with the inhabitants of the said town of Chesterfield and the hamlets belonging thereto, and the P. organ was opened 21st October, 1756.
> Wm. Wheeler, Vicar of Chester [*sic*].

The organ was opened by 'Mr Leyland'. The case was similar to that at Sheffield, with single–storey flats and with the tallest tower in the centre front.

Alexander Buckingham noted the earliest reliable stop–list:

The Parish Church, Chesterfield—An organ with three sets of keys the Great Organ from GG long octaves to E in alt. The Choir Organ the same. The Swell Organ from G below middle C to E in alt consist of the following stops:

GREAT ORGAN				
Op. Diapason	...	...	...	57
St. Diapason	...	...	...	57
Principal	...	...	...	57
Nason	...	...	...	57
Twelfth	...	...	...	57
Fifteenth	...	...	...	57
Sexquialtera 4R	...	...	...	228
Cornet m/C 5R	...	...	...	145
Trumpet	...	...	...	57
Clarion	...	...	...	57
				829

CHOIR ORGAN				
Dulciana	...	...	...	57
St. Diapason	...	...	...	57
Principal	...	...	...	57
Flute	...	...	...	57

Fifteenth	...	...	...	57
Bafsoon	...	...	...	57
				342

SWELL ORGAN				
Op. Diapason	...	...	...	34
Dulciana	...	...	...	34
St. Diapason	...	...	...	34
Cornet m/C 4R	...	...	...	116
Trumpet	...	...	...	34
Hautboy	...	...	...	34
				286

Choir	...	...	...	342
Great	...	...	...	829
Total	...	...	...	1,457

Mrs. Dutton, organist. The Dulciana in the Choir all through of metal. The Cornet in the Swell is from m/C to the top. All the St. Diapasons and Flutes trebles is metal. In a Wainscott case 23 ft. high, 13 ft. 1 in. wide, 7 ft. deep, built by John Snetzler, London, in 1756. Chesterfield, November 13th, 1823, A.B.

The presence here of a Nason on the Great and two Dulcianas (unusual in his later church instruments, and here possibly outward–tapering [2]) should be noted.

The organ case in Chesterfield church

Following work by Francis Jones of Sheffield (he who worked at St Paul's church, Sheffield, no. 21,) in 1842 and 1851, Sperling noted these changes:

Manuals remade to *C–f '''* compass. Additional Open Diapason on Great; Claribel Flute (?replacing Cornet); new or revoiced reeds. Choir Bassoon changed to Cremona; Swell virtually renewed, and extended to tenor C. Five couplers, and 'Grand Pedal Pipes' 16'.

In 1851 the organ was moved to the east gallery of the nave, and to the north transept in 1862. Additions were made in 1891 and 1922, and the organ was again altered 1957–8. Despite these changes, ten stops and the case remained when the organ was virtually completely destroyed by fire in 1961. Four ranks, enclosed in a 'Positif' swell–box, survived (the Choir Stopped Diapason, Dulciana, Flute and Fifteenth), and are incorporated in the present organ.

[1] W. L. Sumner, 'The Organs of Chesterfield Parish Church' (TO 156/165).
[2] Hinted at in Herbert Snow, 'The Organs of Chesterfield Parish Church' (TO 40/241), where he records a postcard from E. J. Hopkins written in 1891 'having reference to the peculiar shape of these dolce [sic] pipes'.

32 Edinburgh, Kilwinning, Lodge Canongate (1756)

F 14; W 105 (9)

A large chamber organ was commissioned 2 October 1754 for this Masonic Lodge, delivered and set up by 4 August 1757. It is apparently labelled *John Snetzler Londini fecit 1756*; clearly its completion and delivery were held up by the other major work of that year.

The first moves to obtain an organ had been made upon a visit by Snetzler to Edinburgh, when he met the Brethren on 18 September 1754. Their Minute Book records that

> when Mr Snetzlear [sic] the organist was here he was brought down by
> some of the Brethren and shown the lodge room and his opinion asked
> what organ would be proper for the room and what the price of a proper
> instrument would be [,] and that Mr Snetzlear then said that it was his
> opinion if the lodge gave him commission for making one organ, at about
> Sixty–five or Seventy Pounds, he thought he could promise at that price to
> make the instrument to give extra satisfaction to the society and also to
> answer to the size of the room, and Mr Snetzlear further said that he
> expected to be in this place about the month of July next year to put up
> one organ for a meeting place in Leith when he could endeavour to have
> the organ for this lodge in case it was commissioned early

It is not exactly clear if an organ for Leith or the one for the Edinburgh Lodge (or even the Lodge itself) might to be 'commissioned early'; but the repeated use of the phrase 'one organ' rings true; it is reminiscent of the famous report at Halifax (no. 67), where Snetzler said that the candidate 'ran over te key like one cat'.

On 2 October, the Lodge met and decided unanimously that 'a bargain be made with Snetzler' at a proposed ceiling cost of £70. On 5 March 1755, Snetzler answered a letter from the Treasurer, Brother Robertson; this correspondence was apparently continued, and Snetzler was urged to build the organ as quickly as

The inauguration of Robert Burns as poet Laureate

possible under the terms of the Minute.

It took a further 28 months before 'R. W.' was able to inform the Lodge that 'the organ which they had some time ago commissioned was now arrived at Leith and therefore desired a committee should be appointed to take care and to proceed with all care and despatch in setting up the organ.' (Leith is the port for Edinburgh – the reference is not to the other possible organ for Leith, no. 22 – and the Kilwinning organ arrived there 6 July 1757.)

The organ was presumably promptly delivered from the docks, as a note dated 3 August 1757 records that 'B. W. reported that Br. Mercer had remitted Fifty Pounds Stg. to Mr Snetzler in part payment of the organ'. Snetzler presumably finished the organ *in situ* immediately, but the final payment was made only when it was noted on 2 February 1758 that it was 'Authorised Bro. Mercer to remit Twenty–five Pounds Stg. to Mr Snetzler in further payment of the organ.' Was the extra £5 for packing and transport costs?

The organ stands now where it evidently always did, in an alcove in the Lodge; it has an oak case, approximately 7' wide by 5' deep by 12' high – a larger version of the usual chamber organ type.

The original stop–list was:

(G, A–e'''): OD [open wood bass], SD, Pr, Fl, Ses b III/Cor tr IV

The keyboard is of blackwood with ivory-capped sharps; three large wooden doors protect the upper front case and the gilded front pipes. A shifting movement takes off the Principal, Fifteenth and mixture.

In 1912, a small separate swell-box to the right of the case was added by Hamilton of Edinburgh. It contains a Salicional and Voix Celeste on pneumatic action, tubed from the original grid. Apart from the more recent addition of some tuning slides which presumably involved retuning and consequent pitch change (and presumably a change to equal temperament in or by 1912), the organ remains in its original state.

33 Hillington, Norfolk, St Mary's church
(1756)

F 63; W 106 (13)

A large house or elaborate church organ which has been variously thought to have been made for the Duke of Bedford for the Music Gallery at Woburn, or for Woburn church. The manual compass would perhaps suggest the latter; if so, it would have been superseded there by an organ by Timothy Russell in 1836. It was moved at an undetermined date to the National Society's Training College at Leatherhead, whence it was acquired by Holdich, who made some additions and sold it to Hillington church in 1857. It was installed under an arch in front of a large, specially constructed transept/vestry, and speaks easily into a church with resonant acoustic properties.

The design of the Rococo mahogany case is a unique survival, and may well have been Leonard Snetzler's conception. It is elaborately carved and moulded, and its front corners are angled back. The front pipes are in the 'normal' three-part arrangement but decorated in red, blue, white, green and gold. The date of these decorations is not known, but it is most likely to be 1857; the central flat of painted dummies seem to be Victorian 'flat-backs'. Their decorative scheme is somewhat reminiscent of that used on the original front pipes in the James Wyatt case of Samuel Green's organ 1790 which Holdich removed from Lichfield cathedral to Armitage parish church in 1861; however, there is also Sperling's report of diapered pipes at Wilton (no. 70). Unusually, parts of the original frames for the rear panels of the casework are still in place. The stop-list is at present:

> Great, upper keyboard, (*G'*, *A'–e'''*): OD [to *G*, the bass octave from SD with
>   helpers], SD [now renamed 'Chimney Flute'], Pr, 12, 15, Ses III,
>   and a blanked-off hole [originally for Cor tr?]
> Choir and Swell, lower keyboard, (*G'*, *A'–e'''*): SD b/tr, Fl b/tr, Dul tr
>   [enclosed], Gamba tr [enclosed, evidently replacing an Hautboy]
> Pedal: Bourdon and Great to Pedal

There are no 'shifting-movement' pedals or double sliders; this auxiliary action would not be necessary in an organ with two keyboards of complete compass. The original stop-knobs are of blackwood; the 'paper labels pasted on the jambs', possibly original, noted by Freeman's reporter, are now replaced by engraved ivory plates – see chapter 4, p. 196 for a possible original layout of the stop-knobs. The natural keys are of blackwood and the accidentals are ivory-capped.

The arrangement of the single M-layout soundboard is a unique survival in Snetzler's output, but it is similar to that in the organ (c1771, probably by Thomas Haxby) at Newby Hall, North Yorkshire. The grooves for the two keyboards are intercalated, with the Choir's top-note grooves nearest the centre of the organ. At the back of the soundboard there are the conveyances for the raised Swell, then the sliders alternate thus: SD Choir/SD Great/OD Great (with basses and 'helpers')/Pr Great/Flute Choir/12/15/17/Ses & Cor [front]. The sliders for the Swell are at the higher level. All the pipes of the two wooden ranks of the Choir have 'moulded' caps; the chimney flutes of the Great Stopped Diapason run down to 'fiddle' G.

Upon the organ's installation at Hillington, which cost £70, Holdich provided pedals, *G'–c*, with an octave of Bourdon pipes, *C–c*, and raised the organ on a 9" plinth on top of the general platform. In 1955, a new 30-note pedalboard, *C–f'*, a Great to Pedal coupler and further pipes to complete the Bourdon's compass were installed.

The organ in Hillington church

34 London, Marlborough House chapel
(?1756 & ?1781)

HR 32; F 67

The chapel, designed by Inigo Jones in 1623 for Queen Henrietta Maria (though intended for the Infanta of Spain, to whom Charles I was first betrothed), contained at first a succession of organs. There were none at all from about 1700 onwards, when the chapel was used by French and Dutch protestants, according to Freeman [1]. From 1781 an organ, given by Queen Caroline, was used by the German Lutheran congregation. There are no recorded details of this organ, but it may not be totally idle to speculate that it was made or supplied by Snetzler, who was then about to retire.

The present instrument is a chamber organ supposed to have been given by William IV c1830, to have come from Buckingham House, and to have been made by Snetzler in 1756.[2] It was rebuilt and enlarged in 1862 by Hill & Son and rebuilt again by their successors in 1938. This firm may have 'attached' the date 1756 to the organ, as they customarily date their 'foundation' to this part of Snetzler's working life. The upper part of the case is still to be seen above the reredos, but the organ does not look like one of Snetzler's making, and Paget [3] seems to confuse it with the chamber organ now at Eton (no. 44). Details of its stop-list and console fittings (brass stop-knobs with paper labels) do not seem to ring true either, and yet the Open Diapason is described as having 'helpers' in the bass. The organ is included in this 'catalogue' largely because of its ancient ascription to Snetzler. [4]

The original (now Great) stop-list of the organ seems to have been:

OD, SD, Pr, Fl, 12, 15, Sesq III, ?Tpt

which is a typical Snetzler chorus. Clearly, some proper evidence from the pipework and Great soundboard is still needed.

[1] Andrew Freeman, 'The Organs of St. James's Palace' (TO 16/193).
[2] Gordon Paget, 'The Rebuilt Organ in Marlborough House Chapel' (TO 71/170).
[3] op. cit.; HR 32 adds 'Buckingham Palace. Now in the German Chapel, St. James's.'
[4] Ellis, in his paper 'On the History of Musical Pitch' cites the organ twice (on p. 39 of the reprint by Frits Knuf, 1968) as being by 'Schnetzler' for 'the German Chapel Royal, St. James's Palace ... formerly at Buckingham Palace'. He recorded its pitch as being equivalent to A = 425.6 Hz.

*

35 Huntingdon, All Saints' church
(?1757)

S II/135; HR 35; F 65

A stop–list in Sperling attributes both date and builder thus:

> Snetzler 1757 Gt GG long octaves to E in alt. Swell to fiddle G.
> [Gt.] OD, SD, Pr, Fl thro', 12, 15, Ses III in halves
> [Sw.] OD, Pr, Hb
> German pedals one octave, choir organ scale, old carved case.

Hamilton [1] mentions the Bryceson organ that had superseded this by 1865. The Earl of Sandwich is supposed to have headed the subscription list with a gift of £50.[2] A connection with the organ now at Theddingworth (see no. 57) has been posited; the two organs are indeed of similar size and content, but the latter is dated 1763.

[1] James Hamilton, *Catechism of the Organ* (1865 edn, repr. Knuf, 1992), p. 163.
[2] BIOSJ 12/57.

36 Gloucester, the cathedral
(repairs 1757)

F 18

Freeman quotes Dr Henry Gee's 'Handbook on the Gloucester Organ' (London, 1921) to the effect that the Thomas Harris organ was repaired – seemingly quite substantially – by Snetzler in 1757 at a cost of £130. The organ has since been rebuilt several times, and no documentary evidence of the actual work carried out by Snetzler is available.

37 London, Cleveland Street, St Mary-le-Savoy Lutheran church
(the second organ for the German Lutheran chapel in the Savoy, 1757; or 1767?)

L 24; S I/200; HR 26; F 36

Freeman dates this organ 1757 without the evidence of a label, but he places it in his list with organs of 1767. Archibald Farmer [1] refers to a 'not very legible tablet which is affixed to it' as reading 1757 or perhaps 1767. William Ludlam, writing in the *Gentleman's Magazine* of December 1772 (see Appendix 7), praises the organ, but he does not date it; nor does Leffler.

Since the organ is clearly of the utmost importance in Snetzler's output and was widely quoted as a model of steady winding, and as possessing a very early set of pedals 'to the laft 12 notes and their femitones' (Ludlam) and a 'Tremblant', it is most unfortunate that its exact year of making is not known. Although one source mentions Snetzler as organist here, there is no evidence for this; the first organist seems to have been Karl (Carl) Friederick Baumgarten (*c*1740–1824) who, it has been said, came to London for that purpose at about the age of 18. [2] If this is indeed the case, then the earlier date for the organ would be the correct one. He was known as a skilled modulator [3] (does this imply that the organ was tuned in equal temperament for this German church?), and in 1783–4 he published *Five Preludes and Fugues*, the first organ voluntaries set out on three staves in a manner implying, if not always requiring, the use of pedals. [4]

The organ was made for what Ludlam termed the 'greater' Lutheran chapel in the Savoy (just north of the Thames, near Charing Cross). It is known that pastors from the Moravian community (including Mr Schlicht of Fulneck) preached here, and they may have become acquainted with Snetzler through the first organ he made for the church in about 1747 (no. 5).

When the remains of the Savoy castle were finally demolished, a new church was built off Tottenham Court Road, and the organ, (and the gallery clock) were transferred to it in 1878. The organ was moved by Gray & Davison, who evidently also remodelled it.

Farmer refers to a stop–list 'dated 1772', which he gives as:

> Great (*F'*, *G'–e'''*): OD, SD, Pr, 12, 15, Ses III, Cor (sc: *c'*) V, Tpt
> Choir (*G'*, *A'–e'''* [*sic*]): OD, SD, Pr, Fl, 15, Bn
> Swell (*g–e'''*): OD, Pr, Tpt, Hb
> 'Pedals up to C, Choir to Great, Tremblant'

If Farmer is correct, then the organ is further remarkable for the manual coupler, which is unprecedented – and is not mentioned by Ludlam. Leffler's manuscript account (*c*1800, written up from a visit by or with William Russell) tallies with this; it adds that the Great Stopped Diapason was 'Metal in the treble', and confirms that 'There is a Copula which adds the Choir to the full organ [his frequent term for the Great], & a tremulant'.

The case comprised two storeys of pipes in the flats; the upper curtains of pipes are no doubt there to screen the swell-box. The organ clearly did not have the Swell on the same keys as the Choir, as in some previous organs: photographs show that there was a horizontal panel above the console to provide access to the 'high' Swell key action. The centre pipe in the case-front was almost certainly the 8' C pipe of the Open Diapason, and not a 12' F pipe as Farmer supposed. This style of case seems to have become a pattern for all sizeable church organs (which may again argue for the earlier date), and the organ was presumably Snetzler's chief London showpiece.

The compass for the pedals as given by Farmer agrees with Ludlam – there are twelve naturals from *F'* to *C*, plus ['and'] their semitones. It seems that there were no pedal pipes, but it is possible that the pedals might have operated separate pallets in the Great soundboard, as Buckingham notes at Nottingham (no. 90). The pedalboard may have resembled those found in the U. S. A. (see chapter 4, p. 221), that is, one with 'long' pedals and not mere stubs.

The organ was rebuilt by August Gern in 1904 with pneumatic action, and by Walker in 1935 with electric action. About ten stops and at least the Great soundboard as well as the splendid case (illustrated on p. 56) survived until they were destroyed by German bombs in 1941.

[1] Archibald Farmer, 'The Snetzler Organ at St. Mary–le–Savoy, Cleveland Street' (TO 67/148).
[2] *The New Grove Dictionary of Music and Musicians* (Macmillan, 1980).
[3] *Grove's Dictionary*, 5th edn.
[4] Christopher Kent, 'GG Compass Pedals and the British Organ Repertoire before *c*1850' (BIOSJ 12/72).

38 London, Hackney, St John's church; Poole, Dorset, St James's church (1757)

L 53; S I/57; HR 22 ('formerly St. Augustine's'); F 19

The organ is thus dated by Freeman, but Sperling gives 1764. He and Freeman thought that the Snetzler organ made for the old church at Hackney (rebuilt after demolition in 1796) went to St James's, Poole. The stop–list they gave for the Poole organ is as follows:

> Great: OD, SD, Pr, 12, 15, Ses III, Mix II, Tpt, Cln, Cor V
> Choir: Dul, Pr, 'Nason' Fl, 15, Crm
> Swell: OD, SD, Pr, Cor V [Sperling, but Freeman III], Tpt, Hb

This would appear to be the stop–list of a new organ by G. P. England, and not a normal Snetzler organ. (See below that a Dulciana did not appear on the Hackney organ until 1828; this stop was reserved for chamber organs by Snetzler after its employment in his earlier church organs.)

While undoubtedly the case went to Poole (a watercolour of it in 1825 published by Betty Matthews [1] shows a two–storeyed case of Snetzler's 'Savoy' type), it would seem from Leffler's manuscript that the organ itself remained to be reinstalled (with a new case) in the new church at Hackney. He recorded it as follows:

> St Johns Hackney
> Organ built by Schnetzler & enlarg'd by Mr England in 1797. Compafs
> from GG long Octave to F. Swell to F.
> Pedals up to C.

[Great]		[Choir]		[Swell]	
Open Diap new	58	Stop Diap	58	Open Diap	37
Open Diap	58	Principal	58	Stop Diap	37
Stop Diap	58	Flute	58	Principal	37
Principal	58	Fifteenth	58	Cornt. 3 rank	111
Twelfth	58	Vox hume.	58	Trumpt.	37
Fifteenth	58	Bafsoon	58	Hautboy	37
Tierce new	58		---		---
Trumpet	58		348		296
Clarion	58		---		348
Sexqa 3 ranks	174	Organist Mr Jnr Groombridge			962
Mixture 2 rank	116	Salary £25 raisd at Easter 1802			----
Cornt. to C 5 rank	156	to £40 succeeded Mr L. Hereux			1608
	---	in 1781 June			====
	962				

This account is confirmed by the *Christian Remembrancer* in *'Organo-Historica No. VIII'* (1833-36), [2] which additionally notes the new case:

> The organ of which we are now speaking was built for the *old* church at Hackney, where it originally stood; but, after the erection of the new church, it was removed thither, and underwent an extensive repair by the late Mr. England, in 1796. The compass of the instrument was then extended, by making it long octave; and another open diapason was added to the great organ, with the addition of a *tierce*; and also new sound boards to the great and choir organ, and an entire remodelling of the whole instrument, with a new case of mahogany.

Freeman noted [3] that the organ at St John's Parish Church, Hackney was 'an extensive rebuild and enlargement of the organ made for the *old* church in 1757'. He goes on to quote Hopkins and Rimbault [4] who have apparently paraphrased the *Christian Remembrancer* extract above, and quotes Leffler, *via* Pearce, as to its stop-list at Hackney. Freeman describes the new case as 'massive in appearance ... in keeping with the architecture of the church. It has four towers, and still retains its original position in the west gallery. The fluted supports to the four towers attract attention: their form is probably unique.'

Subsequent work at Hackney, also noted in the *Christian Remembrancer*, included work by Gray in 1828:

> the addition of a set of double open diapason pedal pipes, the compass of which extending [*sic*] from CC to CCC, – thirteen notes; a dulciana in the choir organ, in the place of a vox humana; two coupling stops to unite the swell and choir organs to the great organ; three composition pedals to the great organ; the swell extended from F, to C in the tenor, with a Venetian swelling front; new pair of horizontal bellows; and octave and a half of *German pedals* ... Those conoisseurs [*sic*] who are capable of judging and appreciating the beauty of Schnetzler's *voicing*, will perceive, at once, that the original quality is still preserved....If any further addition could be

made, we should venture to recommend a *Cremona treble* in the place of the *bassoon*; as such a stop, going all through the instrument, is not in keeping with the instrument [*sc.* bassoon] that it represents, being a bass instrument. The Cremona is a more useful stop ...

Henry Willis made additions to this organ in 1863; it was destroyed in a fire on 18 May 1955.

*

The Poole organ was given to St James's Church by its M. P.; the Vestry Minutes for 30 July 1799 record that a meeting was held

> in order to consult of the propriety of fixing an Organ in the Church, and of the most convenient situation for the same. It is now ordered that Benjamin Lister Esqr be permitted at his own Expence to Erect an Organ in the Middle or Singing Gallery, as far back from the front of the said Gallery, as the height of the same will admit.

Sperling records 'An 8ve of open Pedal Pipes GG to G and 1½ 8ves of pedals added in 1820'. This work actually followed a complete rebuilding of the church between 1819 and 1821.

The organ was rebuilt by Walker in 1875; at this time the upper parts of the casework and the front pipes were removed. The previous casework was recalled by John Harris [5] in 1900 as 'a classical oak case with three half circular towers and plain gilt front speaking pipes'. This description, and the watercolour referred to above, would suggest that the case was made on the pattern of that in the German Chapel in the Savoy.

[1] Betty Matthews, 'The Organs of St. James's Church, Poole, and the Goss Family' (BIOSJ 2/82).
[2] As transcribed in BIOS Reporter no. 13/2, April 1989, p. 6 [*sic*: should be p. 18].
[3] Andrew Freeman, 'Two Organ Builders of Note; the Englands' [part 2] (TO 82/46); he later contradicted this in part 4 of the same study (TO 84/169).
[4] *The Organ...* (1st edn.), p. 462.
[5] In *Musical Opinion* (1900), p. 414.

39 London, German Calvinist chapel in the Savoy
(?1757, or earlier)

L 175; S I/201; HR 27; F 68

It has been thought that this organ was a gift by Snetzler to the chapel where he worshipped. (It is presumably the 'lesser' chapel implied by Ludlam: see no. 37.) Freeman stated this, but did not suggest a date for it. Sperling, not unreasonably, may have inferred the date given above from the date of the organ for the 'greater' chapel but, as we have seen, that itself is not certain. He gives this stop–list:

GG long octs no D sharp to e in alt. total 604 pipes.
1. Open Diapason to EE then Double pipes – 64
2. Open Diapason treble to mid C – 28
3. Stopd Diapason – 56
4. Principal – 56
5. Dulciana to C below middle – 40
6. Flute – 56
7. Twelfth – 56
8. Fifteenth – 56
9. Sexquialtra bafs 4 ranks – 112
10. Cornet treble 5 ranks – 140

This is quoted as Sperling gave it; it seems to have been copied from Leffler's manuscript, with which it is in this instance virtually identical, or from a mutual source. There is a clue as to the possible date of the organ: the omission of the top D♯ is (as far as is known) paralleled only in the 1742 Yale organ, which also has a short–compass Open Diapason. In fact the organ appears essentially to be a large chamber organ, and may be either an early organ or a reworking of an older instrument. It seems there were actually 608 pipes in total and not 604; Leffler's arithmetic gave him 664.

Freeman appears to have had his information from a similar source, but he does not say what became of the organ; nor can we. If it survived until the demolition of the remains of the Savoy castle in the 1860s, it was perhaps lost then. There is, one supposes, the (very slight) possibility that this and no. 34 are the same instrument.

40 Coventry, Warwickshire, Charles Lee
   (1758)

In private notes, the Revd B. B. Edmonds has communicated a letter dated 1934 in Andrew Freeman's archive which referred to an organ in the possession of Charles Lee, organ builder of Coventry (established in 1891). The organ was apparently 'autographed' in the soundboard, and had been obtained 'from a country church'. It was destroyed because it had been damaged by woodworm; no other details are recorded.

41a London or Kedleston, Derbyshire, Nathaniel Curzon
   (1759)

According to his Notebook KC 1, Sir Nathaniel Curzon intended that there should be two organs at Kedleston:

Organ, the great one in the Music Gallery
Organ, the smaller one, in the North drawing room.

The 'great one' was evidently ready by early 1759, as the receipt (KL7/1) [1] for it records:

> 1759 February 5th Recievd [*sic*] of Sr Nathl Curzon Bart the sum of Four
> Hundred and Fifty Pound in full of all demands for an Organ by the hands
> of Mr John Broadhurst £450–0–0 pr John Snetzler.

Whether this organ was ever erected at Kedleston is not certain, as the south wings planned for this house were never built. The rooms proposed for these included a chapel and the Music Gallery (or 'Music Room', as shown on the plan below) with its special place for the organ; it was to be reached by a gallery. Robert Adam designed a case for the 'West End of the Music Room' [*sic*]; it appears to have been intended to stand about 18' high by 10' wide by 3' 6" deep.

There is a slight possibility [2] that the organ was placed in the Marble Hall at Kedleston, but no papers relating to its erection there have come to light. Therefore, it might be suggested that the organ remained at the London home of the Curzons (5, Audley Square) until it was resold to Snetzler for £300 in March 1766 for eventual re-use at the Pantheon (see no. 41b). Its price and possible casework size suggest a three-manual organ of 'church' proportions.

[1] Receipt-book no. KL7/1 in the Kedleston Hall Archives, as kindly communicated by Leslie Harris, archivist.
[2] See no. 69 for further discussion of this point, and concerning the 'smaller one' installed at Kedleston in 1765–6.

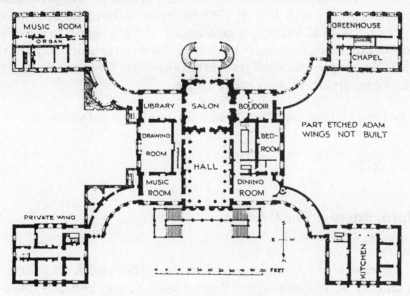

Plan of Kedleston Hall, showing the complete scheme

41b London, Oxford Street, the Pantheon
   (1772)

The Pantheon was built between 1769 and 1772 by Samuel Wyatt to the designs of the young James Wyatt, and opened in January 1772. It was, said Horace Walpole, 'a winter Ranelagh', 'the most beautiful edifice in England', 'Balbec in all its glory'. [1] Samuel had been appointed clerk of the works under Robert Adam at Kedleston Hall in 1760, and he lived there until 1768. Samuel, James and William Wyatt (the last being the business manager) worked closely together until about 1774; their work included the organ cases at Burton-on-Trent (1770–1; no. 84) and the Pantheon. Samuel was a designer in his own right as well as builder – he was nicknamed 'the Chip' because of his origins at Kedleston as a carpenter.

> The rotunda of the Pantheon ... owed as much to Adam's saloon at Kedleston as to its Roman namesake. Like all the major early Wyatt buildings it was executed by the same team of craftsmen as Kedleston, including Joseph Rose II the stuccoist, Biagio Rebecca the painter, Snetzler the organ-builder, and Domenic Bartoli the scagliola-maker.[2]

James Wyatt replaced Adam as the chief architect to the fashionable aristocracy largely as a result of the instant fame of this building, which continued as a place of public entertainment and as a venue for the Handel Commemoration concerts until its destruction by fire on 14 January 1792. It had been converted into a theatre for Italian Opera by James Wyatt, 1790–91. Only its façade survived – on the south side of Oxford Street, near Tottenham Court Road – until 1937.

The *Survey of London* [3] under the heading 'Pantheon' states that 'John Stretzler [*sic*] ... built organ for £300'. Since this is exactly the price Snetzler paid for the Curzon organ on 4th March 1766 (with or without its original case?), the suggestion that the first Curzon house organ of 1759 went to the Pantheon is therefore quite plausible, especially in view of the close relationships of the Wyatts and Snetzler. Nothing is known of its contents or (later?) casework, or if it survived the building's conversion into an opera house.

[1] Quoted in John M. Robinson, *The Wyatts, an Architectural Dynasty* (O. U. P., 1979), p. 25
[2] ibid., p. 26.
[3] vol. xxxi, p. 271.

42 Guildford, Surrey, 'Hatchlands'
   (1759)

The organ, labelled *John Snetzler fecit Londini 1759*, which was formerly in the Methodist church of Wellesbourne (Warwickshire), has recently been privately purchased; it now stands in the staircase hall at 'Hatchlands' in Surrey.

The organ was purchased by the church at Wellesbourne from Barford Hill

'Organ Case for Sir Nathaniel Curzon Bart.' by Robert Adam

House, home of the Smith–Rylands, in 1919 at a cost of £60. It is a chamber organ with a unique case design which presumably was made to fit into the architectural scheme of a particular room (perhaps a Music Room), apparently in Sherborne Hall, Warwickshire. The case is of mahogany with a bold dentilled cornice and a broken pediment; two large pilasters (through the base of which the stop-knobs are drawn) flank two flats of gilded (or painted [1]) dummy metal pipes in lightly carved frames. Only the butts of the hinges of two doors which enclosed the front pipes and the keyboard remain.

The keyboard is an early example, perhaps the earliest, of a retractable type; there is, consequently a sticker and backfall (and rollerboard) key action to the front-facing faceboard. The original stop-list was:

(G', A'–f '''): OD (sc: *c'*), SD [wood] b [up to *b*]/tr, Dul (sc: *c*), Pr b [up to *b*]/tr,
Fl [wood thro'], 15 [thro'], Ses b/Cornett tr

The keyboard has natural keys of blackwood and ivory-plated sharps. The original stop-knobs have been replaced by engraved knobs; signs of earlier labels are faintly visible.

At some time in the second half of the last century, the original feeder and reservoir were removed, and an horizontal one substituted. The Sesquialtra and Cornett gave way to a Keraulophon whose 4' C pipe is inked 'Mifs Ryland's organ'. However, the 'Cornett' trundle survives and is thus marked in ink, perhaps in Snetzler's hand; the 'Principall' also.

Three pedals operate: (a) a swell in the top of the case, modified in the nineteenth century, (b) a disconnected shifting movement, and (c) the feeder. The case is approximately 5' wide by 3' 6" deep by 11' high. Further discussion of the unusual features of this organ will be found under no. 44 and on p. 227, and it is illustrated on p. 49.

It might be recalled, in passing, that the best-known present-day black 'porter' beer was first brewed in 1759.

[1] suggested by Dominic Gwynn, who has found that a 'gold' paint [invented by Pinchbeck? see no. 97] was not unknown in the eighteenth century, and seems to have been used here.

43 London, Westminster Abbey, Novello organ (interior, 1759)

W 109 (21)

The pipework, soundboard and wedge-reservoir from an organ formerly in Clyffe House, Tincleton, near Dorchester, Dorset, were used by N. P. Mander Ltd in 1965 as part of the Vincent Novello Memorial organ.

The original stop-list at Clyffe House was recorded by the Revd B. B. Edmonds as:

OD 'treb', SD, Dul, Pr b/tr, Fl, 15, Ses b/Cor tr II, blank

It is now:

(*G'*, *A'–e'''*): OD [sc: *c'*?], SD, Dul, Pr, Fl, 15, 17, Ses b/Cor tr II

It would appear that the Clyffe House organ was similar in tonal design to that at 'Hatchlands' (no. 42). A new keyboard and key (and stop?) actions were provided when the organ was prepared for Westminster. (See no. 60 concerning the casework used for this organ.)

44 Eton, Buckinghamshire, Eton College chapel (1760)

F 21; W 105 (10)

The organ is dated on its label *John Snetzler fecit Londini 1760*. The 'Hatchlands' organ (no. 42) is therefore the 'pivotal' example of a change of design and layout away from what had been Snetzler's normal chamber organ (with its pin action and three–part pipe display), to a taller organ with a sticker–backfall action. This change may have been brought about primarily for tonal reasons (see chapter 4, p. 227), but one consequence was the possibility of employing the retractable type of keyboard included in the instruments now at Hatchlands and Eton.

The stop–knobs in both organs are arranged horizontally with a similar action, but the Eton organ is additionally the first to have a case with an 'oval' centre flat with seventeen display pipes of wood (but without the later wreath), and two flanking flats of four pipes each. The pediment is gracefully shaped, and an urn in its centre is placed on its own sinuous carved board. Further carvings adorn the panel behind the music desk. The design did not include doors to enclose the case; consequently, there is a lockable flap which can cover the stop–knobs and the keyboard when these are pushed in. (The idea of a retractable keyboard may indeed have come to mind because it was realized that a keyboard could be made to be pushed in behind a covering board just as stop–knobs can be pushed 'off' and covered.)

It was said that the organ was made as a gift for Queen Charlotte from George III (but if this were so its date would have been about 1763), and that she later gave it to the Princess Amelia as a birthday present; there seems to be some confusion here. Upon the sale of many of the royal effects at the end of George's reign, the organ was bought by the Earl of Egremont, and apparently placed first in his house at Bromley, Kent, and then upon loan in St Decuman's Church, Watchet, Somerset. In 1932 it was presented by W. Wyndham, Esq., to Eton College. It has stood in various places in the college; at present it is – appropriately, in view of Snetzler's previous work there – in the larger chapel.

Its stop–list is:

>   (*G', A'–f '''*): OD (sc: *c'*), SD, Dul (sc: *c*), Pr b/tr, Fl, 15, Ses b II/Cor tr II

The stop-knobs are labelled on the horizontal surface under each stop-knob, as were presumably originally those on the organ now at 'Hatchlands' (no. 42).

The keyboard is of ivory with blackwood sharps; this special use of ivory (as on the keyboard of the organ now at Birmingham University, no. 29) suggests a particular and more expensive treatment to suit the royal finger. (Harpsichords had such keyboards since the early part of the eighteenth century but their use in organs, pioneered by British makers, was more common after the mid-1760s.)

A shifting movement takes off all upperwork, and there is a foot-pump.

The organ is illustrated on p. 49.

45 Bisley, Gloucestershire, the Methodist church
(1760)

Despite the changes being made in other chamber organs of 1759 and 1760, the previous 'normal' type of casework was still being produced. The early history of this example is not known, but it may be the same organ as that Andrew Freeman noted [1] as advertised in the *Organist & Choirmaster* for March 1898, by an accountant in Birmingham, Joseph William Blackham, of 180 Corporation Street (and Landsdowne, Olton) as 'Containing 6 stops. Compass BB to E, 54 notes. Suit gentleman's Hall.'

The pin action, soundboard and much of the casework appear to be original, and at least some of the pipework. Its present stop-list is:

>   (*C–f '''*): SD b/tr, OD (sc: *c*), Dul (sc: *c'*), Pr b/tr, 15 (sc: *c*), Oboe (sc: *c'*)

The present keyboard is modern; labels stuck at the sides of the (modern) knobs date from 1982. There are now swell louvres behind the front (an apparently-original roof swell is not in use), and it appears that the central flat of front 'pipes' is not original. There are now eight pipes in the centre as opposed to the usual ten, and all the pipe-shade carvings are missing. The organ has been fitted with an octave and a half of pedals (*C–g*), an electric blower and a hand-pump.

The organ was moved to this church in 1982 and renovated by R. Newton. It was previously in Box Free Church, near Nailsworth, and had been attended to (or perhaps installed) there by Lidiatt in 1938. The original compass and stop-list may have been:

>   (*G', A', C, D–e'''*): OD (sc: *c'*), SD b/tr [?dividing, as now, *b/c'*], Dul (sc: *c*)
>   [or Fl?], Pr b/tr, 15, [/and/or] Ses/Cor [?II] (compare the similar organ
>   made in the same year, now at Bredon's Norton, no. 48)

It seems that the present short-compass Oboe has replaced a mixture treble, and the swell–front has been placed where the Fifteenth and mixture bass pipes stood.

[1] Andrew Freeman, 'John Snetzler and his Organs' (TO 55/169).

46 Valletta (Malta), St Paul's cathedral
(c1760)

L 108; S II/41–2; F 60

The one–manual organ made in 1684 by Smith for Chester cathedral was enlarged by Snetzler in '1760, or thereabouts' (according to Freeman [1]) by the addition of a Choir organ of four stops:

$$(G', A', C, D–d'''): SD, Pr, Fl, 15$$

He also installed a new Trumpet instead of the former Great Trumpet. Leffler's manuscript account confirms these details. A Swell was added in 1814 by Chaliner of Chester.

Although it had been enlarged again in 1823, the organ was removed in 1844 in favour of a new organ by Gray & Davison. It was stored for some years, and then rebuilt and enlarged by the organ builder Robson and taken to St Paul's cathedral, Valletta (built 1843), as part of a gift of essential furnishings. [2] It was placed in a west gallery on its arrival in 1854, and either at this time, or at Snetzler's rebuilding, the main case (originally Smith's) was remade and enlarged. Overhanging sides were eliminated, and the general arrangement of the cornices and the intervening flats seems to be early nineteenth–century in character. It would appear from photographs that both cases are of mahogany; if this is so, then the main case may have been remade or replaced by Robson.

In 1886, the organ cases were emptied and the organ rebuilt at the east end of the cathedral. It was again rebuilt in about 1905, when the Choir department was placed in the old main case and connected to the east console by a pneumatic action. By 1940 the Choir case had been supplied with dummy front pipes: each pipe of the same scale.

[1] Andrew Freeman, 'The Organs of Chester Cathedral' (TO 51/132).
[2] A. G. Smalley, 'The Organ in St. Paul's Cathedral, Valletta, Malta' (TO 76/187).

47 North Walsham, Norfolk, Paston's Grammar school
(parts from a bureau organ of c1760)

An article by Gordon Paget [1] relates the story of a small four–manual organ, at first the house organ of W. J. Birkbeck, made in 1883. It incorporates two Snetzler ranks formerly in a bureau organ, an Open Diapason (presumably a short–compass rank with a new bass) and a Stopped Diapason. The bureau organ was emptied of its pipes, but given new spotted metal copies, and passed to Athelstan Riley; its present situation is unknown.

[1] Gordon Paget, 'The History of a Much–Travelled Organ' (TO 70/118).

48 Bredon's Norton, Worcestershire, the parish church (1760)

W 114 (6)

This chamber organ is, like that at Bisley (no. 45) of the 'normal' standard type, and is labelled *John Snetzler fecit Londini 1760*. It was given to the church by Miss Zula Maud Woodhull of Norton Park, and opened there on 21 May 1907.

The previous history of the organ has been traced, tentatively, by Roy Williamson, to Bishopswood Church (consecrated 1845) near Ross–on–Wye, Herefordshire, to which it had been presented at some time by the owner of Bishopswood House (built 1821). (Bishopstone church, to which parts of the Eton College Smith/Snetzler organ were taken in 1841 is nearby – see no. 14.)

At the time of its opening in 1907, a local newspaper reported that it was 'sweet and mellow' and possessed 'a reversed colour keyboard'. However, the organ has fared badly by the hands of time, neglect and what Buckingham would have called 'unskilful persons'. The case is in poor condition: carvings are broken and missing, the front pipes are not original, the pediment is missing, and the stop action has been altered. The present keyboard has an apparent compass of $B'-e'''$, (the 'short–octave' G', A', C, $D-e'''$ arrangement) which has been clumsily altered to transpose up the original low–pitched pipework, but which has had the fortunate effect of making the cutting–down of the pipework unnecessary. There are now six stop–knobs in a horizontal row over the keyboard, but it would appear that there were originally eight knobs which controlled:

OD (?sc:), SD, Pr b/tr, Fl, 15, Ses b/Cor tr II

Of these, only the Open Diapason, Stopped Diapason, Principal and Flute are recognizably by Snetzler; the present mixture replaced a Dulciana (which itself replaced a mixture) in recent times.

Two slots in the lower front of the case would have housed a foot pump and a shifting movement pedal; the present reservoir is not original, and there is an electric blower.

*

49 Huntingdon, St Mary's church
(c1760 or 1772–3)

L 56; S II/135; F 66

The first date is Sperling's, so is assumed to be approximate. Leffler's manuscript records the organ thus:

> St Mary Huntingdon
> Organ built by Schnetzler has two setts of keys from GG to E long Octave – Swell to G

Open Diap	57	[Swell:]	
Stop Diap	57	Open Diap	34
Principal	57	Dulciana	34
Twelfth	57	Hautboy	34
Fifteenth	57		---
Sexqa 3 ranks	171		102
Trumpet	57		513
	---		---
	513		615
	---		---

> Same front as Lutheran Chapel Savoy.

No further details appear to be known; Freeman says that 'the organ and case have long since disappeared'. Leffler's description of the case rules out this organ as being the one that may have gone from Huntingdon to Theddingworth (no. 57), as F. H. Sutton's drawing of the case there before 'gothicising' [1] shows a large 'wreathed–oval' style of case similar to that at Cobham Hall (no. 99).

The organ has also been ascribed to 'Jones and Snetzler'; if this were correct, it would need to be dated after the time of Snetzler's denization in 1770. Bernard Edmonds and Nicholas Plumley [2] write that the organ was built 1772–3 'at the expense of the Earl of Sandwich', who is also recorded as the part-donor of the other Snetzler organ at Huntingdon (All Saints'; see no. 35).

[1] Nicholas Thistlethwaite, *The Making of the Victorian Organ* (C. U. P., 1990), p. 326.
[2] In 'Thomas Elliot, Organ–builder' (BIOSJ 12/57).

50 London, Hanover Square, St George's church
(1761 [and 1774?])

L 139; S I/30; HR 8; F 44

The Vestry Minutes for 1761 record that a contract was entered into with Snetzler for a 'new' organ inside the existing Gerard Smith case of 1725; the price was £300 plus the old pipes. Freeman gives this stop-list, which is virtually consistent with Leffler's manuscript description:

Great (*G'*, *A'–e'''*): OD, SD, Pr, 12, 15, Ses IV, Cor (sc: *c'*) V, Tpt, Cln
Choir (*G'*, *A'–e'''*): SD, Dul (sc: *G*), Pr, Fl, 15, VH
Swell (*g–e'''*): OD, SD, Cor II [*sic* – Leffler has III], Tpt, Hb, Crm

Leffler's further details include: 'Organ repair'd by Schnetzler ... An Octave of Pedals by England that pull down the Choir organ keys – and there is [a] stop to make them take the full organ in addition ... Organ in the German Lutheran Chapel Savoy a copy of it.' This last statement can only refer to the general tonal scheme, but it might be interpreted to mean that the Savoy organ was made after 1761 and included both a pedal coupler to the Choir and a Choir to Great coupler. However, it is more likely that England installed the Choir to Pedal coupler at St George's, and Snetzler installed the Choir to Great coupler in the earlier Savoy organ from the start (see no. 37).

Richard Grubb, in a letter written in 1762 (see Appendix 4 and no. 61) mentions that John Stanley 'went with me and some Gentlemen who are good judges to try the [Organ] lately finished by Mr. Snetzler for St. George's Church, Hanover square, which had previously undergone the inspection of three master Builders in regard to the workmanship & of three masters of Musick in respect to the excellence of performance, before a crowded audience of the Nobility, when Mr. Stanley & those present entirely approved of the same as an exceedingly good Organ'. Clearly, this organ was important in further establishing Snetzler as a builder to 'the Nobility'.

It was claimed by Hill & Son that, when the organ was taken down to be rebuilt on the lower gallery, the combined Great and Choir soundboard (cf. Hillington, no. 33) was found to be labelled 'John Snetzler, 1774'. One must doubt this in view of the (by that date) unusual soundboard arrangement, and the apparently untypical label. The possibility remains that the organ was further worked on in 1774; as Freeman remarks, the price quoted above is rather low for a complete three-manual organ, even without new casework and – perhaps – front pipes.

The Choir Dulciana (as opposed to an Open Diapason) and the Swell Cremona (not Vox Humana?) are unusual, too; the latter might be assumed to have replaced a Principal were it not for the note of Leffler's that the 'Cornet in the Swell reduc'd to a Principal (the rest taken out [)] by desire of Mr Knyvett 1802'. The organist at the church at the time of Snetzler's work was John Keeble, whose *Third Set of Select Pieces for the Organ* (published 1778) was dedicated to Lord Fitzwilliam, the first owner of the Snetzler organ that Buckingham moved to Wilton House (no. 70). His predecessor was the entirely remarkable Thomas Roseingrave, who studied with Domenico Scarlatti in Italy and died insane in Dublin.

St George's has always been a fashionable church – Handel worshipped there – and the organ as a consequence has always been subject to alteration. Snetzler was followed by England who added the above-mentioned pedals (and coupler?) possibly in 1802, and later by Bishop and by Hill in 1864. The organ was replaced by Hope–Jones (1894–7) and rebuilt by Harrison in 1971. It is unlikely that any Snetzler work survived the Hope–Jones organ, but the 1725 case front, extended and with later front pipes, is still to be seen.

51 Bristol, Horsefair, Wesley's Chapel
(1761)

W 102 (4)

When Freeman noted this organ in 1934, he discovered that the organ had been in Little Plumstead church, Norfolk, for over a century. It was removed to the Rectory in 1911, and eventually purchased at the suggestion of J. T. Lightwood (editor of *The Choir*) for John Wesley's Chapel in Bristol. This was certainly appropriate, as it was to Bristol, to 'methodise' the Society there, that Wesley went after his break with the Moravian Society at Fetter Lane. The organ was restored by R. Spurden Rutt & Co., 1930–1, to as near original condition as then thought possible. At the time of the organ's removal to Bristol, the stop–list was as follows:

(*G', A'–f '''*): OD (sc: *c'*), SD, Dulciana (sc: *c*, grooved), Pr, Fl, 15, Ses b/tr II

The keyboard is of blackwood with ivory–plated sharps.

The mahogany case, of the 'normal' type, is not pedimented – a pediment may be missing? – but it is still fitted with glazed doors. The organ is apparently labelled in the soundboard.

52 Washington D. C. (U. S. A.), Smithsonian Institution
(1761)

This chamber organ, of the 'normal' mahogany–cased type, and labelled *John Snetzler fecit Londini 1761*, was made for Dr Samuel Bard of New York, physician to George Washington. It was purchased for him by an agent; and was the first of a number of organs to be shipped to the American colony in the years immediately before the War of Independence. The organ was passed down to successive members of the Bard/Johnstone family, and for a time was placed in St James's church, Hyde Park, New York. In about 1930, the organ was loaned to the museum of the New York State Historical Association at Fenimore House, Cooperstown; the Smithsonian acquired it from there on 20 June 1968.

The organ was restored between 1968 and 1972 by Douglas Brown. Missing pipe shades, glazed doors and other parts were replaced by analogy with their counterparts in Britain. The stop–list is now:

(*G', A', C, D–e'''*): OD (sc: *c'*), SD, Fl, 15, Ses b/tr II [sic: no Pr]

The present keyboard was modelled on that at Norwich Cathedral, which (as we mentioned) is not of the usual pattern for non–royal organs. It operates a pin action. There is a shifting movement to take off the Fifteenth and mixture, and a pedal to open the roof–swell (a hinged lid behind the pediment). The wind system is original, with a blowing pedal, and all but 16 of the 299 pipes are original. The case measures 7' 2" in height, and is 4' 2" wide and 2' 4½" deep.

53 Oxford, All Saints' convent, St Mary's Road
   (1761)

Robert Pacey [1] noted a chamber organ, moved to the convent in 1986, in its previous location in the chapel of Magdalen College. It is said to be signed and dated, and it contained the following stops:

(*C–f '''*): OD (sc: ?), SD, Pr b/tr, Fl, 15

At a recent rebuilding, the 'non–original' Principal was replaced by a Tierce. The wind system, façade and keyboard (at least) are not original.

Sperling [2] notes an organ 'by Snetzler' at Magdalen College, but he seems to be referring to the large chapel organ, then the one originally made by Swarbrick.

[1] Robert Pacey, *The Organs of Oxford* (Positif Press, 1980), p.41.
[2] S II/219.

54 Blickling, Norfolk, St Andrew's church
   (1762)

W 102 (3)

Yet another Snetzler organ in the area of Norfolk made agriculturally rich (for the landowners) by 'farmer George' and the pioneering work of Coke of Holkham Hall. This chamber organ, with the normal type of case, was almost certainly made for Blickling Hall in 1762, the date which is on a plaque on the organ: 'Built by J. Snetzler 1762/Rebuilt by E. W. Norman'. It was presented to the church by Lady Lothian in 1878, and seems from its casework size to have been a sticker–backfall action organ. In order to fit it for its new use, it was savagely rebuilt by Norman in that year; the dummy front pipes were replaced by new speaking pipes, 6–9–6, to form the tenor of the Open Diapason, and the case was raised to allow the installation of a new pedalboard and an action to an external Bourdon rank. The key– and stop–actions were replaced, but the original soundboard survives, remade and without the Snetzler label. The keyboard seems to be partly original, remade to the new compass; it has blackwood naturals and ivory–capped sharps.

An early stop–list appears from brass labels (2" by ½"), placed next to filled–in square stop–trace holes, with curious spellings which may or may not represent original paper labels, thus:

(*?G', A'–e'''?*): Op diapason (sc: c'?), Stopd Diapason, Dulciana, Principal,
Sesquialtra, Trumpett, Hoboy

The lack of a Fifteenth in this list (and the appearance of one later, unless this was made up from part of the Sesquialtra) raises some doubt as to the exactness of these labels, although the York/Sculthorpe organ (no. 25) and the Kilwinning organ (no. 32) are similar in this respect. The two reeds are also most unusual in such an organ – unless they were originally in a small short–compass swell-box inside the case; if so, this would be an early example of such a disposition.

The 1878 work left the organ with the following stops:

> (*C–g'''*): OD, SD [bass], Pr, Fl, 15 [all of which may contain some Snetzler
> pipes], Hohl Fl [8', from *c*], Gamba [from *c*]
> Pedal Lieblich Bourdon, 30 pipes
> Pedal coupler

All the manual stops except the lower part of the Open Diapason are enclosed in a swell-box.

The overall dimensions of the organ's casework are 6' 6" wide by 12' high by 3' 1" deep, excluding the Bourdon pipes.

55 South Dennis, Massachusetts (U. S. A.), the Congregational church (1762)

Snetzler's second organ in America was made for the Concert Hall in Hanover Street, Boston, by order of its manager/owners, Lewis and Stephen Deblois. It is referred to in correspondence concerning the organ for Trinity church, New York, [1] and arrived in 1763. The Deblois sold it to St John's church, Providence, Rhode Island in 1772, thus removing the organ from participation in the Tea Party of 1776. St John's purchased a new organ in 1834, but the Snetzler organ did not find its way to South Dennis until 1858; its whereabouts in the intervening years is unknown.

The casework is an extended version of the normal chamber type, with five pipe-compartments (3–8–6–8–3) instead of three, protected originally by doors. According to American sources, [2] the front is of walnut (though this is uncharacteristic), with the remaining casework of oak, and it was at one time painted yellow.

The console is somewhat recessed, and includes a 'box' pedalboard of the French type with 13 pull-downs (illustrated on p. 124) thought at one time to have been a later addition, but now thought more probably to be the precious survival of a type used by Snetzler. The stop-list's disposition is in dispute between Barbara Owen and Eugene Nye; the former's conjecture is the more likely:

(*G'*, *A'–e'''*): OD (sc: *G*?), SD, Dul (sc: *g*?), Pr b/tr, Fl, 12, 15, Ses III [?b/tr], Cln b/Tpt tr

The Sesquialtra appears to have been of standard Sesquialtra/Cornet type. The manual's natural keys are ivory-plated, and the sharps are of rosewood.

There had been considerable alterations to the organ in the nineteenth century; restoration work was carried out in the 1970s by the Andover Organ Company, with replacement flue pipes and a new Trumpet rank made by N. P. Mander, Ltd.

The pedalboard of the organ in South Dennis church

[1] see notes to no. 61; John Ogasapian gives the date of installation as 1764.
[2] Barbara Owen, 'Colonial Organs ...' (BIOSJ 3/102); also Eugene Nye, 'The Work of John Snetzler in America' (TO 199/97), and Thomas Murray, 'A Snetzler Organ in America' (*Organ Club Handbook*, 1976), pp. 64–5).

56 Schaffhausen (Switzerland), the Town Musuem (1763)

Like the organ now at 'Hatchlands' (no. 42), this bureau organ has 'surfaced' only fairly recently. It was sold by Sotheby's on 4 November 1982 on the instructions of Mr K. Vaughan of Upton, near Twycross, Leicestershire, and was purchased by Noel Mander. After restoration by his firm, it was sold to Dr Barbara Schnetzler of Schaffhausen (a descendant of Johann) and used for concerts throughout Switzerland. It was placed in the Museum in 1988.

The organ was probably made for the Chandos Pole family of Radburne Hall near Derby. It is labelled and dated 1763. In 1945, the organ was acquired by a farmer in Derbyshire, from whom Mr Vaughan, a veterinary surgeon, obtained it.

It was found, after relatively slight damage had been repaired, that the organ was still tuned in meantone temperament, as is the second organ at Kedleston Hall (no. 69).

The original and present stop-list is:

(*C, D–e'''*): SD, Fl, 15, Ses b/Cor tr

The keyboard is the usual blackwood one with ivory-plated sharps. There are positions at the front and side of the organ for a blowing pedal, and a pedal to open the swell lid. There is also a vertical rod to show the state of winding of the reservoir. The mahogany case has brass carrying handles.

Bureau organ in Schaffhausen Museum

57 Theddingworth, Leicestershire, All Saints' church
(1763)

F 75

The organ, apparently originally a large chamber organ with an 'oval' front, is labelled in the usual way with the date 1763. Its supposed provenance from King's Lynn had caused a date of 1754 (the same as the organ for St Margaret's church there) to be suggested for the organ. Another theory, according to Freeman, was that the organ 'came from Lincoln', and others have suggested that it is one of the Huntingdon organs. We have seen that it cannot be that from St Mary's church, Huntingdon (no. 49).

It had been purchased by the Revd F. H. Sutton, Rector of Theddingworth from 1864 to 1873, who certainly had strong connections with Lincoln*shire*. He discarded the case, designed and 'personally' painted a new one, (as part of an overall decorative scheme for the church), had pedals added and the Swell extended to tenor C. His 'before and after' drawings of the organ case are included in examples of the 'gothicising' of cases in his book *Church Organs* of 1874. [1]

Its original stop-list is not quite clear, but inspection of the rackboards and upperboards, and comparison with analogues, would suggest the following:

> Great (*G'*, *A'–e'''*): OD, SD, Pr, Fl, 15, III [?Ses b/Cor tr]
> Swell (*c* [originally *g*?]–*e'''*): OD, SD, Hb

At some time, a Keraulophon was placed on the Great soundboard and a Double Diapason and Octave (i.e. Principal) were added to the Swell, as well as a pedal-board, a Pedal Bourdon of 30 notes and a Pedal Coupler.

The keyboards are original (and apparently copied down to tenor C on the Swell), with blackwood naturals and ivory–plated sharps.

[1] Reproduced in Nicholas Thistlethwaite, *The Making of the Victorian Organ* (C. U. P., 1990), p. 326.

58 Salisbury, Wiltshire, the cathedral
(1763)

W 111 (26)

The history of this chamber organ can be traced from about 1900, when it was bought by a Mr Wilkins from 'a gentleman's house in the country, north of London' which might be 'Warlies' in Waltham Abbey. It was then passed to his son, C. W. Wilkins, an ironmonger in Gillingham, Kent.

In 1956, it was acquired by F. H. Browne & Sons of Canterbury, who restored the organ and sold it to Michael Thomas, then at Hurley Manor near Henley-on-Thames, Oxon. He sold it to Mr Barry Still, Headmaster of Salisbury Cathedral

School, who placed it in the cathedral.

A new upper case was made for the organ by two joiners of the cathedral to the design of Lord Mottistone in 1961 with funds from the Friends of the Cathedral.

Its disposition is now:

$$(C-f\,'''): \text{OD, SD, Pr, 15, Ses b/Cor tr II}$$

The wind–pressure is 2¼", and an electric blower has been fitted. The organ was further renovated in 1980 by Harrison & Harrison Ltd.

59 Haslemere, Surrey, the Dolmetsch Collection (1764)

F 25; W 105 (11)

A bureau organ, labelled and dated 1764, was acquired by Arnold Dolmetsch from an antiques' dealer in Cirencester, Gloucestershire, about 1930. The dealer alleged that the organ had come from a Convent Chapel, but that is not an unusual way for a dealer to cover his tracks. The organ was restored by Roger Yates.

The stop–list comprises:

$$(C, D-e'''): \text{'Diapafon' [SD of wood], 'Flute' [of wood], '....' [15], 'Sefquialtera'}$$
$$[\text{b, 19–22], '....' [tr, 12–17]}$$

The keyboard is of blackwood with ivory–plated sharps. There is a shifting movement to take off the Fifteenth and mixture, and a pedal to operate the original feeder to the wedge reservoir.

This organ is apparently identical with that seen by Andrew Freeman at The Grove, Cookham, Berkshire, 17 August 1918.

60 London, Westminster Abbey, Novello organ (casework, 1764)

The case of the Vincent Novello Memorial organ belonged originally to the organ made for Mr Kershaw of Halifax, who was, we may presume, connected with the obtaining of the organ for the parish church, the subscription for which was set in hand there in 1764 (see no. 67). It had been in the Roman Catholic church at Great Barr, Birmingham, for some years, unused and unaltered when seen by the Revd B. B. Edmonds in November 1957. He recorded the stop–list then as follows:

$$(G', A'-e'''): \text{OD (sc: } c'), \text{ SD, Dul, Pr, Fl, 15, Ses b/Cor tr II}$$

The case is evidently the second example of the central–oval type used by Snetzler from about 1760 and it includes what was to become customary, a 'wreath' of two palms, knotted at their lower ends, around a nearly–circular pipe display, with a horizontal panel below this to provide access to the faceboard of the soundboard. The design of the casework is thus partly determined by the retractable keyboard and sticker–backfall action.

The 'broken' pediment was supplied as part of the rebuilding by N. P. Mander, Ltd. For notes on the organ's interior, see no. 43.

61 New York (U. S. A.), Trinity church (1764)

F 26

Snetzler's third organ for the American colonies was built at a time when the pace of work, already busy, quickened considerably as important commissions were undertaken.

It was the subject of correspondence [1] between Richard Grubb in London and Goldsbrow Banyar in New York; see Appendix 9 for a full transcription of the three letters and contract. The earliest surviving letter is dated 17 August 1761, and rather amusingly refers to the need to keep the pitch of the organ to 'the lower' because 'we have low voices'. More seriously, and interestingly, there is a proposal for 'a 16 foot Diapason in Front' and suggests that 'the fewer noisy stops there are the better & some are necessary to strengthen the tone of the Instrument. The diapasons are among the musical.'

An enclosure dated 7 October 1761 refers to a '1st plan' of Snetzler's which includes the 16 Foot Open Diapason with, apparently, a specially designed 'frontispiece', at a total cost of £800. Its stop–list would apparently have been similar to that made later for Beverley Minster (no. 79), but with two Principals in the Great organ. As finally contracted–for, the organ's stop–list was as below, but it is not absolutely clear whether or not the front Open Diapason was made at 16' pitch (perhaps on the lines of the King's Lynn so–called 'Borduun'), but it seems that it was not. Buckingham does not make mention of such a pitch at Beverley, but that is presumably because the organ there was double–fronted, with one of the two unison Open Diapasons in each front.

The final stop–list was 'of Mr. Stanley's forming', and it was to be a pattern for many of Snetzler's subsequent large instruments. Leonard Snetzler's role in the design and carving of a 'new & Elegant Frontispiece' is specifically set out in Richard Grubb's letter of February 1762, and this confirms what one could otherwise have only speculated – that not only did he carve the ornamentation of the cases but also had an important, perhaps the chief, part in the design of their overall appearance.

Snetzler contracted on 19 February 1762 to finish the organ 'as soon as possible'; this is a phrase which present–day 'classical' organ builders might find convenient to adopt. It appears that he had verbally promised to have it ready by October 1762, but it was still in London in January 1764 (perhaps because of the ongoing sea-wars with 'the Spaniards'), when Thomas Hayes of Wolverhampton wrote to Goldsbrow Banyar to say that Grubb had broken a promise made to him to hear Stanley play the organ [2], which was then presumably fully put up and finished (in the 'Warehouse' in Dean Street?).

John Stanley's 'Plan' was as follows:

> Great (*G'*, *A'–e'''*): OD ['in front & gilt'], OD ['inside'], SD ['of Wood & mettal'], Pr, 12, 15, 17, Ses IV, Fnt III, Cornet (sc: *c'*) V, Tpt, Cln
> Choir (*G'*, *A'–e'''*): OD, SD ['of Wood & mettal'], Pr, Fl ['of Wood & mettal'], 15, Crm, VH
> 'Eccho & Swell' (*g–e'''*): OD, SD ['of mettal'], Pr, Cor III, Tpt, Hb

Church and organ were destroyed in a major City fire in 1776. On the completion of a new church in 1778, an organ was not made by Snetzler but by Henry Holland of London.

[1] Transcribed in John Ogasapian, *Organ Building in New York City: 1700–1900* (The Organ Literature Foundation, 1977), pp. 6–11.

[2] Burney (in his *General History*, II, p. 1001) comments that 'Where there was a Charity sermon, or a new organ to be opened, he [Stanley] seems to have been preferred to all others' (quoted by Gerald Gifford in his Introduction to Stanley's *Six Concertos*, O. U. P., 1986).

62 Cambridge, Massachusetts (U. S. A.), Christ Church (1764)

HR 9; F 27

Presumably this two-manual (Great and Swell, it seems) organ was delivered at the same time as the one for New York (no. 61), hence perhaps the delay between contract and delivery of the latter. The Lord Mayor of London, Barlow Trecothick, was evidently involved in the acquisition of the organ for Cambridge.

Most of its metal pipes were removed at the time of the battle of Bunker Hill (June 1775) to be melted down for bullets. About fifteen years later, the organ was rebuilt as a one-manual instrument by the Boston builder Josiah Leavitt. It was replaced by a much larger instrument by George Stevens in 1845; exactly how large the organ was originally and how much, if anything, now remains of Snetzler's work is a matter of dispute between American scholars.

A 13-note 'box' pedalboard was found in the cellar of the church; it is similar to that at South Dennis (no. 55). As Barbara Owen reasonably asks,[1] how frequently did Snetzler supply these pedalboards for his British organs?

[1] Barbara Owen, 'Colonial Organs...' (BIOSJ 3/102).

63 Ludlow, Shropshire, St Laurence's church
(1764)

S II/233; HR 10; F 28

An order that 'the Thanks of this Corporation be returned to Lord Powis for his obligeing Letter and handsome present of an Organ by Mr. Town Clerk in the name of the Corporation' was entered into the Ludlow Town Minutes on 21 January 1761. On 5 June 1761, the Earl of Powys's agent Richard Baldwyn wrote to his Lordship that 'The Organ-builder said, he would send down some Plans, to be laid before the Parish here, that They may agree upon the place where the Organ shall stand. But We have heard nothing from him Since he left us.' Snetzler was certainly well-occupied at this time, but he was eventually able to produce the necessary designs: some sketches in the Powys family archives at Aberystwyth show a gallery to be set in front of, and bracketed over, the fifteenth-century rood screen. But as Snetzler desired 'the Gallery may not be raised too high', a third option (thus inscribed) was adopted, and the organ placed rather further westward.

The gallery as actually made was therefore placed squarely under the central tower, and the organ faced down the large nave. A photograph of *c*1858 [1] shows the arrangement. Above the other furnishings of the same period, including a new screen in front of the medieval reredos, the large corbelled wainscot case dominated the interior, visually and musically. The cost to the Earl of this fine ensemble was reported as £1000, which may imply an organ of similar scope as that supplied to New York (no. 61). Or it may have been the 'very Fellow' of the slightly smaller organ made for Halifax (see no. 67).

The organ's original stop-list has to be deduced from sources dating from the early part of last century, but it seems to have been along these lines:

> Great (*G'*, *A'–e'''*): OD, [OD inside?], SD, Pr, 12, 15, [17?], Ses III, Fnt III,
>   Cor (sc: *c'*) [V], Tpt, [Cln?]
> Choir (*G'*, *A'–e'''*): OD, SD, Pr, Fl, [15?], [VH?]
> Swell (*g–e'''*): OD, SD, [Pr?], [Cor III?], Tpt, [Hb?]

The overall case design was of the now-normal 'Savoy' church type, with double-storeyed flats, but with side 'overhangs'. It measured 13' 7" wide by 7' 4" deep at floor level.

Until the church was drastically 'restored' in the 1860s by George Gilbert Scott under the direction of an energetic Restoration Committee, the organ remained nearly unaltered except for work by Joseph Walker in 1837. His work had included the replacement of (?some) front pipes, the installation of a Dulciana on the Choir (perhaps replacing a Fifteenth), and the introduction of 'Double open Pedal pipes 1½ octaves down to GGG', 'German Pedals 1½ octaves' and 'Swell and Pedal couplers' (Sperling).

The organ was removed to the north transept in 1860 by Gray & Davison, comprehensively rebuilt and placed behind a medieval screen, though raised on brick pillars. As this position inevitably made the organ less effective, it was

The organ at Ludlow, c1858

enlarged then, and again in 1883 and in 1891. It was modified in 1901 by Hill & Son, further enlarged in 1950 by J. W. Walker & Sons and rebuilt in 1981 by Nicholson of Malvern. There are about eighteen ranks or part-ranks of original pipework remaining.

A 'Grand Tuba' was added in 1860, the pipes of which projected horizontally through the upper storey of pipes in the flats, which were consequently mutilated, as was their surrounding woodwork. This wonderfully egregious sight was lost in 1981, when the upper storeys were reconstructed – not quite accurately at the junction of the cornices and the centre tower. The corbelling of the upper casework can no longer be seen, and the remnants of the original case now serve merely as a screen to a large transept-full of organ.

[1] Reproduced in Richard Francis and Peter Klein, *The Organs and Organists of Ludlow Parish Church* (Ludlow 1982); from this booklet much of the local historical material above has been gratefully derived.

64 Southwell, Nottinghamshire, the minster (1765)

L 145; B 206/55–6; S II/209; F 24

The history of the organ and Snetzler's major rebuilding of the organ was summed up by Buckingham, who had tuned it from 1819 onwards, thus:

Southwell Minster—An organ with three sets of keys the Great and Choir organs from GG long octaves to D in alt, the Swell Organ from G below m/C to D in alt. A set of pedals from GG to C 17 to act upon the Choir keys and also on the Great Organ keys but on the Great Organ they draw on and off by a stop, contain the following stops:

GREAT ORGAN					Fifteenth				55
Op. Diapason	...	...	...	57					‒‒‒‒
St. Diapason	...	...	...	55					264
Principal	...	...	...	55					‒‒‒‒
Twelfth	...	...	...	55					
Fifteenth	...	...	...	55	SWELL ORGAN				
Sexqualtera 4R	...	...	...	220	Op. Diapason	...	...	...	32
Cornet 3R	...	...	...	81	St. Diapason	...	...	...	32
Trumpet	...	...	...	55	Trumpet	...	...	...	32
				‒‒‒	Hautboy	...	...	...	32
				633					‒‒‒‒
				‒‒‒					128
					Choir	...	...	...	264
CHOIR ORGAN					Great	...	...	...	633
Dulciana to G	...	...	...	44					‒‒‒‒
St. Diapason	...	...	...	55					
Principal	...	...	...	55	Total	...	...	...	1,025
Flute	...	...	...	55					‒‒‒‒

Mr. Edward Heathcote, organist. The Open Diapason ot BB in front the GG and AA is St. Diapason pipe with a helper Principal pipe, metal. The bellows are diagonal, two pairs. The Great Organ case is Wainscott with two fronts but the back front is sham pipes of wood 20 ft. high, 11 ft. wide and 3 ft. 4 in. deep. The Choir case is separate in front of the great organ, 9 ft. 7 in. high, 6 ft. 1 in. wide and 2 ft. 11 in. deep. Southwell, December 5th, 1823, A.B.

Buckingham further noted:

> This Organ Original was built by Father Schmidt in London but was thorough repaired
> and chiefly new by John Snetzler of London in 1765. The Great Organ Open
> Diapason treble the Stop Diapason from C sharp below m/C to ♮ next m/C the
> Principal from G to the top the 12-15-2.3 and 4 ranks of the Sexquialtera Bafs. the
> Cornet. The Choir Organ Stop Diapason and Flute Bafs. and the 15 are the original
> pipes of Father Schmidt revoised by Snetzler and is the only remains of the old
> organ excepting the cases. The Dulciana in the Choir Organ and the Trumpet in the
> Great Organ was added by G. P. England in 1806. The pedals was added by A.
> Buckingham in 1821. The finger movements of the Great Choir and Swell Organ was
> taken out new studs and pivots to the rolers the keys new pins the trackers new wired
> the whole undergone a thorough repair and alterations in order to silence and prevent
> their rattling noise. Also the whole of the pipes taken out cleand regulated and tuned
> March, 1825, by A. Buckingham. It certainly is a very fine instrument and gives an
> wonderful effect more than can be expected from what it contains. New horizontal
> bellows added October 24th, 1833, by A. Buckingham.

Other sources, including Leffler, differ from this in points of detail, but a person
who knew Snetzler's work well and had completely dismantled the organ would
have had a far more accurate knowledge of it.

The organ was completely replaced in 1890 by a new organ by Bishop; the Choir
case (and some pipework?) is supposed to have found its way to a mission church
in north-west Kent. This has so far not been located; there are several Bishop
organs of the period in that area, but none with an old case.

65 Cambridge, Peterhouse chapel
(1765)

S II/31; HR 25; F 29

This relatively small organ for a college chapel was made with a case slightly
scaled-down from the 'normal' church type. It was given by Horace Mann, a Fellow
of the College, and his gift is recorded in a painted text on the case. There is some
doubt as to its exact original disposition, but it appears to have been a
two-manual organ with three divisions:

> Great (*G', A', [?C', D']–e'''*): OD, SD, Pr, 12, 15, Ses III [b/tr?]), Cln b/Tpt
>   tr, Cor V (sc: *c'*) [There are neither Cln nor Cor in Pearce, who has
>   'Sesquialtera and Mixture', presumably following Hill's work; the
>   organ is not included in Leffler's MS]
> Choir (*G', A', [C', D']–e'''*): SD [? b/tr], Pr, Fl [? b/tr]
> Echo, on Choir keys (*f–e'''*): OD, Dul, Hb

If the Great Cornet was indeed 'Mounted' as Sperling records (though this is his
usual appellation, irrespective of the actual position), then the choice of the
tall-centred case becomes logical, especially since the Echo was also mounted
somewhat above the Choir soundboard (behind the Great); it was converted to a
'venetian' Swell in 1836. The Clarion bass was removed in 1852 in favour of a
Trumpet bass. Sperling records the addition of 'Small unison Pedal Pipes ... by
Avory [*sic*] in 1804'.

The organ was rebuilt with three keyboards and pedals with altered compasses, by Hill in 1894 and rebuilt again by N. P. Mander, Ltd in 1963. About ten Snetzler ranks remain. An illustration of the organ can be found in *The Organs of Cambridge* (Positif Press, Oxford, 1983), p. 61.

66 Swithland, Leicestershire, St Leonard's church (1765)

F 30

This organ, the smallest surviving church instrument by Snetzler, was given by the church's patron, Sir John Danvers, together with other furnishings evidently specially designed for the medieval church. Its Gothick–Rococo painted deal case and gilded front pipes remain, but its original side overhangs, seen in the early photograph of the organ on its west gallery (and reconstructed in Michael Pendery's drawing, p. 39), have been lost.

The organ at Swithland, about the middle of the nineteenth century

Its original stop-list was:

> (*G', A', C', D'–e'''*): OD [open to 5' G, then bass from SD with open metal
> helpers], SD [metal from 'middle' C; b/tr], Pr, Fl [from 'tenor' C, of
> metal], 15, Ses b III [17–19–22]/Cor tr [12–15–17]

The original keyboard (lost through misappropriation in the 1970s) was of blackwood with ivory-plated sharps, and the stop-knobs (one of which is preserved) were of ebony. The stop-names were on paper labels next to the original draw-stop holes in the verticals of the panels adjoining the console. A boldly lettered board reading 'John Snetzler Esqre./London/The Builder/1765' was originally the upper part of the music desk, and is still in the church.

When Freeman saw the organ in 1919, it had only recently been moved to the floor from its gallery, and the gallery removed; a new vestry screen and window were being installed as a War Memorial. A Keraulophon had by then supplanted the mixture and the *G'* key had been disconnected. An organist of that period recalled recently that the organ was then in 'unequal tuning'. The organ-builders Taylor of Leicester were instructed in 1926 to make a new two-manual organ within the case, comprising a Great of four ranks, a Swell of five ranks, and one Pedal rank. They re-used nearly all the surviving Snetzler pipes in various ways, but deepened the case and obscured its overhangs.

The organ was rebuilt 1986–7 by Martin Renshaw and Karl Wieneke. The Taylor mechanical actions were retained, but modified, and the Snetzler pipework was reconstituted on the Great in its original format. The front pipes (not used in 1926) were winded again with new metal conveyances; when restored, they were used as a guide to the wind-pressure, low pitch and meantone temperament of the organ. The elaborate carving above the front pipes was restored by Joe Dawes of Felbrigg, Norfolk. The 1926 keyboards and actions did not allow the restoration of the *G'* pipes, all of which had been removed, but the *C♯* key now sounds the *A'* pipework on the Great. A cut-off slider takes off the Great Principal, Fifteenth and mixture. The Swell was altered to form a small complementary chorus, with a new Trumpet in an eighteenth-century style.

67 Halifax, Yorkshire, St John the Baptist's church (1763–6)

S III/62; HR 11; F 31

The organ was actually labelled 1763, according to Freeman. It was therefore already under construction when Henry Bates (the vicar's son) wrote to the churchwardens in February 1764:

> I called upon Mr. Snetzler in London. He had an organ by him just
> finished, the very Fellow of what you are to have at Halifax, and a most
> noble instrument it is indeed. I should be glad to know whether Mr.

Stansfield can possibly prevent the setting up of the organ, for till this be known, my brother cannot engage hands for the Performance of the Mesiah [*sic*] at the opening of it.

Henry's brother was Joah Bates, who was to become well known for conducting the large-scale *Messiah* performances at the Handel Commemoration in 1784. Henry wrote from Cambridge, where he may well have been acquainted with the 1765 Peterhouse organ, but it is more likely that the organ in Snetzler's workshops was the one finished in Ludlow church about August 1764.

The neo-Puritan Mr Stansfield was the leader of a group of men from the township of Sowerby (south-west of Halifax) protesting against the potential cost on their rates of the organ. In fact, a subscription raised £1200 for the organ; nonetheless, the Faculty was opposed. A fighting fund raised a further £720 towards the legal costs of pursuing the Faculty; in the event, only about a quarter of this amount (£194. 5s.) was needed.

But the delay arising from the opposition to the Faculty caused the organ's erection to be postponed; it was evidently completed later in 1764 and was still waiting to be transported to Halifax when Snetzler made a Deposition before Sam Bonner of Carey Street on 6 April 1765 in these terms:

> John Snetzler of Oxford Road in the Parish of Saint Mary-le-Bone in the County of Middlesex Organ Builder maketh oath and saith that by a Contract or Agreement made sometime in the Spring of the Year One thousand seven hundred and sixty three Between him this Deponent and the Reverend Henry Bates and Joah Bates of the University of Cambridge on the Part and Behalf of John Walker and Samuel Waterhouse now or late Church-wardens for the Town or District of Halifax in the County and Diocefe of York And also of others interested in Trustees for or Subscribers to the purchasing of an organ intended to be lawfully erected supported and maintained in the said Parish Church of Halifax by a voluntary subscription only He this Deponent did agree to Build and finish the said Organ thus contracted for in the manner herein above mentioned in the best and most workmanlike manner and to make the same fit and ready for immediate use and Service at the Price and for the Sum of Five hundred and ffifty one Pounds ['and five Shillings' interpolated] which Agreement and Contract he hath since duly and fully performed in his Part And hath further caused the said Organ thus finished by him in the manner aforesaid to be as safely and securely packed up in Cases as the same could be in order to be sent down from his Shop or Warehouse in Dean Street near Oxford Road aforesaid to the said Town of Halifax in order to its being erected and put up in the said Parish Church of Halifax And this Deponent further saith that the said Organ was long ago finished and put up in the said Cases In which it hath ever since remained and been deposited And still and now continues so to be And in this Deponents Opinion and Judgement the said Organ hath already suffered and been injured by remaining in this Condition and will still further suffer and be more injured by remaining longer packed up in the said Cases And this Deponent further saith that according to the best of his Judgement and

belief and in order to prevent the said Organ from being greatly injured & impaired and sunk in its worth Use and Value It will be necefsary to have the said Organ shortly taken out of those Packing Cases and either erected and put up in the said Parish Church of Halifax or in some other Church or Place where it is intended to remain that the said Organ may have the benefit of open Air And also of having its pipes cleaned and their Tone preserved by being sometimes used and played upon which are requisite and necefsary to keep and maintain the several Parts of the said Organ in due and proper order.

[signed] John Snetzler

> Sworn before me at my House in
> Carey Street this Sixth day of
> April 1765
> Saml Bonner

By the time that the Faculty was finally granted on 11 July 1766, fifteen months later, the organ was already in place, and the Leeds *Intelligencer* of the 19 August advertised that

> At the opening of the new Organ, in the parish church of Halifax, Yorkshire, on Thursday and Friday, the 28th and 29th of this instant, August, will be performed, with the assistance of a very numerous band of the most eminent performers, both vocal and instrumental, from various parts of England,
>
> THE MESSIAH
> An Oratorio, composed by Mr. Handel.
>
> Between the first and second Acts, a Concerto on the Organ.
>
> Tickets, 5s. and 2s. 6d. each. Doors to be opened at Nine o'Clock in the Morning each day, and the performance to begin half an hour after Ten. There will be an assembly each Evening at the Talbot.
> N.B. An organist is wanted. Any person who is inclined to offer himself a Candidate may apply for farther particulars to the Rev. Mr. Bates, at Halifax.

This was an early provincial performance of *Messiah*, hence the need to engage performers in London and elsewhere, and not just locally.

A competition was therefore held on the next day, Saturday 30 August, at which Snetzler was present. The six candidates included Wiiliam Herschel, who had led the orchestra at the concert. In Dr Miller's account [1] we read (and hear) what happened:

> They drew lots how they were to perform in rotation. My friend Herschel drew the third lot. The second performer was Mr. Wainwright [of Manchester]...whose finger was so rapid that old Snetzler, the organ builder, ran about the church exclaiming 'te tevil, te tevil, he run over te key like one cat, he vil not give my piphes room for to shpeak'.

The following text appears within the illustration:

CHOIR ORGAN
Open Diapason
Stopt Diapason
Fifteenth
Principal
Flute
Cremona
Bassoon, up to C
Vox Humane

SWELL
down to G in the Tenor

Open Diapason
Stopt Diapason
Principal
Houtboy
Cornet
Trumpet

The Names of the
Stops.
GREAT ORGAN.

Two open Diapasons.
Stopt Diapason
Principal
Twelfth
Fifteenth
Furniture
Sesquialtra
Cornet
Trumpet
Base Larten up to middle C

HALIFAX ORGAN.

The Halifax organ

During Mr. Wainright's performance, I was standing in the middle aisle with Herschel. 'What chance have you, said I, to follow this man?' He replied, 'I don't know, I am sure fingers will not do.' On which he ascended the organ loft, and produced from the organ so uncommon a fulness, such a volume of slow, solemn harmony, that I could by no means account for the effect ... 'Aye, aye,' cried old Snetzler, 'tish is very goot, very goot indeed. I vil luf tish man, for he gives my piphes room for to shpeak.'

Having afterwards asked Mr. Herschel by what means, in the beginning of his performance, he produced so uncommon an effect, he replied 'I told you fingers would not do', and produced two pieces of lead from his waistcoat pocket. 'One of these', said he, 'I placed on the lowest key of the organ, and the other upon the octave above; thus by accommodating the harmony, I produced the effect of four hands instead of two'.

He obtained the position.

On or by 4 May 1765, Snetzler was paid £525, the amount 'as per contract' and a further £26. 5s. for the Choir Vox Humana; these sums totalled the £551. 5s. mentioned in the Deposition. At the same date, his un–named 'servant' was paid cash 'for extra diligence': presumably for repairing the long–crated mechanisms and pipes. The stop–list (as in the engraving opposite) comprised:

Great (*G'*, *A'–e'''*): OD, OD (?sc:), SD, Pr, 12, 15, Ses IV, Fnt III, Cor V
    (sc: *c'*), Tpt, Cln [b only, 'up to middle C', 28 pipes, to 'meet' the Cor?]
Choir (*G'*, *A'–e'''*): OD, SD, Pr, Fl, 15, Bn b/Crm tr, VH
Swell (*g–e'''*): OD, SD, Pr, Cor III, Tpt, Hb

The keyboards were said to be of the usual blackwood/ivory–plated type, though the engraving seems to show them as having white naturals and black sharps; they were replaced by Hill in 1842.

An octave and a half of pedals were added by Greenwood of Leeds in 1810; Double Open Diapason Pipes for these were installed by Gray in 1836, together with a Dulciana to *G* instead of the Choir Vox Humana, with new bellows and several composition pedals. Hill extended the Swell down to *G* in 1842–3, substituting a Cornopean for the Swell Trumpet, and adding a Swell Double Diapason and a 'Coupler to unite the Choir Organ to the Great in the octave below'. The firm also 'sharpened' the pitch of the organ, according to Ellis. [2]

In 1851, the pedals were changed to *C*-compass, and the organ was rebuilt by Hill in 1869 (and tuned to equal temperament [3]), and in 1879 (when the case was destroyed upon the removal of the organ from its gallery to the chancel), modified in 1885 and 1888, rebuilt 1896–7, renovated in 1910, rebuilt by Harrison & Harrison in 1928 and by Walker in 1976. Not surprisingly, after all this, only about five Snetzler ranks are said to remain.

[1] E. Miller, *The History and Antiquities of Doncaster and its Vicinity* (Doncaster, c1804), p. 162.
[2] Ellis, 'On the History of Musical Pitch' (repr. Knuf, 1968), p. 39
[3] *Halifax Guardian*, 1869

68 Belfast, Donegall Square, the Methodist church (1765)

S III/133; HR 30; F 53

Archbishop Robinson (the 'primate Robinson' mentioned in the letter written by Thomas Drew, see no. 4) presented 'a fine-toned and powerful organ, encased in dark oak and being exquisitely carved' to the Dean and Chapter of Armagh Cathedral in about 1765, according to Edward Rogers [1]. It is likely that this was made by Snetzler, as Drew mentioned that his Snetzler organ was originally owned by that prelate.

In 1834, the cathedral was extensively repaired, and the organ stored above the stables in the Archbishop's palace. A new organ was made for the cathedral in 1840 by Walker, who repaired the Snetzler organ and set it up in the concert room at the Tontine where the Music Society met. This Society was dissolved within a few years, and the organ sold to the recently built Donegall Square Methodist chapel in Belfast, where it was placed behind the pulpit. It was opened with a special service on Sunday 2 September 1849; that very same night the church was burnt out. Documents relating to the organ were said also to have been destroyed.

Walker's shop-books, quoted by Boeringer [2], included (1840, 'Concert Room'): 'New backfalls inserted in place of many that were warped; new wood pipe feet inserted instead of some quite rotten: bellows made to act inside room'. This last work may indicate that the bellows were previously placed at a distance from the organ, and this would have been likely in its first installation in the cathedral.

[1] Edward Rogers, *Memoir of the Armagh Cathedral*, p. 106.
[2] James Boeringer, *Organa Britannica*, vol. II, p. 40.

69 Kedleston Hall, Derbyshire, the Music Room (second organ, installed 1765–6)

The 'smaller' organ 'in the North drawing room' at Kedleston that Nathaniel Curzon had intended in 1759 (see no. 41a) apparently arrived about 15 July 1765, when Samuel Wyatt, clerk of the works, reported that

> There came on Saturday five cases which I just looked into as I expected the statues ... I believe they only contain the organ which I presume your Lordship would have remain in the cases.

This seems to refer to an organ sent from Snetzler that was to await his erecting it; the Kedleston ledger KB 12 contains a payment on July 24th 1765 to 'Snetzler Organest [*sic*] – £ 2. 2. 0d' which may refer to packing and carriage costs, for this organ was not new, but rather a reworking by Snetzler of an older organ (previously at Audley Square, in the Curzons' London house?). Buckingham was right to be suspicious, but wrong in his conclusions, in his report of it in 1824 (p. 142):

Robert Adam's 'Organ Case for Lord Scarsdale'

The Right Honourable Lord Scarsdale, Kedlestone Hall, near Derby—An Organ with two sets of keys the Great Organ from CC to E in alt (no CC♯). The Swell from middle C to E in alt and a piano movement.

Open Diapason treble from m/C♯ ...	...	28
Stop Diapason	...	52
Flute bafs and treble	...	52
Sexqualtra bafs 4 ranks to m/C	...	54
Cornet treble from m/C♯ 3 ranks ...	...	81
Hautboy swell on a separate set of keys	...	29
Total	...	296

The 4 rank of the Sexqualtra from CC to FF♯ 6 pipes. The 3 rank in the Cornet is to D in alt. The Swell has a separate set of pallets on the same sound board with conveyance to the Swell box. A handsome mahogany case enclosing the original deal case 9 ft. high, 5 ft. 2 ins. wide, 2 ft. 6 ins. deep. This Organ is one of Snetzler's make but I am of opinion it was one of his first as the work is by no means so well done and executed as his work in general. The sound board is full of runnings. Kedleston Hall, 11 December, 1824. A.B.

It appears from the organ itself that it may have been Buckingham who remade the reservoir into the present single–rise 'horizontal' one, but otherwise the organ is entirely unchanged from the time of his notes. The pipes exhibit an early set of markings in an 'indigenous' style, over–written with Snetzler's marks on the metal pipes, together with some new Snetzler pipes. The $c♯'$ start of the treble stops is uncharacteristic of all but one of Snetzler's organs (no. 3) and is therefore presumably as left by the earlier maker, but the c'–compass Hautboy pipes appear to have been added by Snetzler.

At any rate, this organ was given a new case made, it would seem, after designs by Robert Adam, whose first submission is illustrated opposite. It was constructed by William Johnson and various assistants; the Kedleston ledgers [1] contain detailed accounts for this work:

KC8: Organ case
230 days {To 158 3/4 days of William Johnson
 at 2s 6d {To 71 1/4 days of Thomas Bedson
= £28 15s
     To William Johnson for carving 62 feet of organ mouldings = £2 6s 6d
     To Richd Clark 21 1/2 days at 18d per day = £1 12s 3d
     To Charles Souter – 2 days at 10d per day = 1s 8d
Total of organ case exclusive of money pd. carver = £32 15s 5d
Carving of the organ case
     To Mr. Gravenor for carving the ornaments in the freeze and fastoon of laurel leaves for the pipes to stand upon (see Mr Gravenor's bill) – £3 13s.
     To Mr Brown for carving 8ft 4ins rung [sic] of Base moulding with water leaf & tongue – at 1s 6d = 12s 6d
     To ten ft. 8 ins rung of Cornice
     To   do.   2 mambers carved at 5s 3d = £2 16s
     To carving a festoon of husks – at £1
     [total £8 1s 6d]
     To Mr Gamble for gilding the organ case: £6 16s 6d

Samuel Wyatt reported on 23 December 1765 in a letter to Curzon:

> my men are now fixing the case to the Organ: upon the old one, I am in
> hopes of giving your Lordship great satisfaction in it: as I dare say it will
> have a pretty look when finished, and there will be a very comodious place
> for the Music book just over the Keys, which will fall back enough to be
> quite out of the way.

It is the first phrase of the above that just makes one wonder if the larger organ
had been at Kedleston. Was it now, while the smaller one – indeed an 'old one' –
was being set up, being packed or 'fixed' in a 'case'? The remainder of the report
clearly refers to the present 'old' organ, which indeed has a complicated
arrangement of access doors and music desk.

The Kedleston ledger KB 12 reads: '1766 March 4: Snetzler Organ Maker £9 6s
0d'. A maximum of nearly 160 man-hours would occupy January and much of
February – the season when outside building work was impracticable – so that if
the joiners started as reported just before Christmas, Snetzler would have been
able to complete the on–site finishing towards the end of February. On the same
day, another Kedleston ledger (KB 9) has the following entry: '1766 March 4:
Received of Mr Snetzler for the organ £300 0s 0d.' If this money was paid at
Kedleston, which seems likely, then it is indeed possible that the large organ was
actually there: the reference is to 'the organ' and not to 'an organ' somewhere else.
Was it packed and waiting to go back to London with Snetzler? The difference of
£150 between this figure and the initial cost of £450 for the first organ (see no.
41a) would appear to be the cost of the small organ, its remaking and installation.

The organ has remained in the north–facing Music Room and is still tuned in
mean–tone temperament at low pitch (see pp. 261–3). It has long needed careful
conservation; some work was under way when this book was going to press.

The 1766 case, illustrated overleaf, consists of an almost square flat of 21 gilt
wooden 'flat–backs', with Ionic pilasters, a carved cornice with urns on its front
ends, and a motto 'Si placeo, Tuum est' ('If I am pleasing, the pleasure' – or 'the
credit' – 'is yours') in gilt lettering on the frieze. The casework is overall
approximately 9' high by 5' 5" wide by 3' deep.

The unusual stop–list (which has remained that given by Buckingham) seems
to be a compromise; the mixture is of curious composition:

$$C: 8–12–15–17/ \ G: 8–12–17/ \ B: 8–12–15/ \ c\sharp': 12–15–17/ \ d''': 12–15$$

as if to make up for the lack of a Principal. It is made mostly from older pipes,
some repitched and rescaled, with some new ones in the bass. The two wooden
flutes (Stop Diapason and Flute) are of differing construction, and neither rank is
in Snetzler's usual style.

[1] Kindly made available by Leslie Harris; further details are to be found in Alan Barnes,
The Eighteenth–century Chamber Organ in Kedleston Hall (Richard Alan Publications,
1990).

The Music room organ in Kedleston Hall

70 Wilton, Wiltshire, Wilton House (1766)

B 213/42–3 S III/101

Buckingham is the sole authority for the organ's history up to 1837:

The Right Honble The Earl of Pembroke at Wilton House—An Organ with two sets of Keys, the Great Organ from GG long octaves to E in alt, the Swell from G to E in alt with a Piano Movement.

GREAT ORGAN		SWELL ORGAN	
Open Diapason to CC of Metal	57	Open Diapason	34
Stop Diapason	57	Dulciana	34
Principal—bafs in front	57	Hautboy	34
Flute	57		
Twelfth	57		102
Fifteenth	57	Great Organ	570
Sexquialtera 3 ranks	171		
Trumpet treble	29	Total	672
Clarion bafs	28		
	570		

The Open Diapason to CC below are communicated to the *Stop* Diapason bafs with Metal Principal helpers. The Principal bafs stand in the front gilt: the treble are inside. In a handsome Mahogany Case 13ft. 6in. high, 10ft. 2in. wide, 3ft. 9½in. deep. Made by John Snetzler in 1766 with diagonal bellows. This Organ was Moved from the Earl of Fitzwilliams at Richmond in Surrey and erected in the Cube Room at Wilton House in April 1817 by A.B. Taken from the Cube Room and erected in the Gallery over the Entrance Hall in July 1835 by A. Buckingham.

144

The musical patronage of the Earl of Fitzwilliam and his connection with the music at St George's church, Hanover Square, has already been noted (no. 50).

A new parish church in the Italian style was built at Wilton to the designs of Thomas Henry Wyatt from 1840 to 1845, and this organ was moved into it. An account of the opening of the church in *The Salisbury and Winchester Herald* for 11 October 1845, mentions 'a choir organ, recently enlarged and altered by Mr. Bevington of London, assisted by Mr. Prangley of Salisbury'. That this is the organ from the House is confirmed by Sperling, who notes: 'A chamber organ by Snetzler enlarged by Bevington, fine old case, diapered pipes ... The Swell and Pedal Pipes by Bevington, Great organ by Snetzler'. The stop–list, and Sperling's mention of the 'fine' case with 'diapered pipes' make one wonder if the organ's casework might have been designed along the lines of the 1756 instrument now at Hillington (no. 33), but Buckingham's note of gilt Principals suggests rather Cobham Hall (no. 99).

According to E. G. Caple, [1] when a new Hill organ was given by Lord Pembroke in 1874, the Snetzler/Bevington organ was 're-erected in the gallery of the Great Hall in Wilton House, where it was often played by the late Sir Hubert Parry, but in 1914 it was again dismantled and eventually done away with'.

A Snetzler 'label' dated 1766, found by Bernard Edmonds in Andrew Freeman's collection, may be from this organ.

[1] Edward G. Caple, 'The Organ in Wilton Parish Church, near Salisbury' (TO 68/226).

71 Durham, the cathedral
(1766)

L 88; B 205/7; S II 87–8

Snetzler was evidently in the Durham area in 1766 (when he repaired the Bishop's Auckland organ (no. 72), and may have delivered the chamber organ for Lord Barrington (no. 104), and this year therefore seems to be the most likely for the timing of alterations he made to the 1684–5 Smith cathedral organ. He probably travelled north (via Swithland and Southwell?) chiefly for the installation of the organ at Halifax. The supposition seems to be confirmed by a Chapter note of the 30 November 1765 that 'Mr Dean sent John Snetzler's proposals for repairing the organ, which were agreed to'.

According to Buckingham, writing in August 1823, the work undertaken included additional stops on the Choir (and therefore a new soundboard?); a new Dulciana of 57 pipes 'to G' with its own stopped (wooden) bass; a new Dulciana Principal of 57 pipes 'to C' with its own stopped (wooden) bass; a new Flute of metal throughout, 57 pipes, and possibly some alterations to the 1747 Jordan/Bridge Swell. The Audit Book for 1765–6 notes a payment 'To Mr. Snetzler for cleaning and repairing the organ £130'.

Buckingham does not mention who altered the compasses of the keyboards of the Smith organ from *F'*, *G'*, *A'–c'''* (the contract of 1683 merely specifies 54–note ranks of pipes, so this is assumed to have been the then-proposed compass, though Smith added seven quarter-notes to this, giving 61 pallets in the Great and 'Chair' soundboards), to an eventual compass of *G'*, *A'–e'''* (57 notes) without the quarter-notes. According to evidence published by Richard Hird, [1] this work would seem to have been done by G. P. England and/or Wm. Nicholls who were paid £350 for work in 1815–6, and not by Snetzler. It is interesting, though, that the surviving key-levers are of oak, and their natural platings are of blackwood (with 'white' sharps), and are not made in the 'pianoforte' style with lime key-levers generally current by the end of the eighteenth century. (See also the next entry, no. 72.)

The Dulciana Principal makes a rare appearance here (the stop otherwise called a 'Celestina'), the only instance apart from that in the undated house organ for Miss Bristoe of Southwell (no. 106; it was perhaps delivered in 1765 or 1766). Only the keyboards and parts of the cases remain in various places in and near the cathedral, but there may be some Snetzler pipes in the organ now in the Castle chapel; these are from the former Choir manual, and are now in a swell-box in an organ whose case is that of the 'Chair' of the Smith organ, twice rebuilt by Harrison & Harrison.

[1] Richard Hird in BIOSR, vol. 12 no. 3, pp. 7–8; further details are to be found in *Durham Cathedral Organs* by Richard Hird and James Lancelot (Dean & Chapter of Durham, 1991).

72 Bishop's Auckland, Durham, the chapel of the Bishop's Palace (1766)

B 209/36–7; S II/90

The Smith organ in the Bishop's Chapel was rebuilt by Snetzler, who extended its compass and added a Hautboy in a swell-box that 'measured 2 feet 8 inches high, 2 feet wide and only 8 inches deep'. These facts were recorded by Buckingham, together with other information:

> The original maker was Father Smith in 1680 but repaired by Mr. John Snetzler in 1766 who made new sound board bellows and movements and the Hautboy swell. It appears that Smith made it from AA to C and Snetzler added the GG and the top notes above C to E also the Hautboy, all the rest of the pipes are the original of Smith's.

In other words, Snetzler did here what he is supposed not to have done at Durham Cathedral. Buckingham noted the composition of the mixture thus:

> The Sesqualtra and Cornet: from GG to ♮ next middle C–19–22; from m/C to the top F♯–12–3 [i.e., a tierce rank: a 17th] from G 10 pipes to the top E–12–15.

John Donaldson (see chapter 5, p. 266) was but one of a number of makers Buckingham found to have followed in Snetzler's footsteps here.

73 Sedgefield, Durham, St Edmund's church (1766)

B 207/107; S II/90

Further work in the Durham area included cleaning and repairing the organ built by Gerard Smith in 1708; again Buckingham, who followed Snetzler's trail around these parts, is the authority:

> The following is written on the front of the great sound Bd; This Organ and Loft was entirely built at the Charge of the Revd Dr Theophilus Pickering Rector of the place Sedgefield. And the Organ was made by me Gerard Smith 1708 – Cleaned in 1738 – Repaired and Cleaned by Mr. Snetzler in 1766 – and by J. Donaldson in 1784. Repaired and cleaned by A. Buckingham in 1824.

74 Newcastle-on-Tyne, St Nicholas's church (?1767 or 1768)

L 49; S II/201, 282; F2

Various dates have been given for work by Snetzler at this church (which later became a cathedral), but it would be reasonable to suppose that it was done when other work was being carried out in the area; in fact Leffler suggests 1767, and Sperling 1768. A date as early as 1749 was suggested by Freeman, perhaps because in that year (26 June), the common council ordered the addition of a 'sweet stop'. However, no Dulciana or other 'lieblich' register, which might connect Snetzler with this organ, appears in extant stop-lists.

It is just possible that 'sweet' is a mis-transcription for 'swell', and indeed Sperling cites the addition of a Swell of five stops (Open Diapason, Stopped Diapason, Cornet III, Trumpet, Hautboy [*sic* – no Principal]) to the Harris organ. No detailed information appears to be available from cathedral sources. The organ was repaired by John Donaldson in 1798 (see p. 267).

A crown from the former casework of the organ in this church now adorns the chamber organ now at Birmingham (no. 29).

*

75 Liverpool, the City Museum
(1767)

F 35; W 16

A small chamber organ with an inlaid mahogany case (height 8' 10", width 3' 9", depth 2' 10") similar to the normal three-compartment type, with gilded 'flat-backs' of wood and with pierced gilt scroll work at the top and (originally) doors. According to Messrs Rushworth & Dreaper, it was purchased for £10 at an auction by Mr. William Rushworth from 'Gilbert' at a sale at Ashley House, Frodsham, Cheshire, in April 1925. Whether the organ was part of the furniture of Ashley House, of which Mr Gilbert was the owner, or whether Mr Gilbert acquired the organ on Rushworth's behalf from elsewhere is not clear.

It was part of the Rushworth & Dreaper Collection of Antique Musical Instruments until it was sold, together with the rest of the collection, to the City of Liverpool Museum (now the Liverpool Museum: National Museums and Galleries on Merseyside, or NMGM) in 1967, and is now on display there in a gallery of musical instruments.

The upper frieze is boldly lettered

J. SNETSLER, LONDINI FECIT. 1767.

The stop-list is:

(*C–e'''*): OD (sc: c' [wood]), SD [wood], Fl [wood], 15 [wood bass, metal treble], Ses [labelled "Sesquiltre"] b/Cor tr II

The keyboard, of ivory naturals with moulded boxwood fronts and ebony sharps, is not original. It is not scribed or chamfered in the usual manner and it overhangs the pallet-box of the pin-action soundboard. Its keys are stamped with numbers (not marked in ink) and there are large gaps between the keyboard and its surrounds.

The stop-knobs are of turned ivory, and there are rectangular paper labels. Three slots in the casework base would originally have accommodated pedals for a shifting movement, a swell in the roof of the organ (which is still there, together with a pulley for guiding its operating rope) and a pedal for winding the feeder and wedge-reservoir. This last is now at the right-hand side of the organ case for operation by an assistant, and was probably moved to that position in 1978 in connection with a concert given then.

Although there is no signature inside the windchest (which may be due to some remaking of this part) and there are other deviations from Snetzler's usual practice in terms of the inlaying of the casework, the mis-spelling of the (later?) Sesquialtra label and even of his name, the reversal of 'fecit Londini' and the unusual mouths of the front dummy pipes, there is still evidence that Snetzler made this organ, or was involved in its making. With the exception of the two ranks of the mixture (made by Rushworth & Dreaper), all the pipes are original in construction and marking. The soundboard is basically original, and the original rackboards are safely stored in the Museum. The stop and key actions are typical of Snetzler's work. The instrument is in need of proper restoration and renovation; the casework especially has suffered damage.

76 Bath, the Octagon Chapel
(1767)

The eight-sided chapel was the first 'proprietary' chapel to be built in Bath; it was opened on 4 October 1767. William Herschel did not stay long at Halifax; as Rimbault [1] says, he 'only held the appointment till the following November, when he removed to Bath, where he burst forth from obscurity, and rose to the highest pitch of celebrity in the dignified science of Astronomy'. Even at the time of the competition at Halifax, he had told Dr Miller [2] 'I have the offer of a superior situation at Bath, which offer I shall accept'.

Herschel, in February 1767, 'Wrote to Snetzler, the maker of the organ for the Octagon Chapel, to hasten the work'. [3] The organ was placed in a gallery; the front of the case-work included three towers each of three pipes, the tallest in the centre, with intervening flats. The outer towers were 'surmounted by lyres', and above the centre tower were 'two cherubs sitting back to back, the one on the left represented in the act of blowing a trumpet, while his companion held a scroll of music'. [4]

Precise details of the organ as originally made are not known, but something might be deduced from the stop-list of the organ at the time of its disposal, which had become:

> Great: OD, SD (b/tr), Pr, Fl, 12, 15, Ses, Clarinet
> Swell: Bdn [?], OD, Lieblich Gedacht (b/tr), Gemshorn, Piccolo, VH, Oboe
> Pedals: 2½ octaves

An old keyboard has been displayed from time to time (in 1933, 1947 and 1955); its compass was *G', A'–e'''*, and it was described as 'reversed black and white' (presumably, if original, of the usual blackwood naturals and ivory-plated sharps pattern). It would seem possible that there was originally only this one keyboard of full compass, and the Great stop-list given above represents the original chorus; John Marsh, on playing it in 1781, described it as 'a charming little Organ of Snetzler's'. The Clarinet may have replaced another reed or a short-compass Hautboy in a small swell-box, but a Swell manual with a few stops seems likely, if one might judge from the style of the case-work.

Various parts of the organ were shown at an exhibition of 'Science and Music in 18th century Bath' at the Holburne of Menstrie Museum, from 22 September to 29 December 1977. These included fragments of three pipes (probably from one of the towers) that had been with the Herschel family until 1958, various pipes mounted on a board, and remains of the keyboard.

The organ was advertised in *The Musical Times* for February 1898 as 'a fine-toned church organ with 827 pipes' for £70. For lack of interest, the organ was dismantled.

[1] As quoted by Herbert Snow, 'The Organs of Halifax Parish Church' (TO 37/11).
[2] E. Miller, *The History and Antiquities of Doncaster and its Vicinity* (Doncaster, c1804).
[3] C. A. Lubbock, *The Herschel Chronicle* (Cambridge, 1936).
[4] J. T. Lightwood, *The Choir*, August 1930.

77 Charleston, South Carolina (U. S. A.), St Michael's church (1767)

F 34

Only the casework of mahogany (an expensive timber for a church organ) of the 'Savoy' type (later widened), the smaller speaking front pipes, and the dummies above them, and about 28 wooden pipes remain [1] of what was probably a three-manual organ, apparently of similar tonal size to that made for Andover (no. 85). It was ordered for the colony in 1767 by John Nutt, the London agent (later, partner of Ohrmann), who wrote with the shipping of the organ on 16 June 1768 to the church:

> I have now the Pleasure to address you, with Invoice &ca of the Organ for St. Michael's Church, Charles Town, amounting with Charges to £528. In calculating the Freight – I have abated about one half, and as to my Commission and Trouble, that I beg to present to the Parishioners, as a small tribute of the Gratitude & Respect I bear them – Mr. Snetzler who is now the most considerable, and the most reputable Organ Builder in *England*, assures me that this Piece of Work, is a very perfect one, he puts his Credit & Character upon the Goodness of it, and it will make me very happy to hear, that it gives full *Satisfaction*. The Organ was so well approved and so much admired, when it was tried, that a Gentleman who was present, ordered one of the very same Sort, for a Church in the West of England.
>
> I consulted Mr. Snetzler about sending out a Person to fix it up, & tune it & he recommends Mr. John Spiesegger now in Charles Town, as a person very able and equal to the Undertaking, and at the same Time assuring me, he could not send a better & fitter Person to do it.
>
> I have only to observe, that as I have already paid the great part of the Money for this Organ, & expect hourly to be called upon for the Remainder and as I am afraid you must not depend upon my Friends here for my Reimbursement I must beg you will take an early Opportunity of remitting me, what may be due upon this Account – I very heartily & sincerely wish a *Harmony* and *Happiness* to the Parishioners of Saint Michael's parish ...
>
> P.S. Inclosed please to receive the drawing of the *Frontispiece* which is here allowed to be a very neat one. [2]

Charleston: the organ before 1910

The organ arrived two months later, and was installed by John Speisegger, a pew–holder of the church. He was presumably a relative of Johann Konrad Speisegger, organ–builder of the canton of Schaffhausen, Snetzler's relative and possibly his first master.

George Williams,[2] apparently working from various nineteenth-century reports of the organ, reports that the stop-list was known to have included a wooden Open Diapason (the extreme bass pipes?) and a wooden Stopped Diapason on the Great, a Bassoon (on the Choir, one supposes) and a Furniture (presumably on the Great), and that there were about 900 pipes. But this pipe-total would not allow for a fully-fledged three-manual organ, unless it refers only to the Great. The price paid – which included the expensive case of mahogany, unusually with raised and fielded panels, plus half the freight costs as well as Nutt's commission – suggests either a small three-manual organ or one with a combined Choir and Swell manual ('of the very same Sort' as perhaps at Andover, Hamphire, 1772); the amounts spent on the organ during the first half of the nineteenth century may imply that the organ was then remade as a 'normal' three-manual organ with separate soundboards.

The organ was maintained by John Speisegger and his successors 'for many years'. It was repaired at a cost of $1100 'exclusive of scaffolding and a negroe man as an assistant' and again by Goodrich in 1816. In 1833 Henry Erben, the New York organ builder, suggested that 'the Organ is much in want of Bass, and the deep and Sonerous [*sic*] tones of Pedals will give a grand effect'. He added an octave of pedals and open pipes of twelve notes each from 'GG'; this last implies that the organ's manual compass was 'long octaves' from G'.

During the Civil War, the organ was dismantled and removed from the church, out of danger from Union Army batteries. At this time, a label reading *John Snetzler fecit Londini 1767* was removed from a soundboard, framed under glass, and fixed to the case. The organ was certainly modified from 1865 to 1871 at a cost of $2200. By this time, at least, the 'console' which now protruded from the case contained three keyboards, with ivory naturals and ebony sharps.

The organist wrote in 1894 that this work 'remedied what had become necessary in replacing worn out action, and removing such stops as were no longer capable of being tuned'. He suggested that the organ should be preserved, but in 1910 and 1911 the organ was replaced by a new Austin instrument with 'universal wind-chests'. The case, already at some time widened by the insertion of four blank panels in the upper front, was further widened by swinging the sides of the casework (with new front pipes of equal scale and length) into line with the original front. Further alterations were made in 1939 by Austin.

During 1993, the organ is being replaced by a new instrument made by Kenneth Jones, and the casework is being restored to a carefully-considered reconstruction of its original proportions. The likely layout of the towers and evidence obtained from the still-preserved original pipes in the flats suggest strongly that the organ was originally made with 'long octaves', with the 8' C as its longest front pipe, and scaled along 'Ludlow' lines.

[1] Technical information was kindly detailed by Kenneth Jones in a letter to Alan Barnes, 16 April 1989, and in subsequent conversations with Martin Renshaw.
[2] Historical material is derived from George Williams, 'The Snetzler Organ at St. Michael's Church, Charleston' (TO 131/134) and *St. Michael's, Charleston, 1751-1951* (University of South Carolina Press, Columbia, 1951), chapter viii.

78 Brookthorpe, Gloucestershire, St Swithun's church (1768)

F 91; W 103 (5)

The Wilde (or Wilder, according to Freeman) family of Sulham Manor, Berkshire, possessed this chamber organ from about the beginning of the nineteenth century at least. The Revd H. C. Wilder presented it to the mission church of Tilehurst, Berkshire, in 1932; it was sold to Brookthorpe church in 1938, when it was installed with modifications by Percy Daniel & Co. of Clevedon, Somerset. The case is of the 'normal' type; although the pediment is missing the pipe–shade carvings are in good condition. Apparently, the original stop–list was:

(G', A'–e'''): OD, SD (b/tr), Dul (sc: c), Pr, 12, 15, ?mixture [Ses/Cor?]

There are small–scaled 'helpers' in the bass of the Open Diapason.

The keyboard is of blackwood with ivory–plated sharps; it is balanced and operates a sticker–backfall action. A shifting movement takes off the upperwork. The wind pressure is 2½".

At some time. a pedal–board of 13 notes was added to the organ; this was replaced in 1938 by a 30–note board with a pneumatically operated Bourdon, using some pipes of the extreme bass of the Stopped Diapason, and the case was raised to accommodate the pedalboard and coupler. The original feeder and reservoir were therefore replaced by a new, larger, horizontal reservoir with feeders, and the back panels of the casework were removed. A Keraulophon which had replaced the original Twelfth was revoiced as a Vox Angelica; a Flute to tenor F had replaced an original mixture, probably at the same date as the Keraulophon (that is, the middle of the nineteenth century). Swell shutters were contrived behind the dummy metal (7–11–7) front pipes. The manual compass was unchanged, but some of the G'–B' pipes were removed. Later, a 'home–made' electric blower was installed.

The organ was remade 1980–1 by John Coulson. The 1938 swell–box and pneumatic modifications were removed, and the reservoir and main frame and back panels reconstructed. The thirteen–note pedalboard was preserved, but it is not connected. The Keraulophon/Vox Angelica was removed in favour of a second–hand Twelfth. The Principal's compass was restored to G', and a mixture (G' 17–19 /c' 12–17) installed in place of the Flute. A new electric blower and a reconstructed hand–pump were installed.

The soundboard is dated in the usual manner, and a shifting movement takes off all but the unison ranks. Stop–names, with modern spellings, are engraved on brass plates over the stop–knobs which draw through square holes in the vertical frames of the panels adjacent to the keyboard.

79 Beverley, Yorkshire, the minster
   ## (1767–69)

B 205/12; S III/56; HR 13; F 33

No doubt Snetzler was very much occupied during these three years with the making, carriage, installation and finishing of this, his largest, instrument. Details of the size and materials of the double–fronted case, stop–list, compasses and opening dates of this organ were given by Buckingham thus:

Beverley Minster Yorkshire
An Organ with 3 sets of Keys the Great & Choir organs from GG long octaves to E in alt. The Swell organ from G to E in alt. A set of Pedals to act on the keys 17 from G to C.
   Contains the following stops

Great Organ		Choir Organ		Swell Organ	
Op Diapason	57	Op Diapason	57	Op Diapason	34
Op Diapason	57	St Diapason	57	St Diapason	34
St Diapason	57	Principal	57	Principal	34
Principal	57	Flute	57	Cornet 3 R	102
Twelfth	57	Fifteenth	57	Trumpet	34
Fifteenth	57	Furniture	171	Hautboy	34
Tierce	57	Bafsoon	57		——
Sexqualtra 4 ranks	228	Vox humana	57		272
Cornet 5 R	145		——	Choir	570
Mixture 3 R	171		570	Great	1057
Trumpet	57		——		
Clarion	57			Total	1899
	——				
	1057	Mr. Lambert Organist			

In a elegent wainscott Case with two gilt fronts and the Keys are at one end of the organ for the organist to play
Made by John Snetzler of London   opened with Oratorios
September 20–21 & 22 in 1769
The Pedals were added by Mr. Ward of York

	ft
Width of the Choir within the walls	26.8
From the Choir floor to the ceiling	36.6
From the Choir floor to the Organ Loft floor	19.4
From the Organ Loft floor to the top of the Organ Ornaments	35 –
Width of the Organ case	14 –
Depth of the Organ case	12 –

New horizontal bellows has been added by Ward of York but so badly executed that it requires great strength and labour to blow them.
Beverley July 1823 A B

Rimbault [1] noted that the console was on the north side of the organ case.
   The opening ceremonies consisted of a festival of Handel's music. The installation of the organ was the culmination of a long campaign of repairs to the fabric started about 1716. (In these, Nicholas Hawksmoor was involved; he no doubt derived inspiration from Beverley for his west towers of Westminster Abbey, posthumously built in 1739). The whole work was a remarkable example of 'Gothic survival' of ecclesiastical design and masons' expertise. Even following much Victorian and later 'restoration' there is still excellent eighteenth–century Gothic

craftsmanship to be seen. To this work were added 'a gorgeous wooden' altarpiece and galleries 'on Grecian Models' together with pulpit, reading-desk and font-cover in the same mode. Such a mixture of styles evoked criticism in the early part of the nineteenth century, but the organ-screen (dividing choir and nave, and probably designed by Hawksmoor) was praised by some:

> The organ screen is a beautiful specimen of the Grecian style of architecture with English decorations; but lamentably misplaced amidst such a profusion of pure English ornament

and damned by others as 'the production of corrupt taste and a false idea of magnificence'.

Beverley minster: view from nave

view from chancel

By 1848, the proponents of 'correct' church-building were sharpening their axes:

> a hideous rood-screen [*sic*], of the very worst taste ... filling up the lofty
> and beautiful chancel arch with *red-cloth*, as the clerk informed me – *to*
> *keep the place warm*. He, however, told me that it was proposed to remove
> it, and fill the arch with *glass* instead. Now, the miserable effect of this
> vandalism, every ecclesiologist knows in Lichfield Cathedral, where the
> taste of Mr. Wyatt introduced it.

James Wyatt was the ecclesiologist's favourite scapegoat; he did *not* in fact design the glass screen at Lichfield [2]. Again in 1859: 'another eyesore in the building is the organ-screen, one of the vilest erections, I should think, extant, in a church of any pretensions'.

These effusions [3] show all too clearly the shift in taste and religious sentiment that caused the removal and frequent destruction of eighteenth-century church organs and organ cases, and much other church furniture, throughout Britain. The reader may now more impartially judge the effect of the Rococo–Gothic ensemble from the old photographs.

The process of 'restoration' began in 1824, but the organ screen was not demolished until 1878, when the present screen was designed by Scott. The organ was clumsily re-erected upon it, and was truly an 'eyesore' until the present 'handsome case, designed by Canon Nolloth in conjunction with Messrs. Hill' [4] was erected in 1916.

The Hills' first work was done in 1884 and 1885 upon the completion of the new screen; additions were made to the organ in 1897, 1905, and 1912 before it was enlarged to four manuals in 1916. The organ was again rebuilt in 1962. About fifteen Snetzler stops survive, somewhat repitched, but including a large part of the Great chorus. Part of the Snetzler casework is placed in the entrance to the south choir aisle to conceal a mass of later pipework. Remnants of the organ screen (its iron gates and statues) are still in the church; its stonework was said in 1956 to be in a garden at Cleethorpes.

[1] HR2, p. 251.
[2] See Martin Renshaw, 'The Building of an Eighteenth-century Cathedral Organ', (TO 260/58).
[3] Elegantly documented by Gerald Cobb, *English Cathedrals: the Forgotten Centuries* (Thames and Hudson, 1980), pp. 52–63.
[4] Ibid., p. 56.

*

80 City of London, church of St Andrew-by-the-Wardrobe
   (1769)

W 108 (18)

The introduction of a 'wreath' around the 'oval' in the front of chamber organs in
the years following Handel's death in April 1759 encourages a belief that in some
way this wreath – symbolic of victory – was a conscious tribute to his memory.
This speculation is intensified by its appearance in the case-work of this chamber
organ, made for Lord Hatherton of Teddesley Hall, Staffordshire, a place said to
have been frequented by Handel.

When that mansion was demolished in 1953, the organ was purchased by Noel
Mander, and his firm renovated the organ without making any alterations beyond
the fitting of tuning slides (and change of pitch and temperament?) and the
introduction of an electric blower. Its stop-list is:

> (*G'*, *A'–e'''*): Open Diapason, Stop Diapason, Dulciana, Principal, Flute,
>   Fifteenth, Sesquialtra [b], Cornet [tr]

These names are engraved on circular ivory plates let into the front of the stop-
knobs in a way that was later to become usual.

The keyboard's upper compass only to *e'''*, one note shorter than the *f '''*-
compass on some earlier chamber organs should be noted. The case is of mahogany
and is ornamented with carving above the four-pipe flats and a broken pediment
with a central small plinth. There are seventeen pipes in the 'oval'. Since there are
folding all-wooden doors which enclose the front of the organ from the impost
upwards, it might be presumed that a roof-swell was planned.

The organ was loaned to the church of St Bartholomew-the-Great, Smithfield
(just north of the City), for six years before being placed in the newly restored
church of St Andrew in 1961.

81 Somerset, private collection
   (1769)

This chamber organ [1] is virtually identical with the other 1769 instrument (no.
80), and was presumably made simultaneously. Only the form of its pediment, the
addition of a short-compass reed and its glazed doors differ. It was formerly at Lee
Manor in Devon, where a photograph (not reproduced here) taken early in the
twentieth century shows it in a drawing room.

The organ was given in 1919 to the Congregational chapel in Lynton, Devon, by
Mr and Mrs Polkinghorne as a memorial to a son and daughter. It was sold to its
present owners, Margaret Phillips and David Hunt, in 1992. The stop-list is:

> (*G'*, *A'–e'''*): OD (sc: *c*, grooved to the SD, with 16 helpers), SD, Dul (sc: *c*,
> grooved to SD), Pr, Fl, 15, Ses b/Cor tr, Crm [sc: *c'*]

The keyboard naturals are of ivory with fronts of vertically–veneered pear and the sharps are ebony-plated; the stop knobs are engraved as in no. 80. A shifting movement takes off all except the Open Diapason, Stopped Diapason, Dulciana and Flute. Two (unique?) side–swells – slots for these may be seen in the photograph – and a roof-swell are successively opened by a system of levers and ropes activated by a vertical trace on the pedal–lever. A horizontal reservoir with feeders has replaced the original winding system. The organ is dated inside the soundboard in the usual way.

[1] mentioned briefly by W, p. 118 (21)

The organ in Somerset

82 Drogheda, Louth, St Peter's church
(1770)

The Minute Book of Drogheda Corporation recorded 16 January 1771 an order

> that Mr. Mayor be and is hereby impowered to draw on the Treasurer for
> such sum as will be necessary to pay for the salvage, Freight, package,
> repairing and putting up the Organ lately purchased by the Gentn. of this
> Corporation for Saint Peter's Church which cost £300 in London, the Ship
> wherein part of the said Organ was, being Wrecked at Skerries in the late
> Storm, the same to be allowed in his Accounts.

Which part of the organ suffered in the wreck, and how much the organ cost
above the apparent part–payment of £300, are not known, but the organ was ready
in 1771, as in that year the Vestry Minutes record that an organist and a
bellows–blower was also chosen at a salary of 'Five Pounds Ster[ling], to be levy'd
in like manner as the Organists Sallary'.

The organ evidently contained the following stops:

> Great (*G', A', C', D'–e'''*): OD, SD, Pr, 12, 15, Ses III/Cor II[?]
> Choir (*G', A', C', D'–e'''*): SD, Pr, Fl
> Echo [on the same keys as Choir, in a swell] (*g–e'''*): OD, Pr, Hb

It would appear that the double–storeyed 'Savoy style' case, in this instance
unusually tall and made of deal painted to resemble mahogany, had either become
a standard one for the medium–sized and large church organ whatever its internal
disposition, or that the production system (now that Snetzler took on Jones as a
partner?) did now allow for the earlier rationale. The pipes in the flats are original;
the organ is still in the west gallery.

The organ was maintained by the organist, Anthony Bunting, from 1783 to
1809. In 1874, the organ was repaired by Telford of Dublin, and (possibly) a
Gamba was added to the Great. In 1884, the same firm added a normal Swell
organ with six stops, with a matching keyboard, and rationalized the compass of
the three keyboards to *C–e'''*, though the *G'* (apparent *H'/B♮'*) keys were retained
and copied. Thomas Drew referred to the organ in 1899 [1] as 'not much of an
organ', so it may have been somewhat enfeebled by that date. A pedalboard with
two octaves of open pipes were added; this was extended in 1903. An Oboe was
added to the Swell in 1929, and then the organ was rebuilt with two manuals with
pneumatic action by Conacher in 1934.

The remade Snetzler/Telford keyboards, with blackwood naturals and ivory–
plated sharps, and some other parts of the organ, have been kept in the church.
About six Snetzler ranks remain. [2]

[1] In his letter quoted in no. 4 in this chapter.
[2] TO 280/95 includes further details of the history of the organ; the authors are grateful
to Kenneth Jones for reporting evidence found during his examination of the organ in 1993.

83 Horbury, Wakefield, Yorkshire, St Peter's convent (1770)

A 'small chamber organ' was reported in 1869 [1] to contain these stops:

Great (*G'*, *A'–g'''* [*sic*]): OD 'short', SD, Dul, Pr, 15 (not in *H.G.*), Ses b/Cor tr
('mixture of two ranks'), Tpt
Swell (*c–g'''*): Stopped Diapason, Gamba, 'Principal' (now Geigen Diapason), Oboe
Pedal (now *C–f'*): Bourdon, 'a free reed' (now Flute)
Pedal to Great, Swell to Great

It was built as a 'wreathed–oval' chamber organ for Well Head, Halifax, the home of the Waterhouse family ('prominent in connexion with that [*sc.* the parish church] organ', according to the *Halifax Guardian* article). The Swell and Pedal were 'made by Messrs. Hill', who 'also put in an hydraulic engine to blow the organ'. (In Hill's letter–book for the 1850s and in 1863, what seems to be this organ appears as 'Halifax Chapel'). It was given to All Saints' church, Elland, near Halifax, by Mrs Doherty–Waterhouse in 1915, whence it was purchased by the parents and staff of St Hilda's School, Horbury. After restoration by N. P. Mander Ltd, it was placed in St Peter's convent in April 1958. [2]

[1] 'History of Organs in the parish of Halifax. – No. 8' (*Halifax Guardian*, 1869); thanks to Richard Barnes, Halifax, for sending copies of relevant numbers.
[2] Gordon Paget, 'The Snetzler Organ in Norwich Cathedral' (TO 147/139).

84 Burton–on–Trent, Staffordshire, St Modwen's church (1771)

B 212/123–4; S II/266; F 40

The 'handsome Mahogany Case', in a Classical style along the lines of the case proposed for Sir Nathaniel Curzon (no. 41a), was designed by Samuel and James Wyatt. Nothing now remains of the organ except the case, extended from three original pipe–flats to seven, so Buckingham's description of the organ must serve:

The Parish Church, Burton upon Trent—This Organ has 3 sets of Keys Great and Choir Organs from GG long octaves to E in alt, the Swell Organ from G to E in alt.

GREAT ORGAN		CHOIR ORGAN		SWELL ORGAN	
Op. Diapason	65	St. Diap. bafs and treb.	57	Op. Diapason	34
St. Diapason	57	Principal	57	Principal	34
Principal	57	Flute bafs and treble	57	Cornet 3R	102
Twelfth	57			Hautboy	34
Fifteenth	57		171		——
Sexqualtra 3R	171		——		204
Cornet 4R	117			Choir Organ	171
Trumpet	57			Great Organ	638
	——				
	638			Total	1013

The Open Diapason to CC the 4 lower notes is a St. Diapn and metal principal helpers: added to them is four Pedal Diapason pipes. The Choir St. Diapason and Flute draws bafs and treble. An octave of Pedals act on the Great Organ keys with horizontal bellows in a handsome Mahogany Case 19ft. high, 10ft. 6in. wide, 6ft. 4in. deep made by John Snetzler, London. Erected in 1771. There was only two sets of keys in its original state: the Swell was play'd by the Choir keys. Mr. Anthony Greatorix the Organist added the third set so as to play them separate. Elliot had 105 pounds for new horizontal bellows, an octave of Pedals with 4 double Diapason pipes the GG-AA-BB-♮♮ to the Open Diapason bafs, Cleaning and tuning. Burton, 14 January 1832. A.B

The organ at Burton-on-Trent

It will be noted that Snetzler was still providing combined Choir/Swell divisions, presumably in order to make available a less expensive instrument, as also at Andover and Drogheda. This is virtually the only major work that Snetzler carried out in the West Midlands; the connection is undoubtedly through Kedleston and Samuel Wyatt. In any event, Snetzler's peak of production was past, and the death of Leonard Snetzler in 1772 would have removed an important practical part of the business as well as being a personal blow.

The organ was removed when Hope-Jones provided a new one, 1899–1900.

85 Newquay, Cornwall, the Wesleyan church (1772)

F 41

It is possible that this organ was the one referred to by John Nutt (see no. 77), as it was made for the parish church of the Hampshire town of Andover. An inscription upon it read:

> Given and endowed by Sir John Griffin Griffin, K. B., and Benjamin Lethieullier, Esq., A.D.1772, Benjamin Morgan and Thomas Parry, *Churchwardens.*

The donors were the two Members of Parliament for Andover; the twenty-four members of the Corporation were the electorate in those 'rotten borough' days. The churchwardens cannily made sure that the salary of the organist was secured by a further gift of £733. 4s. in 3 per cent. Consols – hence the 'endowed' of the inscription. A still–extant deed of gift dated 8 May 1772 placed control of the income in the hands of four trustees.

The organ was put in a west gallery and, according to an owner of a copy of John Keeble's *Select Organ Voluntaries*, it was arranged as follows:

STOPS IN THE ANDOVER ORGAN

Ecc. Hautbois [g]	Ecc. Cornet [g]
Ecc. Open diapason [g]	Ecc. Principal [g]
Ch. Flute [bass]	Ch. Principal
Ch. Stop'd diapason [bass]	Ch. Flute [treble]
	Ch. Stop'd diapason [treble]
Gr. Sesquialtera	Gr. Trumpet
Gr. Twelfth	Gr. Fifteenth
Gr. Principal	Gr. Cornet [treble]
Gr. Open diapason	Gr. Stop'd diapason

[signed] Allan Borman Hutchins (May 14th, 1819)

As this would appear to be the layout of the stop–knobs as the organist saw them, the fortunate survival of this description may be added to the small sum of knowledge that we have of Snetzler's practice in this regard. (See chapter 4, pp. 195–9.)

The organ was controlled from two keyboards after the manner of that made for Burton–on–Trent and apparently with an identical stop–list. John Marsh played the organ at Andover in 1781; he describes it as 'put up a few years before by Snetzler', and he 'was much pleased by it'. Bernard Edmonds reports that a Snetzler label was taken out of a soundboard by Hele in 1904 and given to Noel

Bonavia Hunt. A sketch of the organ in the Freeman notebooks, made from a photograph by Arthur Bennett, shows a case with double–storeyed flats in the usual 'Savoy' church manner.

The organ–builder Robert Gray was buried in the churchyard on 15 July 1796; it is possible that Gray & Davison made some alterations around 1836 and again between 1844 and 1846 (at a cost of £85), when the church was entirely rebuilt. At that time, the organ had been removed to London for rebuilding, and was 'said to have met with a serious catastrophe' on its way to London in a road waggon. [1] J. Corps of Reading made additions and tuned the organ to equal temperament. The organ was moved to a new chamber on the north side of the chancel by Bevington on 1872, and further rebuilt, at a cost of £220. The front pipes had by this time deteriorated, and a new decorated front was supplied; only the oak panels of the case then remained.

In 1904, a new Hele organ was supplied, and these builders moved the organ (sold for £175) to Newquay, where it has been rebuilt in 1937 and 1977. Parts of about a dozen Snetzler ranks remain. A Snetzler label is reported to be in the organ.

[1] Arthur Bennett, 'A Traditional Snetzler Organ' (TO 11/129).

86 Hillsborough, County Down, the parish church (1772–3)

HR 29; F 64

The original receipt for the organ, signed by or on behalf of Snetzler survives:

> The Rt. Honble. Earl of Hillsborough to John Snetzler
> 1773

	£.	s.	d.
May. To a New organ with 3 Setts of keys for Hillsborough Church_____	400.	0.	0
To a Wainscott Case in the Gothick Taste for Do. _____	86.	5.	2
To Packing Cases for Do. No. 22 ___	19.	8.	6
	£ 505.	13.	8

> 1777 August 7 I recd the Contents
> of this Bill in full of all
> Demands pr[?] John Snetzler

The organ, with a Gothic double–storeyed case on a Gothic west gallery, was provided for the new church also built by the Earl. The organ's arrival by sea was reported in the *Belfast Newsletter* of 18 November 1772:

> Last week was landed here from England a very grand organ for the Earl
> of Hillsborough's new church at Hillsborough.

Its original stop-list does not appear to be known exactly, but the organ seems to have contained the following stops:

Great (*G'*, *A'* ?–?): OD, SD, Pr, 12, 15, Ses (b/tr) IV, Cor (?sc: *c'*) V, Tpt
Choir (*G'*, *A'* ?–?): [?OD or reed], SD, Pr, Fl, 15
Swell (?*g*–?): OD, SD, Pr, [?Cor III], Tpt, Hb

The original keyboards were blackwood naturals with 'skunk-tail' sharps, a sandwich of blackwood with a centre of ivory or bone. Were these thought to be in the 'Gothick Taste' too? (In the keyboards of some indigenous organs an opposite arrangement of the sandwich was used.) The original keyboards were removed in 1868 by Coombe of Belfast, who shortened the compass in the bass to *C*.

In 1872, a pinnacle of the tower fell into it; curiously, Telford of Dublin reported that the pipes were not damaged, but the Swell soundboard was badly 'twisted' and irreparable. No doubt this was the signal for further work in that department. The organ was rebuilt in 1894, 1924 and 1952, and again 1970–2. Parts of about thirteen ranks of Snetzler pipes remain, together with the Great and Choir soundboards, which are presumably dated 1772.

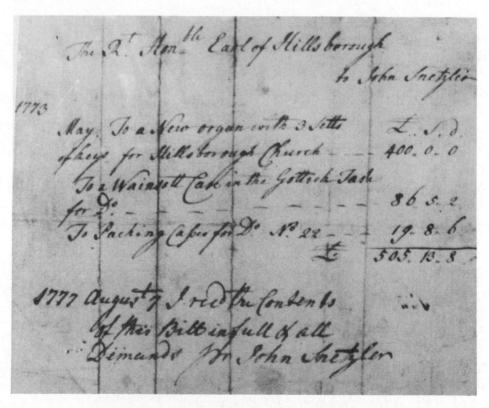

Snetzler's receipt for the organ at Hillsborough

87 Leicester, St Martin's church
(1774)

L [index only]; S II/173; HR 16; F 43

Leicester was a centre of considerable musical activity. The Shire was particularly conscious of its connections with Handel and his music through Jennens of Gopsall Hall and, in the City, St Martin's seems to have vied with the larger, nearby church of St Margaret's. Organs are recorded at St Martin's from medieval times, and an organ was provided after the Restoration in 1660. A replacement for this installed about 1700, was repaired by Mark Anthony 'Dallow' (Dallam) in 1715, and moved westwards 1754–5 with a 'strong Norway Oak Front properly ornamented with Carv'd Work, and Gilding all the front pipes with true Gold' by William Casterton of Langham, Rutland. Upon the appointment in 1765 of Anthony Gretorex of North Wingfield, Derbyshire, (he who was later organist at Burton-on-Trent, and made or had made a third keyboard there for the Snetzler organ of 1771), the possibility of a new organ was canvassed.

An account of current trends in organ–building was published by William Ludlam at the request of subscribers to the organ funds of both St Martin's and St Margaret's churches; it was then reprinted in the *Gentleman's Magazine* of December 1772 (it is fully transcribed in Appendix 7). A subscription was started at St Martin's in 1769 and an organ along lines indicated by Ludlam was opened 21 September 1774. Its stop–list comprised:

> Great (*G'*, *A'–e'''*): OD [front], OD [4 basses from SD, with 4 helpers], SD,
> Pr, 12, 15, Sesq IV, Cor (sc: *c'*) V, Tpt, Cln [?b only: Sperling]
> Choir (*G'*, *A'–e'''*): OD [4 basses stopped], SD, Pr, Fl, 15, Bn
> Swell (*f–e'''*): OD, SD, Pr, Cor III [II?], Tpt, Hb

The organ, dated 1774 in the soundboards, [1] was placed on a west gallery. It cost £500 plus the old organ which was taken in part–payment, the true cost of the new organ being reckoned at £612. 7s. 6d.

An otherwise somewhat off–beam footnote in the *Christian Remembrancer* [2] records acoustic improvements which accompanied the new organ: 'An instance ... ocurred at St. Martin's church, Leicester, where Snetzler erected his last organ, in 1771, and which he pronounced his best. The church having one of the old fashioned open roofs, which was so unfavourable to sound, the parishioners were induced to have it underlined, which had the desired effect'.

The opening concert included Handel's *Dettingen Te Deum and Jubilate*, with the Earl of Sandwich playing the kettle–drums, and Joah Bates conducting a large band led by Giardini. What Omai, the native of Tahiti brought to England by Captain Cook, made of all this is not recorded, but his presence among the auditory was. Further music included *Jephtha* (presumably Handel's) and an *Ode to Charity*, allegedly 'specially composed by Dr. Boyce'.

'Mr Snelsner' was paid ten guineas for work in 1778. Nothing radical was done until Holdich introduced Pedal Pipes (one octave, *C–c*, 16' tone) with Great and

Choir pedal couplers in 1845. He moved the organ from the gallery to the north transept in 1848, and (according to Sperling) removed the 'mounted' Cornet in favour of a Claribella, and supplied Venetian swell-shutters and a new case. The upper compass of the Clarion was perforce completed when the Cornet was removed, and a Cremona supplanted the Choir Bassoon, if it was not already there as its treble.

The central tower and spire were completely rebuilt 1861–7, so the organ was moved then and again in 1870. It was rebuilt by Walker in 1873, preserving most of the Snetzler pipework and two of the soundboards. Upon the elevation of the church to cathedral status, new galleries were built at the west end of the church, and the organ was completely rebuilt on them by Harrison & Harrison 1928–30 and placed in new casework designed by Charles Nicholson. There are about ten ranks of Snetzler pipes remaining.

[1] The 'label' was illustrated in Macnutt and Slater, *Leicester Cathedral Organ* (1930), opposite p. 19; from that booklet the label and some of the history of earlier organs in the church have been taken.

[2] Quoted in BIOSR, vol. 15, no. 1, Jan. 1990; the footnote is to no. X, 'The Organ at St. Stephen's, Walbrook' in the *Christian Remembrancer*'s *'Organo–Historica'* series.

John Snetzler fecit Londini
17 74

Label from St Martin's church, Leicester

88 Wynnstay, Ruabon, Lindisfarne college (1774)

W (illus. 38)

The case of the chamber organ was designed by Robert Adam for the Music Room of Sir Watkin Williams-Wynne at 20 St James's Square, London. Adam's design is similar to one of the rejected designs for Lord Curzon at Kedleston. The organ was moved to 'Wynnstay' and rebuilt by Gray & Davison in 1864. Its present stop-list comprises:

Great [Snetzler] (*now C–?*): OD [?G & D], SD, Dul [?G & D], Pr, Fl, 15, mix III, Tpt [?orig.], Piccolo [replacing or rescaling 12th?]
Swell [G & D]: Double Diapason, Keraulophon, Stopped Diapason, blank [?b], Principal, Fifteenth, mixture II, Cornopean, Oboe
Pedal [G & D]: Grand Bourdon
Four manual and pedal couplers

It is clear that at least part of the Great pipework is by Snetzler.

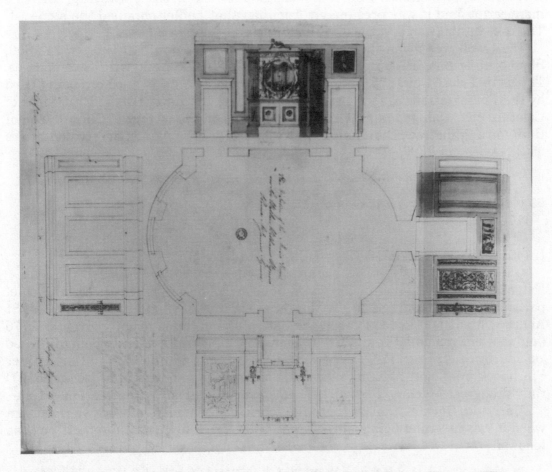

'The elevations of the Music Room in Sir Watkins Williams Wynnes House
St James's Square'

(89) Bath, Brook Street, St Margaret's chapel
1773 or 1775

L 101; S II/240; HR 24; F 45

An organ similar to that made for Andover was made for a proprietary chapel
opened in 1773. The following is abbreviated from the stop-list given by Leffler:

> Organ built by Schnetzler about 1770 ...
> Great (G', A', C, D–e'''): OD, OD, SD, Pr, 12, 15, Ses IV, Cor (sc: c') IV, Tpt
> Choir (G', A', C, D–e'''): SD (b/tr), Pr, Fl (b/tr)
> Swell on Choir keys (g–e'''): OD, Pr, Hb

Leffler described the Swell Hautboy as 'very fine' and added that the organist was 'Mr T. W. Windsor'; he is an ancestor of the present owner of Leffler's manuscript, and it was presumably from him that Leffler obtained the stop-list. The case design was described as 'The same front as the Savoy'.

The Swell was given its own keyboard in 1825 by Smith of Bristol. In 1850, Sherborne of Bath added pedal pipes and rebuilt the console with C compasses. The chapel closed in 1873, becoming briefly 'public baths' [sic] before being used by the Presbyterians. The organ was acquired by the Revd J. J. S. Bird, vicar of Colerne, near Chippenham. While the organ was in the factory of Clark & Son of Bath for a grandiose rebuilding, it was completely destroyed in an accidental fire on 21 December 1889.

90 Nottingham, St Andrew's church
1776–77

L 145; B 206/51–2 and 213/47–8; S II/205; HR 33; F 37.

Extensive tonal remains of the large double-fronted organ made for the chief parish church of Nottingham, St Mary's, are now to be found in the church of St Andrew, Mansfield Road. Though the date of the organ is usually given as 1776 (and it was thus dated in the Great soundboard), it was evidently being finished 'on site' by Snetzler in 1777, as he writes in a letter of 5 June 1777 to Christopher Pinchbeck from Nottingham (a facsimile of which is to be found at organ no. 97) that 'this great Machine I set up here, takes up all/ all [sic] my attention & time'.

Alexander Buckingham carried out a considerable amount of work on the organ when it was in – and being moved around – its original home; he reports on it as follows:

St. Mary's Church, Nottingham—An organ with three sets of keys—the Great and Choir from GG long octaves to E in alt., the Swell from F below m/C to E in alt. A set of pedals from GG to C 17 do not act upon the keys but have a separate set of pallets to the Gt. Organ contain the following stops:

GREAT ORGAN				Fifteenth					57
Op. Diapason	...	...	57	Bafsoon	...	...	...	...	57
Op. Diapason	...	...	61						
St. Diapason ...	...	...	57						342
Principal	...	...	57						
Twelfth	...	...	57						
Fifteenth	...	...	57	SWELL ORGAN					
Sexquil'ta 4R	...	...	228	Op. Diapason	...	...	...	36
Cornet m/C 5R	...	...	145	St. Diapason ...	...	...	...	36
Trumpet	...	...	57	Principal	...	...	...	36
Clarion Bafs.	...	...	29	Cornet 3R	...	...	...	108
			—	Trumpet	...	...	...	36
			505	Hautboy	...	...	...	36
								288
				Choir	...	...	...	342
CHOIR ORGAN				Great	...	...	...	805
Op. Diapason	...	...	57					
St. Diapason	...	...	57	Total	...	...	...	1,435
Principal	...	...	57					
Flute	...	...	57					

Mr. T. Peirson, organist. One of the Op. Diapasons in the Great organ is through in front the other is to CC in metal. The other four notes is a St. Diapason and a helper Principal metal pipes. All of the St. Diapason and Flute trebles are of metal. Three pair of diagonal bellows. In a Wainscott case with two fronts 23 ft. high, 13 ft. wide and 8 ft. deep. Built by Snetzler of London in 1776. It is a very fine instrument, the whole of it mix well together. The Bafsoon and the Cornet in the Swell is the worst stops in the organ. Nottingham, October 18th, 1823, A.B.

The cost of the organ (and gallery?) was £800, according to some (the more reliable) sources; others say 600 guineas. There is a tradition that the oak for the case was given by the King; a crown upon a cushion evidently surmounted one of the fronts, which were, according to Leffler, the 'same design as the Savoy & St. Martin's, Leicester', that is, double-storeyed, as can just be seen in a print dating from the 1840s. [1] The earlier organ was removed to Uppingham parish church, where part of its front case-work survives. The Snetzler organ was set up on a gallery 'in front of the glass screen which separates the chancel from the nave'. [2] Buckingham further notes, following his own work in 1839, that

—This organ was removed from off the gallery or screen which stood in the middle of the church all cleaned the sound boards new palletted brafs plate added to under the wind chest of the sound boards instead of the old leather purses. Also new horizontal bellows with double feeders erected in the new gallery at the west end of the church tuned, etc.—April 19th, 1839, by A. Buckingham. After which a set of 21 pedals with their couplers to the Great and Choir keys and 21 double Diapason bafs. pipes. The four lowest notes from GG to ♮♮ was large Unison pipes then at CCC was double notes 16 ft. long so on up to EE. There was also a coupler movement added to unite the Great and Swell organs together and a new venetian front to the Swell organ all done complete tuned, etc. September 7th, 1839, by Mr. A. Buckingham.

Number of pipes brought over ...	1,435
Double Diapasons added	21
Total	1,456

The cost of this work was estimated at £260. [3]

The cause of the organ's moving was the walling-up of the chancel by the vicar, Archdeacon Wilkins, and the building of a stone west gallery in perpendicular Gothic style to accommodate the organ and the children of the Bluecoat and Parochial Charity Schools.

The church was closed in December 1842, when its fabric was found to be in a dangerously poor condition. After Wilkins's death in 1843, a long and chaotic campaign of 'restoration' was begun under two sets of architects: Cottingham, then Scott & Moffatt. This involved the removal of the nave roof, the emptying of the glazing of the west window and the moving of the western organ gallery, only a few years old, so that the Classical west front could be rebuilt in 'correct' Gothic. Buckingham was again employed in 1846, this time to remove the organ to the north transept and add 'a coupler' and a 'shifting movement'.[4] The church was reopened after five years of work on 18 May 1848, but by then it is likely that Alexander Buckingham had died (probably of despair).

Following an attempt to sell it, the organ was drastically simplified by Lloyd and Dudgeon and moved to the north aisle in 1867 during more 'restorations'. Internal evidence suggests that it was then reduced to 'CC' compasses and repitched a semitone higher than originally.

Upon the introduction of a surpliced choir, it was replaced by a new Bishop & Starr organ, placed in the chancel and opened in October 1871. Snetzler's 'great Machine' was sold to St Andrew's church for £150, and ('tradition' reported) 'the best part of the case [*sic* – what became of the second front and at what stage it was discarded are not clear] ... disposed of and used as a shelter in a private garden for a number of years'.

The organ was first set up adjacent to the sanctuary in St Andrew's church. [5] It was later moved to a new loft north of the chancel and subjected to a number of rebuildings, the first (and most sympathetic) by Conacher in 1898. The organ still contains, randomly placed on various soundboards, virtually unaltered pipework comprising practically the whole of the Great flue chorus including many of the front pipes, some still with their original gilding; but not the Cornet. There exist also much of the Choir pipework and some Swell pipes. Some details of the pipework and its scaling are to be found in chapter 4, pp. 244–6.

[1] Reproduced in Richard Iliffe and Wilfred Baguley, *Victorian Nottingham* (Nottingham, 1976), vol. 17, p. 2.
[2] William White, *History, Gazetteer and Directory of Nottingham* (Sheffield, 1832).
[3] James Orange, *History and Antiquities of Nottingham* (vol. 2: Hamilton, Adams and Co., 1840), p. 532.
[4] See Andrew Abbott and John Whittle, *The Organs and Organists of St. Mary's Church Nottingham* (Rylands Press, 1993) for further details of the 'restorations'. Page 20 of this includes a description of the Snetzler pipework which tallies well with what remains in the organ in St Andrew's church, though it also refers to a mysterious pedal 'Open Diapason of fine metal' previously in the organ; are they Buckingham's 1839 'Dragonetti' basses?
[5] According to Peter Price, the organ's present curator, who kindly permitted a detailed examination of the original pipework.

91 Birmingham, St Martin's church
(1777–8)
and Nottingham, Castle Gate chapel

B 208/183

It appears that Snetzler worked in two churches in Birmingham at this time, and that there is confusion in the sources as a result. (See also no. 92).

Buckingham records work at St Martin's; he says 'I think in 1778'. There was work by the Englands in 1805 at St Philip's [1] costing 400 guineas. Buckingham must therefore be right in thinking that Elliot worked at St Martin's c1823, when the Snetzler parts came to Castle Gate chapel, Nottingham. (Elliot provided a new organ at Christ Church, Birmingham, in 1815, made by Buckingham [2]. It is unlikely that Elliot replaced England's work so soon.)

[1] Andrew Freeman, 'Two Organ Builders of Note: the Englands' (TO 84/170).
[2] B 211/80–1.

92 Birmingham, St Philip's church
   (1777)

F 47

Andrew Freeman, writing of 'Birmingham Cathedral' (in Snetzler's time, the church of St Philip) suggests that 'Snetzler restored and enlarged this organ at a cost of £100', and he refers to TO 35/137 and a Vestry record of the parish church of St Philip, 17 April 1777.

93 Merevale, Warwickshire, St Mary's church
   (1777)

Another Midlands organ, no doubt delivered at the same period as the work in Birmingham and Nottingham. It is a substantial chamber organ of the 'wreathed-oval' type, almost certainly made for Merevale Hall, the home (near Atherstone) of the Dugdale family, descendants of the famous chronicler. An organ made by James Bishop was supplied to the Hall in 1836, [1] and Snetzler's instrument presumably came to the church then. The mahogany case has lost its 'broken' pediment, and some carvings, its roof, its doors, and two dummy pipes of the 'oval'; the kneeboard also appears to have been replaced, probably when the original wind system was also replaced by a compensated double–rise horizontal reservoir with feeders. The key action has been remade, and at some time the compass reduced to C in the bass. A twenty–note Bourdon with small pedalboard was added. The stop–knobs are not original, but probably of the 1830s.
   The original stop–list appears to have been:

(*G', A'–e'''*): OD (sc: *c*, grooved to SD or with separate bass), SD [?*b* up to *B*/tr], Dul (sc: *c*, bass from SD), Pr, Fl, 12, 15, Ses b/Cor tr III, Crm (sc: *c'*)

The organ was renovated by Hill, Norman & Beard Ltd in 1973, and the present *C*–compass keyboard (with rosewood naturals and 'skunk–tail' sharps) dates from then. There are now no *G'–B'* pipes, and the treble Cornet is of two ranks, partly recomposed. The wind–pressure is 2½". A complete restoration to its original state would be possible, by analogy with similar extant chamber organs.
   Alan Barnes's interest in this organ was the reason for the research that led to his thesis, and ultimately to the writing of this book.

[1] Laurence Elvin, *Bishop and Son, Organ Builders* (Lincoln, 1984), pp. 58–9.

*

94 Lightcliffe, Halifax, Yorkshire, the 'Old Chapel' (?c1765–70 and 1787)

The chapel was built in 1529 as a chapel–of–ease to Halifax parish church; in 1775 a new Georgian structure replaced it, using timber specially shipped from the Baltic. Into it was moved in July 1787 an organ by Snetzler, which 'appears from the excellence and finish of its mahogany case to have been first built for a gentleman's mansion', [1] given by William Priestley. [2] The Priestley family of New House, Lightcliffe, and other families were introduced to good church music by the Moravians who in about 1748 settled briefly at Smith House, Lightcliffe, before moving on to Fulneck nearer to Leeds. One of these families included John Walker, treasurer to the Halifax Organ Trustees, and another included John Caygill, who died in 1787. [1]

A photograph of the organ [3] shows the organ and its tall rear extension in the church gallery before its complete destruction by vandals in 1970; the case has the 'normal' three compartment front. The local connection with the Moravians would at least partially explain Snetzler's work at Halifax. We suggest, in default of any definite evidence, that the Lightcliffe organ may have been made and delivered about the time of the Halifax Parish Church organ, and that it was 'completed by his successors, Okeman [sic] and Nutt' [1] in the 'Old Chapel' (so called by Turner because a new Victorian church was built in the 1870s). A seating plan for an orchestra, [4] apparently made in conjunction with the work in 1787, shows the organ with the rear extension. We also suggest that the figure '13' written on the plan (q.v.) may refer to thirteen pedal pipes added when the organ was installed.

Turner, in 1908, related the circumstances of the organ's inauguration, and a version of its stop–list which seems to be based on the *Halifax Guardian* notes:

> The organ was given in 1787 by William Priestley, Esq. It was contracted for by Snetzler, and finished by Okemann [sic] and Nutt, his successors, in July 1787, and was opened the next month, August 24th, when "Messiah" was performed, Mr. Stopford presiding at the organ, and a concerto performed by Mr. Buckley, of Manchester, between the acts ... It has an excellent mahogany case, gilt pipes in front, and is protected by glass doors. There are five drawknobs each side [of] the keys, from GG to F, omitting GG sharp.
>
> On the left there are – blank, principal bass, flute, stopped diapason, open diapason ['bass', *Halifax Guardian*]; on the right – open diapason (wood, treble, substituted for a cornet), fifteenth, principal, open diapason (metal, treble), oboe to middle C. The organ has a manual, seven stops, and 350 pipes ... For entertaining the visitors ordinaries were prepared at ... Mr. Robertshaw's, White Swan, near Hipperholme ...

The 'Mr. Robertshaw' of the second paragraph must surely be of the same family as 'Robertshaw, Organist, Lightcliffe, Halifax' who advertised in *Musical Opinion* of July 1903 a Snetzler organ (possibly this one) for sale, with '1 manual, 7 stops', evidently without success. [5] The 1869/1908 stop–list would seem to be a remaking of a conventional chamber organ stoplist of Snetzler's 'middle period' of work, thus:

> (*G', A'–f '''*): OD (w, sc: *c*?), SD, Pr (b/tr), Fl, 15, Ses b [removed, so 'blank']/Cor tr [removed; wooden Open Diapason installed in its place], Hb (sc: *c'*) [in a high swell–box just visible in the *The Organ Yearbook* photograph, whose conveyances are mentioned by the *Guardian* writer]

The organ Turner described in 1908 would have contained 347 pipes, including the thirteen pedal pipes.

[1] 'History of organs in the parish of Halifax (No. 8)', *Halifax Guardian*, 1869.
[2] T. Horsfall Turner, *Lightcliffe Old Chapel* (privately published, 1908).
[3] *The Organ Yearbook*, no. 7 (1976), p. 117.
[4] Lyndesay Langwill and Noel Boston, *Church and Chamber Barrel Organs* (Edinburgh, 2nd edn 1970), p. 125, Plate 33.
[5] F 88.

95 Rotherham, Yorkshire, All Saints' church (1773–7)

S III/60; HR 20; F 48

The organ, with an oak double–storeyed case in the 'Gothick taste' after the manner of that at Hillsborough (no. 86), was installed on a new gallery in a position similar to that at Ludlow (no. 63); that is, under the eastern arch of the central tower, facing westwards into the nave. The organist, Mr David Lawton, opened it on St Thomas the Apostle's Day, 21 December 1777, when he played the Hundredth Psalm.

The costs of the whole operation are preserved:

MEMORANDA OF THE ORGAN IN ROTHERHAM CHURCH

	£	s	d
Built by Mr. Snetzler	420	0	0
Of packing boards	21	0	0
Carriage of the organ	31	10	0
Organ galleries erected	156	12	2
Organ gallery door, stairs and stool, ladder, benches, shelves and cupboard	2	18	3
Iron work, and curtain rods for organ gallery	10	10	0
Paid Nr. Bradford for moreen curtains and making	3	5	7
Bags and curtains of Miss Bingley	–	14	10
Two sconces and a pair of snuffers	–	8	0
Sam Heathcote for drawing plans, &c.	–	10	6
Treats, given to Mr. Snetzler, and to Mr. Lawton on his election as organist, and paid to the Court of York for the view Faculty	30	11	7
Total	£678	0	11

['moreen' is stout corded material]

Of this total, £615. 2s. 6d. was subscribed in 1774 (the list of subscribers is preserved); the organist's salary was fixed at £20 per annum.

The original stop-list was:

Great (*G', A', C, D–e'''*): OD, OD, SD, Pr, 12, 15, 17, Ses [b/tr?] Cor (sc: *c'* [mounted?]), Tpt
Choir (*G', A', C, D–e'''*): SD, Pr, Fl, Bn
Swell (*g–e'''*): OD, SD, Pr, Cor, Tpt, Hb

The original console and the layout of the stops are still to be seen (see p. 199); the stop-knobs and natural keys are of blackwood, and the sharps are of bone or ivory. In about 1843, the gallery was removed and the organ was placed in the north transept, facing southwards. Around this time, the compass of the Great and Choir was altered by removing the *G'* pipes and keys, and – if the temperament allowed – by making the *A'* pipes sound *C♯*. Gray & Davison also added a Choir Dulciana (or substituted this for the Bassoon?) and added pedals and an Open Diapason 16' from *C'–d'* (27 notes), and couplers (Swell and Great coupled, Choir to Pedals, Choir to Great, Great to Pedals?).[1] A new pedalboard was installed in 1873, and the organ was shortly afterwards put into storage while the church fabric was 'restored'. When the organ was set up again by Brindley & Foster of Sheffield in the north chapel, it was retuned to equal temperament; no doubt it had an actual *C♯* by then.

The case at Rotherham parish church

The organ was rebuilt 1889–90 with two new soundboards with an extended treble compass, and a full-compass Swell, by Abbott & Smith of Leeds, under the supervision of Dr. E. J. Hopkins. All the then-surviving Snetzler pipework was reused (only the Choir Bassoon had entirely disappeared), and this pipework was preserved when additions were made in 1905 by Gray & Davison.

The organ was rebuilt in 1972, when the Great and Swell pipework of an England/Renn organ from Tiviotdale Methodist Church, Stockport, supplanted the Snetzler/Abbott & Smith material and the still-surviving Cornet. A new Choir division was made from, mostly, the Snetzler Great chorus (Open Diapason, Stopped Diapason, Principal, Flute, Twelfth, Fifteenth, Seventeenth, Nineteenth

[?] and Trumpet), and the remaining Snetzler materials were stored on top of the swell–box.

[1] Reginald Whitworth, 'The Snetzler Organ in the Parish Church of Rotherham' (TO 25/19).

96 Alphamstone, Suffolk, parish church
(older organ, installed in Sudbury, St Peter's church, in 1778)

S II/270

Sperling refers to an organ placed in 'Sudbury' in 1841:

> Snetzler 1750. Formerly in St. Peter's Church. Great Organ FF short octaves to E. Swell to mid C. Placed here [*sc.* in St Gregory's church] in 1841.

He gives a stoplist:

> Great: OD, SD, Pr, Fl to mid C, 12, 15, Ses [b?], Cor [tr?], Tpt
> Swell: OD, SD, Pr, Tpt, Hb

Sperling's dating, though vague, is indicative of an organ by Snetzler with an 'early' middle–C compass Swell as in the Fulneck organ of 1748. Sperling also dates the organ more precisely '8 Oct 1778', and this date is that of the Faculty discovered by Betty Matthews: [1]

> 7 October 1778. Sudbury St Peter. Gallery already erected. Permission for organ (already built) 9 foot from north to south [the organ's width]. Depth east to west 6 feet. Height about 18 foot.

The later history of the organ, after it was moved to St Gregory's church in 1841, was related in a booklet published in 1911: [2]

> In the early sixties, an organ, locally known as 'Old Betsy', stood in St. Gregory's Church, having been removed from St. Peter's. This organ consisted of a Great Organ and a Choir [*sic*] Organ, having black naturals and white sharps, and was sold for £20 to the authorities at Alphamstone Church, eventually coming to grief and being disposed of by Mr. George Buttle of that parish.

[1] Betty Matthews, 'George Pike England in Norwich' (TO 256/83).
[2] *St. Peter's Church, 1484–1911, the Fabric and Organs* (privately published, 1911), p. 24.

97 London or Whitehaven, Cumberland, Sir James Lowther (c1777)

B 212/120–1

The letter written by Snetzler in Nottingham has already been adduced (no. 90) as proof of his work there in June 1777. It was written to Christopher Pinchbeck concerning work for Sir James Lowther and Lord Bute:

> Nottingham June 5th 1777
>
> Sir
>
> It is reather somewhat unlucky, Ld Bute & Sr. James Lowther shoud wanted my afsistance so soon affter I left London, however Mr Jones will do what is to be done very well. I think the Bellowes not falling & the Shiffting movement not working, is occasiond by the Dampnifs of the room, & though I have mostly done here, I shall not be able to return to London this 5 or Six weeks, as I must go further downwds no doubt Mr Jones will tacke care, to do it well. this great Machine I set up here, tackes up all all my attention & time, so that I hope you will excuse my Short Scrawl, and believe me to be
>
> Sir,
>
> your very Sincere & Humble
>
> Servent
>
> P.S. when you see Mr Jones
> please to tell him, he will   John Snetzler
> hear very soon from me

In the Lowther of Whitehaven family archives in Carlisle, there are further letters that refer to the barrel organ made for the family. This Buckingham also saw in 1830, after alterations had been made to it by Ward of York:

The Rt Honble the Earl of Lonsdale, Lowther Castle, Westmorland—This Organ plays Finger and Barrel has one set of Keys from GG long octaves to F in alt. The Barrel is from GG short octaves to F in alt. A piano movement that takes off the Prinl 15 and Sexqualtera.

Open Diapason to G of Metal lower Octave Wood	58
Stop Diapason with Metal treble	58
Dulciana to G communicated to the Op Diapn bafs	47
Principal through of Metal	58
Harmonica is Flute bafs and the Treble is a Principal of wood a large scale	58
Celestina a Dulciana Principal of Metal	58
Fifteenth	58
Sexqualtera 3 Ranks	174
Total	569

There is Seven Barrels short Octaves or 55 keys each barrel 4ft. 6¼in. long and 1ft. 5in. diameter. This Organ was made by Mr. Alex Cummins of London short octaves but the Pipes was made and voised by Snetzler and the Barrels played by Machinery. Mr. Ward of York has made it in 1828 long octaves and added the lower octave to the Open Diapason of wood, taken away the Machine and made the Barrels play by a hand winder alone also new Horizontal Bellows with double feeders and the Harmonica treble in the room of the Flute with other alterations. In a new Wainscott Gothic Case 13ft. high, 10ft. 2in. wide, 4ft. 9in. deep, no gilt pipes in front only crimson cloth and also the ends.

Nottingham June 5: 1777

Sir

It is reather somewhat unlucky, Ld Buk & Sr James Lowther shoud wanted my assistance so soon after I left London, however Mr Jones will do what is to be done very well, I think the Bellowes not falling & the shifting movement not working, is occasiond by the dampness of the room, though I have mostly done here, I shall not be able to return to London this 5 or six weeks, as I must go further down—no doubt Mr Jones will take care, to do it well this great Machine I set up here, takes up all all my attention & time so that I hope you will excuse my short scrawl, and believe me to be

Sir

your very Sincere & Humble
Servent

John Snetzler

S.S. when you see Mr Jones
please to tell him, he will
hear very soon from me

Letter from Snetzler to Pinchbeck, 5 June 1777

177

Ward had apparently moved one of the original Snetzler ranks into another organ:

> The Open Diapason to gamut G of metal the lower octave is a Flute bafs. The Flute treble is Snetzler's make and appears to me to have been taken out of the large Organ of Cummins make and the Harmonica put in its room. Who was the original maker I cannot tell but it has been repaired by Mr. Ward of York he has made new horizontal Bellows etc it is a very poor instrument. It stands in a recefs in Lady Lonsdale's sitting room with a new Waincott Gothic case front doors with wire work pannels and silk behind 10ft. high, 7ft. wide, 3ft. 4in. deep. Lowther Castle, 2 September 1830. A.B.

It would appear that the machinery affected by dampness was the shifting movement (worked by the barrel–turning machinery) which would need to be quite free of unnecessary friction. The original bellows would also of course need to fall smoothly under their own weights whether operated by machinery or not.

Of the surviving fragmentary correspondence between Pinchbeck, Snetzler and Lowther, the earliest letter is that from Pinchbeck of Cockspur Street, London (the same street as that in which Bernard Smith had resided, near St James's Palace), to Lord Lowther, dated 9 September 1771. Pinchbeck was the son of a clever maker of automata and the inventor of the 'Pinchbeck Alloy' or 'London Metal', a brass which closely resembled gold.

> May it Pleafe your Honour
> Sir
> I am extreemly Sorry I had not the Pleafure of Seeing you in town when you were so Good as to Call at my Shop – Take the liberty agreable to your Kind direction to my Daughter to write to and intreat you would Favour me with a Draught on your Banker for Three Hundred Pounds, payable to me or Order, and for the better security from Hazards at Seven days after Sight. Your Early Compliance with this requeft will be of great Service to me at this time – who am with the Greatest Respect Your Honours moft Humble and Obedt. Sert.
> Chrisftr. Pinchbeck
>
> P.S. I have already three Barrells Sett two ready for Setting – and should be glad to know how many more you Choofe I should Putt in hand – as the Longer they are made before they are Sett the Better – and hope you will determine upon what Mufick your Honour will next have Sett.

The implication of this is that Pinchbeck was the retailer of the organ and supplied barrels from time to time as required.

About two years later, Pinchbeck wrote to Lord Lowther in some concern:

> May it Pleasfe Your Honour
> Being greatly apprehenfive from not receiving any anfwer to a Letter which I wrote to you on Saturday the 6th inft, with one from Mr Langshaw to me inclof'd in mine – that they have mifcaryed, And as two of your Barrels have been packt up and ready to be Sent away for this week paft – I herein take the Liberty to Send your Honour a Copy of thefe two Letters, and begg to know how you would have me proceed

Copy of My Letter 6th Novr
Hond. Sir
In Obedience to your Direction by Mr Wood on the 19th Ult, I prepared the two Barrells to be Sent away, and have Either been or Sent almoft Every Day since to Toppings Wharf below London bridge, to know if any Veffel was come in to return soon to Lancafter. But none being as yet arrived and haveing two days Agoe Rec'd the inclofed from Mr Langshaw, by which your Honour will see how very uncertain the Bringing them by Sea is (this Barrel having been near two months on Board) and the great Damage they may be Liable to receive from Damps by laying so Long time and by being beat about by Storms & I therefore Sir having on inquiry found that there are Broad Wheel'd Waggons which go Conftantly to Lancaster every 10 or 12 days in which I am opinion if the Barrells are well packt in Stronger Cafes and Well Bedded in the Waggon of which I shall take care, it would be much better to Send them by Land than by Sea on every Account except the Expence which is 14 shillings pr Hundred[-weight.] Each Barrel and Cafe will Weigh about one Hundred & a half – This Opinion I have Mention'd to Lord Bute who thinks it will be the Beft way, as then you will be at some Certainty of haveing your Barrells, there will be some additional Contrivance neceffary in the Packing of which I shall take the Greatest Care and the Moment your Honour favours me with [your] determination I shall Order Cafes and send them away directly [.] I herein send you the List of the Musick you have Chofe, and sh[ould] be Glad to know which you would have on thefe two Barrels, and which on the firft of the two as your Honour by their being brought by Land need not now Stay till both are done – I remain your Honours much Oblig'd and moft Obedt. Sert – Chriftr. Pinchbeck

It appears that the music was arranged and pinned by John Langshaw, the organist of Lancaster Parish Church (as he was described by Buckingham), whose letter of 29 October 1773 to Pinchbeck, sent on to the Earl, did not in fact miscarry, as it is still in the Lowther family archives:

My dear Friend,
I am afraid you will be uneasy that you have not got the Barrel before now. I send this to let you know that no Ships has gone out these six weeks from Lancaster, owing to the Wind being against them, about a fortnight ago the Vefsel with our barrel got out with a little favourable wind, but it blew her back in a few days after, she lies about 30 miles from me, and bad to get to, or I wou'd send this second barrel, I finished it last monday but one, it wou'd be three days in going to the other barrel, in which time the ship may be gone, therefore I shall send it by the first ship to Liverpool, & there are ships often going to London, & by going to Liverpool there will need no land carriage.

I hope they will get safe, the Musick of these two barrels has a better effect than any I have set lately.

I hope this will find you all well. I shall now go to writing my Lords Musick, from your most obledt. Servt.
Jno. Langshaw

The suggested music was copied by Pinchbeck to the Earl thus:

> Meffiah
> I know that my redeemer liveth
> The Trumpets shall Sound
> Let us Break the Bands
> [?Hallelujah] Chorus/
> Father of Heaven – Jud: Mac
> So shall the Lute & Harp awake – Ditto
> The March/
> Your charms to Ruin leed the way – Sampfn
> Chorus of Angels   [–] Deborah
> Bacchus ever fair & Young – Alex: Feaft
> War he Sung is Toil & Trouble – Ditto
> March in the Occafsional Oratorio
>
> Meffiah
> Comfort you my People
> Every Valley
> Since by man Came Death by   }
> man came alfo the Reforection   }
> for as in Adam all Die even so in   }
> Chrift and the Glory of the Lord   }
>
> Judas Maccabeus
> Pious Orgeis
> Arm Arm ye Brave
> Difdainfull of Danger
> Sound an Alarm   a fine Barrell/
> 2d Coro: } Let Judgment and Juftice
> Anthem   }   Halleluja
> 1st Coro: } Zadrock the Preift
> Anthem   } and all the People rejoice
>   God Save the King

A further letter, apparently a postscript from Pinchbeck, is added to the music list, and sent with his copies of his own and Langshaw's letters:

> Sir
> My Lords Barrell mention'd before is not yet arriv'd but Still at Sea – And his Lordfhip who I had the Honour of Seeing Yesterday [Bute?] advifed me to Send one of your Barrels directly to Mr Langshaw (which I have done this morning) that he may See by it how to pack up that Other Barrel of My Lords which he had finifht by him – and which by a Letter Rec'd from him the 16th [the one from Langshaw above] he informs me he has not nor Shall not send by Sea at all – but by Land when he receives Your Honours. I have prefumed to Send you a part of Mr Langfhaws laft Letter for your Honours Confideration as his Opinion therein about the Mufick moft intirely Coincides with Mine in regard to the Species of Mufick moft Proper

to show how much Such a Machine may exceed the Beft Performer – This
I hope you will Pardon – and favour me with your immediate Commands
who am moft Devoted Hum: Sert
Chriftr. Pinchbeck

It would seem from the correspondence that the organ was at this time in
Lowther's London house, or Pinchbeck would have waited longer for a reply from
Westmorland, and instructed Langshaw to send the completed barrels thither; it
may well be that the new 'Gothic' cases were made by Ward so that they could be
fitted into the Lowther Castle rooms. Buckingham notes that there were seven
barrels in total; from the letters it would seem that the organ was supplied in
1771, with the further barrels in 1774. However, the letter of 1777 is the only
documentary evidence for Snetzler's actual involvement in the project, though it
is very likely that he made pipework and perhaps some mechanisms for the organ.

98 Luton Hoo, Bedfordshire, the Earl of Bute
(*c*1777, or earlier?)

Robert Adam (as designer), Christopher Pinchbeck (mechanism and clockwork),
John Snetzler (pipework and actions), John Langshaw (organist and mechanic, and
pinner of the barrels), and Handel's amanuensis J. C. Smith, were all involved in
the construction of the first barrel organ for the Earl's new house at Luton Park
(or Hoo). [1] Its 'frontispiece' (see the sketch dated 1763, p. 48) might also be a
prototype of the 'wreathed–oval' Snetzler cases which made their first appearance
in the early 1760s, not long after the death of Handel.

Langshaw pinned the barrels to music arranged from Handel by Smith 'with so
much delicacy and taste, as to convey a warm idea of the impression which the
hand gives on the instrument'. According to Fétis, [2] Langshaw was employed by
the Earl for more than a dozen years in perfecting the barrels. In 1772 he became
the organist at Lancaster; he died in 1798. However, it proved cumbersome and
awkward to wind up the driving mechanism and to change the barrels of the organ
as made and installed, so Alexander Cumming was asked to make suggestions as
to how the organ might be improved. His suggestions could not be incorporated in
this organ, but they were employed in an organ made in 1787 for the Earl at High
Cliff, near Christchurch, Hampshire. One might presume that Cumming's
improvements were also incorporated in the organ for the Earl of Lowther.

It is not known what stops Snetzler supplied for the Luton Park organ
(destroyed by fire in 1843), but the later (1787) Bute organ, which was broadly
similar, contained a complete chorus and some solo stops thus:

OD (b/tr), SD (b/tr), Dul, 'Violino', Pr (b/tr), Fl, 15, Ses (b/tr), Cor (tr), Tpt (b/tr)

[1] Arthur Ord–Hume, *The Barrel Organ* (Barnes/Allen & Unwin, 1978), pp. 88–90.
[2] op. cit., p. 89, quoting François–Joseph Fétis, *Biographie Universelle des Musiciens*
(Brussels, 1835–44).

99 Cobham Hall, Kent, the Gilt Hall
(1778–9)

W 104 (8)

The large chamber organ, made for the Earl of Darnley's seat near Rochester, is labelled and dated in each of the three sections of soundboards (the Great soundboard is divided internally) *John Snetzler Londini fecit 1778*. The 'Gilt Hall' or Music Room in which the organ stands was previously the banqueting hall; it was decorated by William Chambers with an elaborate ceiling and panels of trophies of musical instruments, and two shallow galleries were installed. The organ was placed in an alcove opening onto the north gallery in 1779. [1] At the same time, Samuel Green appears to have supplied a small chamber organ (now in Hastingleigh church, Kent) dated on the C key 'Oct 29 1778'. This was eventually placed in the 'Chapel', and was sold along with many other effects in about 1962. Both organs had been offered for sale in 1957; the larger organ remains the property of the Department of the Environment.

The two uniquely preserved wedge–bellows (not feeders; there is no reservoir) are raised by detacheable handles placed in slots usually concealed behind sliding panels behind the organ alcove, at the head of an adjacent staircase. The swell–box is placed behind the Great soundboards, and retains its sliding–shutter front with a 'nag's head' action.

The original stop–list seems from internal evidence to have been:

> Great (*G'*, *A'–e'''*): OD [open to C in metal; four lowest notes from SD with
> helpers], SD [metal chimney flutes from *c'* up], Pr, 12, 15, Ses III,
> [17–19–22/15–17–19 at *g♯*/ 12–15–17 at *g♯'*], Cor IV (sc: *c'* [now a
> substituted Clarabella]), Tpt (b/tr [now a Dulciana from *c*])
> Swell (*f–e'''*): OD, SD, Pr, Hb

There is now a pedalboard of twenty notes (*G'*, *A'–d*) which controls 'pull–downs' with seven additional unoriginal large open wooden pipes in the bass winded from a ventil controlled by the Great Open Diapason stop action. This pedalboard is later work, but an aperture in the kneeboard above it suggests that perhaps there was originally a pedalboard of the 'box' type. The keyboards are of blackwood with ivory–plated sharps; there are small nineteenth–century labels above the blackwood stop–knobs. The shifting movement (to additional sliders) cuts off all stops except the Open and Stopped Diapasons on the Great; this may originally have been fitted with a reversing action (see p. 217; for a discussion of the layout of the stop–knobs, see p. 198–9).

The front pipes are taken from the Open Diapason from 6' *F♯* upwards; the six pipes in the side flats and seventeen of the twenty–five pipes in the 'oval' speak.

Apart from the addition of tuning slides and a raising of the pitch of the organ, the pipework is unaltered and is complete except for the Trumpet and Cornet. The key and stop actions and wind systems are virtually as originally made, but an electric blower has been arranged to raise one of the bellows. It would seem that

The Gilt Hall, Cobham Hall

a 14" step about 18" behind the case-front, which brings the bellows very near the key and stop actions, has effectively prevented later substitution of them by an horizontal reservoir.

[1] John M. Robinson, *The Wyatts, an Architectural Dynasty* (O. U. P., 1979), p. 240.

100 Locko Park, Derbyshire, the chapel
(1779)

W 108 (17)

The 'wreathed-oval' chamber organ (with sticker–backfall action) is labelled *John Snetzler fecit Londini 1779* and is now in the chapel of the house. The gilt metal dummies are arranged 3–17–3; doors which enclosed these are now missing, as are parts of the roof and casework sides. The present stop-list comprises:

> (*G', A', C, D–f '''*): SD ['Stopped Diaphason'; W], Dul [sc: *c*], Pr, Fl ['Stopped Flute'; W], Fifteenth (b/tr)

This is surprising. If the Dulciana is original, and there is no Open Diapason, the organ represents a shift from the previous pattern. (Probably the Dulciana is a later insertion, or it is the Open Diapason softened.) A Gamba (dated 1893) had replaced a divided rank, but it is not clear what that was. As there is a disconnected shifting movement (originally affecting the Principal also), it was probably a Fifteenth or (more likely) a small Sesquialtera/Cornet. In 1992, its pipes were 'converted' to provide a Fifteenth on these divided sliders during a general overhaul of the organ. At the same time, an electric blower was added. The lowest pipes still sound the 'apparent' pitches (*B', C, C♯*) of the lowest notes of the short-octave keyboard; tuning slides were fitted to the 'low-pitch' but not meantone-tuned pipework.

The keyboard is of ivory with ebony sharps; this style would be usual for organs of this late date. The stop-knobs are original, but not their labels. The original blowing pedal is disused; the organ can be blown by a later wooden pedal. The wind pressure is 2½".

101 Stevenage, Hertfordshire, Holy Trinity church
(1780)

S III/57; HR 17; F 50

According to notes by Andrew Freeman and Bernard Edmonds, an organ made by Snetzler in 1780 (probably for Scarborough parish church, since this is the only Snetzler organ so far recorded as being made in that year) was taken by Hill & Son in part-exchange for a new one in 1869 and rebuilt by that firm 1890–91 in

Woodhill church, near Hatfield, Hertfordshire. The Great soundboard, now used for a 54–note compass keyboard with six stops, is labelled *John Snetzler fecit Londini 1780*.

The organ was moved to Stevenage in 1977, and an examination of the organ then indicated that a complete Flute, and parts of a Sesquialtra (used as a Fifteenth) and Open and Stopped Diapasons are still extant.

102 Belfast, Clarence Place Hall
(1781)

HR 28; F 51

The church of St Anne, Belfast, was built at the expense of the Earl of Donegal, and was opened in 1776. It has been suggested that he knew about the organ made for his neighbour, the Earl of Hillsborough (no. 86), [1] so that Snetzler was commissioned to make the new organ for the church. It was officially opened on Sunday 24 June 1781 (the Nativity of St John the Baptist) in the presence of the sovereign and of the dignitaries of several Masonic Lodges. [2] The organ was placed on a high gallery at the west end of the church; it was enthusiastically described in a letter written by a former organist, Isaac Nicholl, to the then organist of Downpatrick Cathedral in 1914, thus:

> In reply to your letter, I have much pleasure in giving you all the particulars I know about St. Anne's old organ. I was organist for thirty years. I was appointed 1873, resigned 1903. The following is a description of the old Snetzler organ as I found it in 1873. Two keyboards: top keyboard "great", lower keyboard, "swell"; large keys *black*, small keys very dirty yellowish *white*. Square drawstop rods, names altogether obliterated off the knobs. Stops acted only on half the keyboard, so that when you drew a stop on the right–hand side you had to draw a corresponding stop on the left–hand side. It was a G organ: lowest note on the manuals and pedals, G; next note, instead of being G sharp was A; next note, C.

GREAT ORGAN	SWELL ORGAN
1 Open diapason	1 Open diapason
2 Small open diapason to tenor C	2 Stopped diapason
3 Stopped diapason	3 Flute
4 Clarabella to middle C	4 Principal
5 Principal	5 Oboe
6 Twelfth	
7 Fifteenth	
8 Sesquialtera, 3 ranks	PEDAL ORGAN
	1 16ft.

The great organ was much as Snetzler left it, – of exquisite beauty, fulness, and richness of tone. The full organ *blended* to absolute perfection, forming one grand 8ft. tone. I am not sure the Swell was Snetzler's work.

I have a suspicion that it was an afterthought, but I cannot tell. The wind pressure was 2½ in., – metal *very heavy* and *soft*; wood pipes most *exquisitely made*.

It would seem that the organ was of the short–octave type; the Clarabella may well have supplanted a Cornet. One wonders if the organ was in fact older, with a Swell added in 1781. Nicholl goes on to relate its subsequent history:

> In 1876 Messrs. Hill, London, thoroughly overhauled the organ, putting in new action, adding some stops, and carefully preserving the old case. About 15 years afterwards it was removed to a different part of the church by Conacher & Co., Huddersfield. A tremulant was added. It was re-erected in the present cathedral [of Belfast] by Messrs. Evans & Barr, and finally was removed to Clarence Place (Ch. of E.) Y. M. C. A. Hall, where it now stands, by the same firm. The original case has been preserved: it is of black mahogany.

Hill's rebuilding was done at the expense of Mr John Ferguson, who insisted on the retention of the case, but the original keyboards were then replaced.

The organ was moved by Conacher in 1886, as the *Belfast Telegraph* [3] relates:

> In 1886 it was decided the organ should be moved down from its upper loft at the West end of the church to the West gallery, then occupied by what was known as the Marquis's pew, and this work was carried out by Messrs. Conacher. We read in the *Minute Book* that the church was re-opened after these repairs on the 10th October 1886. Here the organ remained until 27th December 1903, when it was played for the last service held in the old church.

It was erected in the cathedral in a gallery at the east end of the north aisle by Evans & Barr. It remained there only until 1907, when it was purchased by the Revd Joseph Stewart, who presented it to the Clarence Place Hall. It was sold in 1918 to Evans & Barr, who are reported to have scrapped it.

[1] *Belfast Telegraph*, 23 November 1927.
[2] *Belfast Newsletter*, 24 October 1899.
[3] loc. cit.

103 London, Haggerston parish church
   ## (1781)

F 52

Andrew Freeman reports that the archives of St George's chapel, Windsor, note that on 10 August 1781 it was 'Ordered that a compleat swell be put to the organ agreeable to the Proposals given in by John Snetzler wherein he agrees to put the same up for a Sum not exceeding Sixty pounds'.

Snetzler had been called to this organ twenty years before, as it appears from the Windsor archives (Chapter Acts 1743–73 VI B. 7.24, July 1761) that it was then 'Ordered that Mr. Snetzler do inspect and do what is necessary to the organ.

One might suppose that he looked after this organ; it is very near to Eton College, whose chapel organ he maintained for nearly thirty-five years (no. 14). The Windsor organ was replaced by Green's in 1790, and was removed to Haggerston, where it was destroyed during the Second World War.

104 near Zürich (Switzerland), private owner (1782)

Snetzler's last-dated extant organ was found in 1992, dismantled and stored in Switzerland. It has required very little restoration beyond some re-leathering of the wind system and re-hinging of the parchment-hung keys. In almost all respects it is structurally the same as his earliest organs; it was almost certainly made by Snetzler during his first 'retirement' visit to Switzerland. The present restorers comment on its 'ganz hoher handwerklicher Qualität' and say that 'Die Pfeifen sind handwerklich sehr schön gearbeit'. All about the organ seems to confirm what might otherwise have only been suspected: that Snetzler was essentially a small-scale perfectionist craftsman before the order for the large organ at King's Lynn was the spur to a change in his mode of work into one of supervising the making of 'normal' church organs of all sizes. Its stop-list is as follows:

(*C–e'''*): 'Gedeckt', Dul (sc: *c*; lowest octave from the 'Gedeckt'), Fl

The two flutes are made of pine and oak (not of pear); the pipes of the 'Gedeckt' are marked 'Diap'; its basses are of 'tanne' with oak caps (with windways in the caps), and entirely of oak from *c''* upwards. Similarly, the Flute is entirely of oak from *c'* up. Snetzler's reversion to a *C*-compass will be noted.

The natural keys are of blackwood, and the sharps are plated with ivory. The key action is a simple pin action, apparently to pallets immediately under the keys, with the first four notes of the 'sharp' side rollered to the treble. In all respects — the parchment-covered sponselled underside of the grooves, under-slider leather, brass springs, with original pallet leathering in good condition — the soundboard is typical of Snetzler's work from the earliest times. The wind system consists of the usual opposed wedge-reservoir and feeder, and the stop action consists of squares operating the sliders directly from the stop-traces.

The casework, illustrated overleaf, is of simple framed-panel construction, painted grey-olive in the local style of simple furniture; the 'front' is a frame with material stretched across it.

It seems possible that the pipes of the Dulciana may not have been retuned, and that the organ's original pitch (and temperament?) has been preserved in them.

The 1782 Snetzler organ near Zürich

*

105 Durham, Lord Barrington
(undated)

B 205/9

Buckingham is the sole authority for this chamber organ, which he describes in August 1823 thus:

> The Rt. Honbl. Lord Barrington Durham
> An Organ with one set of Keys from GG long octaves to F in alt
> A General Swell on the top of the Organ and a piano movement
>
> Consist of the following Stops
>
> | | |
> |---|---:|
> | Open Diapason from m/C | 30 |
> | Stop Diapason | 58 |
> | Principal bafs and treble of metal through | 58 |
> | Flute | 58 |
> | Fifteenth | 58 |
> | Sexquialtera bafs 2 ranks.. | 56 |
> | Cornet treble 2 ranks | ..60 |
> | Total .. | 378 |
>
> In a Mahogany Case with gilt pipes in front and front doors with pannels and pediment cornish 9 ft 2 in high 4 ft 8 in wide 2 ft 10¼ in deep
> Made by John Snetzler of London
> The Bellows are New Horizontal with two folds
> Durham August 1823   A B

106 Southwell, Nottinghamshire, Miss Bristoe
(undated, but possibly 1769)

B 206/57

L. S. Barnard, the transcriber of the Notebook of Alexander Buckingham, reports only the outline of his entry concerning the instrument in Miss Bristoe's house. It was apparently thought by Buckingham to be a Snetzler organ with four stops:

OD, SD, Dul, Dulciana Principal

It was given new horizontal 'bellows' in 1820. Perhaps the organ was supplied at or about the time when (in 1765) Snetzler worked at Southwell Minster (no. 64).

There is the possibility that this is the organ included in the sale of Willingham House, home of the Boucheret family for several generations, near Market Rasen, described in the catalogue [1] as 'a fine chamber organ containing one manual of 4½ octaves, 4 stops & about 200 pipes' with 'a blowing pedal, swell pedal, and a pedal for shutting off the 4' stop'. The stops were not labelled, but 'may be described as Open Diapason, Stopped Diapason, Dulciana and Principal'. The organ was 'signed' and dated 1769.

The house was purchased by a Captain Barnes, and then a Mr. Wright. The organ's present location is unknown.

A very similar organ, at the other end of the Fosse Way, was advertised in *The Bath Chronicle* for 26 November 1789: [2]

> E. Ashman, No 15 Beaufort Square tunes and repairs Harpsichords ... also to be sold a very good Double Harpsichord, and a Chamber Organ by Snetzler in a very good mahogany case, and has the following [:] stopt, [Open] Diapason, Principal and Flute, and is fit for any drawing room. – May be seen by applying as above.

Did Miss Bristoe take the waters that year?

[1] Dated 11 & 12 June 1907; kindly communicated by Dr Robert Pacey.
[2] Transcribed by Betty Matthews, 'The Organs of the Bath Assembly Rooms', TO 235/44.

107a Hastings, Sussex, South Terrace, the Unitarian church (undated)

F 70

This is an organ with pipework undoubtedly by Snetzler contained in a case that seems to be made partly from a Snetzler chamber organ case. It has a small additional Swell division made in 1837, perhaps by Walker – if so, this is the same year as his work at Ludlow (no. 63). The organ was at one time in the Unitarian chapel (built 1794) at Norton near Sheffield; it was removed from there about 1843 to Banbury, thence to Lewes in 1853 and to Hastings in 1930.

The Snetzler pipework remaining includes a Dulciana from 4' *C*, some small–scaled 'helpers', a wooden Stopped Diapason, part of an Open Diapason, and part of a Principal; all from an organ with a compass evidently *G'*, *A'–e'''*.

107b Derby, William Strutt (undated)

B 208/180

A 'missing' organ with stops containing pipework apparently like that now at Hastings, and which has connections with the Unitarians, is that noted by Buckingham in 1824 as belonging to William Strutt of Derby from 1813 (when it was supplied by Holland). William Strutt died in 1830, and an organ was recorded as being at Norton from about 1836 onwards.

Buckingham's notes on the organ are as follows:

Wm. Strutt, Esq., Derby—An Organ with one set of keys from GG long octaves to E in alt. A Swell from m/C on the same keys and a piano movement that leaves the Diapasons, Dulciana and Flute.

Open Diapason to CC of metal	61
Stop Diapason bafs and treble	57
Dulciana to 4 ft. C metal	41
Principal	57
Flute	57
Fifteenth	57
Sexqualtra bafs and Cornet treble 3 ranks ...	171
Hautboy Swell	29
Total	530

The Open Diapason to CC of metal the GG-AA-BB-♮♮ is a Stop Diapason pipe and a metal principal pipe. A Mahogany Case with a gilt front and sash doors 14 ft. high to the top of the pediment 9 ft. 9 ins. wide—the middle part 6 ft. 5 ins. wide—3 ft. 8 ins. The two outside towers are broken back from the front. The Bellows are diagonal. This Organ is one of Snetzler's make and a very good instrument it is but the Sexqualtra and Cornet is rather too powerful. Derby, 1 December, 1824. A.B.

The relationship, if any, of the Hastings organ to this latter account or to the Ludlow organ may become clearer during much-needed work of renovation at Hastings.

108 Ickham, Kent, St John's church
(undated pipework)

In the Walker organ of 1897 originally made for the billiards room of Brockhampton Court near Leominster, Herefordshire, and installed at Ickham, near Canterbury, in 1951, there is an 'Open Diapason' rank whose pipes comprise various Snetzler ranks. The largest Snetzler pipe is the 4' C; the stops used in this rank include 27 pipes marked 'Princ gt' (the 4' C♯ is not by Snetzler, which may imply that the Principal pipes came from a short-octave Great) [1], a 'GG Sesq 2' (from the '19th' rank), one pipe from a 'Sesq 1' (a '17th') rank, together with a 'C Forn 1' and other pipes from the '22nd' rank of a Furniture stop.

This unusual organ also includes four ranks of Schulze pipes, and a Hill rank [2]. It is not clear how and when these were brought together, but the Snetzler pipes could have originated in any of a number of his organs later worked on by Walker. The style of the Snetzler pipes would suggest a middle-period date; from this possibly short-octave organ it would seem that a Principal, Sesquialtera and Furniture were removed. Sperling reported an incredibly early ('1731') organ at Leominster (see chapter 5, no. 1, p. 268), but there remains the ghost of a chance that Snetzler did some work at some time in or near that town – or is Ludlow, not far away, also a possible source for this pipework?

[1] For details of a pipe from this rank, see chapter 4, pp. 238–40.
[2] Further details of the organ are included in Michael Edwards, 'Some Organs in Kent' (TO 224/177).

109 Hemel Hempstead, Hertfordshire, Marlowes Baptist church (undated)

Bernard Edmonds records [1] an organ formerly in St Matthew's church, Duddeston (built 1840), that had been enlarged by Hill, and moved to Hemel Hempstead by Banfield in 1889. It was rebuilt by Kirkland in 1899. On a visit in 1952, Herbert Norman and Bernard Edmonds found 'several' stops to be by Snetzler, 'not all complete'.

[1] BIOSR, vol. 12, no. 2 (April 1988), p. 10.

110 London and Orkney, private owner (undated)

In a private communication, Robert Shaftoe reported that he repaired a small Snetzler chamber organ which subsequently belonged to the composer, Peter Maxwell Davies. It was apparently destroyed in a house fire.

111 Rotherham, Mr Walker (? *c*1783)

An organ by 'Snetzler & Jones' is referred to in the letter (see chapter 1, p. 15) of 1783 from the churchwardens of Holy Trinity, Hull, in which they 'desire Messrs. Snetzler & Jones to examine the organ' with a view to making repairs 'when they come to erect Mr. Walker's organ at Rotherham'. This may well refer to an organ actually made by Jones, as it is likely that Snetzler was not at this time in London.

Snetzler's previous work in Hull has been cited (no. 23).

112 London, the Strand, King's College (undated)

W 109 (19)

This is a bureau organ, similar in size to the others known, but with some details that might give one cause to question its frequently–supposed maker. Its stop–list is:

$$(C, D–e'''): SD, Fl, 15, II (b/tr)$$

The keyboard is of blackwood with 'sandwich' sharps; these have (untypically) a wide centre of ivory or bone, and narrow outer blackwood edges.

The stops are worked by metal levers; there is a shifting movement taking off the Fifteenth and mixture, and a blowing pedal. A small knob of ivory slides along a horizontal aperture over the rear of the keys to show the state of the winding of the reservoir; this is not a typical Snetzler detail (but can be found on organs made in the 1830s).

The organ was previously owned by Thurston Dart, and was placed at his death in 1971 in the College where he had been King Edward Professor of Music.

113 Wyke, near Halifax, the 'Unitas Fratrum' (possibly 1759)

The *Halifax Guardian* article ('No. 8', 1869) on the 'History of organs in the parish of Halifax' mentions a Snetzler organ in the chapel of the 'Unitas Fratrum' or 'united brethren'. The Revd B. B. Edmonds, in a private communication, has also reported an 'anonymous' note regarding a Snetzler organ 'dated 1759' formerly in the Moravian church at Lower Wyke, near Bradford, and 'sold in 1788 for £8. 10s.' This might, of course, be the same organ as others above dated 1759 or thereabouts, but no further details are known.

*

Snetzler's 1777 console at Rotherham

4 His techniques

I Church and larger house organs: mechanism

1 Consoles: stop-layout and nomenclature

Because of the loss of so many organs or their severe alteration during the past two hundred years, it is now quite difficult to reconstruct even the consoles of the mid-eighteenth-century British church organ. Indeed, there is no completely unaltered Snetzler church console, but piety and poverty have left some clues from which various aspects of Snetzler's designs might be discerned. If to English-speaking people some of which follows seems very 'alien', they may be excused that impression – even the use of the very word 'console' to mean the part of the organ at which the player sits is scarcely a hundred years old, and we have now to go back in imagination for two hundred and fifty years. John Marsh's *Preface* (Appendix 9) is a good starting point for a more complete understanding of the task of the organist in Snetzler's time, but at present the relationships of organs, their church music and the forms of worship of the time are under-explored, and even the fingering technique of the organist in mid-eighteenth-century Britain, are not well or widely understood.

The earliest-dated surviving church organ 'console' (the then-current description was simply 'keys') is that of 1756 at Hillington in Norfolk. From it three divisions are playable from two keyboards and the pipework is winded from one soundboard (see chapter 3, no. 33). Two flutes which comprise the Choir together with its two enclosed ranks which form a 'Swell' or 'Eccho' are controlled from the lower keyboard, and the Great chorus is played upon the upper keyboard. The unenclosed Choir ranks are divided so that they might form a bass to the short-compass 'Swell' Dulciana, or an accompaniment to the 'Swell' Hautboy (which has been replaced at some time by a Gamba).

Though the console may be rather confusing at first sight, this organ is cleverly arranged to give a small instrument a maximum of flexibility. Its general principles seem also to have been applied to somewhat larger church organs, so that although the mechanisms of these have been much altered, it may be possible to reconstruct their original layout.

The spelling of the stop-names overleaf is based on that used at Andover (see below), as the console is now fitted with ivory stop-name plates. Over the years, the layout of the right-hand jamb seems to have become somewhat muddled, and at present the Great Sesquialtera and Cornet sliders have been linked, and are controlled by the Sesquialtera knob only. The original stop-knobs are laid out as overleaf:

[LHS:] Eccho Dulciana [from *g*]   [RHS:] Eccho Hautboy [from *g*]

Choir Flute [bass]   Choir Flute [treble, from *g*]
Choir Stopd Diapason [bass]   Choir Stopd Diapason [treble, from *g*]

Great Sesquialtera [III]   Great Cornet [III; ?from *c*]
Great Twelfth   Great Fifteenth
Great Open Diapason   Great Principal
    Great Stopd Diapason

The 'keys' of the Cobham Hall organ

A note was made in 1819 of the stops contained in the console of the organ made by Snetzler for Andover church in 1771, and this was later found in a copy of Keeble's Voluntaries (see chapter 3, no. 85). It seems to preserve the original arrangement of the stop-knobs, and it may also be a transcription of the original spelling of the stop-labels:

[LHS:]	Ecc. Hautbois [RHS:]	Ecc. Cornet
	Ecc. Open diapason	Ecc. Principal

	Ch. Flute [bass]	Ch. Principal
	Ch. Stop'd diapason [bass]	Ch. Flute [treble]
		Ch. Stop'd diapason [treble]

	Gr. Sesquialtera [thus spelt]	Gr. Trumpet
	Gr. Twelfth	Gr. Fifteenth
	Gr. Principal	Gr. Cornet
	Gr. Open diapason	Gr. Stop'd diapason

'Ecc.' is short for 'Eccho(e)', the common name for the Swell at the time (cf. the original engraved labels on the organ at Newby Hall, made in the same year, chapter 5, no. 266). Conservatism ensured that the name used for a division previously enclosed in a non-'swelling' box continued to be used for a while for one that could now 'express Pafsion'. 'Gr.' was the normal abbreviation of 'Great' at this time, too; on two organs by Stephen White (1794–5 and 1801), engraved stop-knobs are thus distinguished: 'Gr.' and 'Ch.'.

Other organs with two manuals but three divisions were made, for instance, for Burton-on-Trent, Drogheda, Peterhouse Cambridge) and Sheffield. In all of these, the Swell and the Choir were played from the same keyboard; at Andover, the stop-knobs' layout suggests that this may have been the *upper* one. If so, there had been a change from an earlier practice exemplified at Hillington and, in an organ not made by Snetzler, at Leatherhead (chapter 5, no. 5), where the Swell or Eccho was originally a short-compass (*c'*) division played from the *lower* keyboard. By 1772, when William Ludlam wrote to the *Gentleman's Magazine* (Appendix 7) it may have been that the Swell had come to be regarded as the secondary rather than the tertiary division: he rather implies this. Certainly, at Newby Hall in *c*1771 (in the organ probably by Thomas Haxby of York, see chapter 5, p. 266), and in Snetzler's organ of 1778 at Cobham Hall (see below), the *g*-compass Swells were controlled from the upper keyboards. At Newby Hall, the soundboard arrangement (similar to that at Hillington) would have allowed either keyboard disposition, so it seems that the upper two and not the lower two keyboards of a three-manual console had, by the early 1770s if not earlier, become the general model for a two-manual layout.

The two Choir stops that formed the bass for the 'Swell' stops were quite logically placed on the left-hand (or bass) stop-jamb. The divisions are also arranged as on most British organs, with the stop-knobs for the 'upperwork' (and reeds) above those for the lower-pitched ranks. The arrangement of the pipework on the soundboards may therefore be deduced – particularly that on the Great, where there is less room for variation between the positions of the stop-knobs and their associated mechanism because the soundboard is situated almost above the console and just behind the front pipes. The stops on the two stop-jambs must therefore control alternate sliders so that there is enough room for the trundles' arms and the slider backfalls. So it is likely that the ranks of pipes on the Great soundboard at Andover would have followed this order:

[Front (lowest knobs):]   Open diapason (with some pipes in the case front)
                            Stop'd diapason
                            Principal
                            Cornet
                            Twelfth
                            Fifteenth
                            Sesquialtera
                            Trumpet
[Back, with tuner's access between Great and Choir/Eccho soundboards.]

It is possible that the exact nature of the Cornet can be discerned from this arrangement, which (if correct) shows clearly that the stop is a 'solo' one and not merely the treble to the Sesquialtera, but not one mounted high above the other pipework as in eighteenth-century French organs. Indeed, its position nearer to the tuner than the Stopped Diapason and Principal would suggest that it was placed at, or only just above, the level of the other pipework in the manner of the surviving Green soundboards at Armitage (1790) and Chatham (1795), otherwise the ears of the metal Stopped Diapason trebles and the trebles of the Principal pipes could not be reached by the tuner.

By contrast, the stop-knobs of the 1778 two-manual chamber organ at Cobham Hall, Kent, are laid out thus:

[LHS top:]   Sw Open diapason   [RHS top:]   Sw Stopd diapason
               Sw Principal   Sw Hautboy
               Trumpet bass   Trumpet treble
               Sesquialtera   Cornet
               Twelfth   Fifteenth
               Principal   Flute
               Open diapason   Stopd diapason

Later alterations are reversed, but the spellings are not necessarily original.

It will be seen that the layout is similar to that at Andover, but that the Cornet is in a different place. The Sesquialtera has survived as a three-rank mixture of full compass (see chapter 3, no. 99 for details of this), but the Cornet has been displaced by a Clarabella. Its position on the soundboard can again be 'calculated' using the system of 'alternation' actually employed in the Great stop action of this organ:

[Front:]   Open diapason – pipes from this are in the 'front'
             Stopd diapason
             Principal
             Flute
             Twelfth
             Fifteenth

Sesquialtera
Cornet [*c'*]
Trumpet bass & Trumpet treble [now a Dulciana to 4' C]
[Tuner's access here, between Great and Swell soundboards]
Sw Hautboy
Sw Principal
Sw Stopd diapason
[Back:]   Sw Open diapason

Although the pipes of the Cornet are now missing, the original soundboard indicates that it was placed at the same level as the surviving full-compass Sesquialtera and that it comprised three ranks of pipes. Early stop-list compilers would not have made clear that it was a separate mixture unless they also specified the number of pipes in each stop; this may be one of the reasons for (e.g.) Leffler's doing so. It was noted previously that Sperling distinguished between the two types by calling the 'solo' Cornet a 'mounted' cornet, even when this was not literally the case.

The purely logical arrangement of stop-knobs exemplified in these three organs, in which 'form follows function' seems to have changed towards the end of Snetzler's career, perhaps when he allowed others to take a more prominent part in the design of his organs as he passed his sixtieth year. The console preserved at Rotherham, made in 1777 (chapter 3, no. 96; console illustrated p. 194), exemplifies the change:

[LHS top:]		[RHS top:]	
	Sw Trumpet		Cornet
	Sw Hautboy		Trumpet
	Sw Cornet		Sesquialtera
	Sw Principal		Tierce
	Sw Stopd Diapason		Fifteenth
	Sw Open Diapason		Twelfth
	Ch Bassoon		Principal
	Ch Flute		Stopd Diapason
	Ch Principal		Open Diapason
	Ch Stopd Diapason		Open Diapason

The stop-labels are not Snetzler's (or Ohrmann's?); later stops are omitted.

Here, all the Great stop-knobs are on the right-hand jamb, and the Swell and Choir stop-knobs are placed in two groups on the left-hand jamb: a practice that was to become universal during the following century. The logical connection of knobs and sliders is disturbed, and it is no longer clear where exactly the Cornet is placed, or if it was 'mounted'. So not only does this console exemplify changes made during Snetzler's working life, but it also emphasizes some of the uncertainties over details which have to be resolved when early stop-lists are scrutinized.

The Rotherham layout is virtually identical with that used by Green at Lichfield Cathedral in 1790, where an early account seems to show the arrangement of the stop-knobs overleaf:

[LHS top:]	SWELL	[RHS top:]	GREAT-ORGAN
	Hautboy		Cornet
	Trumpet		Trumpet [treble]
	Cornet		Trumpet [bass]
	Principal		Sesquialtera
	Dulciana		Firneture [*sic*]
	Open Diapason		Terce [*sic*]
	Stop Diapason		Fifteenth
	CHAIR-ORGAN		
	Fifteenth		Twelfth
	Flute		Principal
	Principal		Stop Diapason
	Stop Diapason		Open Diapason
	Dulciana		Open Diapason

This scheme is taken from John Jackson's *A History of the City and Cathedral of Lichfield* (1805), in which he has apparently tried to copy the stop-knobs' engraving (and paper 'department labels'?) at the keys. The still–surviving Cornet in this organ (now at Armitage) is not placed behind the Trumpet, but between the Stopped Diapason and the Principal; the original stop action is awkwardly arranged to accommodate this arrangement. It is possible that some such layout may have been used by Snetzler in all his later larger instruments, but there seems to be no evidence except for the consoles from which to draw any conclusions.

It will by now be clear that the console's layout is bound up intimately with the layout of the organ as a whole. When a Snetzler organ is rebuilt substantially (for instance, in order to alter combined Eccho or Swell and Choir divisions so that they are played from two separate keyboards and soundboards) the console is likely to be among the first parts to be lost. It is, however, an important first step towards an understanding of his organs to know what the organists who played Snetzler's instruments would have found in front of them.

Spelling and nomenclature: After the general layout of the stops had been understood, the organists' attention might next turn to the information given on the stop-labels. As noted above, the Andover stop-list appears mainly to coincide with Snetzler's own spelling as it can be found written on pipes, parts of wind-chests, stop actions, and in contracts. For instance, the spellings 'Hautbois' and 'Hautboy' are both to be found. Other stops are idiosyncratically spelt, and it is possible that Snetzler's regular stop-labels did not always follow his personal style in this respect. For instance, he wrote 'Cornett' on actions and rackboards in the organ now at 'Hatchlands' (1759), in the bureau organ now in Schaffhausen Museum (1763) and in the organ at Merevale (1777). An analogous 'Trumpett' appears in the contract for Trinity church, New York (1762), and the largest wooden pipes in the 1742 Cuckston organ are inked 'Diapaison'. (See also Snetzler's letters to Fulneck, Appendix 3.)

The original stop labels of John Byfield (on the organ of 1765–6, now at

200

'Finchcocks', Kent) and Hugh Russell (on the organ made in 1798 for St Runwald's church, Colchester, now at St Clement's church, Thurrock, Essex) are cut from sheets of paper with stop–names printed from an engraved plate or block. Small variations in the borders of the cartouche of each label make it possible to see that (for instance) the borders of the two 'Stop Diapason' labels in an organ with a divided Stopped Diapason are identical, but that the borders of other stop–names are slightly different. It is therefore likely that all the various stop names were printed from a single engraved plate. Indeed, at 'Finchcocks' the faintly–engraved lines along which the labels were cut out of the printed sheet are visible – the lines are like those used on the sheets of the first postage stamps upon their 'invention' in 1841 by Rowland Hill. Generally, only the 'ghosts' of Snetzler's labels remain, often under layers of paint or varnish, but those that have been studied (at Swithland, 1765, for instance) show that they are of similar rectangular format and size, 2½" by 1". The survival of the Byfield and Russell labels, dating from 1765–6 (the time of Snetzler's peak output of work) and from 1798 respectively, must show that these printed sheets had a lengthy currency in London; only because there was so restricted a range of stop–names in a British organ would such a labelling method be possible.

The labels are made of paper, not parchment which is difficult to glue cleanly in small pieces onto hardwoods; they have therefore been very vulnerable to wear and to 'improvers'. It was no doubt partly their fragility that led to the adoption of engraved ivory inserts in the faces of the stop–knobs. These seem to have been first used by Snetzler occasionally from about 1769, but the idea was taken up more consistently by Green, who appears to have used them at Lichfield Cathedral as well as at Heaton Hall and on his chamber organs, despite the reduced legibility of this arrangement in candle– or rush–lit churches and music rooms.

Perhaps a further reason for the ultimate adoption of engraved inserts was that the stop–knobs' layout necessarily became more compact as the organs became larger. The stop–knobs at Rotherham (and indeed at Hillington, a much smaller and earlier organ) were 'staggered' diagonally. This arrangement is taken for granted now, as it was virtually universal in nineteenth–century British organs, and it was introduced so that where there are many knobs to be accommodated, the 'reach' to the highest knob is not so great. It would have been more straightforward mechanically to set out the knobs in a single vertical line, and such a procedure allows the console opening to be narrower. Therefore this was done in smaller organs with built–in consoles, so that satisfactory proportions between the lower casework panels and the console opening could be maintained. In the smallest church organ at Swithland and in the larger chamber organs, the stop–knobs were drawn through the vertical frames of the panels next to the console, and the console opening was only as wide as the overall width of the keyboard and its cheeks.

Music desks: Organists would have found a capacious music desk in the church instruments. Obvious, one might think, but the strange thing is that the chamber organs of Snetzler's contemporaries and successors often appear to have made no such provision, and even his own chamber organs rarely possess original desks (see chapter 2, p. 59). The need for music desks in a church organ seems to us to be perfectly evident – but how much were they used two hundred and fifty years ago, and what was in fact placed on them? No doubt organists used substantial bound volumes of Voluntaries, together with bound and manuscript copies of versified psalm hymns (their music, if not always their words, according to Marsh) as well as 'thorough bass' scores of anthems, but it was expected that a high proportion of their music would be freely improvised.

A test of the candidate's skills of improvisation was an important feature of an audition or 'trial' for an organist's post. William Hayes, writing in 1765 (see Appendix 5), even implies that the term 'voluntary' arose because *extempore* music came, as he put it, 'voluntary from the mind' of the performer. Voluntaries were expected during the service as well as before and afterwards; no doubt their musical result was often that neatly described in Peter Ackroyd's 'historical' novel *Hawksmoor* (1985; p. 174): 'There was indeed a pleasure ... and nothing to burden the memory after: like a voluntarie before a Lesson it was absolutely forgotten, nothing to be remembered or repeated'.

At Swithland the upper part of the music desk – plainly visible over the gallery front – was used as an advertisement for the builder. It proclaims *John Snetzler, Esq., London, The Builder, 1765* in large shadowed gilt capital letters. At King's Lynn, the lettering above the console opening still can be read: *JOHANNES SNETZLER/Londini fecit 1754*. These may seem to us the very essence of pomposity and self-regard, and they do not seem to have been used by previous British builders, but they parallel plentiful lettering on gallery fronts and text- or charity-boards, as well as the Lord's Prayer, Creed and Commandments on the reredos of the altar-table – all intended to be studied by a society proud of its wide literacy. Perhaps Snetzler had seen such lettering elsewhere – in Holland (on the Rückpositiv of the Müller organ at Haarlem?), or indeed in Germany or France. In the cathedral at Albi, for instance, the organ builder's name is displayed in gold capital letters on an arch over the western 'high' altar.

2 Keyboards and key actions: compasses and temperaments

It will be clear from Snetzler's work-list (chapter 3) that his preferred 'house style' was to use blackwood for natural keys and ivory-plated stained pear for sharps. Further details of the keyboards will be discussed below, but as certain aspects of the keyboards are peculiar to British practice, they must be addressed first.

The compasses of the keyboards would be surprising to anyone from any other organ culture; indeed, they seem to have somewhat confused Snetzler at Fulneck in 1748 (chapter 3, no. 9). The *upper* termination of the compass there (to e''') was higher than the usual continental practice at the time, but the Moresby Hall claviorgan's keys even went as high as f''', presumably to match the Shudi harpsichord. The 1742 Cuckston organ also has this extended keyboard compass. His church organs, however, universally terminate at e''', a compass adopted by most other organ builders in Britain from about 1760 onwards, but Snetzler's other chamber organs go up to *e'''* or *f '''* without apparent standardisation. The only organs which deviate from these 'norms' are the 'Yale' and German Calvinist Church organs, which freakishly omit the *d♯'''*, and terminate at *e'''*.

Although the Fulneck contract states: 'The temperament shall so far as ever possible be installed in such a way that all keys can be played', it is not now possible to discover if Snetzler actually tuned the Fulneck organ (made without a low *G♯'*) in anything like equal temperament. As the organ was made for a German community, such a temperament might well have been considered, but the matter is made the more confusing because the keyboard of a bureau organ of near date (1751) and supposed also to have been made for, or at least to have come from, Fulneck has a high *d♯'''* but not the lowest *C♯*.

Whatever may have been done at Fulneck, it is meantone temperament, doggedly adhered to in church work for at least another century – 1875 seems to be the point of general capitulation to equal temperament – that, together with the general preference for a low *G'* (or even *F'*) compass rather than one to *C*, that shaped the *lower* termination of British organ keyboards. This has little to do with the lack of pedals, as has been supposed – pedals did not supply 16' tone generally until the compasses of both manual and pedal keyboards were shortened to *C* – but, as Charles Pearce pointed out in 1912,[1] the old compasses were the '*vocal organ range*'. In other words, the organist was able to accompany the normal range of the human voice and to support it at will at the octave below, just on the keyboard(s), using 'The ordinary manner in four parts' (the right hand playing the upper three parts), as Hamilton's '*Catechism*' put it.[2] Pedals were therefore required only to help as a 'third hand' (as the Italians would say), until later composer/organists such as William Russell saw the musical potential in using pedals to play a separate or contrasted line.

A meantone temperament makes undesirable frequent use, except for special effects of musical coloration, of root–position chords of F♯ major (though F♯ minor is wonderfully anguished), G♯ major (though G♯ minor is 'acceptable'), or C♯ major (but again, the minor key is quite 'playable'). As the pipes of these lowest notes of the lowest octave are large and expensive, they and their keys were generally not provided. How many were omitted depended on the size of building (and therefore the size of case and its gallery) and the depth of the church's collective pocket. There were two systems in use.

First, there was the 'long octaves' system. This simply left out the lowest *G♯'* pipes and keys in a *G'*-compass organ. In the larger and more expensive *F'*-compass organ, the *F♯'* was omitted but the retained *G♯'* could be used as the minor third of a chord on F, if not as the root of a major chord of G♯, the chord containing the 'wolf fifth', G♯ to E♭. Therefore, 'GG long octaves to e in alt.' as the sources would describe it, implied a compass of 57 notes: four notes in the lowest octave, forty–eight in the middle octaves, and five in the highest 'in altissimo' octave.

Second, there was the 'short octaves' system. It will be seen from the photograph of the Rotherham console (p. 194) that there are blocks of wood between the bass–end key–cheek of Great and Choir keyboards and the lowest C keys. These blocks are later substitutions for a natural key of full width from front to back (like a top F or C key on a pianoforte), a key which could at first sight be mistaken for a *B'*. In fact, this key would be connected to the pallet for the *G'* pipes, and there would be no *G♯'*, *A♯'*, or *B'* pipes, pallets or actions; and since there is no urgent musical need for a *C♯*, this, now the lowest accidental key, is used to work the action, pallet and pipes of *A'* instead. Although this may seem bizarre, because the actual sequence of keys from the bass upwards becomes G–C–A–D, the fact that the keys fall into dominant and tonic pairs (G–C and A–D on adjacent keys) makes the system musically quite logical. In the lists of organs in chapters 3 and 5, we have shown the 'short–octave' arrangement as (*G', A', C, D–e'''* or *f'''*) for the sake of clarity, but it should be borne in mind that this is not the order of the notes or keys as the player sees, feels and hears them.

The primacy of the 'long–octave' over the 'short–octave' system is also shown on the Rotherham console: there are gaps between bass and treble key–cheeks and their respective stop–jambs each equivalent to the width of a natural key. The console was evidently made to a 'standard' long–octave width, presumably for the sake of the convenient organization of Snetzler's various workshops.

As with all logical systems, where mechanical and structural arrangements are intimately bound up with the requirements of music and temperament, any interference with the original logic begins a progressive breaking–down of the entire system. So when, as at Rotherham, a *C* pedalboard with pipes of sub–unison tone is introduced into a short–octave organ, the *G'* key appears to be superfluous. It is therefore disconnected, and replaced with a wooden 'blank', and the organ builder makes off with any *G'* pipes that are not in the front and are easily removable. He also supplies a Great to Pedal coupler with which (to some extent) to make up for the lack of 'sub–vocal' tone. The organist then feels and hears low pitches (*C'* to *F♯'* from the pedal pipes) which he has not experienced before, and wants more – apparently forgetting that the harmony–binding effect of the whole chorus sounding on the *G'* and *A'* keys, much more musically satisfying, has now been lost.

The organ builder is now also faced with what to do with the *A'* pipes which were played from the low 'apparent *C♯'*' key. A conscientious man would make new pipes of the correct scale for this note in each rank. In fact the usual procedure is to find the nearest equivalent from the now–redundant *G'* and *A'* pipes, and place them, cut down as necessary, to sound from what has now actually become a normal *C♯* key. The back of a front pipe previously sounding *A'* (or *A* on the Principal) is cut down ruthlessly by means of extra tuning windows or a large slot. This process weakens the structure of the pipe because it now speaks at a pitch a major third higher than originally. All wooden *A'* pipes of Stopped (or Open) Diapasons are sawn off *in situ* until they reach the new pitch. The (usually) terminal decline of the organ – hastened by its being removed from its gallery – has now begun, and the process of attrition is further advanced when, later still, almost every pipe is cut shorter in a general retuning to equal temperament. This unpleasant tale is no fantasy: the evidence for it is easily to be found in almost every surviving late eighteenth– or early nineteenth–century British church organ.

As noted above, the upward termination for Snetzler's church organs was invariably e'''. This was higher than the then–common d'''; later, the 'post–Green' generation of builders, observing that Snetzler (in some chamber organs and in his claviorgans) and Green (in chamber organs) took the compass to f''', was to adopt this as the top note in their church organs. This became the 'standard' for the next thirty years or so, until upward pressure from the pianoforte (itself subject to compass–inflation), together with a vogue for duet-playing, provoked further extensions.

The upper e''' termination explains also to a large extent why soundboards and mechanisms scarcely survive from Snetzler's church organs. A 'short–octave' soundboard of 54 notes might be adapted to a $C\text{--}f'''$ compass, but not a greater one; and although a 'long–octave' soundboard of 57 notes might be adapted to a $C\text{--}g'''$ compass of 56 notes, even this soundboard would not be extensive enough for the later 58- and 61-note compasses which appeared in conjunction with continental–Romantic orchestral transcriptions and octave couplers.

The operation to change a 'long octaves' organ to a C compass is more straightforward. The pipes of the four lowest keys are simply removed, and if the action is altered, the upper compass can be raised by three notes to g''' by using three of the now–redundant (if rather large) pallets. Such an operation would usually require new keyboards (with ivory naturals and ebony sharps) with the new $C\text{--}g'''$ compass. In fact any upwards extension of the compass meant the removal of the original keyboards and, usually, their destruction. Only two complete sets of Snetzler's church–organ keyboards seem to have been preserved: three keyboards in the 1777 Rotherham 'console', and the two original 1770 keyboards at Drogheda. Until it was taken during the 1970s, there was also a single 1765 keyboard at Swithland.

The lower termination of the compass of the Swell keyboard at 'fiddle g' (g) or the adjacent f is due largely to the design of the swell-box itself. This was a solid timber box with a sliding–shutter front somewhat like the pop-holes of hen–coops and duck-arks, and it was supported by four vertical legs over the Great pipework (when not combined with a Choir division and played from the Choir keys), and was placed just behind the central tower and the flanking upper storeys of front pipes' flats. In this high position it could not contain longer pipes without becoming unwieldy and even unsafe, because for every further octave of lower–pitched pipes that the box might contain, it would have to be made twice as tall and nearly twice as wide. But any apparent disadvantage in compass was turned to advantage musically. The sound of the Swell was direct, and it was capable of sustaining solo melodic lines on the reeds (singly or together) or of 'leading' the congregation in a hymn-tune using the bright Cornet-topped chorus. It was the British equivalent of the eighteenth-century French Récit, but with powers of crescendo and diminuendo which equipped it even better to 'tell a story'.

Any enlargement of the Swell would therefore lose this characteristic directness. Only the lessening of the importance of the Choir as a secondary keyboard during Snetzler's working life (for various reasons, including the introduction of shifting movements for the Great or Full Organ into church as well as chamber organs, and

– ironically – his pioneering use of Choir stops to complete otherwise short-compass Swell stops with potential for accompaniment) made it possible for the Swell to be considered as an accompanimental division rather than a solo division. Viewed in this new way, it could instead be placed at the back of the organ either over the Choir or, instead of the Choir, behind the Great soundboard. Here it would inevitably lose its soloistic character. This trend was exemplified in Green's long-compass Swell (to 'gamut' *G*) at St Katherine-by-the-Tower, made in 1778, the same year in which both builders supplied organs to Cobham Hall. It reached its peak (or nadir) in an organ made in 1821 by Flight & Robson for St Nicholas's church, Harwich, whose Swell was (like its Great) of *G'*, *A'–f '''* compass.

The Rotherham Swell keyboard does not continue below *g*; there is a solid block of wood in the bass. Organs by other builders sometimes have 'false' immovable keys in the bass (as at Newby Hall, 1771, attributed to the harpsichord and piano maker, Thomas Haxby of York, who would have been used to making two keyboards of complete compass for his harpsichords), and Snetzler supplied these in more expensive organs, as at Cobham Hall. Later builders were to try to make up for the loss of the Choir bass in a two-manual organ by making the Swell keys press down the corresponding keys on the Great, and consequently adjusting the shifting movements (later, if not in Snetzler's time, called 'piano' movements) to provide a quiet Great (for instance, Stopped Diapason and Dulciana) when required. This indeed was a 'shift' in the old English sense of 'making do', as well as in the literal shifting of the movement's sliders.

Basic styles of church organs Snetzler's church organs appear to have been made to four basic tonal, mechanical and casework designs which allowed for a range of musical, acoustic and financial circumstances:

(i) A small organ for a small church; an organ with one full-compass keyboard, whether 'short' or 'long' in the bass. In the earliest instances, as at Durrow (long-octave, 1748), and possibly Fulneck (long-octave, also 1748), this keyboard operated a pin action. In later organs, as at Swithland (1765, with short octave), the keyboard controlled a sticker-backfall action. These organs cost about £240, according to Ludlam.

(ii) A small organ with two keyboards which controlled, generally, a long- or short-octave Great and a short-compass Swell whose pipes were placed over the Great pipework.

(iii) A two-keyboard organ of moderate size, with short- or long-octaves' compass, in which (in the earlier examples) the lower keyboard controlled both unenclosed ('Ch.') and enclosed ('Sw.') pipework. The unenclosed Choir was envisaged as the main accompanimental or secondary (antiphonal) division, but at least two of its ranks were divided so that (usually) the Stopped Diapason bass and Flute bass could provide a suitable bass to the Swell stops when some of these (for instance, the Open Diapason, Stopped Diapason, or Dulciana) were also needed for accompanimental purposes. The later and larger version of this type might also have a Bassoon in the

'Choir bass' to 'carry down' the Hautboy. In this type, the Swell, though it was somewhat raised above the Choir soundboard on metal conveyances, would speak less directly in this position and so lose its solo function to some extent. However, this type of organ was economical in that it saved space and used fewer mechanical parts. It is likely that in later organs the 'Swell' idea predominated over the Choir and that the combined divisions were played from the upper manual, though the evidence for this is tenuous. The cost of these were set by Ludlam at between £325 and £340.

(iv) A larger organ with three keyboards, as at Rotherham; here the swell–box might be placed over the Great and tuned from the Great access (the reeds being at the rear of the box), or over the Choir, where if it contained more than one reed rank it would presumably have to be tuned from the rear of the organ. The Choir pipework was placed behind the Great soundboard, or even occasionally on combined Great and Choir soundboards. These organs seem to have cost around £450.

It should be noted that these prices are very moderate – even low – by contrast with the prices which Hopkins[3] stated were obtained by earlier builders. He instances the cost of £700 for the 17–stop double–fronted Smith organ at Durham in 1683, the 1,000 guineas for the 21–stop Schrieder organ at Westminster Abbey in 1730, as well as the prices obtained by Green. Snetzler's prices did not of course have to take account of separate Choir cases, but one is left with the worrying thought that this very moderation (no doubt aided by the zeal and application of his ascetic 'Swiss mechanic' colleagues) contributed somewhat towards the low prices obtained for organs current in the middle of the nineteenth century, and their consequent doubtful quality, which caused Hopkins some concern. Snetzler would also have exerted considerable commercial pressure on his contemporary indigenous builders: we know that, in 1765, John Byfield was reported by the London agent of Sir James Grant (for whom he was making the organ now at 'Finchcocks') to be 'starving'.

II Design and construction of key- and stop-actions

We have already seen how the layout of the stop-knobs might be one of the indicators of the internal arrangement of an organ. Since not one of the large Snetzler organs survives without serious alteration, their exact layout can be reconstructed only from this and many other (often slight) clues. It may not be possible to determine some matters: for instance, even something as basic as whether the Rotherham organ was made with its Swell over the Great or over the Choir. Something might be told from the original depth of their cases and any surviving vestigial remains of soundboard and action supports, but all the larger organs have been rebuilt – some many times – so that often only fragments even of their casework remain, let alone any other evidence.

The only two-manual organs that remain nearly as first made are those at

Hillington and Cobham Hall, and their original key and stop actions can be studied. Of these, the organ at Cobham is the less altered mechanically, and its wind system is a unique survival. In this respect, and in others, it also seems better to represent Snetzler's larger-scale practice (see also chapter 3, no. 99).

In the Cobham Hall organ, the Great key action is a sticker-backfall action, the Great stickers passing through cut-outs in the Swell keys, with a large open-framed rollerboard and one roller for each key. The Great pipework stands on one soundboard which is divided internally and so winded in 'sides', and is (typically) deep rather than wide. The stop action is 'conventionally' arranged: the sliders are drawn by wrought-iron backfalls worked through trundles to the draw-stops. Because the Swell is behind the Great, the 'chamber' or alcove not allowing it to be above, the action to it is more complex. Its key action employs a backfall, two sets of brass squares and a rollerboard; its stop action uses trundles, squares, and iron rollers at the sliders. The organ's mechanisms are supported on a separate internal frame, as there is casework at the front only, as well as some relatively lightly constructed panelling at the back of the organ alcove.

Its two bellows are raised alternately by two detachable handles inserted into slots through holes normally concealed within the panelling of the wall of a staircase landing behind the organ chamber. The floor-level wind-trunk into which the bellows disgorge through valves runs across the width of the organ at the front, just inside the case. The divided Great soundboard is winded by two trunks, and the Swell by a smaller subsidiary trunk taken from the 'treble' Great trunk.

This general arrangement must represent in essence that of the larger organs. We have seen on p. 38 that their cases were, where necessary, designed so as to allow the bellows to be accommodated within them. In large organs, the area that three such bellows occupy would be at least as much as the superficial area of the Great and Choir soundboards, and it is clear from the surviving cases of Green's late eighteenth-century organs at Armitage (from Lichfield Cathedral, built 1790), Salisbury (1792), and Chatham (1795), that it was the volume of wind-raising apparatus required, and not the size of the soundboards and pipework, that primarily determined the depth of their casework. Each of these organs was able to contain later pedal pipes without any increase in their depth, as long as their original bellows were simultaneously replaced by a horizontal reservoir with feeders which took up only half the space of the original bellows. Only when the bellows were placed at a distance from the rest of the organ could the casework be made no deeper than the soundboards required. The organs at Ludlow and Nottingham originally stood on substantial eastern galleries, and could have been winded from behind or from one side; the wind system at Nottingham was therefore altered by Buckingham when he moved it to a later west gallery.

The effect on the size of the casework of placing the bellows a distance from the organ may be observed in contemporary French organs. In the abbey church of St Guilhem-le-Désert, Hérault, for instance, the c1782 J.-P. Cavaillé organ, though similar in tonal size to the Lichfield organ, is contained in a main case half the depth of the English organ.

Although it is difficult to envisage the larger Snetzler organ as a whole, there is sufficient evidence to allow an understanding of its various parts to be built up into a general picture. The following sections attempt this by describing the various mechanical parts in detail.

Balanced keyboards in church and house organs

The pair of keyboards at Cobham Hall (1778) are levered with a mechanical advantage to the player of 4 : 3. The backfalls and rollerboard arms are all of equal (1 : 1) ratios, and therefore the pallets were made to open sufficiently by attaching the action to them at only three-quarters of their opening length as measured from their hinged ends. The result of these leverages is to decrease the amount of movement of the various parts of the action, but only by an extent that still allows for their adjustment. The precision of the action depends on crucial points being silenced with thin (not 'split') leather; any modern felting or baizing of the sticker ends or the use of any baizes placed over the leather adjusting buttons would immediately affect the action and tend to make it feel 'sponge-like'.

Like the Swell keyboard at Cobham Hall, the 1779 Locko Park keyboard is contained in a frame of four rails between substantial cheeks. The front rail is not pinned, but supports only bedding material to quieten the impact of the keys' fall and the front vertical 'slip'. A second rail with ⅛"-diameter brass pins guides the keys at a point just behind the visible natural and sharp platings. These pins are set low enough – just to the height of the top of the key-stocks when they are in the raised 'ready to play' position – to allow a 'thumper' rail, typically of 2" by 1" section, over them. (A similar arrangement is used in the much earlier 1755 organ made for York, now at Sculthorpe.) The balance rail is more substantial, and higher, and would allow a maximum depth of movement of the keys of about ½". Because the pins on this rail are staggered (at Cobham, at least), with the sharps' balance pins ½" behind those of the naturals, the undersides of the oak key-levers are relieved a little where they pass over the bevel of the rail. A rear rail serves only to help ensure that the whole keyboard frame remains rigid and square.

This additional rail is also employed where the keyboard is the upper one of a pair, or slides into the case when not in use: at Eton College (1760), a ramp at the rear of the key-stock is 5" long overall, and rises ⅜" to engage the action when the keyboard is pulled out.

The keys are sawn from edge-glued planks of oak finished 11/16" thick and are mortised through at the front guide pins, but the mortises at the balance rail are eased only just sufficiently to allow for the movement of the keys on the pins. Careful finishing and regulation of these mortises is crucial to the keys' quiet but easy working; they were not baized, and there was only a thin baize 'washer' under each key at the balance rail.

Naturals The normal Snetzler keyboard employs a blackwood as a ⅛" plating for the natural keys. This wood was normally a species of ebony, and not – as used elsewhere – a cheaper dark brown wood, such as grenadil, stained black. The natural keys are 'scribed' with a number of parallel lines in front of the sharp, a form of decoration which has a functional origin. The expensive ebony was not wasted by cutting out each sharp-indent, but was applied in two closely fitting pieces: the narrow rear 'tail' and the wider front 'head'. The joint between them was then disguised by running one or two pairs of lines along the heads, the rearmost line being the actual joint. Snetzler habitually scribed two pairs of lines. Even when the plating was made from one piece, these lines were retained as a decorative feature, and the rear line was the one to which the back of the 'head' was cut to give clearance to the sharp. The most forward line also had its origins in a mark from which the key-maker chamfered the sides of the natural plating, at about 20 degrees to the vertical edge. This chamfer extends to the front of the key and enables the player to glide readily from one key to the next; it is particularly accommodating when players use 'early' fingering techniques.

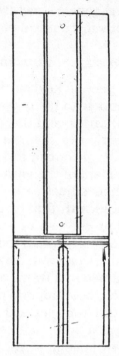

The vertical fronts of the keys are decorated to conceal the oak stock from which they are made. Snetzler generally used a mahogany veneer with its grain set vertically, but he also used 'arcades' of semicircular mouldings and other features which are detailed in chapter 3.

Typical natural and sharp keys

Accidentals The accidentals are normally made of pear, stained with a permanent 'legal' black ink, and plated with a thin (1/16") 'veneer' of ivory. These recall the keyboards of 'early' Viennese pianofortes. Indeed, the form of Snetzler's natural keys and their scribing are also practically identical to those in the pianofortes made by Rosenberger and Walther.

The great majority of Snetzler's surviving keyboards, from first to last, are made with these materials. The exceptions are apparently those for special chamber organs commissioned by particular, usually royal, patrons. These include the organs now at Birmingham (1755/6), Eton College (1760) and in the church of St Andrew-by-the-Wardrobe (1769). The first two of these had close royal connections, and the organ in St Andrew's was evidently made for an aristocrat, a keen admirer of Handel. All these instruments have keyboards with ivory naturals (with butted heads and tails) scribed in the same way as the normal blackwood ones, and with black sharps made from stained pear with an ebony veneer. The Locko Park organ (1779) also has this type of keyboard (called by this date a 'piano' keyboard), but with sharps of solid ebony. This may simply be because of its later date rather than for any special reason, as by this time Green and other builders had made it the norm for chamber organs. Unfortunately, the design of the original keyboard for the organ at Merevale, made two years before, is not known for certain – a previous keyboard with ivory naturals was removed as 'unoriginal' – so that no definite conclusions about the dating of Snetzler's adoption of 'piano' keyboards can be drawn.

As far as we know, the keyboards of the church instruments were also of the 'normal' style, but there do seem to have been some exceptions. The Rotherham keyboards (1777) are made with plain bone sharps, as are those in the secondhand organ at Kedleston. The keyboards at Hillsborough (1773) are said to have been of the 'skunk–tail' pattern: one in which the sharp 'combs' are made as a sandwich of bone or ivory and ebony with the ebony in the centre, the natural keys being black – a technique used by British–born organ builders and spinet makers up to about 1760. The chamber organ (1755) at Clare College, Cambridge, has a reversed version of this, as has the bureau organ at King's College, London; the latter with an unusually wide central piece of bone. However, so many keyboards have been destroyed without any precise documentation of their design that it is not possible to say whether or not these distinctive keyboards were as rarely made as now appears.

Sample measurements of keys made for the early organ of 1742 (Cuckston) and the late instruments at Rotherham (1777) and Cobham Hall (1778) are as follows:

		1742	1777	1778
natural keys:	platings' length:	4¾"	Gt; 4¾"	5" overall
	heads' length:	1½"	1 9/16" (Sw)	1½"
	scribings:	¼" overall	¼" overall	¼" overall
	platings' thickness:	3/32"	⅛"	3/32"
	octave span:	c6¼" to 6⅜"	6⅜"	c6⅜"
	G'–e''' span:	31½"	—	31 5/16"
key–levers:	stock thickness:	7/16" oak	7/16"	⅝" oak
sharps:	overall length:	3¼"	2¾"	3⅛"
	width at base:	7/16"	—	⅜"
	width at top:	5/16"	—	5/16"
	overall height:	7/16"	15/32"	7/16"
	ivory thickness:	1/16+"	[bone]	1/16"

Both keyboards are made of the same materials, and both are scribed with two double lines; only the vertical fronts of the naturals are different, as noted previously. The setting out of the keyboard is not equally 'tempered', so that there is a wider natural 'tail' between the C♯ and D♯ keys than between the F♯, G♯ and A♯ keys. Exactly which system Snetzler used to set the keyboard out is not clear, but it seems not to be that described by Dom Bédos.

Sticker–backfall key actions

The common description of a normal British–made mechanical action organ as 'tracker'–actioned is misleading. Properly speaking, the 'tracker' is but one part of an action, and it is a component used in so–called 'suspended' actions as well as in actions which employ balanced keyboards, stickers and backfalls. There is no evidence that Snetzler employed back-pivoted keys 'suspended' directly on the pallet springs; even the short-compass (*c'* upwards) Swells in the early instruments, as at Fulneck (chapter 3, no. 9 and Appendix 3) were apparently set too deep inside the organ for this kind of action to have been used.

Snetzler's habitual design of the various action components is as follows:

Stickers These are either rectangular in cross-section (approximately ¼" by ⅛"), where there is a need for them to pass through a register (as in the organs with a sliding keyboard), or round (¼" in diameter), and made from red, or Scots', pine (*pinus sylvestris*). They are 'pinned' with 1/16" diameter brass wire, pushed into them and cut to leave ¾" of its length visible.

Backfalls These are made of laths of pine or oak, ¼" or 5/16" in thickness; it seems that oak was used in the larger organs where they might be subject to more torsion. At their rear and front ends where they are pushed by the stickers and pull the trackers respectively they have variously shaped taperings, most characteristically done in a curve. They are pivoted on a beam (at Cobham 2½" wide by 2⅛" deep) made as a laminate equally of pine and oak, with the backfalls' slots cut 7/8" into the oak. At 'Hatchlands' the beam is papered; the paper might have been used in its setting-out. The pivot is a continuous length of brass rod, apparently 3/32" in diameter.

Roller-boards The Cobham rollerboards are made as frames in ¾" pine. The rollers are of pine, irregularly octagonal in section, made from ¾" wide by ⅝" high material. The corners of the rollers are planed off to allow them to be set closely above one another. They are pivoted with brass wires through the eyes of short iron 'studs' whose centres are set at a distance of ⅝" from the face of the rollerboard. These 'studs' are made in a similar way to the roller-arms, which are of ⅛" iron, hammered flat and bored at one end. The arms' effective mechanical length is 1⅝" (in the Swell action) or 2" (in the Great), and they are fixed in the rollers by means of a rough thread at a distance of 1" from the ends of the rollers. The rollers and the rollerboard-frame are all marked in ink with their respective note-names.

Trackers These are rectangular strips of clear pine, about ¼" by about 3/64" in cross-section. Through two holes near each end is threaded a piece of slightly softened (annealed) 1/16" brass wire in the manner shown. The wire at the upper end of the tracker is hooked through the eye of the roller-arm, or the pull-wire, and at the lower end it is threaded to receive a leather 'button' for the adjustment of the action. Very few original leather buttons survive from the eighteenth century, but those

Trackers and wires

which have been found (e.g., under the 1788 Green organ at Attingham Park) are nearly spherical; this shape makes it possible to understand why they were called 'buttons' in the first place.

Pull-wires The action passes through the underside of the pallet-well, where it has to be wind-sealed, by means of a leather pouch or 'teat' held to a brass wire by being glued to the ends of two short sections of ¼" diameter dowel made from what appears to be straight-grained ash (not made, it seems, from the willow recommended by Dom Bédos). An eye formed in the wire through which the tracker is connected holds the lower dowel in place. At Cobham, there is no eye above the upper dowel as there would be in a system that used a 'chest hook' – a short piece of S-shaped wire connecting an upper eye to the pallet – so it must be presumed that the upper dowel is held in place by being pushed over a threaded or file-roughened length of the wire and glued. The pull-wire is loosely looped over the pallet eye with a little slackness left between this and the 'teat' assembly to allow for any tightening of the leather pouch as it dries out. The teats are formed from strips of thin leather (possibly goat- or kid-leather, which can be more easily 'moulded' than sheepskin) glued to the upper (inner) surface of the oak that forms the 3" or so of the pallet-well board nearest to the face-board. The lower dowel is guided in a countersunk boring in the oak, as shown.

Pallets An eye ¼" in diameter was formed from brass wire pierced through the pine pallet and turned over on its top surface, underneath a single layer of white sheepskin leathering. The pallets are generally of the same length throughout the compass (approximately 8½" at Cobham Hall, in the Great soundboard) and are either somewhat graduated in width (as at Cobham Hall) or are of the same width (as at Merevale). The pallets are marked on their front faces with the pitch of the keys to which they relate, and are of the cross-section shown. They are hinged with leather and glued to the bars and fillings of the grid, which are themselves covered with a single layer of leather or paper.

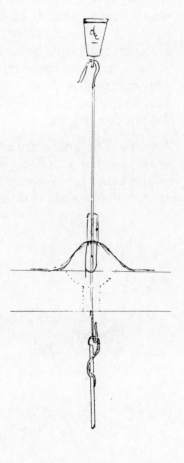

Connection of tracker to pallet

Pallet springs The brass springs at Cobham Hall are triple-wound at their ⅝" eyes, with 5" legs placed in indentations in the pallet and in a guide rail, which is on a continuous support of 1" oak. In the 1742 Cuckston organ, there is no hole in the pallet underside, and the springs are shaped to glide along a shallow groove in it; there is only one turn at their eyes.

Stop actions

Draw-stops Since the names of the stops are given on paper labels, the actual knobs are of plain turned hardwood, generally a blackwood. They are not like drawer handles, as in other contemporary builders' organs, but quite dainty and usually of a characteristic profile. The diameters of the 'faces' of the knobs are small, from about 1" to 1¼" and the overall visible length of the knob is a little over 1½". The similarity of a surviving knob at Swithland with those in the Cobham Hall and Rotherham consoles suggests that such knobs were used for all sizes of organs. The stop-knobs on the Eton College chamber organ are of ivory and different in profile, probably because the 'normal' shape would be rather too fragile in that material. The stops draw 1½" in the smaller chamber organs, and 1¾" in the larger.

Shanks The knobs are set in shanks of mahogany of nominal ¾" or 13/16" square cross-section which, beyond the jambs, are spliced and screwed to 'traces' of oak of the same cross-section. The stop name is written on the oak traces in ink, so that any subsequent alterations to the stop-list or layout should be identifiable.

The traces in the organ at 'Hatchlands' (1759) are marked as follows:

Op Diapason
Principall treble
15th
Cornett

Diapason [i.e., Stopped Diapason]
Dulciana
Flut
Principall Bafs
Sefq [?; almost illegible]

Stop-knob from Swithland

Trundle–backfall action This is the usual draw–stop action in the larger house organs and one therefore presumes it to have been employed in the church organs. The trundle is a stout vertical post, usually of pine but sometimes of oak; generally about 1¼" square in the chamber organs, and up to 2" square in the larger organs. It is made octagonal by planing its corners off and is pivoted in upper and lower rails with ¼" diameter iron pins, the lower pin being driven into the trundle, and the upper passed through an upper pivot rail. Tapered wrought iron arms of approximately ¼" material are spiked through the thickness of the trundles. At Cobham, the centres of the L–pin holes in these arms are 5" and 4½" from the pivot centre of the trundle, at the drawstop trace and backfall trace connections respectively. Clevises cut in the traces are connected to the arms by ⅛" diameter straight 1" pins of brass whose top ends are hammered flat and splayed to prevent their falling through. The trundle works simultaneously to change the direction of the action and to raise it, so its

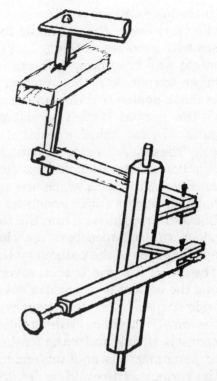

Trundle–backfall action

connection to the backfall which transmits the action to the slider is generally higher than that to the draw–stop. The pivot pin of the vertical wrought–iron backfall is held in a shallow slot in the top surface of a horizontal plank in whose thickness the backfall is housed.

The backfall is of a maximum size at the pivot point of 1¼" by ¼", and it has a leverage of about 6" to 15" at Cobham Hall. It is slotted into the slider end without reinforcement, and is pinned at its lower end to a horizontal trace connecting it to the trundle arm. The 1¾" draw of the stop–knob is thus 'geared down' in two stages, at the trundle and at the backfall, to give a slider movement of ⅝", and to include a small allowance for slack or lost motion.

This whole system can be scaled down or up according to the size of organ and the consequent length of the draw–stop actions and the amount of the sliders' movement.

Soundboards and shifting movements

Soundboards Both of the soundboards which survive from 1742 (see chapter 3, nos. 3 and 4) are made in the Germanic fashion with 'filled' bars. Since the soundboards at (for instance) Hillington (1756), and in the 'Hatchlands' (1759) and the Cobham Hall (1778) organs and the organ in Switzerland (1782) are also made in this way, it might be assumed that all surviving soundboards were also made in this manner. However, since those who come into close contact with these mechanisms all too rarely report in writing on what they find upon removing the sliders, or when they examine the undersides of the soundboards, it is difficult to say with absolute certainty that such is the case. A large church organ soundboard might well have been different in a number of respects from the 'large chamber' organ soundboards that remain, or it might have been Snetzler's normal practice to make double soundboards in 'sides' for all large divisions.

The normal British soundboard was made with a grid closed on its upper surface by the 'table', a series of planks over which leather is laid and the sliders run. These planks run at right angles to the bars of the grid, and therefore any significant alteration in the climatic environment of the soundboard sets up considerable strains which are usually resolved by the tables' cracking along their lengths. Such a construction was used by Snetzler's British contemporaries, but Snetzler brought with him the Germanic 'sponselled' or 'filled-in' arrangement in which the softwood bars are closed completely, top and bottom (except for the opening area of the pallets) by tightly fitting glued-in ¼"-thick strips of dry oak. The top of the grid is then covered with strips of leather, laid under the sliders, and the bottom is papered or covered with parchment reinforced at intervals with wide strips of pine. As the sponsels run parallel to the bars, the climatic stress on the construction, as it dries out, is lessened. All that might happen is that the sponsels shrink under the leathered top-side or tend to fall out from the paper- or parchment-covered underside, and the initial process of assembly and gluing the various parts could be designed to minimize these possibilities.

Snetzler's typical soundboards (and this includes the pin-action soundboards) are framed in oak with strong dovetailed corners, with (as far as one can see) pine bars and oak sponsels. All other parts are made of oak, including the 5/16" thick sliders and ⅜" bearers (to allow for the 1/16" leathering usually under the sliders, but in one organ observed to be over them; see chapter 3, no. 10), the doubled upperboards (when there are shifting movement sliders between them) and the 5" tall spigoted ½" by ⅝"-section rack-pillars and ¼" rackboards. The soundboard bars were assembled (presumably after 'dry' trial) with hot 'animal' glue and then 'flooded' with hot glue to seal pores in the timber and any minor flaws. Many of these well-made soundboards are in use in the smaller organs with little or no alteration, the generally damp British climate having kept the sponsels firmly in place.

The oak used is a straight-grained Baltic (called 'Danzig') or Austrian timber, not the inconsistent and heavier British *quercus robur*. Fittings on the pipework are also made with this oak (imported via King's Lynn?), as are the key levers and the oak parts of the stop action. The pallet-opening in the underside of the grid is covered with a fine white paper (hand-made, of course, and acid-free), or – in the 1742 Cuckston organ – in leather. The use of leather over the pallets was not necessarily Snetzler's idea; the 1629 organ made for Dean Isaac Bargrave of Canterbury has parchment to close the bars and a double layer of leather at this point also, and it may have been a common British technique at the time. The oak face-board, leathered all over its internal face and over its edges, is invariably recessed into the pallet well. It is made removable by thongs of leather and held in place by iron clasps or wooden turn-buttons or by tightening a large 'cheese-head' screw fixed vertically through the underside of the well-board halfway along the length of its front.

The oak rackboards, and often the upperboards, are marked with the ranks' names – 'Cornett' and 'Sesquialtra' are typical spellings – and where the layout is potentially confusing they are marked also with the pitches of the individual pipes. The pitch of each pallet is inked on the front edge of the front rackboard as a guide to the assembly of the pipework, both in the workshop and on site. This marking would be particularly necessary when the organs were shipped abroad or sent great distances from London. The organs could then be assembled with local labour, and Snetzler himself would only be required to finish the organ tonally (as at Lulworth, apparently; see chapter 3, no. 24). But the other reason that so many components are marked (and Snetzler's organs are not the only ones of this period with many marks) may be that the 'journeyman' system of using labour meant some discontinuity of work, and that it was necessary for a workman coming fresh to an organ to know quickly and exactly about any particular layout. The markings on mechanical parts and on pipework are very consistent; their spelling and 'German' style of notation suggest strongly that they are by Snetzler himself, and (less strongly) they may suggest that he used 'German' workers. It is anyway unlikely that they were necessary because of an 'assembly-line' system of widespread sub-contracting of the normal essential mechanical components; it was probably one of Snetzler's ways of keeping the work flowing as steadily as possible.

Shifting movements The appearance of any kind of registrational device in British organs (apart from the duplication of stops 'by communication' in Renatus Harris's organs, as at Backchurch – see Appendix 1) seems to be contemporary with Snetzler's arrival; at least, they appear in his organs from 1742 onwards as 'shifting' movements operated by a pedal. (The 'machine' pedal in the harpsichords dates only from the 1760s, and may have been developed in emulation of it.) Snetzler and his imitators and colleagues (Haxby, Donaldson and Richard Seede) seem to have made only a system using additional sliders. In Snetzler's organs, these extra sliders are placed on a separate sub-upperboard above those operated by the drawstop action and are connected through a single wrought-iron horizontal trundle or a large oak bar via a vertical trace to a pedal. The extra sliders are put 'off ' by the pedal's movement, and a spring of wood or metal returns the action and opens the extra sliders when the pedal is released.

At Cobham Hall, the 'shifting' action, placed to be operated by the player's left foot but not at present connected, incorporates an arrangement resembling a later type of mechanical 'poppet' reversing action. This mechanism would have required lead weights, now missing, to counter-balance the weight of the extra shifting-movement sliders, but if the system is original – which would be most remarkable – the presence of the poppet implies that the player would press the pedal once to reduce the registration to 'piano' and again to restore the stops as set by the draw-stops and that there would be no need to hold the pedal down. Some such mechanism would in fact be necessary in an organ with a pedalboard, the player's right foot being engaged in winding the organ and opening the swell-box front.

There are signs that a pedalboard was provided at Cobham Hall, and the device need not immediately be dismissed as a later addition. It would have been required in those organs (for instance that at the 'Savoy' Lutheran church, chapter 3, no. 37), known to have been equipped with pedalboards from the start. However, it may be that a 'notch', suggested by the 1748 Fulneck contract (chapter 3, no. 9), was all that was required.

Where there are shifting movement 'over-sliders', the drawstop sliders, and therefore the draw-stops, do not move. In a 1783 Seede organ, springs were inserted into the sides of the draw-stop sliders to prevent their being dragged 'off' by the over-sliders, which here (and in other builders' work apart from Snetzler's) are placed directly upon the draw-stop sliders. The 'sub-upperboards' used by Snetzler circumvented this problem, which would be particularly evident in a small chamber organ soundboard (or a 'narrow' church-organ soundboard) with short sliders of relatively little mass, but only one example of a 'British-built' organ (a large chamber organ apparently made in London) which uses sub-upperboards is known to the authors.

Snetzler used only a system with two sliders, not the 'cut-off slider' between two separate grids, as in the 1766 Byfield organ at 'Finchcocks'. It neither resembles the later special designs of Samuel Green or of John Abbey and Timothy Russell, nor is it at all to be compared with the draw-stop moving 'combination actions' of Flight, James Bishop and the later nineteenth-century builders. Its function is confined to cutting off wind to the upperwork and reeds momentarily, so that an instant 'piano' may be obtained. The system was never applied to the Swell stops – nor to the Choir stops, as far as we know – and logically it was not required at all when a Choir division could be used for 'piano' passages in a two- or three-manual organ. It is designed to give to a Great manual the musical potential of two manuals, and it is clear that the Handel concertos rely on its use. Some 'foreign' music, such as C. P. E. Bach's *Preludio e 6 Sonate* (1790) seems to be written for a small organ with a similar sort of registration device, so Snetzler may have seen it in Vienna.

Usually, the shifting movement silences all the stops drawn except any unison stops and the Flute. It is perfectly flexible, in that it will reduce any combination of the group of stops that can be affected by it to any combination of the group of stops unaffected by it. Combined with an open or shut Swell (or 'Eccho'), four distinct gradations of tone (or 'terraced dynamics', as one used to call them) are immediately available from 'one-and-a-half' keyboards.

Ecchoes and swell devices

The Echo box, from which the eighteenth-century concept of the Swell was developed, was originally a wooden enclosure for short-compass (and therefore short-length) ranks of pipework designed to 'echo' sundry corresponding stops on the Great. This incidentally produced a distant 'piano' tone in the organ which could be exploited musically in its own right. Since the Choir division's pipework already produced quiet tones in larger organs, the simple suggestion (by the

Jordans in 1712) that a lid to the box might be hinged, and thus a 'swelling' effect produced when the lid was raised, had an obvious musical use; the idea was therefore taken up, at first gradually but later universally.

The short–compass (*c'*) 'Ecchoe' box could be contained in the space above and behind the top keyboard, and below the Great soundboard(s). Such a position was described by Snetzler regarding the organ for Fulneck, 1748, 'with a separate keyboard just below it'. Here space was tight and the pipework not easily accessible; Snetzler thought that at Fulneck a proposed reed rank should be left out as it could not be tuned readily.

Later and larger swell–boxes were placed above the Great. The change from an 'internal' echo box to this new position might be seen in the front casework of the Smith organ at Great St Mary's church, Cambridge, where a 'diall' or clock gave way in 1766 to pierced carving, presumably because the clockwork would be inaccessible, or in the way, when an Echo/Swell was placed high in the front of the organ by the Parkers.

Instead of the lid–opening box, a sliding shutter–frame was designed for the high Swells, perhaps inspired by the recently introduced sash–window. All eighteenth–century shutter fronts, including Green's versions, are normally closed (that is, their pipework is still thought of as 'Ecchoes') until they are opened by the action of the pedal. When the pedal is released, they close again, the shutter falling gently by the aid of levered counter–balances. It is likely that any notching of the pedal slot to latch the box open is later work, required by an organist used to the Victorian 'trigger' swell–pedal.

Though the Swell was generally controlled from a second keyboard in the church and larger house organs, it was sometimes winded from the same soundboard as the Choir pipework (as at Hillington, 1756, where their keyboard is the lower one,) and was even occasionally part of the tonal scheme of a single–manual organ, as John Sutton says:[4]

> He [*sc.* Snetzler] made very beautiful Chamber Organs, and ufually introduced a hautboy stop upon another wind chest in a fmall swell box, the action of which he attached to the ordinary action, thus saving the expenfe of another fet of keys.

The solo 'swell' stop mentioned by Sutton was in fact conveyed through a tall groove–block from the normal upperboard, as in the organ at Clare College, Cambridge (1755), and the two stops in the swell–box at Hillington are also thus winded. The small organ at Kedleston (chapter 3, no. 69) is not typical, in that there is a separate keyboard and action solely for the Swell Hautboy; this is an additional sign that this organ was an older, rebuilt instrument.

In Snetzler's smaller chamber organs, the action to lift the shutter–frame was often simply a cord running over pulley–wheels fixed in the roof of the casework and descending to the swell–pedal, but there were more sophisticated arrangements of wooden levers where space allowed.

The Cobham Hall organ Swell is unaltered, and typical of the standard late eighteenth–century high Swell in everything except its position. Its internal aperture is carefully shaped to allow only a small opening upon the first pressure of the pedal; clearly, it was designed to produce as steady a crescendo as possible.

Perhaps because of the 'nodding' action of the horizontal lever that lifts the shutter-frame, the nickname 'nag's head' was applied to it. Clumsily designed actions, or those that were not carefully counterbalanced and allowed the shutter-frame to shut audibly, might have made such a term of ridicule seem apposite, but the device was of real interest to musicians. The earliest English organ music with crescendo and diminuendo symbols – of the same kind as those in Geminiani's violin scores – was the mid-eighteenth century D minor *Voluntary* by William Walond, 'Organist at Oxford' (actually an assistant organist at New College). It was presumably written for a recently-installed Swell-box.

Some Snetzler chamber organs (of all dates, but only those equipped with doors) had lids in the otherwise solid tops of their cases; these 'roof-swells' were lifted by a sturdy roller placed just behind the pediment. In one instance (chapter 3, no. 81) at least, there were also small solid shutters behind grille-like slots in the upper sides of their casework. The swell in the 1745 Kirkman–Snetzler claviorgan employs an opening hinged panel analogous to some early harpsichord 'lid–swells'. Actually, this and the 'roof-swells' *do* look like nags' mouths, and are visible – unlike the Swell inside an organ case. The term 'nag' might anyway refer to a 'scold', or a 'jade' of the *human* variety; as with a 'Vox Humana', it is necessary to hear the authentic sound of an early Swell fully to appreciate the appellation.

It is perhaps instructive to note that the Cornet-topped chorus in the high Swells remained longer in favour than the Great Cornet. Despite the decline of the Cornet voluntary *per se* by the end of the century, this high Cornet was still a valuable and well-placed sound for the 'giving out' of tunes and – *pace* John Marsh who set out stringent instructions for the musical use of the Swell (see Appendix 9) – for leading a congregation, especially following the introduction early in the nineteenth century of a Swell to Great 'coupla movement'.

Pedalboards, couplers and tremulants

The organ at the German Lutheran church in the Savoy (*c*1757, see chapter 3, no. 37), was famous in its time for its pedals which, according to Ludlam (1772), were connected to the last twelve notes of the Great 'and their semitones'. This may very likely mean not that the keys of the Great were connected through a coupler mechanism of the nineteenth-century British type, but that they winded the Great through separate pallets in the same way as that described by Buckingham at St Mary's church, Nottingham (chapter 3, no. 90):

> A set of pedals from GG to C 17 do not act upon the keys but have a
> separate set of pallets to the Gt. Organ

One wonders if the organ in St Martin's church, Leicester, was also made this way, in view of Ludlam's connection with this church. It seems that the earlier-dated organ at Halifax (chapter 3, no. 67) did not possess pedals – hence Herschel's need for lead weights. Did he therefore have pedals at Bath (no. 76)? Music he composed appears not to give any clues.[5]

Samuel Wesley was quoted by Pearce[6] as saying that 'he could well remember the time when the only organ in London to which Pedals were affixed was that in the German Church in the Savoy, built by Snetzler'. Rimbault[7] instanced a letter (probably the same) from Charles Wesley which says that this was the first organ in this country provided with a pedal clavier.

There are counter-claims to this assertion relating to the organ at St Paul's Cathedral, which possessed toe-pedals from at least 1721 onwards (later played by Handel, as related by Burney),[8] and the advertisement issued by John Harris and John Byfield I about their 1726 organ at St Mary's Redcliffe, Bristol, which had pedals to the lowest octave of the *C'* compass Great. These, and the possibility raised by the organ concerto op. 7 no. 1 in B♭ that pedals (albeit temporarily) were available to Handel in 1740, may show that the Wesleys' claim should not be taken to be absolute.

Nonetheless, this was very probably the first organ in England (or in London) to have been designed with pedals that were more than short toe-pedals, but consisted of a complete pedalboard which might have been playable by the heels as well as the toes. Since two sets of 'box' pedals (each of thirteen notes) survive in America in association with Snetzler organs of 1762 and 1764, it may well be that this was the style of pedalboard or 'clavier' employed. (See chapter 3, nos. 55 and 62.) They are similar to classical French pedalboards, so that when the longer-still toe-and-heel *C*-compass pedalboards were introduced in the first part of the nineteenth century and were called 'German pedals' (probably because of their compass), the distinction made then should not confuse us now. Buckingham does not describe the Nottingham 'set of pedals' at all precisely, and in fact he does not use either of the terms 'pedalboard' or 'German pedals', so their actual design is not clear from his reports.

What appears to be original recessing of the lower part of the console of the organ at Cobham Hall (chapter 3, no. 99) and the fact that its knee-board is shorter than the present pedalboard requires (but would be right for a pedalboard that sloped upwards towards its inner edge) suggest that a pedalboard was supplied when the organ was made in 1778. If there was one, it did not operate separate pallets in the Great soundboards – probably because a step in the floor just behind the console would have made the necessary action difficult to arrange, and because the width of the alcove in which the organ is placed restricts the number of pallets which could be accommodated in the Great soundboards. If a connection was made from the pedalboard directly to the Great keyboard, this is not now obvious because of a later pedalboard and coupling system, but signs of an original arrangement might be found upon any dismantling of the organ.

Couplers Leffler's slightly confused account of the couplers at St George's church, Hanover Square (see chapter 3, no. 50), leaves open the possibility that this (and other?) organs originally included inter-manual couplers – here, there was a Choir-to-Great coupler, one also included in the Savoy organ: 'a Copula which adds the Choir to the full organ'.

Buckingham did not visit these organs, and does not record any other Snetzler couplers. He does, though, record his own addition of inter-manual and manual to pedal couplers to a number of Snetzler's organs.

Tremulants The only recorded 'tremblant' made by Snetzler is that in the Lutheran chapel in the Savoy (chapter 3, no. 37). Ludlam, in remarking on the stable wind in that organ (Appendix 7), also says that 'the foreigners' (which could presumably include those in England's immigrant churches) employ the device to make 'the whole organ sigh and sob most dolefully, and is therefore used at funerals'. A charming idea!

Drum– or Thunder–stop Although Ludlam does not specifically mention it as part of the 'Savoy' organ – he calls it 'A very absurd imitation of the kettle-drum ... made by two great pipes, out of tune to each other' – Christopher Smart (see pp. 34–5) did mention it apparently in that context. The very fact that Ludlam mentions it in a survey of British organ-building may be indicative of its occasional existence; perhaps it must also be presumed to be an effect that appealed only to benighted 'foreigners'.

III The mechanical design of chamber organs

Because the mechanical designs used in the various chamber organs influenced, and were influenced by, the requirements of their tonal design, it is necessary first to classify them by types. The system used here is based on the outward design of the cases, but the 'evolution' of the organs' mechanisms is complex and not absolutely clear. It would seem that Snetzler may have kept some 'stock' organs (and certainly he made several in batches) which were sold some time after they were made; their chronology is therefore difficult to determine, especially since it is known that there were some other chamber organs whose contents and exact format were not recorded.

Type A: organs (usually) with 'normal' cases:
    A1: with pin actions, in two sizes:
        (*a*) with 6–10 (or 13)–6 front pipe displays, or
        (*b*) with 7–10–7 front pipe displays
    A2: with sticker-backfall actions and 7–11 (or 13)–7 displays
Type B: 'bureau' organs
Type C: organs which, in general, have 'wreathed-oval' fronts with either
        (*a*) 4–17–4 front pipe displays, or
        (*b*) 3–15–3 front pipe displays
            and which employ sticker-backfall actions
Type D: 'claviorgans'
Type E: early instruments which do not fit the above types
Type F: larger chamber organs with two manuals, or those remade or designed for a
    specific location

The chronology of the chamber organs whose contents are known seems therefore to fall into these categories:

Type A:

A1(a)	1750	Picton Castle, *G' (long)–f'''*
A1(b)	1754	Norwich Cathedral, *G' (long)–f'''*
A?	1755	Clare College, *G' (long)–f'''*
A1(a)	1755/6	Birmingham University, *G' (long)–f'''* [with ivory natural keys]
A2	1756	Kilwinning, *G' (long)–e'''*
A1	1755	Sculthorpe, *G' (long)–e'''* [for York Assembly Rooms]
?	1760	Bredon's Norton, *G' (short)–e'''*
A1(a)	1760	Bisley, *G' (short)–e'''*
A1(a)	1761	Wesley's Chapel, Bristol, *G' (long)–f'''*
A1(a)	1761	Smithsonian, *G' (short)–e'''* [not now with its original keyboard]
A2	1762	South Dennis, *G' (long)–e'''*
A2	1762	Blickling, *G' (long)–e'''* [?]
A1(a?)	1763	Salisbury Cathedral, *C–f'''* [altered]
A1(a)	1767	Liverpool Museum, *G' (long)–e'''* [not original keyboard]
A2	1768	Brookthorpe, *G' (long)–e'''*
A2	?1777	Lightcliffe, *G' (long)–e'''* [probably of earlier date]

? undated Barrington, *G' (long)–f'''*
? undated Bristoe (4 stops)

Type B:

1751	Johnson, *C, D–e'''*
1752	New Haven, *C, D–e'''*
1754	Mersham–le–Hatch, *C, D–e'''*
1763	Schaffhausen, *C, D–e'''*
1764	Dolmetsch, *C, D–e'''*
undated	King's, London, *C, D–e'''*

Type C:

1759	Hatchlands, *G' (long)–f'''* [special casework front]
?1759	Clyffe/Westminster Abbey (mechanism) *G (long)–f'''*
1760(a)	Eton College, *G' (long)–f'''* [with ivory naturals]
1764(b)	Great Barr/Westminster Abbey (case) [*G' (long)–e'''*]
1769(a)	St Andrew–by–the–Wardrobe, *G' (long)–e'''* [with ivory naturals]
1769(a)	Somerset, *G' (long)–e'''* [with ivory naturals]
1770(a)	Horbury, *G' (long)–e'''* [with original ivory naturals?]
?1774	Wynnstay, *?–?* [Adam–designed front]
1777(a)	Merevale, originally *G' (long)–e'''*
1779(b)	Locko, *G' (short)–f'''* [with ivory naturals]

Type D:

?1731	Moresby Hall, *C–f'''*
1745	Wemyss, *G' (long)–f'''*

Type E:

1742	Cuckston, *G' (long)–f '''*
1742	Yale, *C–d''', e'''*
?1748	Durrow/Mirrey, *G' (long)–e'''*

Type F:

?1755	Sandbeck Hall/Handsworth, ?–?
1756	Hillington, 2-m, *G' (long)–e'''*
1759	Curzon/Pantheon, ?3-m, ?–?
1766	rebuilt organ at Kedleston, *C, D–e'''*
1766	Fitzwilliam/Wilton, 2-m, *G' (long)–e'''*
1766	rebuilt organ at Bishop's Auckland, *G' (short)–e'''*
1778	Cobham Hall, 2-m, *G' (long)–e'''*
undated	William Strutt/?Hastings, large 1-m, *G' (long)–e'''*
c1762 or 1777	Lord Bute's barrel organ (parts)
c1777	Lowther barrel organ (parts)

To this list should be added organs (not certainly by Snetzler) so far untraced which Freeman noted in various advertisements:

1745: '5 stops, one added later', *Musical Opinion*, July 1903; this might be the same as the one advertised in *Musical Opinion*, May 1878 from Revd W. H. Whitworth, Ratlinghope Vicarage, Shrewsbury, as having '6 stops, ped bdn Hill £50'
1759: bureau organ, 5 stops thro', mahogany case; *Musical Opinion*, February 1891
1766: 9 stops, general swell, mahogany case; *Musical Opinion*, February 1891/June 1905
undated: 5 stops, mahogany case, pedals, foot/side blowers, *Musical Opinion*, April 1907
undated: 6 stops, 202 pipes, height 7'6" depth 28", 4½ octaves, pedals, *Musical Opinion*, October 1925
and Freeman's note of a 'small organ in an upper vestry of St George's Chapel' (TO 55/168) [also noted by Harvey as in the 'Belfry Tower' at Windsor in 1882]
and a 'decayed' one–manual organ at All Saints' church, Cambridge, removed in 1864

From these lists, inevitably incomplete in detail, certain points can be made:

(i) At least twice as many Type A organs were made as Type C; the earliest Type A being made in 1750. But pin–action organs had been made earlier (as early as 1742) and were employed in church organs, which shared certain features of their construction, (as at Durrow, 1748). The 1767 Liverpool organ seems to be the latest positively–dated Type A1, but the outward design of the upper front case of this type was used until at least the next year (Brookthorpe, 1768).
(ii) Type C appears about 1759, and was made almost until the end of Snetzler's career. Indeed, the dates of the last two (1777 and 1779) splice neatly into Green's first definitely–dated chamber organs at Appleford (1777) and Cobham Hall (1778). In these, Green used a revised version of the 'oval' front, where the removeable middle 'oval' panel extends right down to the impost and is not placed in Snetzler's manner on another plain panel that conceals the face–board of the soundboard.

(iii) Type B bureau organs make their appearance at about the same time as the first Type A1 organs, but were apparently not made after 1764.

(iv) The compasses of the Type A and Type C organs are generally $G'-e'''$, with short- or long-octave basses; but, for some reason which is still not clear, the upper termination was f''' in some early-to-middle period Type A organs, and in at least three of the nine Type C examples. There does not appear to be any pattern to this; the higher compass seems not to have been used after about 1763. It is unlikely that someone like Green would have influenced a change from f''' to e''', as in Green's output only the 1777 Appleford organ terminated at e''', and all his subsequent chamber organs extend to f'''. Contemporary chamber organs, as at Great Packington (made by Bridge or Parker) and 'Finchcocks' (Byfield, 1766) were made or first designed with a compass only to d'''; Snetzler's different practice has led one to speculate that his early work with claviorgans may have influenced the f''' compass of his earlier organs. If this were so, one might have expected this compass to have been adopted as a standard one, and it is difficult to see why it was not; visual considerations (for instance, of keyboard symmetry, where the pattern of keys in the bass and treble match) do not seem to be involved. Snetzler's larger chamber organs, and his and Green's church organs, universally extend only to e'''. As far as Snetzler is concerned, therefore, e''' should be taken as the 'norm' for his church and chamber organs; from this norm only the claviorgans, the 1742 Cuckston organ and about eight chamber organs deviate.

(v) It can be seen that the surviving chamber and larger house organs account for nearly half the total number of organs known to have been produced in Snetzler's workshops. Of course, this is not the proportion of work involved in the total manufacture of pipework, mechanisms and cases, but such an output (some fifty instruments) certainly indicates the rather sudden popularity of these organs as well as a recognition of the Snetzlers' expertise in their construction and ornamentation.

(vi) A high proportion of the secular organs seems to have survived, and the construction of these instruments indicates that Snetzler maintained to the end some features (for instance, sponselled soundboards, elaborate key-frames, single-rise wedge-reservoirs) completely at variance with contemporary or later indigenous instruments. What these 'foreign' techniques might indicate about Snetzler's workshops (did he employ mostly immigrant workmen – such as Ohrmann? – and if so what happened to them subsequently?) suggest further lines of enquiry outside the scope of this present study.

Characteristic key and stop actions of each type

Type A1 The fixed keyboard assembly protrudes from the case; immediately below it is a natural key's length elongation of the soundboard grid with the pallets under it. The keys, which are hinged at their rear with parchment, push down short 'pins' of 3/32" brass which pass through a leather strip and a tight hole into each 'groove' and directly open the pallets. In the extreme bass, several keys act upon rollers to the extreme treble end of the soundboard under the wide key-cheek blocks, so that the layout of the soundboard for the bass notes which require more wind is not restricted to the chromatic 'scale' of the keyboard. (The 'scale' is the lateral layout of the keys at a point just behind the front of the sharps, where the leather–padded keys contact the stickers.) The brass 'pins' are also angled further up the bass octave; the scales of keyboard and pallets match from about *G* upwards, and in the extreme treble the pallets are laid out to a scale narrower than the keys so that here again the 'pins' are angled.

The soundboard is therefore only as wide as the overall width of the keyboard plus the key–cheek blocks. The longest pipes are positioned along the inner sides and rear of the case, away from the soundboard grid and over or beyond the stop action which extends to the slider ends from stop–knobs or stop–levers placed each side of the keyboard/grid assembly. Access to the pallets is obtained by removing a mahogany assembly fitted around and below the keyboard and soundboard grid extension, and by taking out the flush–fitting oak 'face–board' below the soundboard grid.

Every Snetzler organ was 'labelled' on the vertical inside face of the 'soundboard bar', a strong softwood rail beyond the pallets and their springs that, together with the pallet–well's sides and bottom and the face–board, forms the enclosing wind–box into which the wind from the feeder and reservoir is ducted through a wooden wind-trunk.

Type B and Type D These organs have similar pin–actions, except that in these the stickers are made longer, since the soundboard is placed nearer floor level. Their pipework is behind the stickers and stop–action, and the soundboard grid is only slightly extended to receive the sticker ends.

Types A2, C and F Since the width of the soundboard was restricted by the keyboard scale and some extra width gained under the wide key–cheek blocks, the Type A1 design – perhaps derived from Swiss models – was necessarily limited to a few ranks only. It could not cope with the addition of a short–compass reed (either in a swell–box, or on a rear or front slider), or the extension downwards of the Open Diapason (often wooden in the early A1 organs and of short (*c*) compass) to one descending in metal to *C* or lower in wood or metal, or even with the addition of an extra rank to the mixture. Such extra stops created demands upon the design of the wind system (and especially the narrow soundboard grooves) that the pin–action soundboard could not be expected to meet.

The soundboard in organs of these types is therefore raised within the casework (itself therefore made taller), and a sticker–backfall action connects keys to pallets. As the backfalls can be 'fanned' outwards, the scale of the soundboard can be considerably increased (though Snetzler's soundboards and their grooves were never made as wide as some of Green's because of the constraints of their sponselled construction) and vertically stacked rollers allowed more large pipework to be placed at its treble end.

The process is elucidated in the following stop–lists:

Type A1 organs:

1750	Picton	OD sc: *c'*?SD	Pr	Fl	15	Ses/Cor	
?1754	Norwich	OD sc: *c* SD	Pr	Fl	15	Ses/Cor	
1755	Birmingham	OD ?sc SD	Pr	Fl	15	Ses/Cor II	
1761	Smithsonian	OD sc: *c'* SD	?	Fl	15	Ses/Cor II	
1767	Liverpool	OD ?sc SD	Pr	Fl	15	Ses/Cor	

Type A2 organs:

1755	Cambridge	OD ?sc SD	Dul	Pr	Fl	15	S/C III Hb	
1756	Kilwinning	OD (*?C*) SD	–	Pr	Fl	15	S/C III/IV	
1755	Sculthorpe	OD SD	–	Pr	Fl	–	S/C III	
1762	Blickling	OD SD	Dul	Pr	Fl	–	Sesq or Tpt	Hb
1768	Brookthorpe	OD SD	–	Pr	Fl	15	? mix	Hb

These lists show how the enlarged organs built after 1755 necessitated a modification of the action, and that this happened before the change to the Type C casework a few years later. In this respect, the development of the design of the long-delayed organ for Kilwinning (ordered in 1754 but delivered in 1757) may have been crucial; it is as if Snetzler was obliged to adapt the key action of a 'British' small church organ to this larger chamber organ.

Type C organs:

1759	Hatchlands	OD sc: *c'*SD	Dul	Pr	Fl	15	Ses/Cor	
1760	Eton	OD sc: *c'*SD	Dul	Pr	Fl	15	Ses/Cor II	
1769	Wardrobe	OD SD	Dul	Pr	Fl	15	Ses/Cor	
1769	Somerset	OD SD	Dul	Pr	Fl	15	Ses/Cor	Crm
1777	Merevale	OD sc: *c* SD	Dul	Pr	Fl	15	Ses/Cor III	Crm

These Type C stop-lists are more standardized than those of Type A2; it would seem that the short-compass Cremona was introduced into them after the eventual abandonment of the Type A casework.

No doubt these organs were made, whenever possible, in 'batches'. The delayed delivery of the organ for Kilwinning, the various near-'twins', (for instance, those at St Andrew-by-the-Wardrobe and in Somerset), the fact that Snetzler seemed able to plan well in advance to work in particular areas of the country, and that the various types were made over long time-spans – all these suggest that he had a considerable 'waiting list'. Since he also was prepared to wait lengthy periods for payment for large organs (as at Halifax and Hillsborough) it would seem that he had indeed accumulated some very necessary capital in his early years.

*

Wind systems in Types A, B, C and D

The wind-raising system occupies the whole of the space below the keyboard, soundboard and stop action, and it is made accessible through two hinged panels in the case front. The usual wind system consists of two connected parts, each made with oak or pine 'ribs' and boards leathered together. The first part is a 'feeder' (wedge-shaped in elevation) which, as the blowing pedal is pressed down, rises from its resting open position and closes up. Air is thus forced through valves into the upper part as the external valves in the underside of the feeder shut under the pressure of the wind now pressurised within it.

The upper part is a larger wedge-shaped lead-weighted 'reservoir' for the wind; it is often inaccurately called a 'bellows' because of its resemblance to fire-bellows. Its free end rises with successive influxes of air from the feeder. As a precaution against over-filling, an arm screwed to a hinged 'safety valve' is allowed to trip open upon a part of the soundboard support frame when the reservoir is sufficiently filled. There is an indication to the blower of the fullness or emptiness of the reservoir by means of a rising stick; this was often superseded later by a dangling 'mouse' tell-tale, claimed to have been 'invented' c1804 by Thomas Elliott (or Buckingham?). (Bellows, because they are raised alternately – one just as the other closes – require other ways of ascertaining their state of winding.)

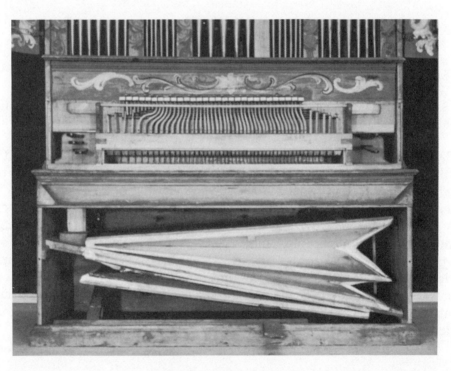

Wind system, stop action and key action of a 'Toggenburger' organ made by Joseph Looser, 1788

In order to make the system more compact, the feeder and reservoir 'wedges' are contra–disposed, and the dividing board between them (with the connecting valves in it) is elongated so that it can be supported at an angle on an internal frame or on the casework. As we noted above, this form of construction appears to have been new to Britain at the time of Snetzler's arrival; it may have been derived from a Swiss or south German tradition that included a wind system of this kind in its small organs – including the 'Toggenburger' organs – from the seventeenth to the nineteenth centuries. (The English organ had by this latter time developed more 'sophisticated' systems, pioneered by Alexander Cumming and Samuel Green.) Although Snetzler's system very cleverly saved space and eliminated the 'bellows only' winding of previous small organs, it did not ensure a perfectly steady wind supply.

As the wedge–reservoir fell under the influence of its weighting, and of the taking of wind from it to the various pipes through the wind–trunk, pallet–well, pallets and grid–chambers, it did not give out a flow of wind at an equal pressure under all conditions of demand, or at all positions of its weighted top board. If the reservoir were allowed to fall under its own weight without being replenished by the feeder, a difference in pressure (in fact, a rise of about one–fourteenth is the accepted calculation) would be audible to a sensitive ear – a variation particularly trying to a person tuning the organ. Snetzler's single–fold reservoirs were perhaps more aurally noticeable in this respect than were some contemporary British–made multi–fold ones, especially where the size of his system was restricted by the smallness of the lower casework. There is also a tendency for the relatively small reservoir to rise by a series of 'jerks' if the feeder is operated clumsily. Therefore, as Thomas Drew said (in his letter of 1899; see chapter 3, no. 4), the organ has to be 'humoured'; but when operated by a careful and sensitive blower/player, this design can yield expressive musical results. It should be remembered that generally the player was expected to wind these small instruments, and it was – and remains – therefore part of a musician's expressive art to produce a music-enhancing result from his or her management of the blowing pedal.

The iron pedals and their mechanisms for operating the 'shifting movement' and any swell–box arrangement are situated in the lowest part of the organ, under the wind system.

Wind system in a Type F organ

As the organ at Cobham Hall (1778) is the largest surviving little–altered Snetzler organ, and has readily been made accessible for measurement, some basic details of its wind system follow. These may to some extent represent the arrangement originally used in the smaller church organs:

(i) The two single–fold bellows seem to have been made 36" wide by 72" long at first, though they are now somewhat smaller because their pine planks have dried out, with ribs 13¾" wide at their maximum. They are weighted with bricks and, as they rise, sliding wooden 'springs' work upon their upper surfaces with increasing effect. These springs are apparently intended to maintain the higher pressure, created by the internal encroachment of the ribs, as the bellows become nearly empty. A similar arrangement is described by Hopkins[9] as being used in the organ at Backchurch (1724) where 'Renatus Harris applied accumulative springs to the four bellows for this purpose' [*sc.* for equalizing the wind–pressure]. Hopkins goes on to describe German improvements in the system which included the following: 'To counteract any greater influence which the inward folding ribs might still exercise, a long wooden spring was applied, which operated during the earlier stages of the bellows' sinking, in addition to the surface weights; but by degrees ceased to do so as the influence of the ribs was more and more felt.'

Hopkins also notes[10] that 'while small and moderate–sized organs have from 2 to 6 diagonal bellows, many large instruments have 8, 10, 12 or even as many as 14'. From the context, it may be inferred that the maximum in Britain was 6; the higher numbers refer to continental organs that were very large by British standards.

(ii) At Cobham Hall, the pumping handles raise the bellows some 12" to give them a capacity of about 8 cubic feet of air each.

(iii) The bellows empty through 'beaks', each measuring about 10" by 3" internally, and through valves into a main trunk 5" square internally which runs across the whole width of the organ at its front. From it rise two trunks 4" square internally which supply the Great soundboard through the well–board's extreme front corners; these trunks each include two right–angled bends.

(iv) The Great pallet well has a cross–sectional area of approximately 12" by 3⅜".

(v) The Swell is winded by a smaller trunk (about 2" by 3½" internally) taken from the treble–end Great wind–trunk just before it enters the Great soundboard.

(vi) The wind–pressure given by the system using the bellows alone seems to be a maximum of 3", but it is difficult to measure this because the bellows are in poor condition.

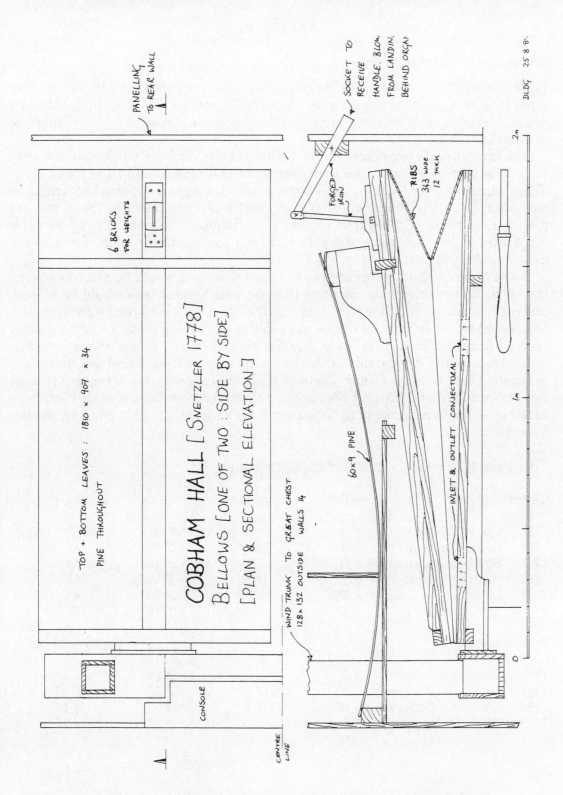

The labels within the drawing read:

PANELLING TO REAR WALL

SOCKET TO RECEIVE HANDLE. BLOW FROM LANDING BEHIND ORGAN

DLDG 25·8·81

2m

6 BRICKS FOR WEIGHTS

RIBS 343 WIDE 12 THICK

FORGED IRON

COBHAM HALL [SNETZLER 1778]
BELLOWS [ONE OF TWO : SIDE BY SIDE]
[PLAN & SECTIONAL ELEVATION]

TOP + BOTTOM LEAVES : 1810 × 907 × 34
PINE THROUGHOUT

INLET & OUTLET CONJECTURAL

60 × 9 PINE

WIND TRUNK TO GREAT CHEST
128 × 132 OUTSIDE WALLS 14

1m

CONSOLE

CENTRE LINE

0

Plan and elevation of the bellows in the organ at Cobham Hall

231

The layout of the pipework

Since the organs are most easily tuned from the front (where the tuner can remove pipes for access, play the notes required and perhaps even also operate the blowing pedal), the internal layout of all the chamber organs is similar, and is arranged to practical advantage.

The largest pipes are placed at the back and sides, and the winding of the very longest is 'conveyed' from the upperboards of the soundboard to a lower level. Those ranks with the next-longest open or stopped pipes are placed according to size directly on the soundboard. Within relatively easy reach of the tuner are placed those ranks of pipes that require most frequent attention. These comprise the Flute, of stopped wood, the Fifteenth and the relatively small pipes of the Sesquialtera and Cornet.

If the organ originally included a Dulciana, this rank would be placed between the Open Diapason and the Stopped Diapason; its longest pipe would be 4' long, and reachable over the Stopped Diapason. If a short-compass reed were supplied, this would be set in front of the Cornet, so that its tuning wires could be readily reached from the front. It is likely that the organ's owner, or one of his servants, would be expected to tune this rank when necessary. A reed placed in a swell-box (as in the Clare College, Cambridge, and Kedleston organs) would require at least two persons for its tuning, but the majority of the chamber organs could have been tuned by a single reasonably agile person, even without any help from an electric blower.

Case sizes of chamber organs and bureau organs

Chamber organs		width	height	depth	type
1755	Clare College	5' 0	9' 0"	3' 0"	A2?
1756	Lodge Canongate	7' 0"	12' 0"	5' 0"	A2
1761	Smithsonian Institute	4' 2"	7' 2"	2' 4½"	A1
1762	Blickling church	6' 6"	12' 0"	3' 1½"	A2
1767	Liverpool Museum	3' 9½"	8' 10"	2' 10"	A1
?	Lord Barrington	4' 8"	9' 2"	2' 10"	?

Bureau organs					depth reducing to
1742	Yale University	3' 8"	5' 6¾"	2' 3½"	1' 2"
1751	Sir Ronald Johnson	3' 9"	3' 9"	2' 2"	1' 2"
1764	Dolmetsch Collection	3' 9"	3' 9"	2' 5½"	1' 0"
?	King's College	3' 9"	3' 9"	2' 3"	1' 3"

*

IV Pipework

Introduction

The 'archaeological' study of pipe–scaling was established by David Wickens in *The Instruments of Samuel Green*.[11] He discusses Snetzler's pipework scaling, partly in order to set Green's practice into a wider perspective and partly because, he suggests, there is a close resemblance between the pipework of the two builders. He also suggests that in fact Green may have been his own pipemaker.

In fact, although there are some resemblances between the styles of the two builders (especially in terms of the scaling of the pipework), there are also divergences. Nonetheless, as David Wickens points out, the years between Green's official apprenticeship with Pyke which ended after seven years in 1761 and his partnership from 1768 with John Byfield (the third of that name, who died in 1799) remain to be accounted for. There are indeed several pieces of evidence that do not seem to 'ring true' and need to be more fully explained. First, Green's apprenticeship with Pyke – chiefly a maker of clocks (including organ clocks) – would, on the face of it, have seemed more likely to have produced a maker of barrel–organs and mechanical contraptions than a serious organ–builder who was able to plan the large–scale making of organs of all sizes. Where then did he obtain this experience? Second, why did Green not train with the Jordan–Bridge–Byfield 'establishment', as John Sutton suggested?[12] Or indeed with Snetzler? There are possible answers to the first question: in 1754, the younger Jordan's health was failing (see p. 12); though Bridge was still active, he was of advanced years; perhaps Byfields II and IV were too busy training each other. As to the second question: Green evidently chose to train with someone who would give him an introduction to the City of London and the royal court. Snetzler could not give him the former, nor until 1760 the latter.

The following chronology is conjectural, but is fitted round the facts as they are at present known:

1754–61 Green trained 'officially' with George Pyke in Newgate Street, but probably actually learns organ–building with the associated builders just along Holborn in Theobald's Road. These included the Byfields, the Englands and perhaps Hugh Russell. (Or did Green learn from his relative Charles? Or was there a link between his father Henry Green, distiller at Wheatley near Oxford, and Leonard Snetzler, carver to the University, towards the end of this period?) In the last two years (1759–1761) Green, by then experienced in making pipes, makes pipes for Snetzler in a 'style' of pipes (itself similar to pipework used in Byfield organs at this time) which can be found in Snetzler's organs from at least 1759 onwards.

1761–1768 Upon completing his apprenticeship with Pyke in 1761, Green worked directly for Snetzler. These years, and especially the middle years of the decade, saw many large organs made for churches throughout the Midlands and the north of England. When Snetzler travelled around and (it seems) left a capable person in charge in London, he would have needed the help of an energetic colleague or 'servant' – the one who was paid extra cash at Halifax in 1765, perhaps – who materially helped to supply and finish the organs built in that period. Such a person could not become a partner because Snetzler was not a British citizen until 1770.

1768–1772 Green found a 'partner' instead in John Byfield III, but this arrangement finished in early 1772.

1772 onwards Even when he had become independent, and had married Sarah Norton, the daughter of a clock maker, it would have been possible for Green to have worked for Snetzler. Green's first personal commissions (at Sleaford, 1772; Walsall, 1773; and Leigh, 1777) could have been made alongside work for Snetzler during those years. In fact, Snetzler's last organ of consequence, made for St Mary's, Nottingham, in 1776 and erected in 1777, was made just before Green's first large organ at St Katherine's (a royal foundation) in 1777–8. The next Snetzler organ, at Rotherham 1777, was evidently master-minded by Ohrmann (see p. 18), but the Cobham Hall organ, dated internally 1778 but possibly not erected until the next year, is again 'Green-like'. Green apparently completed only two chamber organs in 1778, one of which, dated 29 October 29 1778, was made for Cobham Hall. After these, and the quite small 1779 organ for Bangor cathedral, Green was constantly occupied, and Snetzler seems gradually to have detached himself from involvement in organ-making.

An odd circumstance is that Green made no barrel or other mechanical organs, but that Snetzler did participate in a number of schemes involving these, apparently from the mid–1770s onwards. But after Snetzler's retirement, it seems Green did make or repair some organ parts to harpsichords by the Shudi workshop.[13]

Rather more problematical is some of the pipework still in the organ at Hawkesyard Priory, Staffordshire (chapter 3, no. 14) which may date from 1750–1 (or later?), and which was mistaken for Green's by commentators and organ-builders 150 years ago. There is indeed the possibility that there was some confusion because of the nearby presence of another organ purchased by Josiah Spode: the Green organ from Lichfield Cathedral, which he presented to St John's church, Armitage, in 1862. There is no suggestion in the Eton College records or elsewhere that Green worked there (and Snetzler maintained the organ until 1784), but the pipes in question clearly bear a strong resemblance to Green's. However, there are a number of organs by Green that were rebuilt or replaced by the two builders associated with this organ during the nineteenth century (Holdich and, later, Hill) and it is not certain when these pipes were introduced.

It should be made clear that the discussion centres on the construction of the pipes, and not their marking-out. All Snetzler's pipes, from the early 1750s until the later 1770s, are marked consistently in 'his' style. However, the 1777 Rotherham pipework is marked in a style different from that at Cobham Hall of the next year and, perhaps coincidentally, *c*1777 is mentioned by David Wickens as being about the time at which Green's pipe-markings took on a characteristic 'hook' to his B natural ('♮') script; this style is to be found in Green's small Cobham Hall organ, made in 1778.

Furthermore, David Wickens notes[14] that the scaling practice in Green's earlier organs (during the 1770s) is similar to that used by Snetzler at Ludlow (1764) and Rotherham (1777), and that there is considerable circumstantial evidence – strong hints in correspondence, too – that Green may have made at least some, if not the majority, of the pipes for his own organs himself, as well as marking them out. Much more work needs to be done in examining the practical organization of the eighteenth-century workshop before it can be established how many persons were required to make the pipes for the through-put of the organs made either by Green or by Snetzler, but modern practice would suggest that, after making allowance for improved productivity in other branches of modern organ-building because of the use of machinery, two or three metal pipe-makers could have coped. Snetzler seems not to have been one of these, but Green may have been. Would this have been a neatly complementary arrangement while it lasted?

Analysis of pipe-metal and solder

Although Snetzler has been accused[15] of using 'poor' metal (by including too high a proportion of lead in the alloy), this view is factually untrue. It is also anachronistic, based as it is upon the supposed superiority of 'spotted' metal and the modern fashion for using tin-rich alloys. Recent analyses of pipe-metal from Snetzler's organs have shown that over a reasonably wide time-span his preferred alloy was one containing around 27 per cent or more tin:

Year	Place	Type	Rank/pitch	Lead : tin proportion	Analyser
1742	Cuckston	chamber	15 bass 8ve	65 : 35	Renshaw
1756	Whitehaven	church	– –	80 : 20	Dixon
1760	Bredon's N'n	chamber	Sesq c'	70 : 30	Barnes
1765	Swithland	church	OD c'	70 : 30	Barnes
			Pr c'	70 : 30	Barnes
			Pr –	73 : 27	Renshaw
1765	Peterhouse	chapel	– –	76 : 24	Dixon
1775	Bath, Marg St	church	– –	81 : 19	Dixon
1777	Merevale	chamber	15 c'	76 : 24	Barnes
			12 $c\#'$	76 : 24	Barnes
			12 c'	75 : 25	Barnes
			Ses $c\#'$	76 : 24	Barnes
1777	Nottingham	church	'diap' –	86 : 14	Dixon
1779	Locko Park	chamber	Pr $c\#'$	72 : 28	Barnes

The contrast of modern research with George Dixon's measurements made c1909 (probably by chemical analysis) is obvious, and may partly be due to modern methods of analysis. Alan Barnes's measurements were obtained around 1980 by atomic absorption and Martin Renshaw's by electron microprobe, 1987–90. Perhaps Dixon's values for the organs at Nottingham (removed from St Mary's church, c1870) and for the Bath organ (destroyed in 1889) should not be taken as those for undoubted Snetzler pipes; in fact, these values are suspiciously close to known front pipes' alloys of the period. The Whitehaven organ was, however, moved to Arlecdon c1904, and Dixon should have been able to identify the internal Snetzler pipework for himself.

Other analyses instigated by Martin Renshaw found that three builders working towards the end of the eighteenth century (Russell, England and an unknown maker) used alloys with tin percentages of 27 per cent, 26 per cent and 25 per cent respectively in their finer work, and that only more common work might use alloys of about 18 per cent. No lower value for internal pipework has yet been found from this period, but the metal used in the nineteenth century was often much less rich: a 'value' as minimal as 4.8 per cent tin was found in a Hill chamber organ of 1847.

The most recent analyses have all failed to find antimony, even when specifically searched for, but a small amount of copper was found to be present in both pipe-metal and solder alloys. The copper is probably a residue in the Cornish tin lode which earlier smelting techniques did not remove. Its accidental presence seems to have been an important reason why Cornish tin was the preferred choice of organ builders throughout Europe. A small quantity of copper has recently been found experimentally to make alloys that are otherwise hard and 'difficult' to work (but tonally very useful) appreciably more malleable. The percentage of copper found in the 1742 Cuckston and 1765 Swithland alloys is around 1 per cent of the tin content; precise percentages are as follows:

	Lead	Tin	Copper
1742 pipe-metal alloy:	64.9%	34.74%	0.36%
1765 pipe-metal alloy:	72.748%	26.91%	0.253%
1742 solder alloy:	46.4%	53.12%	0.48%

Pipe-marks on metal pipes

After the pipe-metal had been cast and planed, it was cut into plates of suitably graded thicknesses for the bodies and feet of each complete rank. These plates were gradually sorted into two separate piles, and the actual sounding pitch of the pipe was scribed on each body-plate and its corresponding foot-plate with a sharp-pointed scribing tool. These marks were made at the lower left-hand corner of the outside of the body plate, and the upper left-hand corner of the foot plate. When the pipe was assembled, therefore, the pitch marks were to be found at the back of the pipe to the right of the vertical seams of the body and foot as viewed from the back, above and below the languid seam.

As Snetzler's usual practice was to make all metal ranks in the same organ to the same general scale, virtually all the metal pipework apart from the front pipes could be set out simultaneously and sorted into piles of plates according to the largest plate of each rank. Each stop was then marked with its rank name and pallet-pitch (in the case of off-unison ranks this pitch would vary from the nominal pitch already marked) and the mouths' widths were marked out with dividers.

Snetzler's pipes (unlike Green's) exhibit parallel vertical scribe-lines which extend somewhat beyond the eventual upper positions of the ears, and slightly-angled short lines below the mouth. These scribings are made on the inside of the body and foot plates to facilitate the formation of their upper and lower lips and the alignment of bodies and feet during assembly. The matching parallel short scribing on the foot-plate (which becomes angled inwards, as seen from the front, when the foot is formed into a cone) enables the lower lip to be 'flatted' in towards the languid to form the wide flues and to give the pipes their characteristic profile.

His usual pattern of marking on the front of the pipe-plate was to scribe the pitch directly above the rank name, at about a quarter of the total length of the pipe above the mouth – somewhat higher on smaller pipes. (The wooden pipes are marked in the same way and in the same position, in ink.)

A typical set of markings is as under:

Bass octave

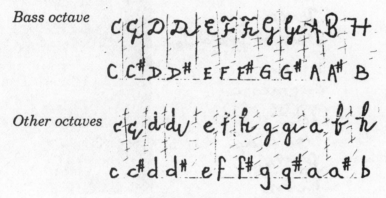

Other octaves

Pipe markings: pitch marks

The characteristic 'hook' which denotes the sharpened note will be observed; note also that this is a system that differentiates the octaves from C to H (that is, C to B♮), in contrast to the English system of distinguishing the octaves from G to F♯. However, Snetzler (or his pipemaker) commonly formed a scribed 'bay-leaf' on each of the larger metal pipes, up to the F♯ pipe 3' long. In the earlier and smaller organs, perhaps made entirely by Snetzler himself, this 'bay-leaf' continues to the B♮ pipe 1' long.

Doubled upper-case lettering is used for pipes in the lowest part-octave (*G'–H'*). In the bass octave (*C–H*; see above), the marking is in single capitals. The lower-case letters shown above are used for pipes in the tenor octave (*c–h*). Because there might be confusion as to which higher octave is meant (as, especially, in the layout of mixtures), each succeeding octave above middle C (*c'*) is designated by one or more horizontal lines above the lettering:

Middle octave (c'–h / b♮): one line, thus:

Treble octave (c''–h'' / b♮ ''): two lines, thus:

Top octave (c'''–h''' / b♮ '''): three lines, thus:

Pipe markings: upper pitch marks

Individual ranks of mixtures are additionally distinguished by a rank number in arabic numerals (the largest rank being numbered 1) scribed below the other marks.

The various ranks are named on the pipes by means of abbreviations, and they relate to the pitch–marks as shown:

Fifteenth	*15 Fn*
Flute	*Flut*
Dulciana	*Dulci*
Sesquialtra	*Sesq or Sesy or Ses*
Principal	*Princ*
Cremona	*Cremona*
Twelfth	*12 Th*
Open Diapason	*Op Diap*
Stopped Diapason	*St Diap*
Cornet	*Corn*

Pipe markings: rank marks

Assembly

The actual method of assembly of the pipes was determined to some extent from a Principal A pipe (just over 2' long, from the 'bass' octave) from the organ at Ickham, Kent (see chapter 3, no. 108) that had been badly damaged by the collapse of its foot. The pipe was taken apart at the languid joint (unlike those pipes which required restoration at Swithland, where later increased cutting–up was remedied by taking them apart just above the body–languid seam,) and the languid was removed. So it was possible to measure precisely the languid angle (63 degrees) and how much the languid tapered (from a maximum of 0.101" at the front to 0.045" at the back – about the thickness of the body metal at that point of the back). It was also possible to note (i) that the underside of the languid was marked with an 'a' formed in the same way as the normal pitch marks; (ii) that there was a slight counterface on the languid (not measurable because of disturbance by the nicking); (iii) that the internal edges of the seam inside the foot were very tightly brought together; and (iv) that the metal for the foot had been scraped to its finished thickness at right angles to the seam.

The thickness of the metal of the foot at the lower lip was 0.055"; the body was 0.04" thick at the languid end and tapered to 0.03" at the top. The circumference of the pipe was 7¼" ; its diameter 2¼". The mouth height ('cut up') was just under one-quarter of its width (the mouth width and average height were approximately 1¾" and ½" respectively) and there were fifteen nicks across the languid (the front of which was just over 1¾" wide). These nicks seemed to have been made after the assembly of the pipe because there were corresponding slight marks on the inner edge of the lower lip, but one nick was made so close to the extreme right-hand edge of the languid, right behind the ear, that it might have been nicked when the languid had only been tacked to the foot (with two small tacks of solder only a short distance back from the flue) before the body was soldered on, or before the ears were fixed. There was no evidence of tacking at the rear of the languid, though it might have been held there during assembly by a slight extension of the seam of the foot. The languid seam held together the body, languid and foot simultaneously but showed no signs of 'sealing' the languid to the foot, contrary to general current practice and to Dom Bédos's instructions for the assembly of larger pipes.

Nicking on the languid of the C pipe of the Twelfth at Merevale (1777)

As can be seen from the illustration above, the nicks slope like a grave accent (\), as viewed from the front. It has been suggested therefore that Snetzler was left-handed, but even the extreme right-hand nick observed in the pipe from Ickham might have been inserted at this angle by a right-handed person holding the pipe upside-down in his left hand, as some voicers do. It was also noticeable that the metal pipes in the 1742 Cuckston organ which needed repair almost always needed the front-view left-hand side of their languids refixing. This weakness, primarily caused by omitting the 'sealing' process, might suggest that the body/foot/languid seam was started at the opposite side by a person holding the iron in his right hand and the pipe in his left hand.

The Ickham pipe was evidently very carefully washed after assembly, as no remnants of the 'size' used to prevent the solder running beyond the seams could be found, internally or externally.

It is not possible to date the Snetzler pipes at Ickham, and their provenance is not known, but the pipes are wholly typical of his 'middle-period' work. The evident care with which the pipe described above was made is fully comparable with the work of Green as described by David Wickens.

Mouths, ears, languids and feet of metal pipes

The earliest front pipes to survive are the nine pipes in the towers of the case at Fulneck (1748). They seem to be of high tin content (about 70–75 per cent tin) with scribed 'bay-leaf' lips, and have small ears quite different from the 'Green-style' ears of the later organs. These are the only original pipes to survive in this organ; unfortunately, the front pipes in the flats were replaced only a few years ago. In the original contract of 1748, it was specified that the pipes should be polished, and the extent of their original polishing can still be seen, even though they are now sprayed with 'gold' paint. They appear to have no original pitch-marks, probably because they were made with the case 'on the spot', but they are no longer winded.

It was a tradition among the older employees of the firm of Hill, Norman & Beard (which claims descent from Snetzler's workshops) that their 'foundation date' of 1755 represented the year in which Snetzler set up his workshop production on a permanent basis. This may or may not be accurate, but it does seem that many of the 'typical' aspects of his work, such as the style of pipework, date from about that year – just after the King's Lynn organ was successfully completed. 1756, it will be recalled, was the year noted in the genealogical register at Schaffhausen where Snetzler was described as: 'Orgelmacher ... London'.

Ears of the type shown above were used on all Snetzler's normal chorus pipework, and were soldered to the larger pipes in each rank, ceasing at the 1' C. (Again, this is in contrast to the 1742 Cuckston organ, where they cease at the 1⅓' G pipes.) The extent of the nicking in the smaller pipework has been noted at Merevale; the number of nicks in the Sesquialtera C pipes were as follows: rank 1, thirteen nicks; rank 2, twelve nicks; rank 3, eleven nicks.

Only the Dulciana pipes were equipped with ears throughout the compass. They were of a special type, a 'box-beard', designed to aid the speech of the small-scaled pipes and consisting of ears extended in a single piece of pipe-metal into a horizontal 'fender' set somewhat below the lower lip. They help to steady the speech of the pipe and they aid the voicer to make it speak more promptly and brightly than it otherwise could.

Generally, the metal chorus pipework's mouths are 'cut up' to a height of around a quarter of their width. The commonly-used expression now implies that the mouth is 'cut up' higher from a lower opening left by the pipemaker, but in fact the mouth height can be much more readily cut out during the course of the assembly of the pipes, to leave only final adjustments by the voicer. There is some slight evidence, gained by careful observation of the upper lips of the pipes, that this might have been the practice of Snetzler's workshops – a busy builder-voicer would find this a considerable saving of his time. It would seem that his final adjustments of the mouth height consisted of chamfering the upper lip (at about 45 degrees) to reduce the thickness of metal there, and on occasion he slightly arched the upper lip where more power was required without concomitant wind noise.

We have seen above that Snetzler nicked the languid's edge as a matter of course. By contrast with Green's normal style, and even more with that of the early nineteenth-century builders, the nicking is widely spaced. Since the flue is also characteristically wide, that part of the nicking which serves only to enlarge the area of a flue is not required and the nicking is used instead mainly to reduce or remove unwanted sibilants or inharmonic overtones. Despite the impression given by the Halifax incident, when Snetzler was evidently upset by Dr Wainwright's not giving his pipes 'time to speak', his pipes do not actually speak particularly slowly. They may not have the promptitude of the Byfield pipes at 'Finchcocks' which gives that organ its bold and splashy character, but they are rather firm, full and bright – and generally more attractive at a distance than at close quarters.

The perceived speed of a pipe's speech is regulated mainly by the relative positions of the languid and the lower lip (a languid angle of 63 degrees allows much more control over the speech than the 'steep' angles used in the 1742 Cuckston organ), but a voicer is also aware of the need to maintain a relationship between the areas of the flue and the tip-hole of the pipe foot in order to produce a steady tone at various dynamic levels. An additional factor, much more difficult to quantify, is the effect on a pipe's speech of the capacity of its foot. Snetzler seems deliberately to have made his pipes' feet rather longer than was usual among his contemporaries (and they do not shorten as the pipes shorten), probably because a larger foot capacity slightly slows down the build-up of pressure at the flue, and allows the voicer more control over the exact onset of full speech. Although these various individual factors may seem to have a marginal effect in terms of the speech of one pipe, the overall musical result of an organ and its characteristic voicing style depend ultimately on such minutiae. Only an attempt to understand (and, where necessary, to copy) a particular style carefully can really reveal the processes at work. It may be thought (and was said) that an organ is only a machine up to its pipes' feet, but that is only a partial truth. Some present-day builders are beginning to rediscover that the pipes are only a part of the organic whole, and that they can carry out what Charles Fisk[16] called their 'transducing' function of turning wind into musical sounds only in relation to the wind system that supports them and the acoustic that transports their tones. This approach has obvious implications for the restorer and would–be copier of old organs.

The relationship becomes clearer only to the intelligent voicer who works in the building which houses the organ, and carries out as much as possible of the voicing there, and not in a 'voicing room' in a factory. How much Snetzler's output allowed him to voice every large organ 'on the spot', we do not know for certain. The very short time he apparently spent at Lulworth (chapter 3, no. 24) to complete a largish house organ, contrasted with the implication in the letter from Nottingham (see nos. 92, 97 and 98) that he was there for some considerable time, promotes the obvious conclusion that the chamber organs were voiced almost completely in the workshops and could be erected in their eventual location by someone else, but that but that he personally supervised or actually carried out the erection and voicing on site of the larger church instruments. The Halifax Deposition (quoted in chapter 3, no. 67) speaks of that organ's being 'long ago finished', but does that phrase mean that it was only mechanically and structurally complete? It seems rather that the larger organs – for King's Lynn and New York, certainly – were completely assembled and largely voiced in the 'Warehouse' (at a lower pitch, one supposes, so that they could be tonally 'finished' on site) and were demonstrated to the London 'gentry' and musical public by way of advertisement.

Pipe–scaling

Open metal chorus pipework In theory, each organ's pipework can be especially designed for the building in which it is to be heard. However, in historical organ–building practice, it seems that this was thought to be neither necessary nor even entirely desirable. Most organ–builders, because of their received background and training, learned methods of work and a style of pipe–making and voicing that previous experience found satisfactory. Although builders naturally sought to improve their instruments in points of detail – Green certainly did so – they did not start afresh with every organ. They could not, because the continuous production of new organs necessitated a degree of standardisation of the eventual 'product'. The modern idea, occasioned by discontinuous production and the individualistic demands of organists and architectural contexts, that each organ should be entirely freshly designed, was not thought of. The 'work' that the organ had to do was well known and generally understood, so the cost of an organ of sufficient resources would be taken into account from the start, and the competent builder would be fit to supply what was necessary at a 'normal' cost.

He was therefore equipped with a number of systems of proven worth by which the main choruses of the organ could be 'scaled' to its building. His 'scaling' systems adjusted the actual sizes of the whole range of pipes employed, from the largest Open Diapason to the smallest pipe of the Fifteenth or mixture rank, according to the general 'scale' chosen.

Until David Wickens's study of Green's scaling methods was published, information on the process of designing the sizes of pipes was either ignored altogether or made to appear more complicated than is necessary. Organ-builders used (and pipe-makers still use) quite simple means of determining the scales of pipes, derived directly from their experience in the workshop, where complex mathematics are inappropriate. Since the bodies and feet of pipes are cut out from flat sheets of lead/tin alloy of lead, a full-size method of determining the sizes of the rectangular bodies is necessary. Usually pipe-makers now use a marked 'rod' (a rule or template) of wood or a sheet of zinc or other hard metal to ascertain the width of the pipe-body and they measure the likely maximum finished (tuned) length of the body-plates from a 'length rod'. The width of the mouth, and any internal scribing, are marked directly on the body- and foot-plates with dividers, using simple geometry; dividers are also used to set the length, and therefore the angle, of the feet-cones.

The way in which the rods and templates are marked out can be shown simply on a linear graph where the horizontal axis is the theoretical relationship of one octave to another, and the vertical axis is the actual width of the pipe-body-plate. The horizontal axis is divided into sectors which proportionately represent the halving of the pipe-length for each octave displayed. Within each octave sector, its twelve chromatic notes are generally set out as ratios of the whole octave according to the proportions of the theoretical scale called 'just intonation'. This horizontal axis is compressed, as there would be no need to show the exact lengths of the pipe-bodies even if it were practicable to do so. These can be taken from a normal 'length rod'; this includes a sufficient extra allowance for the voicer and tuner later to cut the assembled and voiced pipe shorter by stages to its final tuned length in the organ. As the octave sectors on the horizontal axis of this graph are set out in the proportion of 1 : 2 (the proportion of the pipe lengths from one octave to another), this display is called a '1 : 2 octave ratio scale'. It seems to be the format in which the majority of Classical scales were re-created for practical use at the time; it is therefore the one in which they can be displayed efficiently. Some builders, it seems, used a 3 : 5 octave ratio scale, but even their scalings can be displayed on 1 : 2 graphs.

A straight line drawn on a 1 : 2 graphical display will give, depending on its angle, either disproportionately large body plate widths in the bass or very wide-scaled and therefore unvoiceable treble pipes. Either way, there is no properly balanced progression from bass to treble. The builder-designer also has to consider those two extremes: the largest pipes must be scaled to the proportions of the case of which they form the front, and the smallest pipes must not be either too shrill or too insubstantial, depending on the acoustic properties of the building. Snetzler's experience of these problems led him to the use of 'broken' scale-lines which allowed the basses' plate widths to taper to relatively smaller values (and thus produce pipes that are not ponderous in tone) and the trebles to taper similarly; at the same time he maintained sufficiently large values in the middle register which comprises the greater number of pipes to allow the chorus as a whole to be appropriately full as well as bold in tone.

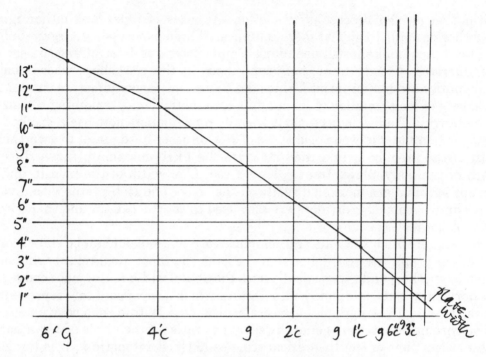

Ludlow: general scaling system
note that the scalings for Rotherham and Nottingham are the same as this

The scales can therefore be adjusted to the size of building by 'breaking' the scale-lines on this graph. Since the middle register determines, in general, the output of the organ, the values of its plates' widths can be varied either as a proportion of the larger scale or produce a line of values at an angle to it.

The advantage of the graph is that it shows visually, to an extent, what will be heard, if the voicing is regular – particularly when the chorus scaling is entirely based upon it. Accordingly, a scale where the line of the values of the trebles is at a steeper downward angle might be more suitable for a building with resonant acoustics that will 'absorb' the additional overall brightness; conversely, the pipework for a building with little or no resonance requiring a somewhat more sombre tone may be designed from scales whose shallower angles will produce somewhat larger-scaled pipework in both the treble and bass portions.

The way in which the angles on the graphs are usually described is slightly confusing unless the theoretical zero value on the horizontal axis is considered. It would follow that a pipe with no length would have no body-plate width; the body-plate width-line on the graph would therefore be presumed ultimately to descend and pass through the 'origin', the zero point on the vertical axis. In practice, the scale-line does no such thing; if it did so, the scale of a 1' pipe would be disproportionately small as compared with that of a 4' pipe, for instance. In order, therefore, to make the unison pipework of the vocal compass (that is, from the 5⅓' G to ⅔' G) regular and even in sound in a particular circumstance – and the beauty of the 'straight-line' chorus is that the rest falls into place if the unison scaling is judged correctly – the scale-line is angled to pass the horizontal zero at a point higher on the vertical axis. The value of this point, measured up from zero, is called an 'addition constant'.

Above the 'vocal compass', and below it, for both acoustic and practical reasons, the angle of this line has (as we have seen) to be modified. If it were to be maintained in the extreme treble, it would give values for the smallest pipes of the chorus rather too large to match the middle-range pipes in perceived power and brightness, so the values on the line are modified by means of its 'breaking' to pass the horizontal zero at a point somewhat lower on the vertical axis (that is, with a reduced addition constant). For practical reasons, an addition constant of ½" is the minimum from which the highest pipes of a Fifteenth ascending to *f '''* was made; there was no pipe in a mixture except for the tierce rank of a Cornet smaller than this, and such a pipe (even in a chorus-mixture Cornet) would usually have its diameter increased by 'scale-transposition', as is described later.

The effect of the reduced addition constant on the treble pipes is thus to decrease their scale, but – perversely – the addition constant must be *increased* in order to decrease the scale of the bass pipes proportionately, because the angle of the scale-line in the bass 'rotates' about the first break at the lower end of the vocal compass. The scale-line for a large organ, running from pipes 10⅔' long to the smallest, therefore usually has three angles and two breaks (see the Ludlow, Rotherham and Nottingham graph above). A smaller organ, containing pipes of 5⅓' speaking length and smaller, would require only two angles and one break (see the Swithland graph below). A still smaller organ necessitates no breaks at all (see the 'Cuckston' graph overleaf).

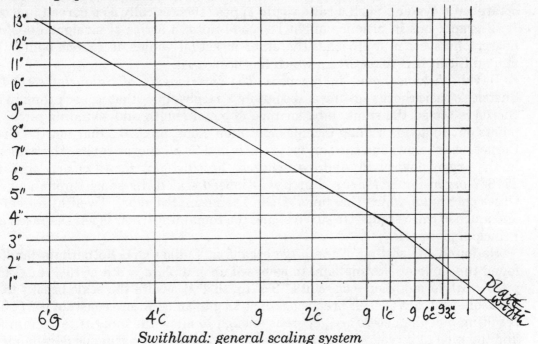

Swithland: general scaling system

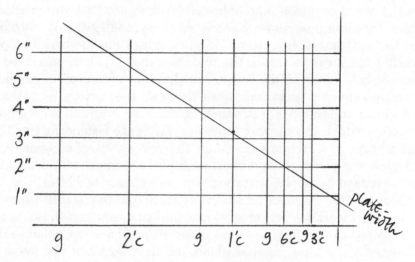

'Cuckston': general scaling system

Snetzler seems generally to have arranged the breaks on C pipes (presumably as a result of his background of *C*-compass organs), but which Cs were used varied according to the number of breaks, as can be seen from the graphs. A scale–line with more than two breaks might be capable of interpretation as part of a 3 : 5 octave ratio system. Such a ratio would appear theoretically as a curved line on a 1 : 2 graph, but in practice might be made up of a series of straight lines; the nearer one system approaches the other in actual values at salient points, the more difficult it is to ascertain which has been used.

David Wickens noted in his book *The Instruments of Samuel Green* that Snetzler's basic chorus scaling is absolutely 'straight–line': that is, each rank in the chorus is scaled the same, pipe for pipe of equal length and sounding pitch. He points out that this scaling includes mutation stops, mixtures (but not the Great Cornet – see below) and the surviving Choir and Swell chorus ranks. The evidence in the organ now in St Andrew's church, Nottingham, shows clearly that the 1776–7 organ for St Mary's church was indeed scaled the same throughout the Great chorus (of which the 'inner' Open Diapason, Principal, Twelfth, Fifteenth, and much of the Sesquialtra survive) and the remaining Choir Open Diapason and Principal pipework.

He found the scaling of the large organs at Ludlow and Rotherham (and we found the same at Nottingham) to be based upon a plate width of 13½" at G (5⅓' pitch) with an addition–constant of 3½" up to 4' C, where the scale breaks to an addition–constant of 1"; it breaks again at ⅔' g to an addition–constant of ¾". The resulting pipe diameters are generous enough to allow the mouths to remain low and the pipe to be voiced with some power as well as full harmonic development; the trebles are also midway between the practical extremes, and so can be bold and firm as well as bright, as would be necessary in these large buildings. The 8' C pipe would have a diameter of a little under 6" on this basis; both at Ludlow and Nottingham it was part of an imposing facade in a dominant gallery at the east end of the nave (see chapter 3, nos. 63 and 90). The diameter of the 8' C front pipes made by Green for Lichfield Cathedral in 1790 is greater than this by only ½". It used to be thought that Green's bass–pipe scales were especially large, but they are not; it is probable that observers were mislead by the fact that Green's organ case–fronts frequently contained one or (as at Lichfield) two open 'GG' pipes of 10⅔' speaking length, whereas it seems that Snetzler's longest front pipes were normally the 8' C pipes.

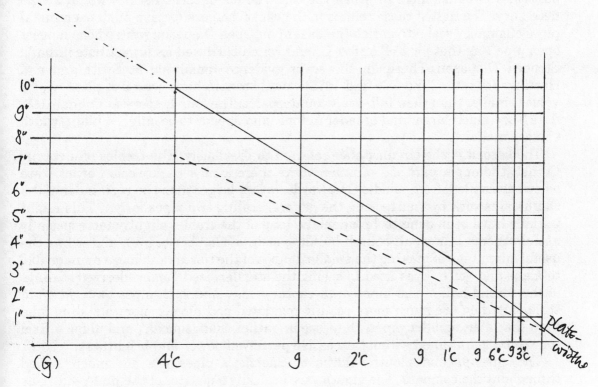

Merevale organ scaling: chorus pipework and Dulciana

The overall scaling of Snetzler's chamber organ at Merevale is much smaller, as would be expected. The plate–width of the 4' C pipe is 10", with an addition-constant of 1"; the scaling line breaks once at the 1' C (plate–width 3¼") to an addition–constant of ½" for the trebles of the pipework. The actual values for the small church organ at Swithland (1765), which follow this break–pattern, fall almost precisely midway between the Ludlow and Merevale scalings. It would seem that Snetzler did not simply transpose pipes within a general scaling scheme as some later builders did, but that he used several distinct systems according to the size of the organ and its location, presumably in order to preserve overall tonal consistency in varying conditions.

Scale-transposition would have been carried out by taking, say, the Ludlow scheme and making a smaller-scaled organ by choosing the plate-width values for the D or E pipes and making C pipes to these values, and so on throughout the whole compass of the scaling. As David Wickens points out, later builders were to do this in particular for smaller-scaled ranks (such as Dulcianas); it is true, too, that Hugh Russell, in 1794–5 at least,[17] did this to differentiate ranks within the chorus – his Open Diapason being one scale larger than the general scale, and parts of the upperwork one or two scales smaller, after the reported manner of George England.[18]

Snetzler, however, appears to have transposed scale values in the only two particular circumstances in which the construction of special scales would not be necessary. The first of these relates to the use of 'helpers' (octave pitch open metal pipes of smaller scale) to enrich the bass of an Open Diapason rank whose longest open pipe was that for 8' C or 5⅓' G, and which borrowed its lowest notes from a Stopped Diapason. These, in the scant evidence remaining at Swithland and Hastings (chapter 3, nos. 66 and 107a) would seem to have been five plate-width values smaller than their full-scale counterparts. The four 'helpers' at Cobham (*G'*, *A'–B'*) are much larger and broader in tone, and appear to be only 1½ plate-width values smaller.

The second is the circumstance referred to previously. The trebles of a chorus Cornet (the upper part of a mixture where there is no separate solo Cornet – see below) are scaled, from middle C upwards, rather larger than the remainder of the chorus pipework by transposing the general scaling two pipes larger. This might initially have been done to 'broaden' the tone of the trebles slightly (an especially useful scheme in a small church building or in a chamber organ), and it has the useful advantage of making the smallest pipes of the tierce rank more manageable to make and voice. Eyes used to seeing the standardized Töpfer-derived scalings of the second half of the nineteenth century, may find such pipes quite large in scale, but they are much more readily regulated and have a more blending tone than the later, smaller pipes: they 'speak' rather than 'squeak', and allow a firm tone to be maintained without excessive perceived power and brightness.

The cut-ups and mouth widths of Snetzler's pipes are not much varied throughout the compass. The mouths are basically a quarter of the plate width; as we have seen, they are also cut up in this proportion – only a little lower than this in the bass, but precisely a quarter or only slightly higher in the treble. This is in contrast to the practice of British builders of this period who narrowed the mouths of the pipes and raised their cut-ups proportionately as they ascended in pitch. Snetzler's technique gives a firm and bold tone to the smaller pipes, and it is one reason (perhaps an important one) why his organs were perceived as bright and lively.

Dulcianas 'The dulciana stop, brought hither by Snetzler, is a tall, delicate, narrow pipe, of an exquisite sweet tone, without a reed; on which account it stands in tune equally with the Open Diapason.' (Burney's article in Rees's *Cyclopaedia*.)

The Dulcianas at King's Lynn are of outward-tapering construction (see chapter 3, no. 16), but the 'normal' Snetzler rank thenceforward (possibly apart from the organ at Chesterfield) was to be cylindrical. 'Box–beards' are used for the mouths of every pipe in each rank.

The Lynn Dulciana's diameters are as follows; the former Swell rank is now at 4' pitch on the Choir, but both ranks (marked 'Choir' and 'Swel') are evidently made to the same scale:

	Mouth	Present top	Source
8' C:	'about' 4"	'about' 5"	TO 26/82 (H. Norman & W. A. Roberts)
E:	3 9/16"	3 15/16"	R. Barker
4' C:	'about' 2⅝"	'about' 2⅛"	TO 26/82
2' C:	1¼"	1 7/16"	R. Barker
1' C:	¾"	13/16"	R. Barker

At Merevale (1777), the scaling–line of the Dulciana has no break, but it runs straight as if from a theoretical plate width of 10" at G; the rank starts at c, and was at some time transposed up a semitone. This value happens also to be the plate–width of the 4' C of the chorus–scale in that organ. The Dulciana might therefore be described as being six plate–widths smaller than the chorus generally, but such a description would disguise the fact discernible from the graph above that the discrepancy between the two scale–lines varies from this to a maximum of nine plate–widths smaller in the extreme treble, because of the lack of a break in the Dulciana line. The effect of its scaling is that the tone of the Dulciana pipes gradually becomes proportionately smaller, and consequently quieter and more gentle, as the rank ascends to the high treble.

The Lynn Dulcianas are nicked in the same way as the other metal flue pipes: a 2' pipe with a mouth width of 1" has sixteen nicks.

Solo Cornets The only surviving solo Great Cornet of five ranks (at Rotherham, 1777) is scaled somewhat larger than the chorus pipework. David Wickens[19] gives the scale, and suggests that its moderate dimensions might be derived from southern German practice; he cites the very similar scaling of the Cornet by Holzhay (1792) at Rot-an-der-Rot, and contrasts this with Clicquot's wide scaling at Souvigny (1782), and other Classical French work.

We noted above that the plate–width values for the normal Cornet part of a Great mixture, when this was the only mixture and was a divided Sesquialtra and Cornet (17–19–22 in the bass, breaking to 12–15–17), appeared to be transposed from the general chorus values, and it is possible that the Rotherham Great Cornet values could be interpreted in a similar way. It would be logical to transpose both types of Cornet if they were intended not only to be used from time to time as 'solo' stops in church organs but also to be combined with the Great chorus.

As noted above, evidence obtained during the restoration of the tonal scheme of the Swithland organ (1765) suggested that the Cornet of three ranks (12–15–17), the treble of the divided mixture, was made to a scale transposed two values larger than those of the corresponding pipes in the chorus generally. It would seem that the Rotherham Cornet values were similarly calculated.

Stopped metal flutes Snetzler used a 'chimney flute' construction for the trebles of Stopped Diapasons and Flutes in all organs where these ranks were not made in wood throughout (as they were in the bureau organs and some chamber organs). Its general form and sample scalings are given below; it is clear that Snetzler did not vary the scaling of the pairs of flutes within an organ, or even of all the flutes' trebles in an organ (as at Rotherham and Ludlow). In the 4' Flute rank at Swithland, the largest chimney flutes' mouths were cut up 1 : 3 (at tenor C, the 1' long pipe), the cut-ups rising to 1 : 3.5 (at middle E) and then to 1 : 4 for the highest octave (from treble F upwards). The upper lips are very slightly arched and a little pulled out; the substantial metal of the upper lips is not chamfered through all its thickness.

The 'German Flute' in the Swell of the King's Lynn organ was a chimney flute of about three times the normal length, voiced to produce its first harmonic, a twelfth above the ground tone. The scale suggested by Wedgwood's data,[20] a diameter of 1¾" at middle C (i.e., a plate width of 5½") produced from a pipe the length of the F a twelfth below, indicates that this stop was at the (usual) octave pitch rather than the '8ft. tone' he reports. Wedgwood also noted that the mouths of this rank were arched; as that contrasts with the nearly 'straight' mouths of Snetzler's normal chimney flutes, the pipes have probably been revoiced and been transposed by a semitone. Since the rebuilding of this organ in 1890, this stop has apparently been at 8' pitch (with, presumably, a later tenor octave) on the Choir soundboard; perhaps Wedgwood's findings were confused by these transpositions.

The disc that forms the top of the pipe, and the chimney itself, are both marked with their pitch; the chimney is soldered to the disc at its underside. No chimney has been observed to have been made 're-entrant' – that is, hanging from the disc, inside the pipe.

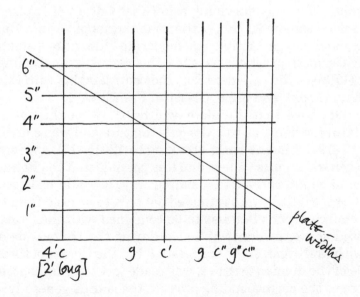

Cobham Hall and Nottingham: chimney flute scalings

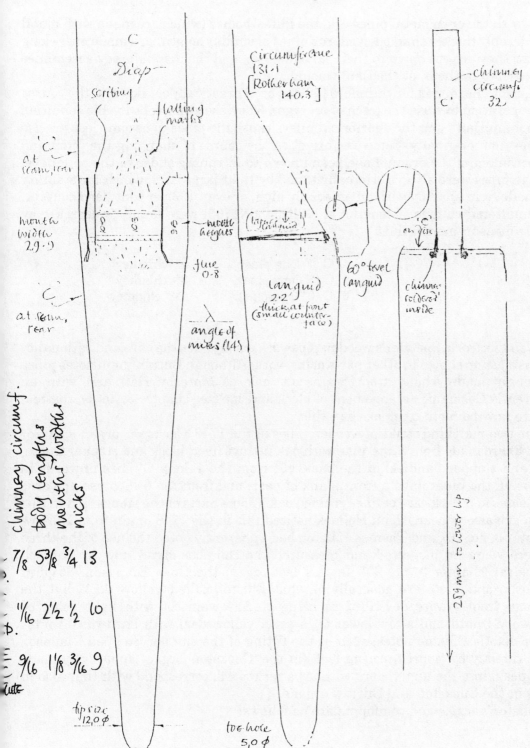

C

Diap-

scribing

flatting marks

Circumference
131·1
[Rotherham
140.3]

chimney
circumf.
32

'C'
at seam, rear

'c'

mouth
width
29·9

mouth
heights

flue
0·8

(stopped end)

60° bevel
languid

on disc

chimney
soldered
inside

'C'
at seam,
rear

languid
2·2
thick at foot
(small counter-
face)

angle of
nicks (14)

chimney circumf.	body lengths	mouths widths	nicks
7/8	5 3/8	3/4	13
11/16	2 1/2	1/2	10
9/16	1 1/8	3/16	9

b.

flute

tips oc
12,0 φ

toe hole
5,0 φ

287 mm to lower lip

Cobham Hall: Great Stopped Diapason trebles and Flute

As with the open metal pipework, the flutes' bodies (which are made with metal considerably thicker than open chorus pipes of similar length) are made over-long at first; they are cut down to their tuned length, and the disc/chimney assemblies are soldered to them, at the final voicing stage.

It is not uncommon for chimneys to have been drastically cut down in the course of an operation to raise the pitch of an organ (they are at present in this condition at Cobham Hall), and the shorter chimneys cause the pipes to become less precise in tone than originally. Some 'restorers', in the course of changing the pitch and temperament of the organ, have been known to fit tuning slides to the chimneys, but the pipes were always originally tuned by their large ears, which for stability are made from an alloy with an especially high, or even 100 per cent, lead content. The unaltered chimneys' lengths at Swithland (1765) were found to decrease by simple measurements, thus:

2' C (1' long pipe):	6" chimney
1' C (6" long pipe):	3" chimney
6" C (3" long pipe):	1½" chimney

Wooden pipework Snetzler's wooden pipework exemplifies the care and rationality of construction shown in other parts of his work. Although Buckingham notes pipes seemingly made wholly from 'wainscott' oak at Moresby Hall and with an apparently Germanic arrangement of block and cap (see chapter 3, no. 1), the real picture may be more complex than this.

The two matching ranks of wooden pipes in the 1742 'Cuckston' organ (chapter 3, no. 3) are made from Scots' pine with oak fittings (feet, block and stopper fronts, caps and stopper handles) in the bass, but from the 1' long C pipes upwards in each rank the pipes have a front plank of pear, and from the 6" C pipes upwards their sides and backs are of fine-grained oak. (Some parts of the stop action in this organ are also of pear.) John Holmes noticed this in the 1748 organ from Durrow (chapter 3, no. 10), and Thomas Elliston had apparently noted the use of the three timbers when he inspected and measured the chamber organ now in Norwich Cathedral (chapter 3, no. 20). In this last organ, the Open Diapason, Stopped Diapason and Flute are generally of what Elliston called 'yellow deal', but the extreme trebles were described as being of 'fine wainscot with light-coloured hardwood fronts' and a few lower ones as 'of yellow deal with hardwood fronts'. Other details Elliston notes, such at the fitting of the smaller Stopped Diapason pipes directly by 'short tapering feet' (in the 'Cuckston' organ, apparently made from pear) into the upperboard without a rackboard, correspond with the wooden pipes in the Cuckston and Durrow organs.

Elliston's scales and comments are as follows:

Keys hinged with leather. Single feeder bellows ... The open diapason is of wood throughout, the CC, 8 ft. tone, being a stopped bass.

Open diapason   Ten. C 2 13/16 in. x 2⅛ in. mouth, ⅝in. high

Mid. C 1⅜ in. x 1⅛ in. base

Treble C 13/16 in. x 9/16 in. full

The top six notes are made of fine wainscot with light–coloured hardwood fronts, the next seven notes below being made of yellow deal with hardwood fronts, the remainder of the pipes being entirely of deal.

Stopped diapason   GG 5⅛ in. x 4 1/16 in. mouth ¾ in. high

CC 3 13/16 in. x 3 1/16 in. mouth ⅝ in. base

Mid. C 1¼ in. full x ⅞ in. full

Upper eighteen notes (from C) having fine wainscot sides and back and light–coloured hardwood fronts.

Flute   GG 2 11/16 in. x 2 in.

CC 2⅛ in. x ¾ in.

Ten. C ⅞ in. x ¾ in.

Mid. C ¾ in. full x 9/16 in. full

The upper pipes of wainscot with hardwood fronts.

All the pipes are well made and of good quality of tone. The stopped diapason has no rack–board. The small pipes are held up by having very shart tapering feet which fit tight into their holes in the upperboard to the depth of about half an inch. Some of the largest of the others are hooked up, and the rest are prevented from falling by a wooden lath or spline.

It may be that what Buckingham saw at Moresby Hall were also pear–fronted pipes and that he did not identify them as such; under a harpsichord in poor light, they would be difficult to distinguish clearly. Such finely made pipes are very suitable in a small chamber organ, but inappropriate in a large chamber organ or a church organ; in these the extant wooden pipework is of Scots' or red pine with oak fittings.

Snetzler's typical wooden pipes are built around a block of pine faced with oak; into this a narrow 'throat' is cut to take the wind from the (separately made) foot towards the cap. Three planks are glued with natural 'animal' glue to this block: the first two are the side planks, which are cramped to the sides of the block; when the glue begins to dry, the sides are planed level and a third plank is glued onto the back of the block and sides. This is pinned to the block and to one of the sides with small wooden pegs to help prevent the assembly slipping while it is re-cramped. The three planks are sized internally with thinned glue, and finally the front plank, sized and with the bevel above the mouth already formed, is glued and cramped to the side planks, and positioned on them with further pine pegs. The mouth height above the block has to be determined at this stage; although there are various ways of doing this, it is not clear from his pipes which procedure Snetzler adopted.

The stopper handle is made separately and glued into a short piece of the block material set aside for the purpose. Although the oak face can be seen in the stopper's upper surface, the front edge of the stopper handle is marked with a small gouge for ready identification of the front of the stopper when it has been leathered and fitted inside the pipe body. Original stopper leathering in the 1742 'Cuckston' organ is cut carefully at each corner of the stopper block, with the French–chalked nap outwards; the rather thin leather is tightly fitted within the pipe, and the longish stopper-block is slightly bevelled. The pipe foot is prepared from a square–section piece of pine which is bored through, singed, and then planed as a regular octagon; its spigot and tip are rasped and filed. The underside of the block is bored through to the throat to receive it. When the pipe has been planed externally it is marked in ink and fitted with the bevelled and moulded oak cap characteristic of Snetzler's work from at least 1756 (Hillington) onwards.

This, in brief, is how it would seem Snetzler made the wooden pipework for the basses of Stopped Diapasons and Flutes and, with variations of stopper handle shapes, for complete ranks on occasion. The techniques involved are common enough in pipes of the period (though a number of indigenous London builders used a different arrangement of the pipes' planks),[21] but two points of detail need to be noted.

First, the caps, though often 'moulded' on their upper edges, are fitted so that their grain runs the same way as the pipe–planks: this direction makes it easier to cut out the internal shaping of the flue–way (a gradual curve, not the rather sudden curve typically found in British makers' pipe–caps), but rather harder to create the moulding. Indeed, there is no obvious reason why such trouble was taken to plane a moulding across the grain, except – one might be allowed to suggest – that this, together with a characteristic slight bevel on the finished lower edge of the cap, is a kind of 'thumb–print' of a conscientious and even enthusiastic woodworker.

Second, the upper surface of the blocks of the larger pipes (more than 2' actual length) are not level. Their oak facings are apparently quite deliberately positioned to protrude above the pine, but only slightly: to a maximum of about ⅛". Again, there is no obvious necessity for this unless it was to aid the pipes' speech. One wonders if Buckingham made a mistake about this too when he was peering under the Moresby Hall harpsichord and thought he saw a 'Germanic' sloping block.

The front top edge of the block is bevelled; the lower edge of the bevel must be no lower than the top of the cap in its final position. It is also sparingly nicked with nicks formed in the same way as those in Green's wooden pipes, apparently with a special tool for the purpose.[22]

David Wickens reports that the scales of the wooden bass pipes at Ludlow[23] seem to be derived from the circumferential plate widths of the metal chimney flute trebles, plus addition constants, and this may be the way in which they were calculated, though it seems to involve more complicated calculations than might have been possible two hundred and fifty years ago. Snetzler's method of making a pipe would have involved a final facing of the front and back of the block during assembly to 'true up' the edges of the side planks; this and subsequent shrinkage through natural drying will leave the blocks slightly undersize, and will distort any measurements that might be made now.

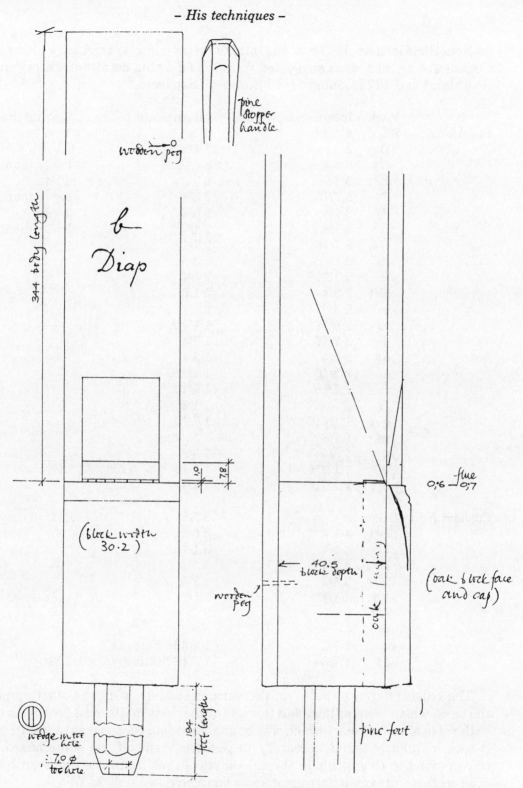

Cobham Hall: Great Stopped Diapason bass

Nonetheless may be that the blocks' sizes simply originally decreased by fractions of an inch, as is suggested from the following details of the original 1765 Swithland and 1778 Cobham Hall Stopped Diapasons:[24]

	Pitch	Internal depth (")	Internal width (")	Cut–up proportion
Swithland:	8'C	4 1/4	3 1/2	1 : 4
	D	4	3 1/4	
	D♯	3 3/4	3	lower than 1 : 4
	E	3 1/2	2 7/8	1 : 4
	F	3 7/16	2 3/4	lower than 1 : 4
	F♯	3 1/4	2 5/8	1 : 4
	G	3 1/8	2 1/2	lower than 1 : 4
	G♯	3 1/16	2 7/16	
	A	3	2 3/8	
	B	2 13/16	2 1/4	
	H/♮	2 3/4	2 1/8	
	4'c	2 5/8	2	
	c♯	2 9/16	1 15/16	
	d	2 7/16	1 7/8	
	d♯	2 1/4	1 3/4	
	e	2 3/16	1 11/16	
	f	2 1/16	1 9/16	
	f♯	2	1 1/2	
	g	1 15/16	1 7/16	
	g♯	1 7/8	1 13/32	
	a	1 3/4	1 3/8	
	b	1 11/16	1 5/16	
	h/♮	1 11/16	1 1/4	
Cobham Hall:	GG	5	3 7/8	
	BB[♭]	4 1/2	3 5/8	
	8'C	4 1/4	3 1/4	
	D	3 3/4	3	
	E	3 1/2	2 3/4	
	F♯	3 1/4	2 1/2	
	G♯	3	3	
	B	—	—	
	4'c	2 1/2	1 7/8 [= Flute CC]	
	f♯	1 7/8+	1 7/16 [Flute 1 7/8 x 1 3/8]	

The chief differences between the various scalings were the starting points in the bass, which were adjusted to the size of the division (largest for the Great) and to the size of soundboard which was to accommodate these large pipes. In practice, it was frequently found necessary to position them off the soundboard, and to convey wind to them; this is normal Classical practice in the eighteenth century even in those organs whose compasses venture down only to *C*.

Other details, such as the heights of the blocks and stopper handles, the thickness of the caps and the bores of the feet, are matters more to be decided by experience than theory, and are of lesser importance than the scales and mouth heights. It is important, though, for a restorer to find out what the finished lengths of unaltered wooden pipes of a particular scale should be, as these will indicate the power originally obtained from the pipes at a particular wind pressure – this power might well have been greater than that established in any later re-regulation of the pipework; signs of changes would be pushed-down stoppers or ragged pipe-tops cut down by later tuners.

A smooth transition of tone-colour from wooden pipes to metal was facilitated by piercing the stoppers of the wooden pipes from G to B adjacent to the first metal 1' C pipe. It would be interesting to know whether or not Snetzler had any particular tonal reason in any particular circumstance for breaking to metal pipes at this 1'-long C or at the G below. On the Swell, as we have noted, he carried the metal chimney flutes down to 1⅓'-long G or F; below this note he would have found, as others have since, that the tone of pipes with bored-through stoppers or with chimneys tends to become unsteady.

The same methods of construction as above pertain for the open wooden pipe-work. As was noted regarding the organ at Fulneck (chapter 3, no. 9), Snetzler used wood for the Open Diapason because the low headroom there would mean that its basses would need to be mitred. He also made wooden Open Diapasons for some of the early chamber organs (see *re* Norwich Cathedral, above, but also see chapter 3, no. 94) for reasons that are open to speculation, as these ranks are of short compass, to *c* or *c'* and not to *G'*, and did not need to be mitred. There is the possibility that in some early church organs, a second Open Diapason might have been made of wood.

Since the construction of the portable bureau organs necessitates a certain amount of mitring of pipes in bass and tenor octaves, wooden Stopped Diapasons and Flutes were naturally employed in these for this reason, as well as because they are less liable to damage and less heavy to carry about, and easier to re-tune, than ranks with metal chimney flute trebles.

Reed ranks

Trumpets and Clarions It seems that the original Great Trumpet of the 1777 Rotherham organ, now on the Choir, may be the only complete surviving representative of this stop, but it has been revoiced with new shallots and tongues. Its resonators have been slotted, probably during a revoicing and raising of the pitch of the organ, but their overall lengths may represent the original resonator lengths. In common with general practice at the time, Classical British reed resonators were not slotted but were cut to length during the final voicing. The essentials of the processes involved were described by Dom Bédos.

One Great Trumpet pipe (*e'''*) survives at Cobham, having been placed in the Swell when the pipes of the Hautboy were moved at a change of pitch; otherwise there are only a few odd pipes left in various other places. The 1771 Trumpet rank at Newby Hall (from *c'*) seems to be original in every respect; as much else in that organ seems to be derived from aspects of Snetzler's practice, it may be useful evidence for a somewhat smaller scaling, perhaps a Swell scaling, for which there is no direct evidence remaining.

As far as is known, no Clarion survives, but it may perhaps be assumed by analogy that its scaling was the same as the Trumpet it paired.

Organ/pipe	Top diameter	Top circumference	Resonator length
Rotherham 4'C:	(2 13/16")	8 13/16"	42 3/16"
2'C:	(2 1/8")	6 5/8"	19 15/16"
Newby 2'C:	2 1/16"	6 7/16"	
Rotherham 1'C:	(1 13/16")	5 3/4"	9 1/2"
Newby 1'C:	1 13/16"	5 3/4"	
Newby 6"C:	1 3/4"	5 5/8"	
Cobham top E:	1 1/4"		3 3/8"

Rotherham, Newby Hall and Cobham Hall Trumpets

Hautboys There are original Hautboys in the Swells at Theddingworth, Kedleston and Cobham Hall. Dimensions of the Cobham Hall example are given opposite. Their shallot sizes are much the same as those for the Trumpet and Vox Humane at Newby; it would seem that modifications of tone–colour rather than variation in output were sought from the various resonator forms used. Original Hautboys are not capped, slotted or 'pierced', but completely open – William Hill's firm was still making them this way for at least a century after Cobham Hall's organ was built – and, judging from examples made by later makers,[25] they were scarcely quieter than a Swell Trumpet and not very different in timbre, as were their eighteenth–century 'orchestral' counterparts.

Bassoons, French Horns, Cremonas and Vox Humanas The Newby Hall 'Vox Humane' seems to be a short–resonator Cremona with a 'choke' in it, and again may be the only representative of its kind. The Bassoon, generally used by Snetzler as a bass to the Cremona, was presumably a small–scale Trumpet, as it is in the 1792 Green organ now in St Thomas's church, Salisbury. There is nothing else surviving that can be measured. The 'French Horn' at King's Lynn was evidently a large–scale Hautboy, and such a stop was in the Harris organ that Burney played in St Dionis church, Backchurch. One wonders exactly which of their contemporary 'orchestral' instruments these stops were intended to 'imitate'. For instance, the Clarinet was not at this time generally included in any 'orchestral' ensemble, so was the 'Cremona' in fact intended to imitate the violin, as its punning name suggested – hence the lack of 'strong' string–toned flue stops?

The reason for the virtually complete destruction of Snetzler's reeds is not that they were indifferently made; Sutton says that they were much better than those built before Snetzler's time, and he must have included Renatus Harris's and the older Byfield's often–praised stops in this judgement. Rather, their desuetude was occasioned by two later, virtually contemporaneous, factors: first, the predilection for more ingratiating, soft–toned stops which echoed their mid–Victorian orchestral counterparts and, second, the purely practical one of a rise in pitch of nearly a semitone during the hundred years following Snetzler's mature work.

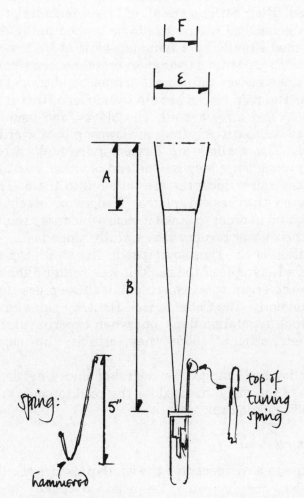

Dimensions in inches:

	A	B	C ϕ shallot	D ϕ nut	E circumferences (plate widths)	F
f♯	6⅞	30	⅜+	1	7	4¼
c′	5	21⅛	5/16	1	6½	3⅞
c″	2 13/16	10	¼+	15/16	5½	3
c‴	1 5/16	4½	7/32	⅞	4⅞	2⅞
e‴	–	3⅜	7/32	⅞ [the only Trumpet pipe]	–	

[boots are all 7⅛" long]

NB The original f Hautboy pipe is missing, and f♯ has been put in its place, hence the use of a Trumpet pipe for *e‴*.

Cobham Hall: Swell Hautboy

Certain details of the constructional features of the reeds at Newby Hall and of Snetzler's Hautboys are to be noted. Their fittings are all of brass, including the 'French style' tuning spring which is notched where it is to be tapped up by the tuner's reed knife; it is also hardened slightly by a hammer-blow at its lowest curve. The Newby reed springs are also filed into a triangular cross-section where they engage the tongue, but this unnecessary refinement cannot be observed in Snetzler's own work, or in Green's. The reed blocks are almost modern British in form, except that they are less deep and large overall. The blocks, and usually their 'boots' or 'sockets', are numbered consecutively from the lowest pipe upwards, and are not marked with a pitch. The shallots are formed individually from rolled-up brass cylinders left open along their length. One end of these is cut at 45 degrees, and closing plates of the same thickness are soldered to them. The pipes' pitches are marked in ink on the 'beaked' plates. Wedges of beech or sycamore hold the parallel tongues, and in order to make it clear which way round these tongues should be inserted their lower corners are carefully nipped off.

Because of the very dirty condition of the Hautboy pipes in the swell-box at Kedleston (probably the least-altered example of the rank) it was rather difficult to assess them tonally at the time the organ was inspected, but those pipes that spoke did so very promptly and pungently. The Cobham Hall Hautboy pipes have been transposed and fitted with small regulation flaps, but when experimentally re-tuned to something like their original pitch they exhibit the same characteristics.

The composition of the 'brass' alloy has changed considerably since Snetzler's time, and research into the nature of the metal he used for the reed tongues and wires (and pallet springs) is yet to be carried out.

Wind-pressure, pitch and temperament

Wind-pressure Buckingham appears to have measured the wind-pressure of only two of the organs he visited, but the 'machine' he used to make these measurements gave readings that we are not at present able to interpret:

> Bridport, an organ by 'Nichols' in 1815: 'The wind is 10½ by my machine'
> [TO 210/20]
> Penzance, an organ by 'Crabb' before 1842: 'too light at 8½'
> [TO 213/47]

If nothing else, Buckingham's readings confirm that a more sophisticated method of measuring and recording wind-pressure 'on the spot' was in use than the one in which a note was made of the weight of stones to be placed on the reservoir when the organ was finally set up – an expedient no doubt adopted to save the expense of carrying weights over toll-roads or along canals. What system Snetzler used is not known, but an indication of the pressures he used has been given in the list of organs in chapter 3, where there is reliable evidence.

For the smaller chamber organs, the range seems to have been from 2" (1742 Cuckston) to 2½" (Yale, Locko Park and Brookthorpe), measured by water gauge.

The small church organ at Swithland, where the front pipes had not been much altered and could be used to establish both pitch and pressure, seemed to speak at its best on 2⅝". The Great chorus at Beverley Minster, which is the most extensive tonal scheme to survive, now speaks well on 3", but the pipework has almost certainly been re-regulated to some extent. The organ in Hillsborough church – a much smaller building – is now speaking on 2½". Since the wind-pressure at Cobham Hall may have been as high as 3", such a pressure, or something near it, may quite possibly have been used in the larger buildings or (as at Cobham Hall) in difficult acoustical circumstances. Snetzler is most likely to have decided the pressure to be employed only when the organ had been delivered and set up, and made ready for final tuning, so there is scope for variation in wind-pressures between instruments of similar size.

Pitch An organ fitted with tuning slides has irretrievably lost all evidence of its original pitch and temperament unless there are speaking front pipes which are unaltered or have only been cut or slotted below their original rounded 'windows'. Such evidence as there is suggests that Snetzler's pitch may have been about a quarter of a tone lower than 'treble' C = 513 Hz, the present 'norm':[26]
  (i) The pitch of Kedleston organ at 52 degrees Fahrenheit (11 degrees Centigrade), was -52 cents at *c* in February 1985; the temperament was evidently meantone, a tuning probably dating from before Buckingham's visit in 1824.
  (ii) The restored pitch of the Swithland organ, when some of the tuning windows of the front pipes (the Open Diapason) were temporarily restored to their original arrangement at 58 degrees Fahrenheit (14 degrees Centigrade), was -45/46 cents at 2' C, or -47 cents at 4' C (approximate values; the pipes had then to be blown by mouth); their finished pitch (April 1987) at 2⅝" wind-pressure and 60 degrees Fahrenheit (15 degrees Centigrade) was -45 cents.
  (iii) The 1742 'Cuckston' organ was found to speak at its best at a pitch where a meantone middle A was found to sound 423 Hz. at 55 degrees Fahrenheit (13 degrees Centigrade).
  (iv) Ellis[27] instances two 'Schnetzler' organs (in the 'German Chapel Royal, St James's and at 'Halifax'; perhaps the parish church, chapter 3 no. 67, or possibly no. 83, q.v.) whose original pitch he 'presumes' to have been A = 425.6 Hz.
  Ludlam's comments on pitch (see Appendix 7) suggest that organ were tuned to bells – or at least that they should be. Sperling's interest in bells (also recorded in his notebooks) may also suggest that there was at one time a closer connection between the pitches of bells and organs – very necessary when the two are sounded together, perhaps as in an opening voluntary – than has been recognised hitherto.

Temperament Christopher Kent[28] has pointed out that three organs by Snetzler are associated with composers who wrote music that would seem to challenge the musical potential of a meantone tuning. He suggested that a *Preludium XI* headed 'Arbitrary Modulations' was written by William Herschel with the Halifax (parish church) organ in mind. As the MS includes registrations for a three-manual organ which included a Vox Humana and no pedals are indicated, this would indeed seem to be the likely intended organ. The music wanders into fairly 'extreme' keys (including D♭ major and F♯ major), so the beginnings of a case that this organ was tuned in some modification of meantone might be made.

'Evidence' perhaps just as strong is that the organ was opened with a performance of the tonally wide-ranging *Messiah* with a band of instrumentalists; if the organ had an important role in this performance, its tuning may well have been modified away from strict meantone. On this basis, the tuning of the organs at Beverley Minster ('opened with Oratorios' according to Buckingham) and Leicester (whose opening featured choral music by Handel and Boyce) might have been similarly treated. However, it was reported of the Halifax organ in 1869[29] that it

> was not finally perfect until Sunday last [Summer 1869]. Mr. Roberts, the present organist, is now able to present some of Bach's best figures [*sic* – fugues?] in the exact form in which they were written; the pedal bass having in it no inversions; and the equal temperament of the organ enabling the modulations to be given without the offensive effect upon the ear of the barbarous unequal temperament...

which plainly indicates that the original temperament of this organ, howsoever modified, cannot have been anything like an equal one.

Herschel's *Organ Concerto in D* was written as part of the inauguration of the Snetzler organ in the Octagon Chapel, Bath, in October 1767, and Christopher Kent suggests that passages in this work also require an organ with an 'extended' temperament. It is not unreasonable to suggest that a scientist of Herschel's capabilities would have taken a great personal interest in a tuning scheme for this organ, particularly as it was in effect being made for him. The individual owners of chamber organs may also have requested 'special' tunings – Burney indeed said that meantone was used 'for church organs' and he meant to imply by this that other temperaments were employed in other places.

Finally, the music of Baumgarten, organist at the Lutheran church in the Savoy (see chapter 3, no. 37) and, perhaps significantly, well-known as a skilled modulator, employs harmonic techniques typical of the later eighteenth century; it would seem likely that this organ may have been tuned along lines hinted at in the Fulneck contract: 'in such a way that all notes [*sic*] can be played'.

However, there is one chamber organ, still where Snetzler put it, which defies the evidence so far adduced. The temperament of the organ at Kedleston Hall (chapter 3, no. 69) was investigated in detail on 5 February 1985, and notes made then by Martin Renshaw included the following:

> The Open Diapason rank, from middle C♯ upwards, was removed and [their mouths] carefully cleaned with a soft brush so that the pipes could speak. The inscriptions on the pipes were transcribed and, after the pipes were reinstalled and time for cooling had been left, metered readings of their pitch were taken.
>
> [Two sets of readings were recorded.] If the general pitch of the organ is taken to be –52 cents at C, then the average of these readings may be compared with normal quarter-comma meantone as follows:

Average readings:		Quarter-comma meantone:
C	0	0
C♯	−24	−23 or −24
D	−8/10	−7
D♯	+10/11	+10
E	−14/15	−14
F	+1/−1	+3
F♯	−23	−21
G	0/−3	−3
G♯	−29	−27
A	−8	−10
B	+6	+7
♮	−20	−17

These figures correspond sufficiently for it to be reasonably clear that the organ is indeed still tuned in meantone temperament. The last recorded work on the organ is that of Alexander Buckingham's visit on 11 December 1824. Since he noted that there were runnings [and a major one is still to be found], it is likely that he then tuned the organ. On this or a later visit he may have converted the reservoir to its present horizontal form – work he carried out elsewhere – and may have partly repaired the runnings. He thought that the organ was older than 1766, and this [supposition] is borne out by the varied markings on the pipes.

I was told on 5 February 1985 that the Curzon (Baron Scarsdale's) family was not in residence for many of the middle years of the last century, and Dr Michael Sayer was told by the second Viscount Scarsdale (1898–1977) that he could not recall the organ's being tuned in his lifetime.

This evidence points to the great likelihood that the organ maintains the tuning of 1824 and possibly even that of 1766.

It is ironic (in view of the fact that it was not wholly made by Snetzler) that the Kedleston organ may be the only one of 'his' now in Britain that appears to retain nearly its original pitch and tuning. The bureau organ now in Schaffhausen (see chapter 3, no. 56) is said to have been 'found' in an unaltered condition, but precise details of its pitch and temperament have not been published.

The Kedleston Hall organ's uniqueness highlights the changes suffered by the vast majority of eighteenth-century organs in Britain. As a result of these changes, their original condition has become so remote that they are now difficult fully to comprehend, technically or musically. This book has aimed to help us all towards a better understanding of these instruments and to further a general re-evaluation of a potentially splendid heritage from this period – and in doing so to celebrate the achievements of a particularly remarkable man.

*

Endnotes

1. In the Preface to the second volume of his edition of part of Henry Leffler's MS, published as *Notes on English Organs...* (London, 1900), p. v.

2. James Hamilton and Joseph Warren, *The Catechism of the Organ* (4th edn, 1865, Cocks & Co., London, reprinted Frits Knuf, Buren, 1992), p. 43.

3. HR 2, p. 306.

4. John Sutton, *A Short Account of Organs* (1847), p. 75.

5. See BIOSJ 14/24–5.

6. Charles Pearce, *The Evolution of the Pedal Organ* (London, 1927).

7. HR 1, p. 149.

8. See Cecil Clutton and Austin Niland, *The British Organ* (Batsford, 1963), p. 82.

9. HR 2, p. 13.

10. HR 2, p. 11.

11. Macmillan Press, 1987, pp. 62–98.

12. John Sutton, *A Short Account of Organs*, pp. 79–80.

13. See Raymond Russell, *The Harpsichord and Clavichord* (Faber and Faber, 1959), p. 83, fn. 2.

14. Op. cit., p. 77.

15. William Sumner, quoted by Freeman (TO 55/171).

16. Cited in *Charles Brenton Fisk, Organ Builder* (Westfield Center, 1986), vol.2, p. 141.

17. As in the organ (1794–5) now in St Guthlac's church, Branston–by–Belvoir, Leicestershire.

18. HR 2, p. 156 (para. 695).

19. David Wickens, *The Instruments of Samuel Green* (Macmillan, 1987), p. 84.

20. James Wedgwood, *Dictionary of Organ Stops* (London, 1907), p. 186.

21. Wickens, op. cit., p. 86.

22. Ibid., p. 87.

23. Privately communicated by David Wickens.

24. A 'practical working' scaling method for wooden pipes is given in J. W. Hinton, *Organ Construction* (3rd edn, Weekes and Co., London, 1910; repr. Frits Knuf, Buren, 1992), p. 60.

25. For instance, the reeds made by Timothy Russell in 1824 for Holy Trinity church, Newington Butts, London.

26. The following three paragraphs are taken from various reports by Martin Renshaw.

27. In his paper 'On the History of Musical Pitch' (reprinted Frits Knuf, 1968), p. 39.

28. See BIOSJ 14/22–27.

29. In 'No. 7' of the series of articles entitled 'A history of organs in the parish of Halifax' published in the *Halifax Guardian* in 1869. They were first brought to notice by Richard Barnes of Halifax in BIOSR, vol. 11, no. 4 (Oct. 1987), pp. 6–7; his help in supplying the pertinent copies of these is gratefully acknowledged.

5 Instruments previously attributed to Snetzler

I Work by identified contemporary builders

1 James Jones

Only three organs by Snetzler's one-time partner have yet been identified:

(i) *Fritton, Norfolk, the parish church* A rebuilt chamber organ, ?1774.

(ii) A small chamber organ noted by Alexander Buckingham (TO 210/18) as made by James Jones, Hyde Street, Bloomsbury, and belonging to Mr C. F. Younge of Sheffield. The transcript of Buckingham's notes does not list the stops, but records only that it contained four, and was given 'new bellows and keys and a set of 12 pedals' by him in 1827.

(iii) *Betchworth House, Surrey* Labelled in the soundboard 'James Jones London fasit 1780' [1], this is a chamber organ also of four stops:

$$(G', A', C, D\text{--}e'''): \text{OD (sc: } c'), \text{ SD, Pr, Fl}$$

The keyboard natural plates are of ivory, with sharps of stained pear with ebony veneers (cf. Locko Park, 1779 (chapter 3, no. 100) on key-stocks of oak. The Stopped Diapason trebles (from middle B [*sic*]) and the Flute (from *C* upwards) are metal chimney flutes. The wind-pressure is 1¾", and middle A is 80 cents flat of 440 Hz.

A pedal takes off the Principal and Flute, and there is a blowing pedal to a feeder with a single-rise wedge reservoir. The mahogany case, not of a Snetzler style, measures 4' 8" wide by 2' 3½" deep by 9' 6" high; the front pipes are arranged 3–19–3, the six outer pipes being the bass of the Principal.

[1] details of this organ are published by courtesy of Christopher St John Stevens, who also notes that the abridged diaries of John Marsh (in the Cambridge University Library) contain an account of his wanting some pipes for an organ in 1786; he went first to Green, but was directed to James Jones, who supplied them although he was on the point of retirement.

2 Thomas Haxby

Haxby, who lived and worked in York all his life, was born in 1729. At the age of twenty-one, he was appointed Parish Clerk of St Michael-le-Belfry, and a singing man at the Minster. He opened a music shop in 1756, and was encouraged to take up instrument-making by the precentor of the Minster. Haxby attested to the fact that he knew Snetzler (see chapter 1, p. 20). He made numerous keyboard and stringed instruments of all kinds (including a Cittern for George III), maintained the organs in the Minster and St Michael's, and is known to have worked on the following organs:

1760	Leeds parish church	– repairs
1762	St Mary, Scarborough	– new organ
?1767	Nostell Priory	– new organ (now at Wragby)
1767–8	Louth parish church	– new organ (B: TO 210/17)
1782	Aston parish church	– new barrel organ

An organ of *c*1771 made for Newby Hall near Ripon, North Yorkshire, is still *in situ* and has been circumstantially and technically attributed to Haxby. As in the Snetzler organ at Hillington (chapter 3, no. 33), the soundboard pallets and grooves of the two manuals are intercalated. The organ originally contained the following stops, and was restored to this form in 1981 by Martin Renshaw and Karl Wieneke:

Great (*G'*, *A'–e'''*): OD, SD, Pr, Ses b IV/Cor tr IV, Tr (sc: *c'*)
Eccho (*g–e'''*): Dul, Vox Humane

3 John Donaldson

A notebook compiled by J. W. Knowles about a hundred years ago repeats the suggestion that John Donaldson worked for Snetzler, but there is as yet no proof of this. He was born about 1747, and died in York in 1807. He first set up in business in Newcastle in the early 1780s, and moved to York about 1790. Like Haxby, he also made and repaired fortepianos.

Stephen Bicknell compiled the following list of his work (BIOSJ 11/32):

1783	St Paul, Aberdeen	– new organ or rebuilding
1784	Sedgefield, near Durham	– repairs (B: TO 207/107)
1785	St Andrew, Newcastle	– new organ
1785	St John, Newcastle	– repairs
1786	Bradford parish church	– new organ
*c*1788	St Andrew, Glasgow	– addition of 5–stop Swell to Snetzler organ (chapter 3, no. 7)
?1789	Ripon Cathedral	– repairs [new pipework also]
1790	Knaresborough parish ch.	– new organ
1790	Belvedere House, Dublin	– new organ
1791	Leeds parish church	– repairs
1791	Sowerby parish church	– new organ
1792	Pontefract parish church	– new organ
1792	St Mary, Beverley	– new organ
1792	Trades Hall, Glasgow	– new organ

1792	Sacred Music Inst., Glasgow	– new organ
1793	Auckland Castle, Durham	– repairs (B: TO 209/36–7) to organ previously repaired by Snetzler (see chapter 3, no. 72)
1794	Mansfield parish church	– new organ (B says 1795; TO 206/54)
1796	All Saints, Newcastle	– new organ
1797	East Retford parish ch.	– new organ
1798	St Nicholas, Newcastle	– repairs
1798	St Andrew, Newcastle	– repairs
1798	St Paul's chap., Aberdeen	– repairs
1799	Altyre House, Morayshire	– new organ
1802	Doncaster parish church	– new organ
1802	St Andrew's, Newcastle (R C)	– new organ
1802	Handforth Chapel, Cheshire	– new organ
1803	Penistone parish church	– new organ
1807	Leeds parish church	– repairs
undated	St James, Sheffield	– new organ (B: TO 210/19)
undated	Mr Lambert, Beverley	– new organ (B: TO 212/126)
undated	St Nicholas, Whitehaven	– repairs (B: TO 208/176–7)

Mr Lambert was (at least by the time of Buckingham's visit in 1823) organist of Beverley Minster. (B) indicates new organs, or repairs, detailed by Buckingham. The 1790 Belvedere House organ is now in the Holywell Music Room at Oxford; a full description of the organ and a comparison of its scaling with typical Snetzler practice were also given by Stephen Bicknell.

II Organs attributed to Snetzler by various authors

Both Sperling and Freeman list a number of organs which have been ascribed to Snetzler. More recently, unlabelled organs in styles inconsistent with Snetzler's known work have been attributed to him by Michael Wilson, Noel Mander and others, sometimes on the basis that these are 'early' instruments.

Snetzler's habit of 'labelling' his work, from his earliest extant organs of 1742 onwards, would have made conclusive demonstration of their true maker perfectly possible, if it were not for various difficulties. There has been a high rate of destruction of church–organ soundboards within which the labels were glued. There is still the occasional difficulty of access to a soundboard within a working organ, and there are a few detached labels in private collections. It has not been possible for the authors of this book to make a personal inspection of every *in situ* label; where they have not done so, they have relied on published reports of their existence and their dating only when these are consistent with other independent accounts and observations.

Snetzler's organ cases, too, are generally so characteristic that there should be no problem in recognizing them. But, again, there is the unsettling fact that at least two later cases exist (made in 1812 and 1814 by the Lincolns) which are quite close copies of his most-used church organ 'frontispiece'. Bernard Smith's four-tower case design was also copied during the eighteenth and nineteenth centuries, quite consciously as an act of homage to a builder of high reputation. Such homage was also, more obliquely, paid to Snetzler by the attribution to him of a number of organs mostly dating from the middle of the eighteenth century that were actually made by indigenous builders. The firm of J. W. Walker, in particular, moved several instruments of this kind which thenafter became associated with Snetzler.

The following critique divides the attributed organs into groups according to their various attributors. In most cases it is not at present possible to demonstrate the actual maker, since 'archaeological' research into 'anonymous' eighteenth-century instruments has scarcely begun.

1 Sperling's attributions

Apart from those also listed by Freeman, Sperling attributed the following additional organs to Snetzler. It is very hard to know what credence should be given to his details of instruments that have now disappeared, or had even gone by Sperling's own time. Those organs dated vaguely or in 'round' figures (e.g., '1750') are the least convincing.

(1) Leominster, Herefordshire, the Priory church (1731)
S II/126
There is no information at Leominster, and the date looks most improbable – but it is the same year-date that Buckingham thought he saw in the claviorgan at Moresby Hall, chapter 3, no. 1. See also chapter 1, p. 3, and chapter 3, no. 107.

(2) Pontefract, St Giles's church (1744)
S III/64
Because of damage inflicted in the Civil War, the old parish church of Pontefract, All Saints', became unuseable and the congregation migrated to St Giles's, which was used as the parish church, though not officially designated as such until about 1789. Sperling gives the following stoplist:

> Great (*G',A'–e'''*): OD, SD, Pr, 12, 15, Sesq IV (b ?), Cor IV (tr ?), Tpt
> Swell (*g–e'''*): OD, Dul, Pr, Tpt, Hb

He further says that the organ was removed in 1842 and sold to the Revd. F. Maynard Branwilt near Doncaster. (Should this perhaps rather be F. Maynard at Kirk Bramwith or South Bramwith near Doncaster?) A vestry meeting at St Giles's, 15 February 1792, decided that the old organ should not be repaired but that a new one should be purchased; whether nothing was done, or the organ moved into All Saints' (by then partly restored?) is not clear.

(3) London, Westminster, St John's church, Smith Square (1744)
S I/28
Some sources ascribe work here to 'Griffin' who was a barber-surgeon as well as an

organ–builder; others (including Sperling) mention Snetzler. Who actually made the organs Griffin supplied is not known, nor is the precise date of an organ made for St John's after a fire or the storms of 1741.

(4) Barnsley (Yorkshire), St Mary's church (1747)

S III/73; B 212/119

Sperling notes: 'Great Organ by Snetzler 1747. Erected here 1780', but Buckingham attributes the organ's origin as a one–manual to Parker 'in a handsome Wainscott Case' (also attributed to Smith because of its four–tower design) with a 'Choir organ added by whom I do not know ... Swell organ was added by Greenwood of Leeds'. There are no Snetzler pipes in the organ.

(5) Leatherhead, Surrey, church of St Mary and St Nicholas (1750)

S I/169; HR 7; F 20

The approximate date is Sperling's; as Freeman gives 1760, the exact date is obviously not clear in the sources. The case is said to have consisted of 'square towers', and the following stop–list is given by Sperling:

> Great (*G', A', C, D–e'''*): OD, SD, Pr, Fl (sc: *c'*), 12, 15, Ses III, Tpt, Mt Cor
> V (sc: *c#'*)
> Swell (*c'–e'''*): OD, SD, Tpt, Hb.

The history of the organ has now been traced to some extent: it began as a one–manual organ with an upper compass to *d'''*, and was enlarged by the addition of a second (lower) keyboard for a middle C Swell and its compass was extended to *e'''*. It was installed at St. Mary's parish church, Watford, by 1766. Walker made a new (smaller) organ for this church, and removed the old one to Leatherhead in 1843 [Shop Books 7 : 269]. That firm enlarged the organ in 1857, 1873 and 1885, and it was rebuilt by Kingsgate, Davidson & Co. with pneumatic action in 1927, and partially revoiced in 1956 by R. H. Walker & Sons.

The organ was disused after 1983, and damaged in a fire in 1989. During the dismantling of the organ in January 1991, it was possible to find and store many of the 'original' (that is, pre–1843) components, including the front pipes, the Great soundboard, and much of the Great and Swell pipework. A pair of keyboards which had been preserved in a vestry are from the same organ. The Great keyboard is the upper set, and the sharps are of the 'skunk–tail' kind paralleled in London–made organs by British builders in the 1730s, '40s and '50s. There is no element of the surviving old parts that can be ascribed to Snetzler. The case was one in which the pipes stood in three 'towers' (straight in plan), with two intervening 'flats', disposed 3–8–3–8–3; it survived until 1885.

The pre–1843 stop–list has been established as follows:

> Great (*G', A', C, D–e'''*): OD (thro'), SD (b/tr), Pr, Fl (thro'), 12, 15, Ses
> IVb/Cor IV tr, Tpt (b/tr); all stops dividing *c/c#* [upper keyboard]
> Swell (*c'–e'''*): OD, SD, Pr, Hb [lower keyboard]

(6) Berwick–on–Tweed, Holy Trinity church ('1750')

S 2/203

Sperling, whose dating is not to be trusted implicitly, is the source for the attribution. He gives a stop–list:

Great (*G', A', C, D–e'''*): OD (metal to *D*, then wood to bottom), SD ('in
    halves'), Pr, Fl (metal to 'fid. g' then wood bass), 12, 15, Ses b
    III/Cor tr III, Tpt ('in halves')
Swell (*g–e'''*): OD, SD, Pr, Tpt

Sperling notes that 'In 1850 the organ was repaired by Nicholson of Newcastle, who made
the compass of the Great organ BB to E in alt. [i.e., as the keyboard 'looked'], carried down
the Swell to tenor C, and added a Dulciana and Double Diapason, also a slide for another
reed. The work was done in a very inferior manner'. Sperling does not mention that
Nicholson had divided the organ each side of the west window, and added pedal pipes. The
organ was extensively rebuilt by Thomas Harrison in 1869, who retained most of the
previous pipes. It was rebuilt by Harrison & Harrison in 1880. (See L. Elvin, *The Harrison
Story* (Lincoln, 1973), pp. 44–5 and 77.)

(7) Worcester, St Swithun's church ('c1750')
S II/303
Another of Sperling's vague dates. The church was newly built in 1736 on an old site, but
the organ would seem to be mid–eighteenth century at the earliest. It was traditionally the
oldest organ in the city after that at the cathedral. The console retains its original black
non–Snetzler stop-knobs (now engraved); the Swell and the pedal pipes were added by
Nicholson of Worcester *c*1843, and the case deepened.
    The church is now in the care of the Redundant Churches' Fund. [Grateful ack-
nowledgements to James Berrow and Watkins Shaw for some of this information.]

(8) London, Westminster, Christ Church (1760)
S I/35
Freeman notes that the (then) church was built in 1842, and suggests than any previous
Snetzler organ may not have been transferred to it.

(9) London, Charterhouse chapel
S II/95
For a discussion of this organ, see chapter 3, no. 5.

(10) Belper, St Peter's church (1754)
S II/76
Sperling is the sole authority for this organ. He gives an unlikely compass and mixture
composition; the organ does not seem to coincide with any other known Snetzler organ in
the area, and no further information has been found in the church archives. It was
replaced in 1853.
    Sperling gives this stop-list:

(*G', A', C', D'–d'''*): OD, SD (b/tr), Pr, 15, Ses b V/Cor tr V, Tpt

(11) Ellesmere, St Mary's church (1754)
S II/232
An entry in the Vestry Book of the church reads:

At a Vestry Meeting held on Tuesday 18 June 1754 it was ordered that the
organ lately purchased by subscriptions be set up in the Church in some

proper and convenient place provided it is to be supported by a voluntary subscription and no tax upon the parish...

The organ was erected on the gallery in the south transept; it was described as 'diminutive but very powerful and sweet–in–tone'. It was replaced in 1849 by a Holdich organ.

Sperling is the sole source for the attribution: 'Old organ, Snetzler 1760, is now in the Vicarage [crossed out] Town Hall'.

(12) Stockton–on–Tees, St. Thomas's church (1759)
S II/89
Sperling is the only source for the attribution, date and stop–list of this organ, which he gives as:

> Great (*G', A', C, D–e'''*): OD, SD, Pr, 12, 15, Ses b/tr V, Tpt
> Swell [or 'Echo'] (*c'–e'''*): OD, SD, Pr, Fl, Cor III, Tpt
> 'Swell keys to GG, acting on St Diapason and Principal of Great.'

The short–compass Echo/Swell would seem to indicate an earlier date, if this is a Snetzler organ. The large Great Mixture is apparently similar to that noted at Belper.

(13) Lancaster, St John's chapel (1761)
S II/153

> 'Snetzler 1761. A row and half of keys, GG to E, Swell to fid. G.'
> Great: OD, SD, Pr, Fl, 15, Ses b III/Cor tr III, Tpt b/tr
> Swell: OD, SD, Tpt, Hb

There is no other information about this organ, but these details are plausible. Buckingham (see chapter 3, nos. 96 and 97) describes John Langshaw, who pinned the barrels for Lord Lowther's barrel organ, as organist of Lancaster parish church. Whether or not he was previously organist at St John's chapel is not certain; the organ in the parish church was made by G. P. England in 1811 (TO 83/111).

(14) Richmond (Surrey), 'old' church (1770)
S I/167
Freeman could find no reason for this attribution by Sperling, who has 'Snetzler 1770, additions by Handcock', and he suggested that the organ was made by Knight in 1770. The case front (of which there is a photograph in TO 26/123) is unlike anything known to have been made by Snetzler, and the pitch–marks on the front pipes are of the type used by indigenous makers – perhaps Byfield, Wilcox and Knight (as at Banbury, no. 24 in this section)? The attribution may have been mistakenly connected with the organ made in 1766 for the Earl of Fitzwilliam at Richmond (see chapter 3, no. 70). HR 1, p. 148, also includes this location, and adds that the organ was 'The gift of S. Sprags, Esq.'.

(15) Witney, St Mary's church (1771)
S II/223
Sperling, uncorroboratedly, provides a stop–list:

'Snetzler, 1771 [replacing 1774]. Great and Choir organs GG to E in alt.' [*G', A'–e'''*?]
    Great: OD, SD, Pr, 12, 15, 17, Ses III, Tpt
    Choir: OD, SD, Pr, Fl
    German pedals [nineteenth century] '1½ 8ves.'

(16) 'Bradfield', (undated)

S II/13

Sperling does not say which of the five possible Bradfields is involved, and it has generally been assumed that Bradfield near Reading, Berkshire, is the one. However, it is possible that when the Revd Dr L. G. Hayne left Eton College in 1871 to succeed his father in the benefice of Bradfield, Essex,[1] he took with him (among much other organ material) the Choir organ from Snetzler's rebuilding of the College organ (see chapter 3, no. 14). If this were so, it would account for his using Snetzler parts at this period, as some of those from Eton's Choir organ are otherwise unaccounted for until 1899; though what happened to these parts between Hayne's death in 1883 and their reuse at Hawkesyard in 1899 is less certain. They may have been in the Hill firm's possession, as the correspondence over their work at Hawkesyard rather implies.

[1] See notes by Bernard Edmonds in BIOSR, vol. 15, no. 1 (January 1991), pp. 14–15.

(17) London, Paddington Chapel (undated)

S I/204

Sperling reports that this organ was installed in 1848 as 'a second–hand organ from Brown's Lane Chapel'. According to Walker's shop–books it was 'An old organ by Snetzler' with a Walker Swell. Sperling noted this stop–list:

    Great (*G', A'–e'''*): OD, SD, Pr, Fl, 12, 15, Ses b III/Cor tr III
    Swell (*c–e'''*): Double Diapason, OD, SD, Pr, Tpt, Hb
    Pedals 'GGG–D' unison pedal pipes.
        Shifting movement.

He noted a mahogany case, 14' by 7' by 6', with gilt speaking pipes.

(18) Bicester, the parish church

S II/222a

(19) Walcot, St Swithin's church (1780)

S II/248

Sperling gives what is probably an approximate date, and rather delightfully describes the builders as 'Snatchbull and Jones'.

2 Andrew Freeman

Of the list of work given in Freeman's articles on Snetzler, the following organs were either possibly or certainly made by other builders:

(20) Lewisham, Roman Catholic church (1750)
F 4

Freeman notes an organ supposed to have been labelled 'John Snetzler, fecit, Londini, 1750' in a church in Lewisham. He was told that the organ later found its way to a cinema proprietor in north London, but he was unable to trace it. The date does not suggest any other surviving organ, though the cinema may well be the one noted in chapter 3, no. 19.

(21) Louth, parish church
F 38 (also HR 12)

This organ is now known to have been made (1767–8) by Thomas Haxby of York (see above). Another estimate for an organ at Louth was sent to a 'Rev. Mr. Ball' of Great Portland Street, not apparently in Snetzler's hand.

(22) Edmonton parish church
F 42

Freeman notes that this was also ascribed to the 'elder' (by which he meant George) England, 1772.

(23) West Bromwich, St Andrew's church (1777)
F 49

An organ from St Gabriel's church, Weoley Castle, near Birmingham, recently restored in East Anglia and offered for sale in London, is dated 1777 on a brass plate. It has been attributed to Snetzler. The organ is not labelled, and there are no apparent technical grounds for the attribution.

(24) Banbury parish church
F 54

Freeman notes that the organ contained Snetzler pipes, but that the case no longer existed. Bernard Edmonds, quoting Jackson's *Oxford Journal* for 27 November 1756 (in BIOSR, vol. 5, no. 1, p. 10), noted the report of its being made in 1765 by John Byfield II, George Wilcox and Thomas Knight. See also chapter 3, no. 107a, which may have confused sources when it was briefly in Banbury.

(25) Bath, Moravian chapel
F 55

Ascribed to Snetzler in *The Choir*, January 1914. The Moravians were settled in Bath in November 1765, and moved to Charlotte Street in 1840.

(26) Beeleigh Abbey (Essex)
F 58; W 101 (1) (dated 1747)

This is an unlabelled organ with a case unlike Snetzler's normal work, and with a stop-list with divided Principal and Fifteenth. Details of the keyboard and stopper handles are also unlike Snetzler's practice.

(27) Devizes, St. John
F 61

Freeman could find no justification for this attribution. What is left of the case is certainly old, but not of a normal Snetzler pattern.

(28) Hereford, the cathedral
F 62
There is no record in the cathedral archives of any work by Snetzler here, though Boeringer reports a proposal by Snetzler and Jones (1772) to add a Swell to middle C and a Choir Dulciana. For various reasons – in particular, the short–compass Swell at such a late date, and the untypical suggestion of a church–organ Dulciana – these details do not have the ring of truth.

(29) London, East Dulwich, St Anthony's church, Lordship Lane
F 69
Freeman records an organ in St Etheldreda, Ely Place, London, rebuilt in 1873 when the church, originally used by Welsh Episcopalians, was taken over by Roman Catholics. At this time, the original case and most of the original pipes were removed. The organ was sold to St Anthony's and rebuilt there in 1922. Its attribution must remain doubtful in default of further evidence.

(30) Nottingham, St Peter's church
F 71
(31) Painswick, St Mary's church
F 72
These two organs were made by the Lincolns in 1812 and 1814 respectively. Both organs are contained in casework reminiscent in its overall pattern of the 'normal' double–storeyed Snetzler case, and this has misled various recent authorities. However, all the early organ–list sources, and the two churches' records, document these as new organs by 'Lincoln' (as discussed in *Historical Organs Information Notes*, no. 6/7, pp. 14–18). One wonders if the elder (John) Lincoln had some particular connection with Snetzler or his successors. He worked on the Snetzler organs at King's Lynn and St Paul's, Sheffield, and was known to label his organs (for instance) 'Johannes Lincoln, Londini, Fecit 1789' (see BIOSJ 1/11), somewhat in the Snetzler manner.

(32) Tiverton, St Peter's church
F 76
The organ was made by Christian Smith in 1696. No evidence has been found to back the repeated assertion that Snetzler repaired it.

(33) Whaddon, Cambridgeshire, the parish church
F 77
Freeman says that the organ was brought to the church in 1857 after enlargement by Walker, and that the case dated from then.

(34) York, All Saints' Pavement church
F 79
The two stops (a Dulciana and a Flute) that Freeman mentions could more likely have come from an organ made by Thomas Haxby, whose workshops were nearby. In the organ, ascribed to him, at Newby Hall, the Eccho Dulciana is fendered in the Snetzler manner, and the upper part of the Great Stopped Diapason is a metal chimney flute in the Snetzler style.

(35) Newbury, St Nicholas's church
F (TO 27/158)

In an article on the organ of this church, Freeman says that he had seen a note to the effect that 'Upon opening the great organ windchest in 1875, Messrs. Bevington found "Jno: Snetzler" written on the wind bars'. The organ was made (or supplied?) by Byfield and Green in 1771, and the old one removed to Bethnal Green, St Matthew, London, where it was destroyed by fire in 1859. The Newbury organ has since been rebuilt twice, in 1927 and c1972. It still contains some Byfield and Green pipework, much altered, but the present Great soundboard has no obvious label.

(36) Oxburgh Hall, the Chapel
F 98 [*sic*: should be 90] W 110 (24)

Freeman lists this organ upon the recommendation of Gordon Paget. Although the organ has glazed doors (the feature that Paget found suggestive), it is not 'labelled' and neither its casework nor any other details conform to Snetzler's normal workmanship. It appears to date from the first half of the nineteenth century.

3 Michael Wilson

In his book *The English Chamber Organ*, Michael Wilson includes these organs in his Snetzler list:

(37) Cambridge, University Music School
W 103 (6)

He notes that it deviates from Snetzler's usual practice. It does, in many detailed respects, and it is not labelled.

(38) Candlesby, St Benedict's church
W 104 (7)

He notes that this organ has eight stops and is 'signed and dated 1775'. At St Andrew's church, Brocklesby Park, Lincolnshire, there is an organ by Knight (dated 1773), formerly at Candlesby, with a Swell by Greenwood (1820).

(39) Colonial Williamsburg (Virginia, U. S. A.)
W 111 (28)

This unlabelled organ, which in many ways recalls Byfield's work, was built in 1760 for Lord Kimberley of Kimberley Hall, Norfolk. Its compass to d''' and its stop–list, casework and internal details do not conform to Snetzler's usual practice.

Not in Wilson's book, but analogous to the above, is:
(40) Edinburgh, St Cecilia's Hall
The unlabelled organ here is similar to the Williamsburg organ, and the John Byfield organ of 1765–6 at 'Finchcocks', and so might also be by Byfield.

In Wilson's 'Anonymous' list is:
(41) Duror, St Adamnan's church
W 115 (12)

The organ is suggested by Michael Wilson to have been made by Snetzler, but although it contains some eighteenth–century pipework, this is not marked in Snetzler's manner. The organ is not labelled and is not of his general style of manufacture.

4 Other attributions

(42) Openwoodgate, Derbyshire, St Mark's church

Largely because the organ contained an outward–tapering Dolce (actually of nineteenth–century manufacture) it was locally attributed to Snetzler. In fact, it belonged to G. B. Strutt of Belper, and was reported upon in detail by Buckingham (TO 208/175), who attributed it to Stephen White; a suggestion consistent with other known work by that builder. From internal evidence, it can be dated 1794–5; it is now in private hands in North Yorkshire.

(43) Eastcote (Middlesex), the Methodist church

The organ, wantonly destroyed c1950, appears to have been of native rather than Snetzler's manufacture, and to have dated from the middle of the eighteenth century. It had 'skunk–tail' sharps and a short–octave $G'-e'''$ compass. The upper front of the case was enclosed by glazed doors.

(44) Bath, King Street, Methodist chapel (not positively dated)

Michael Hemmings, a local carpenter and prominent Methodist, was said to have entered into an agreement with the Chapel that he would lend it an organ by Snetzler, his own property, which could be removed at any time.

There is, however, no trace of any such agreement in the church records. In a discussion by Betty Matthews (TO 235/40–43) of the various organs in the Bath Assembly Rooms, she reports that Charles Green made an organ for the Octagon Room in 1771 (for which Snetzler had been asked to quote also) at a cost of £126. An organ was advertised for sale in 1789, but whether this was one made by Seede (who offered it) or one said to have been installed by Snetzler in New King Street chapel in 1779, or even one from Lulworth Castle (see chapter 3, no. 24), is not at all clear.

A new chapel at Walcot, opened 30 May 1816, replaced the King Street chapel, and seems to have then had a secondhand organ, installed (with a new case–front) by Holland.

(45) Scremby, Lincolnshire, church of St Peter and St Paul (1775)

The chamber organ with a mahogany case and a sloping toe–board for the front pipes (but not arranged in Snetzler's normal style) has been in the church since 1905. Dr Robert Pacey has found that it was previously at Hatcliffe parish church, where it was installed in 1862; the inauguration of the organ then being 'presided' over by Mr and Mrs Josiah Spode of Hawkesyard Park. The present stop–list is:

$(G', A'-e''')$: OD (11 basses from SD), SD, Pr, Fl (b/tr), 15, Ses b II/Cor tr II

The keyboard has ivory naturals with arcaded ivory heads and ebony sharps; the shifting movement takes off the Fifteenth and the (originally three–rank) Sesquialtera and Cornet. The stop-knobs are of rosewood with ivory faces, engraved. There is an illiterate nameboard above the keys: 'Snetzler London, Fecerunt 1775'. The style of pipework makes it difficult to accept the organ as one made by Snetzler, but one might wonder if the inscription suggests Jones (see above) as author or remaker of both organ and nameboard. Dr Pacey reports that 'Snetzler' also appears written on woodwork inside the organ.

(46) London, Soho Square, St Patrick's R. C. church
The organ here (much rebuilt, and for a time at Mill Hill R. C. church in north London) is apparently eighteenth–century in origin, but its pipes and soundboards are not in Snetzler's style.

(47) Great Packington (Warwickshire), St James's church
The ascription to Snetzler of the Choir division of this organ was made by William Sumner (TO 153/40–1). There is no documentary support for this suggestion. In fact, the organ was made by one builder, although Handel (in a letter to Charles Jennens in 1749) had specified a one-manual organ which might be built by Bridge, a builder 'very well' approved of by Handel.

It was installed at Gopsall Hall, Leicestershire: Jennens's home. Upon his death, many of his effects were removed to the home of the Earl of Aylesford at Great Packington Hall. The organ was moved to Packington church about one hundred years ago. It was brought to public notice by Lady Susi Jeans and Thurston Dart. It was used for recordings of the Handel organ concertos in 1959 by E. Power Biggs and the Royal Philharmonic Orchestra, at which time it was fitted with an electric blower and, controversially, tuned to the higher modern standard pitch and fitted with tuning slides.

The stop–list comprises:

> Great: (*G'*, *A'–d'''*): OD, SD, Pr, Fl, 12, 15, 17
> Choir: (*G'*, *A'–d'''*): SD, Fl, 15

The Great Tierce is original, and conforms to Handel's suggestion that there should be no reed in a 'country' organ. However, it is clear from its original rackboard that a Trumpet was originally planned.

5 Hopkins & Rimbault

The list of Snetzler's organs in HR 1 (pp. 148–9) includes, in addition to the above organs:

(48) City of London, St Clement's church, Lombard Street (undated)
HR 23
We have previously noted the entire lack of authenticated organs by Snetzler in the City of London, and the likely reason for this (p. 23).

(49) Leeds, parish church (undated)
HR 31
See John Donaldson's work–list above.

*

Charles Burney at home: 'A Sunday concert', 1782

C. L. Smith (1751–1835) sketched this distinguished company: from left to right, Cariboldi (double bass), Lady Mary Duncan, Hayford (oboe), Cervetto ('cello), Bertoni (keyboard), Paccierotti (castrato), Salpietro (violin), J. C. Fischer (oboe), Langoni (violin), Pieltain (horn); in the foreground, Burney talks to Polly Wilkes. The figure on the far right is unidentified, but may be the artist. Fanny Burney described these gatherings as 'harmonical coteries', and said that such was her father's reputation that 'there was hardly a musician in England who, if called upon, would have refused his services'.

Appended Documents

Appendix 1 The organ in St Dionis's church, Backchurch, City of London

The Harris organ, opened 15 June 1724, was a large organ with a three-tower case (the central tower the largest), and with double-storeyed flats. It cost £525.

The stop-list given in the contract, and copied from this by Cecil Clutton [1], is as follows:

Great organ (G', A–d''')	Choir Organ (G', A'–d''', 'the undersett of keys or choir organ')
Open Diapason	Half Open Diapason 24 pipes [plus 27 by Communication from Great]
Stoped Diapason	Stoped Diapason [G up from Great]
Prinsipal	Prinsipal
Great Twelfth	Fflute
Fifteenth	Ffifteenth
Tirce	Bassoon
Larigo	Half French Horne (27 pipes)
Sesquialtera [4 ranks]	Clarion by Communication
Trumpet	
Cremona	
Clarion	
Cornet [5 ranks, sc: c']	

Echo organ ('the thired sett of keys [meaning the bottom or top set?] are for the Ecchoes and Swellings and to commence on G–sol–re–ut')

Open Diapason
Stop Diapason
Principal Full Bodied
Trumpett
Cremona
Vox Humana
Cornet [III]

No pedals or coupler
Four bellows
[The Great and Choir were evidently on the same soundboard]

279

The organ was moved to St Mark's church, Walworth, after the demolition of St. Dionis' church in 1879, and was 'rebuilt' after water damage in 1885. In fact, at this time only the case front and the front pipes were retained, and the organ went to Darenth Training College at Dartford, where it was rehabilitated in 1924. Ten Harris ranks survive in the 1966 Mander organ in the Livery Hall of the Merchant Taylors in the City of London.

It is clear from the organ's condition in 1924, and from the Leffler MS, [2] that the organ was built with slight variations from the contract stop–list.

The records of the church (transcribed by Sumner, [3]) for 15 December 1722 note that:

> The Church–Wardens agree that Mr. Renatus Harris of Bristol should build an organ under certain conditions, e.g. ... the touch to be entirely to the satisfaction and good liking of Mr. Philip Hart ... to be submitted to the judgment and determination of the following persons: John Loeillet, William Babel, George Frederick Handel, Dr. William Croft, and Mr. R. Courteville, all of them Professors and Masters of Music, or the majority of them.

How much the design of this organ influenced Burney and Snetzler in their design at King's Lynn may be debated (see chapter 3, no. 17) but the stop–list of the King's Lynn organ does seem to be an up–dating of that at Backchurch, and it may be that the 'communicated' Great/Choir suggested the combined Choir/Swell arrangements at Lynn.

[1] Cecil Clutton, 'Livery Hall of the Worshipful Company of Merchant Taylors in the City of London' (TO 183/98)
[2] L 19 and 192
[3] William Sumner, 'George Frederick Handel and the Organ' (TO 153/44)

*

Appendix 2   A dozen labels from Snetzler's soundboards

To call Snetzler's labels 'signatures', as some have done, is inaccurate. When he wrote in German, his natural rapid and extrovert handwriting is to be seen; and he made his German signature in the correspondence relating to the 1748 organ at the Moravian settlement at Fulneck, thus:

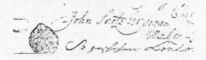

By contrast, the labels in the organs are, as one would expect, the careful and deliberate hand of a person writing in a foreign language. When he wrote English words, as in the Fulneck letters (see Appendix 3), he wrote them in an 'English–Italic' manner quite different from that of the text generally, and he signed the Contract on 15 February 1748, like this:

His letter from Nottingham (chapter 3, no. 97) is entirely written in this hand.

The earlier of the two labels dated 1742 would seem to be that in the organ now owned by Alan Cuckston (chapter 3, no. 3). It is a chamber organ containing a label thus:

The latinized form of his christian name and his German surname are obviously appropriate in this early context, but the other organ of 1742, now at Yale University, is labelled:

where the *John:* seems to be either a punctuated contraction of his Christian name or a deliberate anglicizing, and – perhaps uniquely – the date is not below the rest of the text.

The next-dated label is apparently that from the 1743 organ for Fetter Lane, but it differs from the 1742 and 1745 labels in two vital respects. First, the surname is spelt with a 'long z'; second, the Christian name is clearly *John*, and his surname is anglicized. These points inevitably lead one to suspect a reading of the date as 1743, which is indeed not clearly written: the '4' is unlike that in the others, and might be interpreted as a '6', though this would be a variant (see other labels below). A third detail, but one that would seem to suggest an earlier rather than a later date, is the form of the initial 'J', which closely resembles the Yale 1742 signature but no other, all later ones having a high or low loop in that letter, (low in the 1760s). However, the forms of the 'S' and the initial letter of 'fecit' do resemble those written in the 1760s:

Next comes the label in the Wemyss claviorgan, 1745:

where an anglicized surname is preceded by a semi-anglicized Christian name, perhaps because the organ was made in conjunction with the analogous *Jacob Kirckman fecit Londini* of the harpsichord nameboard. In other words, this label is a 'throwback'. The confident terminations of the 'z' and the 'L' were not always repeated, as will be seen from the following selected labels, which span the remainder of his creative life.

Snetzler's labels are written on paper glued to the vertical face of the main 'bar' which runs across the rear of the pallet-well of each soundboard; they are therefore quite easily visible when the face-board is removed. Their format is, after 1745, absolutely consistent, with a completely-anglicised *John Snetzler* followed by *fecit Londini* and the date. The 'final' label is, for obvious reasons, the only one not to follow this pattern.

Durrow/ Mirrey, 1748:

Norwich Cathedral (as 'traced' by B. B. Edmonds; see chapter 3, no. 20), 1748:

– Appended documents –

King's Lynn, 1753:

John Snetzler fecit Londini 1753.

Sculthorpe, 1755:

John Snetzler fecit Londini 1755

South Dennis, 1762:

John Snetzler fecit Londini 1762

Nottingham, 1776:

John Snetzler fecit Londini 1776

Merevale, 1777:

Switzerland, 1782:

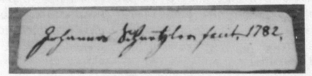

Johannes Schantzloor fecit 1782,

Appendix 3 The Fulneck Letters

The original German texts have been transcribed and translated as literally as possible by Dr Eric Poole; underlined words are those written in a 'formal Italic' (as opposed to normal German script) and square brackets show where original words are illegible:

Letter 1 John Snetzler, London, to Mr Schlicht, 16 December 1747

Hochgeertester Herr!

Nehme die freiheit, mit gegenwartigem beschwerlich zu sein, weilen vernehmen, daß die löbl. Congregation in Loco wo sie sich befinden, gesinnet eine Orgel in dero Capell verfertigen zu laßen, sie hatten die gutheit meine arbeit alhier in London zu recomandieren und hoffe es were zur Satisfaction, ersuche die selbe deß nahme von der güte zu sein und daß Wort der [three illegible words], solten sie darin Success haben, versichere daß meine bestes Thun werde mit guter und wohlfeiler arbeit aufzuwarten, kan mir eines Theiles beßere Satisfaction zu geben, versprechen, wan die Orgell particular vor dem Platz darin sie zu stehen und vor die stärke von der [one illegible word], soll besprechen werden, die difficultat weiters soferne von London kan leichtlich gehoben werden, wo sie gedenken daß es von nötig die Orgel selber auszurichten ich werde die reise als eine lust reise ansehen und die Zeit welche darzu erfordert wirdt nicht estimieren die umkösten können daß nahen so groß nicht sein gedenke bey solchem stük arbeit, daß es beßer etwaß weniges nicht anzusehen, und guter arbeit versichert zu sein, als auf ungewüß zu waagen. Ersuche daß nahen die selbe durch eine beliebige antwort nachricht zu ertheilen, recomendiere mich in dero Gunst und verharre unter Göttes erlaßung

> *Hochgeehrtester Herr*
> *Dero gantz ergebenster Diener*
> *Johann Schnetzler*
> *Orgelmacher*

London
den 16 December / 1747

Most honoured Sir,

I take the liberty of troubling you with this present letter, because I hear that the worthy congregation, in the place where you are, is thinking of having an organ set up in your chapel. You were so kind as to recommend my work here in London, and I hope it was to your satisfaction. I beg the same whose name [ ] to be so kind and [ ] the word. Should you have success in this, I assure you that my best performance can be expected, with good and inexpensive work. I can promise better satisfaction to some extent, if the organ is to

284

be specially discussed for the place where it is to stand and for the strength of the [ ]. Further, the difficulty of being so far from London can easily be overcome, when you consider that when it is necessary to erect the organ itself I shall regard the journey as a pleasure trip, and shall take no account of the time demanded. The expenses cannot be nearly as great for this piece of work, and I consider that it is better not to regard anything less, and for good work to be ensured, than to venture into the unknown.

I beg you to impart to me a favourable reply to the same, commend myself to your favour, and remain under God's providence

> Most honoured Sir,
> Your entirely devoted servant,
> Johannes Schnetzler
> Organ maker

London, 16 December 1747

Letter 2 *John Snetzler, London, to Mr Schlicht, 16 January 1748*

<u>London</u>, den 16ten <u>January</u> 1747/8

Hochgeehrtester Herr,

Dero geehrtes habe erhalten; es thut mir aber leid, daß sie bey daro <u>recomendation</u> den geringsten Punckten gegen mir solten auszusetzen haben, jedoch der ersten Punckt wegen aufschieben, der Orgelldekels ist also würklich geholffen auf die Weise wie sie gemelt der Zweite, aber bite mir zu der Zeichen, wan darin mich so sehr geirret in meiner <u>opinion</u> ware es, daß sie mir vermeldet daß die halfte deß gelts gleich baar könte bezahlt werden, dem rest aber eine Zeitlang darnach, welches ich vor 2 oder 3 Monat <u>supponiert</u> weil sie es aber auff 12 Monats war es ein großes Mißverstandniß von mir, und versicherlich k[] Mißtrauen, es solte auch bey einiger <u>accord</u> sehr schwer vor mich sein die bezahlung so lang zurük zu setzen, weilen ich nur ein anfänges und bey einem verfertigten stük mir helffen muß, ein anderes wider zu unternehmen, hoffe dieses wirdt unvergeßen sein.

Die bemelte Orgel betreffend so können nicht wohl beßere <u>Register</u> aufgesucht werden, als die gemeldet werden, daß unglük ist freilich daß nicht mehr höche zu solchen <u>Registern</u> verhanden, und wan bemelte Zunehm <u>Register</u> als <u>Trumpet</u> und <u>Hautbois</u> sollen hinein gemacht werden, so wirdt die <u>Gallery</u> schwerlich diess genug sein, weil alsdan muß platz gegeben werden, hinder der Orgell bey zu kommen, um solche zu stimmen wenigstens 1½ fuß und dan 1½ fuß wenigstens von voran bey dem <u>Clavir</u> vor den <u>Organisten</u> zu spielen so daß vor die tieffe der Orgel nicht mehr dan 3 füß übrig, welches doch zum wenigsten 4 füß sein solte zu allen diesen <u>Registern</u> wird also wenigstens 7 füß dieff von der <u>Gallery</u> erfordert und weil nicht Hölze genug müßen viele von der grösten Pfeiffen gekröpfet werden. N.B. die groste Pfeiffen G muß 12 fuß lang sein, solte es aber sein daß nicht so viel Platz kunte gegeben werden, so glaube daß folgende <u>Disposition</u> eine [ ] <u>Complete</u> Orgel ausmachen solten namlich <u>open Diap.</u> vom Holtz durchauß / werden die Pfeiffen von Holtz können die gröste leichtlich gekröpft werden. N.B. in der Orgell in <u>Fetter Lane</u> sind nur 3 <u>Octaven</u> die grösten sprechen in <u>Stop Diap.</u> so daß in den <u>Bass.</u> zu <u>Stop Diap.</u> und <u>Open Diap.</u> nur eine Pfeiffe ist. Ich hab davon zu Herrn Brokmer gesprochen er hoffet daß in Zeit etwas gelt soll auff-[ ] werden eine <u>Addition</u> von disen Pfeiffen zu machen, welches die [ ] *ein Merkliches verstärken wirdt.*

1.	<u>Open Diapason</u> *von Holtz durchauß* }	*nebst einem doppelten Zug*
2.	<u>Stop Diapason</u> *von Holtz* }	*bey welchen die 4*
3.	<u>Principal</u> *in front* <u>Mettal</u> }	*Registers stehen bleiben*
4.	<u>Open Diap.</u> *halb* <u>Mettal</u> }	*die anderen 5 aber können an*
		und ab gezogen werden
5.	<u>Twelfth</u> <u>Metal</u>	
6.	<u>Fifteenth</u> <u>Metal</u>	
7.	<u>Sesqualtra</u> *in* <u>Bass</u> <u>Metal</u> }	*Separiert wie gemelt*
8.	<u>Cornet</u> *in* <u>Discant Metal</u> }	
9.	<u>Solicional</u> *von* <u>Metal</u> *hat im thon alswie ein* <u>Violoncello</u>	

Hat die gleiche dieffe als ein <u>Open Diapason</u> *welches sehr anmutig weiß nicht wie eine schwell könte anderst angebracht werden als durch ein* <u>Aparte</u> <u>Clavir</u> *welches halb durch gehet und die Pfeiffen in einen klein Kasten gantz oben und Mitl von der Orgel mit duon 4 Registern als 1* <u>Diap.</u> *2.* <u>Solicional</u> *3.* <u>Cornet</u> *4.* <u>Trumpet.</u>

Weil sie eine Front mit Türen verlangen, habe diese Zeichnung wornach unsere Orgel in der hoch Teutschen <u>Capelle</u> *gemachtet habe, mit überschicken wollen, welches ungefehr die größe von der Platz ist.*

Der niedrigste Preiß solche Orgell zu machen will sein 150 £ und ohne schwell 125 £ sterling, und wen es soll gemacht werden mit den gemelten Zeugen Registern will es zu 160 £ sterling kommen ohne schwell.

Wen es verlangt wirdt, kan solches Werk in Zeit von 4 Monat zu liefern verstrechen.

Ich verharre nebst freundlicher <u>Salutation</u>

*Meines hochgeehrtesten Herrn
gantz ergebenster Diener
Johannes Schnetzler*

P.S. Ich habe es in underschiedlichen Orten in Teutschland gesehen daß wo die Kirche nicht hoch genug gewesen daß sie wo die Orgel zu stehen kamen die da etwa 3 Fuß höher gemacht welches eben nicht schlecht außgesehen.

London, 16 January 1747/8

Most honoured Sir,

I have received your honoured letter, but I am sorry that in your recommendation you have the least point to find fault with me about. However, to deal with the first point, the organ cover is really helped in the way you informed the second one, but I beg to refer to the drawing. What led me so far astray in my opinion was that you notified me that half the money could be paid as cash down, and the rest a certain time later. I supposed this would be 2 or 3 months, while you took it to be 12 months. It was a big misunderstanding on my part, and assuredly [no] mistrust. In any contract it would also be very difficult for me to set back the payment so long, while I have only made a start and must help myself, with a completed article, to undertake yet another. I hope this will not be forgotten.

As regards the organ that was ordered, better stops cannot well be sought out, as they were ordered. Unfortunately, such high stops are no longer available, and when the increased stops that were ordered, such as <u>Trumpet</u> and <u>Hautboy</u>, have to be brought in, the gallery is hardly enough for this, because space also has to be allowed for coming round behind the organ: at least 1½ feet to allow for this, and then at least 1½ feet in front of the keyboard for the organist to play, so that for the depth of the organ not more than 3 feet is left over. To this, there should be at least 4 feet for all these stops, so that at least 7 feet is required in depth of the gallery, and because there is not enough wood, many of the biggest pipes have to be bent. N.B. The biggest pipes, "G", must be 12 feet long, but should it be that so much space cannot be allowed, I believe that the following arrangement should provide a [ ] complete organ, that is, <u>Open Diapason</u> of wood throughout. The pipes will be of wood, and the biggest ones can be slightly bent. N.B. In the organ in Fetter Lane, there are only 3 octaves. The biggest correspond to <u>Stop Diapason</u>, so that there is only one pipe in the bass, to <u>Stop Diapason</u> and <u>Open Diapason</u>. I have spoken about this to Herr Brokmer, and he hopes that in time some money will be [ ] for making an addition to these pipes, which will strengthen the [ ] perceptibly.

1.	<u>Open Diapason</u> of wood throughout	}	with a double 'gear' [sliders]
2.	<u>Stop Diapason</u> of wood	}	by which the[se] 4 stops
3.	<u>Principal</u> in front metal	}	remain as they are, but the
4.	<u>Open Diapason</u> half metal	}	other 5 can be pulled on
			and off
5.	<u>Twelfth</u> metal		
6.	<u>Fifteenth</u> metal		
7.	<u>Sesqualtra in Bass</u> metal	}	Separated, as ordered
8.	<u>Cornet in Descant</u> metal	}	
9.	<u>Solicional</u> of metal; has a tone like a <u>violoncello</u>.		

It has the same depth as an <u>Open Diapason</u>, which is very pleasant. I do not know how a Swell could otherwise be fitted in, but through a separate keyboard which goes halfway through, and the pipes in a small chest, quite above, and in the middle of the organ with perhaps 4 stops, such as 1. <u>Diapason</u>, 2. <u>Solicional</u>, 3. <u>Cornet</u>, 4. <u>Trumpet</u>.

As you require a front with towers, I have had this drawing made of our organ in the High German Chapel, and will send it over. This is about the size of the available space.

The lowest price for making such an organ will be £150, and without a swell £125 sterling, and if it is to be made with the stop gear as ordered it will come to £160 sterling without swell.

If it is required, such work can be completed in a period of 4 months for delivery.

I remain, with friendly greetings,
My most honoured Sir,
Your most devoted servant
Johannes Schnetzler

P.S. I have seen in various places in Germany, that where the church has not been high enough they have made it some 3 feet higher where the organ was to stand, which has not looked bad.

Letter 3   John Snetzler, London, to Mr Schlicht, 26 January 1748

London 26 Jan: 1747/8

Geehrtester Herr!

Es ist mir lieb daß vorgeschlagene Proposition der Orgell ihnen gefällig, und bin versichert, das die von ihnen bemelte Disposition ein Completes Orgell Werk außmachen wurde es thut mir aber leid daß es mir nicht möglich ein solches Stück Arbeit vor den bemelten Preis zu verfertigen wünschen daß ich es thun könte, bite aber sie wollen Considereren waß for arbeit [da]rzu erforderet wirdt haben daß nahme alles auff das genaueste überleget 140 £ ist das geringst daß ich darvor nehmen kan, vor weniges Kunte solches nicht undernehmen, solten sie sich zu diesem resolvieren können, so sollen alle bemelten Punkten genau observieret werden und sie können versicheret sein, daß sie ein Gutes und wohlfeiles Orgelwerk haben sollen, wie ich den Offeriere daß verständigen in diser Arbeit so wohl gutniß als Preises halbe möge examiniert und taxiret werden und bey einigen Klägden darvon antworten werde.

N.B. Solicional hat einen gantz differenten Thon wie Open Diapason es ist eine lange Pfeiffe von gantz schmalere Mensur welche keine Kröpfung findet so daß die Pfeiffen so weit in die dieffe hineden gehen solten als die hohe der Orgel erlauben will welches ohngefehr in daß G gehen wirdt die dieffeste Octav spricht in Open Diap.; die Schwell kan nicht dieffer als C kommen weil es die höhe der Orgel nicht erlauben will.

Wegen übersendung der Orgel gedenke daß es Ziemlich wohl getheilt und ehender schwere for mich wan die pak Kästen welche ein merkliches kosten werden und die reise und auffsetzen über mir selber nehme, und weil so in loco vielleicht beßere gelegenheit finden können die Orgell hie zu schaffen sie dieses über sich nehmen stellen in erwartung beliebes anthwort verharre

> *Geehrtester Herr, dero*
> *bereitwilligster Diener*
> *Johannes Schnetzler*

London, 26 January 1748

Most honoured Sir,

I am glad that the proposition for the organ, as set before you, pleases you, and I am sure that the arrangement you have ordered would provide you with a complete organ job. However, I am sorry that it is not possible for me to instal such a piece of work for the price you have offered. I wish I could do it, but beg you to consider how much work is required for it. I have gone through everything as closely as possible, and £140 is the least that I can take for it. I could not undertake such a job for less, and if you should be able to decide on this, all the points you have ordered will be exactly observed, and you may be assured that you will have a good and inexpensive organ system. The way I offer an understanding of this work, both as to goodness and price, may be examined and assessed, and I shall reply to any complaints about it.

N.B. Salicional has a quite different tone from Open Diapason. It is a long pipe of much narrower diameter, and has no bend, so that the pipes should go as deep as the height of the organ will allow. It goes to about "G", and the deepest octave corresponds to the Open

<u>Diapason</u>. The swell cannot come deeper than "C" because the height will not allow it.

As to dispatch of the organ, I think that it is fairly well divided. It would be difficult for me sooner if I take personal responsibility for the packing cases, which cost quite a lot, and the journey and erection. Because it may perhaps be possible to find a better opportunity on the spot, to build the organ here, you may wish to take responsibility for this. Awaiting your kind reply, I remain

> Most honoured Sir, your readiest servant
> Johannes Schnetzler

Letter 4   John Snetzler, London, to Mr Schlicht, 4 February 1748

<u>London</u> *den 4 Febr: 1747 / 8*

Hochgeehrtester Herr,

Dero letsteres habe ich erhalten, der Vorschlag die Orgell in <u>Leeds</u> zu machen ist sehr wohl und dank ihnen vor der Gutheit und Mühwaltung, es solte mir aber sehr nachteilig sein, meiner Kundschaft alhier vor so lang zu verlaßen und kunte mich zu solchem gar nicht <u>resolvieren</u>, und bey überlegung finde, daß sehr wenig könte erstarret werden, es ist zwar sehr wohlfeil alda zu leben wie ich vernehme, jedoch die <u>Materialen</u> wurden daß gleiche Kosten und viele sachen nicht so wohl zu haben sein als hier beyseits die einrustung und werkzeug der darzu erfordert würde.

Als for den Platz wo die Orgel zu stehen komt, weil ich daß Maaß darvon habe, ist es schon genug biß es zum aufsetzen komt ich wurde die gantze Orgel also <u>Ordinieren</u> daß die Bälge unden in den Kasten kommen sollen und daß gleich voll sehr wenige oder gar keine Pfeiffen sollen gekröpfet werden, daß <u>Solicional</u> betreffend, so ist est viel natürliches, wan die Große <u>Octav</u> und vielleicht nicht die gantze, welche höhe halber etwan nicht können hinundergebrachtwerden in <u>Open Diap.</u> gehen sollen, als gedekte Pfeiffen darherzumachen, es werden ohne dem die <u>Bässe</u> sehr stark werden, in dem sie von viel weiteren <u>Mensur</u> sollen gemacht werden als in <u>Fetter Lane</u> jedoch wan sie gedekte Pfeiffen haben wollen sollen es gethan werden.

Geehrtester Herr ich gebeichene solches nun recht zu überlegen wan solch bemeltes Orgellwerk solle wohl <u>executieren</u> werden, waß darhin erfordert wirdt, so werden sie finden, daß sie gar keine ursach haben, sich deß Preißes halber zu beklagen und möchte sie etwa jemand finden der es vor einen Geringeren Preiß unternehmen wurde, ich wünsche, und wolte uns haben daß es wohl möchte gethan werden.

Ich will zum überfluß noch dieses Thun, weil sie gedenken daß daß herschaffen, so viel kosten wirdt ich will alle die umkösten über mir selber nehmen, und ihnen die Orgel in meinen umkösten hinschaffen und aufsetzen, wan dahingegen die letster Halfte des Geltes anstatt 6 <u>Monats</u> in 3 <u>Monats</u> Zeit kunte bezahlt werden, wan sie um dieses zu viel zu sein gedenken so muß ich in Gottes Nahmen ihnen überlaßen zu thun waß sie gedenken daß beste zu sein.

> *Verharren indeßen*
> *Hochgeehrteste Herrn dero*
> *Ergebenster Diener*
> *Johannes Schnetzler*

N.B. *Ich versichere sie, daß es mir solte eine freude sein ihnen zu dienen und zwar in dem allergenauesten weg ohne sich selber scheiden zu thun.*

London, 4 February 1748

Most honoured Sir,

I have received your latest letter. The proposal to make the organ in Leeds is very well, and I thank you for your kindness and the trouble you have taken. However, it would be very disadvantageous to me to forsake my customers here for so long, and I could not resolve to do this, and I find on consideration that very little could be left unattended. It is admittedly very cheap to live there, as I understand, but the materials would cost the same, and many things are not so easy to get as here, besides the equipment and tools that would be required for it.

As for the space where the organ is to be placed, because I have the measurements for it, it is enough until it comes to fitting it up. I would arrange the whole organ so that the bellows would come underneath in the chest, and very few or no pipes would be bent. Regarding the Salicional, it is very natural, when the big Octave and probably not the whole, which because of their height could perhaps not been brought underneath, should go in the Open Diapason, to bring it along as covered pipes. Without this, the Basses would become very strong, in that they would be made of much greater diameter than in Fetter Lane. However, if you want to have covered pipes, it shall be done.

Most honoured Sir, I now [beg] you to consider definitely if such an organ system as was ordered should indeed be carried out as is requested. You will find that you have no cause whatever to complain about the price, and if you were able to find someone who would undertake it for a lower price, I wish, and should like us to have it, so that it might so be done.

I want in addition to do this, because you consider that the construction will cost so much: I shall take all the expenses upon myself, and build and set up the organ for you at my own expense, if in return the last half of the money, instead of being paid in 6 months, could be paid in 3 months. If you consider this too much, I must leave it to you in God's name to do as you think best.

Awaiting in the meantime, most honoured Sir,
    Your most devoted servant,
      Johannes Schnetzler

N.B. I assure you that it would be a pleasure to me to serve you, in every detail, without our separating.

*

Letter 5   The contract, 15 February 1748

*Herr Johannes Schnetzler, Orgelbauer in <u>London</u>, verspricht der Gemeine in <u>Fulneck</u>
bey <u>Pudsey</u> in <u>Yorkshire</u> eine Orgel zu machen mit folgenden Registern &c.*

1. *<u>Stopt Diapason</u>, von Holtz vom <u>Contra</u> G bis zum höchsten E, i.e. 58 Pfeiffen.*
2. *<u>Open Diapason</u>, von Holtz – eben so.*
3. *<u>Viola di Gamba</u>, von <u>metal</u>, die letzte <u>octave</u> im bass spricht in <u>open diapason</u>.*
4. *<u>Solicional</u> von <u>metal</u>, vom mittler C bis ans höchesten E.*
5. *<u>Principal</u> – von <u>metal</u> – 58 Pfeiffen.*
6. *<u>Octav</u> – von <u>metal</u> – 58 dito.*
7. *<u>Cornet</u> – von <u>metal</u> 3 oder 4 <u>Ranks</u>.*
8. *<u>Sesquialtera</u> von <u>metal</u>. N.B. eine <u>Octave</u> tieffer als die in <u>Fetter Lane</u>.*
9. *<u>Trumpet</u> gantz durch [ ] also auch 58 Pfeiffen.*

In diese Orgel wird ein <u>Swell</u> gemacht mit folgenden 4 Registern.

1. *<u>Open Diapason</u>, von Holtz, vom mittleren C bis zum höchsten E.*
2. *<u>Open Diapason</u> von <u>metal</u> – eben so.*
3. *<u>Principal</u> 8 fußen; von <u>metal</u>, auch so.*
4. *<u>Cornet</u> 3 <u>or</u> 4 <u>Ranks</u> von <u>metal</u>, id.*

*Die Zwey <u>Manuale</u> zur Orgel und dem <u>Swell</u>, wurden mit schönen schwartzen Holtz und
die <u>Semitonia</u> mit Helffenbein wohl ausgelegt, und von solcher Länge gemacht wie die in
<u>Fetter Lane</u>.*

*Zu den Pfeiffen soll recht gutes Holtz und <u>Metal</u> genommen werden, und eine jede soll
recht rein ansprechen.*

*Die <u>Fronte</u> von diesem Werk wird mit fünf Thüren gemacht, und mit hübschen
<u>Ornamenten</u> und Schnitzwerk versehen werden.*

*Das Schnitz- oder Laubwerk und die Simpße, an den orten wo sehr schickt, sollen schön
verguldet, der Kasten aber &c. schön angestrichen werden.*

*Die Pfeiffen vom <u>Principal</u> in der <u>Fronte</u> werden also nicht verguldet, sondern recht weiß
und schön <u>polist</u>.*

*Ein jedes der lauten Register wird mit einem doppelten Züge gemacht, zu welchem unten
ein Tritt ist, der von der Seite geschoben wird, so, daß man weder beym anziehen noch
ablaßen deßelben einiges Gekrische oder <u>alteration</u> im Spielen vermerken.*

*Das gantze Werk soll mit Wind recht wohl versehen werden, und die <u>Ventile</u> &c.
so wohl verwahrt seyn, daß man vor dem so genannten Heulen der Orgel gesichert ist.
Jedoch muß der <u>Touch</u> leicht und <u>regulair</u> seyn.*

*Die <u>Temperatur</u> soll so weit als immer möglich, so eingerichtet werden, daß man aus
allen Tonen spielen könne.*

Kürz, es soll alles mit allem fleiß, dauerhaft und schön gemacht werden.

*Vor dieses Werk nun, welches Joh. Schnetzler in 4 Monathen zu lieffern ver-
spricht, werden Ihm von gedachter Gemeine Hundert und vierzig Pfund Sterling, bezahlt,
die eine Halfte davon, wenn fr[ ]fes Werk gantz fertig an Ort und Stelle geliefert und
aufgesetzt hat, und es <u>probirt</u> und dem <u>Contract</u> gemäß befunden werden, die andere Halfte
in einem 4teljahr darauf.*

*Es sind aber allen Ankosten der fracht von <u>London</u> und so weiter, bis zum Platz wo
die Orgel hinkommen soll in diese 140 £ eingeschloßen.*

Daß mir hierüber eins worden, bezeugen hiermit durch eignhändige Unterschrift

Charles Metcalfe	Vorsteher
John Snetzler	Organ Maker
Wm Bell	Gevollmächtigter besagter Geneiur

So geschehen <u>London</u> den 15ten <u>Februarii</u> 1747/8
Paul John Brockmer als Gezeuge

Herr Johann Schnetzler, organ builder in London, promises to the community in Fulneck, near Pudsey in Yorkshire, to make an organ with the following stops etc.

1. <u>Stopped Diapason</u>, of wood, from <u>Contra</u> G to highest C, i.e. 59 pipes.
2. <u>Open Diapason,</u> of wood – just the same.
3. <u>Viola di Gamba</u>, of <u>metal</u>, the last <u>octave</u> in the bass corresponds to <u>open diapason</u>.
4. <u>Salicional</u> of <u>metal</u>, from middle C up to highest E.
5. <u>Principal</u> – of <u>metal</u> – 58 pipes.
6. <u>Octave</u> – of <u>metal</u> – 58 ditto.
7. <u>Cornet</u> – of <u>metal</u> 3 or 4 <u>Ranks</u>.
8. <u>Sesquialtera</u> of <u>metal</u>. N.B. one <u>Octave</u> deeper than the one in <u>Fetter Lane</u>.
9. <u>Trumpet</u> right through, [will] thus also [have] 58 pipes.

In this organ a <u>Swell</u> will be made with the following 4 Stops.

1. <u>Open Diapason</u>, of wood, from middle C up to highest E.
2. <u>Open Diapason</u> of <u>metal</u> – just the same.
3. <u>Principal</u> 8 feet; of <u>metal</u>, also the same.
4. <u>Cornet</u> 3 <u>or</u> 4 <u>Ranks</u> of <u>metal</u>, id.

The two manuals on the organ and the Swell will be well inlaid with beautiful black wood, and the semitones with ivory, and made of such length as the one in Fetter Lane.

Wood and metal of the best quality shall be used for the pipes, and each shall respond clearly.

The front of this work will be made with five towers, and provided with attractive ornaments and carvings.

The carvings or foliage, and the cornices, in the places where very appropriate, shall be beautifully gilded, but the case etc. shall be beautifully painted.

The pipes of the <u>Principal</u> in the front shall also not be gilded, but quite white and beautifully polished.

Each of the loud stops will be made with a double pull [slider], to which there is a pedal underneath, which is pushed from the side [notched?] so that either on pulling or release any squeaking or alteration in the playing may be observed.

The whole work shall be properly provided with wind, and the pallets etc. protected that as to make sure that there is no so–called 'howling' of the organ. However, the touch is to be easy and regular.

The temperament shall so far as ever possible be installed in such a way that all tones can be played.

In short, everything shall be done with all diligence, durability and beauty.

For this work which Johann Snetzler promises to deliver in 4 months, the said community shall pay him One hundred and forty pounds sterling, half thereof when the work is delivered and installed on the site ready for use, and it has been found to be proved and in accordance with the Contract, and the other half one quarter of a year later.

However, all expenses of carriage from London, and so on, to the place where the organ is to be installed, shall be included in this £140.

I hereby testify with my signature by my own hand that I agree to this.

Charles Metcalfe, director
John Snetzler, organ maker
Wm Bell, aforesaid fully authorised engineer

Given at London, the 15th day of February 1747/8
Paul John Brockmer, as witness.

Letter 6   *John Snetzler, London, to Mr Slicht, 18 February 1748*

London den 18 Febr. 1747/8

Geehrtester Herr,

Dero letsteres habe erhalten und obschon der Differens, in veränderung der Registern, arbeit halber nicht so gering, als sie gedenken habe jedoch um nicht mehr Zeit zu verlieren keine Difficultet machen wollen, und den aufgesetzten Contract den sie an Herrn Benzien geschikt underschriben und wurde auch zugleich den anfang in der arbeit machen, um daß Werk sobald als möglich zu verfertigen.

Weil sie um daß Solicional aus der Schwell wollen in der Orgel haben, welches ich freilich lieber in der Schwell hatte weil es zum schwellen eine properen und anmütigen Thon hat so muß Principal in der schwell 4 fuß thon sein, weil op. Diap von Metal und Principal 8 fuß thon daß gleiche ist den op. Diapason ist nichts anders als ein 8 füßiges Principal wurde es also nicht so wohl sein 3 op. Diap. in der schwell zu haben.

Es thut mir eines Theils leider daß sie diese Veränderung in den Registern gemacht, nicht so wohl, weil es mir mehrere arbeit gibt als aber der Orgell halbes.

Ich hatte mir vorgenommen die großen Pfeiffen in op. Diap hieden an die Orgel zu setzen und sie gantz hinniden biß auf den boden kommen zu laßen, so daß sie dan alle ihre gantze länge behalten [marginal note: und nicht nötig sie zu knäpfen] bey eine Trumpet aber müßen sie gantz anderst kommen und dan muß der Trumpete halber der Orgel viel schärfferen Wind geben, als zur lieblichkeit der Subtilen Registern erfordern wirdt, und [   ] es ist freilich die Trumpete in schönes Register wo sie stärke halber erfordert wirdt ich glaube aber die Orgel wirdt ohne Trumpet voll stark genug werden, und bey den übrigen Registern zu lieblicheren veränderungen dienen bey seits der Mühe der Stimmung halber übrigens stehet es in dero belieben, und wan sie solten etwas zu anderen haben ist es noch Zeit genug, ich versichere sie indeß daß mein besten Thun werde also anzugehen daß wan deß Werk gethan es den Meisterloben möge verharren undeß
meines Hochgeehrtesten Herrn
    Dero bereitwilligsten Dieners
    Johannes Schnetzler

P.S. Bite so gut zu sein und mir den Skiß mit gelegenheit zu übersenden daß daß Maas zu dem Kasten darnach nehmen Kan. Werde nicht ermanglen ihnen wüßen zu laßen bevor die Orgel wirdt gethan sein.

Die Hohe, Weite, und Tieffe deß Platzes weiß ich sehr wohl.

London, 18 February 1747/8

Most honoured Sir,

I have received your latest letter, and although the difference, in the altering of the stops, is not so small as regards the amount of work as you have supposed, nevertheless so as not to lose more time we shall make no difficulty about it, and are signing the contract that has been drawn up and which you sent to Herr Benzien, and would also like to make a beginning with the work, so as to get the job completed as soon as possible.

As you want the Salicional out of the Swell in the organ (which I would rather have in the Swell, because it has a proper and agreeable tone with the Swell), the Principal in the Swell must be 4 feet tone, because Open Diapason is of metal and Principal 8 feet tone, the same. The Open Diapason is nothing other than an 8-foot Principal, so that it would not be so well to have 3 Open Diapasons in the Swell.

I am rather more sorry that you have made this alteration in the stops, not so much because it gives me more work, than for the sake of the organ.

I had intended putting the big pipes in Open Diapason lower in the organ, and to make them come right down to the floor, so that they would then retain all their full length, and it would not be necessary to bend them. However, with a Trumpet they must come quite differently, and then for the sake of the Trumpet the organ must have much sharper wind than is required for a pleasant effect in the subtle stops. [ ] however, the Trumpet is a beautiful stop in which it is required for the sake of strength. However, I think the organ will be quite strong enough without the Trumpet, and will serve for pleasanter alterations with the other stops, beside the trouble on account of tuning. After all, it must be as you wish, and there is still time enough if anything has to be altered. I assure you that my best efforts will be devoted to it, so that when the job is done it may deserve the praise of a master.

My most honoured Sir,
Your ever willing servant,
Johannes Schnetzler

P.S. Please be so good as to send me the sketch when you have an opportunity, so that the measurements for the case can be taken from it. I shall not be lacking in having your wishes carried out before the organ is completed.

I know the height, width and depth of the available space very well.

Letter 7 Revised contract: Schlicht to Johann Schnetzler, 21 February 1748

Pudsey 21 Februar 1747/8

Verehrtester Herr Schnetzler,

Wir sind's gleich zufrieden, daß die Trumpete wegbleibt, sie ist nur [hi]nein kommen, weil

*viele davon waren.   Alsdenn aber ist die <u>disposition</u> diese folgende, <u>und bey der sol's</u>
<u>bleiben</u>:*

1. <u>*Open Diapason of wood*</u>, *da Sie denn die Pfeiffen so setzen können.*
2. <u>*Stopt Diapason, of wood*</u>, *wie Sie gemeldet.*
3. <u>*Open Diapason of metal*</u>, *halb durch.*
4. <u>*Salicional, metal*</u>, *gantz durch, so weit's gehen will.*
5. <u>*Viola Di Gamba, metal*</u>, *halb durdh.*
6. <u>*A pretty Flute*</u>, *ganz durch.*
7. <u>*Principal, metal*</u>.
8. <u>*Cornet,*</u>   *4 Ranks }* *eine octave tieffer als gewöhnlich.*
   <u>*Sesquialtera, 3 Ranks}*</u>
9. <u>*Twelfth*</u>.
10. <u>*Fifteenth*</u>.

Zu dem <u>Swell</u> Kommen:

1. <u>*Open Diapason OF METAL*</u>.
2. <u>*Salicional of metal*</u>.
3. <u>*Hautboix*</u>, *recht niedlich.*

*Die <u>Cornet</u> und <u>Swell</u> werden wir selten brauchen. Sie ist also leicht wegzulaßen, und ich
denke diese 3 Reisterzen [?] werden recht <u>charmant</u> klingen zusammen, oder 2 und 2, weil
ich auch der Gedanken bin, daß holzerne Pfeiffen im <u>Swell</u> nicht viel taugen, so wollen wir
das <u>Open Diapason</u> von Metal machen, wie gemeldet.*

*Und das wäre eine <u>admirable disposition</u> von einer [kleinen] Orgel, und gerade so wie
ich sie gern hätte, ich glaube auch Sie selbst werden nichts daran auszusetzen finden.*

*Sie können also in Gengenwart Herr Benziens nur halten am <u>Contract</u> eine [N.B.]
machen daß die <u>Register</u> so wie ich sie jetzt gemeldet choosiert [?] wewrden, oder es kan
dieser Brieff da vergelten, das übrige bleibt, wie im Contract schon gemeldet.*

*Ich denke Sie sind ziemlich überzeugt daß Sie sich von nichts böses zu
versehen haben. Wir handeln ehrlich und ohne falsch, versprechen uns auch
von Ihnen ein gleiches, besonders ich der eh' von herzen bin*

> *[Herrn] Schnetzlers,*
>   *aufrichtiger Freund und Diener*
>   *C. F. L. Schlicht.*

*P. S. Ich hätte den Riß schon zurückgeschickt, wenn ich gewust hätte daß sie ihn brauchten,
weil ich aber geglaubt Sie hätten einen andern und er ein wenig zu dick ist <u>per posta</u>
herumgeschickt zu werden: so habe es bisher unterlaßen, indeßen komt es hierbey auf Ihr
Begehren. Ich hoffe daß die Orgel–Fronte den Riß weit übertreffen wird. Ich werde mich
freuen Sie zu sehen, wenn Sie die Orgel aufzusetzen zu uns kommen. Ich denke doch daß
die Simpse der 2 aufrechten großen Thuren gantz an den Balken oder <u>Sealing</u> kommen
werden.*

To Mr Schnetzler, at London.

Pudsey, 21 February 1747/8

Most honoured Herr Schnetzler,

We are equally satisfied that the <u>Trumpet</u> is left out, it has only come in because there were a lot of them. The arrangement is then the following, <u>and is to remain accordingly</u>:

1. <u>Open Diapason of wood</u>, as you can then set the pipes so.
2. <u>Stopped Diapason, of wood</u>, as you stated.
3. <u>Open Diapason of metal</u>, half through.
4. <u>Salicional, metal</u>, right through as far as it will go.
5. <u>Viola Di Gamba, metal</u>, half through.
6. <u>A pretty Flute</u>, right through.
7. <u>Principal, metal</u>.
8. Cornet,   4 Ranks } an octave lower than usual.
   <u>Sesquialtera, 3 Ranks</u>}
9. <u>Twelfth</u>.
10. <u>Fifteenth</u>.

To the <u>Swell</u> there come:

1. <u>Open Diapason OF METAL</u>.
2. <u>Salicional of metal</u>.
3. <u>Hautboix</u>, really pretty.

We shall seldom need the <u>Cornet</u> and [*sic*] <u>Swell</u>. It is therefore easy to leave them out, and I think these 3 registers will sound really charming together, or 2 and 2, because I am also of the opinion that wooden pipesare not much use in the <u>Swell</u>, so we want to make the <u>Open Diapason</u> of metal, as stated.

And that would be an <u>admirable disposition</u> of a [small] organ, and just asI should like to have it. I also believe that you yourself will find nothing in it to find fault with.

You can thus at present only hold Herr Benziens to the Contract to make a [N. B.] that the Registers are chosen [?] as I have now stated them, or this letter can repay it. The rest remains as already stated in the Contract.

I think you are fairly convinced that you have no harm to expect of us. We deal honourably and without falsehood, and promise ourselves the like from you, especially I who am from my heart

        [Herr] Schnetzler,
           Your sincere friend and servant
           C. F. L. Schlicht.

P. S. I would already have sent back the sketch if I had known that you need it, but because I thought you had another, and it is a little too thick to be sent around by post, I have hitherto refrained. In the meantime, it comes herewith at your request. I hope that the organ front will far surpass the sketch. I shall be glad to see you when you come to us to set up the organ. I think however that the mouldings of the 2 big upright towers will come right up to the balcony or the ceiling.

To Mr Schnetzler, at London.

Letter 8   John Snetzler, London, to Mr Schlicht, 9 April 1748

London, den 9ten Aprill 1748

Hochgeehrtester und Wehrtester Herr,

Bite nicht übell zu nehmen, daß mit gegenwartigem sie molestiere*. Sie haben mir in einem von ihrem schriben vermeldet daß sie gute Schreiner in* loco *haben, ich finde bey vielfaltiger überlegung, daß es viel beßer wäre wan der Orgellkasten kunte alda gemacht werden, weil sonsten, wan ich ihn hier machen solte, müßte solcher in* aparte *pakkisten auff gepakt werden, welche ohngewöhnlich groß sein müßten mich also in sehr große umkösten, so wohl der pakkasten als aber der* fracht *halber bringen wurde, ersuche sie deß machen wo sie es gut befinden, von der güte zu sein mir vor eine gelegenheit darvor umzusehen, es will diser Platz davon sie mir gemelt überauß wohl thun oder aber einiges wegen nähes bey Hand, ich wurde alles zur Orgell belangende hier in* London *(*)* verfertigen, außert die Orgelkasten und den Blasbalg welcher ein großes gewicht außmacht, und ihne so wohl alda als aber hier machen kann.*

Ich gedenke meine arbeit hier fertig zu haben, in dem ende deß Monats Mey da dan bey meiner ankunft in Yorkshire *gleich kan* Ordre *geben vor den Orgelkasten und so lang diser in arbeit ist kan ich dan bloß Balg in der Zeit verfertigen welches nicht viel über 14 Tage Zeit auffnehmen kan übrigens gehe ich mit der arbeit mit* plaisir *an, weil mir vorher verstrechen kan, daß es ein wohlklingendes und angenehmes Werk werden würdt.*

Ich habe noch eine frage an sie zu thun, weilen gerne ein Completes *Werk haben wolte, daß ist, in die Schwelle sollen nur dise 3 Register kommen als* Op. Diapason, [Violon *crossed out]* Solicional *und* Hautbois *welcher 3 gleich Klingende Stimmen sein und also vor eine Schwelle nicht den gewünschte* effect *haben wurden so gedenke viel beßer zu sein, anstatt der* Hautbois *zwey andere Register hierin zu machen als ein* Principal *und eine* Cornetin *welches ein überauß angenehmes Register. Ich habe dise Wochen die Ehre, Herrn* Benzien *und H.* Brokmer *bey mir zu haben, und hate just eine Orgel bey mir worin dises Register welches ihnen beyde überauß wohl gefallen. H.* Brokmer *gedekt auch daß es sicherlich beßer were, beseits der mühe die sie des stimmens halber haben werden, weil zu der Schwel nicht so gemächlich zu kommen hoffe also durch ein beliebigen Antwort von ihnen zu vernehmen der ich mit verharrung* etc.

Verbleibe Hochgeehrtester Herr dero
Ergebenster Diener
Johannes Schnetzler

(*) *Marginal note: 'in Leeds'.*

London, 9 April 1748.

Most honoured and most esteemed Sir,

Please do not take it amiss that I trouble you with this present letter. You instructed me in one that you wrote to me, that you have good cabinet-makers on the spot. I find on thinking it over many times, that it would be much better if the organ case could be made there, because otherwise, if I made it here, it would have to be packed in separate crates, which would have to be unusually large and would thus involve me in very great expense both for the crates and for carriage charges. I request you to do this where you think good, and to be so kind as to look out for an opportunity for me. This space of which you have instructed me will be well used, or else one near at hand for the sake of nearness. I should like to do everything relating to the organ here in London (*), apart from the organ case and the bellows which amount to a heavy weight and can be made on the spot as well as they can here.

I expect to have my work finished here at the end of the month of May. Then, on my arrival in Yorkshire, orders can be given for the organ case, and as long as work is in progress on this I can get the bellows ready at the same time, which cannot take much more than 14 days. Moreover, I am setting about the work with pleasure, because I can look forward to it being a well–sounding and agreeable job.

I have one more question to put to you, because I want to have a complete job done, and that is that in the Swell there are only to be these 3 stops: <u>Open Diapason</u>, <u>Salicional</u> and <u>Hautboy</u>, which are 3 equally sounding voices and so do not have the desired effect for a Swell. I therefore think it is better to make two other stops instead of the <u>Hautboy</u>, such as a <u>Principal</u> and a <u>Cornetin</u>, which is an extremely pleasant stop. I have this week the honour of having Herr Benzien and Herr Brokmer on my premises, and had just such an organ there, in which there was this stop, which pleased both of them very much. Herr Brokmer also thinks that it would certainly be better, besides the trouble there will be about tuning because it will not come to the Swell so conveniently. I thus hope to receive a favourable answer from you, and with perseverance etc. I remain, most honoured Sir,

> Your most devoted servant,
> Johannes Snetzler

(*) Marginal note: 'in Leeds'.

Letter 9   John Snetzler, London, to Mr Schlicht, 8 November 1748

<u>London</u>, den 8ten 9bris 1748

Hochgeehrtester Herr,

Sie werden mir vergeben daß gegenwertige nicht ehender überschiken können ich könte solches nicht ehender von dem Bildhauer gethan bekommen, habe zugleich eine Zeichnung vor die seitenflügel übersenden wollen, welche ohne Zweiffell eine große Zierath vor die Orgel sein wurden, sie werden ohngefehr wan sie vergüldet zu 5 oder 6 <u>Ginees</u> zu stehen kommen sie können also nach dero belieben <u>Ordre</u> geben ich hoffe die Orgell ist in gut <u>Ordr</u> und gibt <u>Satisfaction</u>, wovon mir lieb sein wirdt zu hören und wan etwaß zu meinem Vortheil könte gehoret werden, so bitte meinen nicht zu vergeßen womit nebst Gottes empfehlung verbleibe

> *Hochgeehrteste Herr*
> *Dero Willigster Diener*
> *Johannes Schnetzler*

P.S. Nebst freundlicher begrüßung an alle freund. Es wundert mich auch wie das <u>Clavicimbal</u> außgefallen.

London, 8 November 1748

Most honoured Sir,

You will forgive me that I have not been able to forward the present enclosure sooner. I could not get it done by the sculptor sooner, and wanted to forward at the same time a drawing of the side wings, which without doubt will be a great adornment for the organ. They will come to about 5 or 6 guineas when they have been gilded. You can therefore give orders as you wish. I hope the organ is in good order and gives satisfaction, and shall be glad to hear about this. If anything can be heard of to my advantage, I beg you not to forget me, whereupon with God's commendation I remain

> Most honoured Sir,
> Your most willing servant,
> Johannes Snetzler

P.S. With friendly greetings to all friends. I also wonder how the Clavicimbal has turned out.

Letter 10   John Snetzler, London, to Mr Schlicht, 13 December 1748

London, den 13 December 1748

Hochehrender Herr,

Dero schreiben habe erhalten, und thut mir leid daß überschikte Ornament nicht geliebet werden. Hate mir flatiert daß solche in disem Platz überauß wohl sich zeigen wurden ich glaube gar nicht daß ein Ornament welches den gantzen Platz außfüllen wurde, wohl stehen solte und for ein rundes habe ich niemahls gesehen es wird [ ] ehrentheil ein Wappen in solchen Platz gemacht, und gedachte daß solches so wohl als einiges Wappen sich zeigen wurde es ist mir sehr lieb daß die Orgell so wohl thut es solten freilich anstatt der Höltzernen Pfeiffen Metalerne die Orgel stecken machen, weil sie aber in ein großes gewicht lauffen, so sind sie auch kostlich und kunten under 30 £ nicht wohl gemacht werden und weil sie keine Kröpfung leiden, solte etewelche die just under der Schwell zu stehen kommen, welche Difficultet machen, es könte zwar die zwey Octaven im discant von Holtz bleiben wan ohngefehr ein oder andrer gelegenheit verfallen solten daß nötig were nach Yorkshire zu kommen, könte solches leichtlich gemacht werden.

Wegen deß Harbsicord klang, kan nichts melden ohne solches zu sehen wan es aber zu schwer spielen thut kan leichtlich in der palance geholffen werden.

Der brieff den ich vor etwaß Zeit von H. Mitcalve empfangen habe, hat mich nicht wenig unruhig gemacht in sonderheit wan ich in dem Contract nach der Zahl der Pfeiffen gesehen, und solche auff einem Clavir nachgezelt, welches ich zuvor nicht gethan, weil nur der Compass von doppel GG zu e in alt schon genug war, und G X niemahl gedacht wirdt hoffe aber sie werden bey aller meiner arbeit daß gegentheils überzeugten sein, so daß hoffentlich nicht nötig sein wirdt den brieff zu beantworten ich verharre

> *Hochehrender Herr, dero*
> *Willigster Diener,*
> *Johannes Schnetzler*

London, 13 December 1748

Most honoured Sir,

I have received your letter, and am sorry that the ornament I sent you is not liked. I had flattered myself that in this place it would show exceedingly well. I do not believe at all that an ornament that filled out the whole space would look well, and as for a round one, I have never seen one. A coat of arms is put in such a space [as] a mark of honour, and I thought that this would show as well as your own arms.

I am very glad that the organ is doing so well. Admittedly, instead of the wooden pipes, metal ones might be put into the organ, but because they come to a great weight, they are also expensive and could not well be made for under £30, and as they will not permit any bending they would have to be put just under the Swell, which causes difficulties. The two Octaves in the Descant might indeed remain of wood. If some opportunity or other should occur, making it necessary to come to Yorkshire, this could easily be done.

As to the sound of the Harpsichord, I cannot advise on anything without seeing it. However, if it is too hard in the playing, it can easily be helped in the balance.

The letter that I received from Mr Mitcalve some time ago has disquieted me considerably, particularly when I reckoned by the number of the pipes in the contract, and counted them on a keyboard, which I had not done previously, because only the compass of Double GG to high e was already enough, and G X [♯] is never thought of. However, I hope that in respect of all my work you will be convinced of the contrary, so that I hope it will not be necessary to answer the letter.

I remain, most honourable Sir, your most willing servant,
Johannes Schnetzler

*

Appendix 4 Letters relating to the organ for Trinity church, New York

Three complete letters and a stop–list relating to the organ for this church are given in full in *Organ Building in New York City: 1700–1900* by John Ogasapian (The Organ Literature Foundation, 1977), pp. 6–10.

The first two letters are preserved as (probably abbreviated) drafts of correspondence from Goldsbrow Banyar, a vestryman of Trinity Church, to Richard Grubb, Snetzler's agent. That dated 17 August 1761 includes:

> Mr. Snetzlaar the builder may be desirous to raise the Pitch of the Organ as high as possible, which will be a trifling advantage to him, but we have low voices and the Pitch should on that account be the lower. He is the most eminent Builder, and being full of Business require[s] as long as they were in procuring the New Organ at Boston. [Presumably the organ for the Deblois' Concert Hall, chapter Three, no. 55, dated 1762 and installed in 1764.] Accelerating the payments may hasten the work. It will not be long before we may have Peace which is the only objection we should have against its being ship'd immediately if made in the time it could possibly be made in. If there are any new Improvements in the Organs, we shall be glad they were extended to this, if not too complicated or expensive and the proposal of a 16 foot Diapason in Front must be left to those who are better judges ... I will close on this general observation, that the less Noisy the composition, the more musical and consequently the more agreeable. It follows that the fewer noisy stops there are the better & some are necessary to strengthen the Tone of the Instrument. The diapasons are among the musical...

A second letter, dated 7 October 1761, was included with the first:

> Since the inclosed I have seen a letter of the 7 August last from Mr. Snetzlaar to our Organist who desired to know what addition it would make to the cost if the Front open Diapason in the Great Organ was of 16 Feet and a Cremona or a Bassoon which Mr. Snetzlaar says is the best stop, 30 pounds, makes for a whole 680 pounds exclusive of Packing Cases. And if the open Diapason be of 16 Foot which he much approves of, he says the whole cost with frontispiece agreeable to his 1st plan sent to our organist will be 800 pounds sterling exclusive of packing cases. I have not had time to consult Messrs. Harrison, Walton and Bache on this Head: If we can raise the cash they will have no objection. In the mean time Mr. Snetzlaar may proceed so far on the first plan of 600 pounds sterling as not to interfere with the proposed addition should it be agreed to. It appears to me that the Great Organ in the 800 pound plan will be louder than necessary. If the Furniture and one of the principals in the great organ and

301

the Sesquialtra and the open Diapason in the choir organ might be omitted without seriously injuring this Plan it would reduce the price to about 650 pounds or at most 700 pounds I should be glad to know whether there is any material objection to leaving out these 4 stops, what Price will then be, and whether he can make no abatement of the 800 pounds in case it should be determined to adhere to his largest Plan which is subjoined.

The copy of the contract is included with a letter from Richard Grubb, evidently written in late February 1762:

To George Harrison, Jacob Walton, Theophil. Bache, Esqs. New York

Gentlemen:
... Mr. Stanley who has been remarkably obliging & ready in giving his advice respecting the Organ in your Church, went with me and some Gentlemen who are good judges to try the one lately finished by Mr. Snetzler for St. George's Church, Hanover Square, which had previously undergone the inspection of three master Builders in regard to the workmanship & of three Masters of Musick in respect to the excellence of performance, before a crowded audience of the Nobility, when Mr. Stanley & those present entirely approved of the same as an exceedingly good organ – add to this that the same Builder has lately [*sic*] finished one of a larger size for the Town of Kings Lyn which has been highly approved & I have the opinion of Sign. Giardini, Mr. Butler, Mr. Keeble & other eminent Masters that no one builder at this time gives a finer Tone than Mr. Snetzler, he having also so much practiced of late in Church as well as small Organs & is allowed to be greatly improved and to excell in his way – wherefor in order to do justice to your recommendation, as I am divested of partiality or attachment. & that I find he now stands as high in reputation as any of the Business. I have on mature deliberation & the best advice receeded from my intention of employing Mr. Byfield & Contracted with Mr. Snetzler to build your Organ for Six Hundred & fifty Pounds, as you will perceive by a Copy of the Contract on the other side, which I hope you will approve; the Plan being of Mr. Stanley's forming, who will be ready to do everything in his power towards the perfection of the Instrument. You may depend no time has been lost in consulting about this Business & determining who to employ, as both these eminent Builders have their hands full of work this Winter to finish what was engaged, but now your organ goes on with great application, & in order that you may have a new & Elegant Frontispiece, Mr. Snetzler is gone to Oxford, to engage his brother (who is Carver to the University) to form a new design and Undertake that Branch of the Work.
    Mr. Snetzler will do his best to finish the Organ by October whereof I shall keep you advised & as to payments he hopes & I have promised to accomodate him with some part while the work is carrying on.

Richard Grubb completes his letter with a reference to the current 'price of Gold & Silver' as 'Gold a £3. 19' and silver as 5 shillings, 6¾ pence, 'lower than has been for some time past but may be expected to rise unless some large prises [*sic*] are taken from the Spaniards'.

His copy of Snetzler's contract is as follows:

Proposals for an Organ to be built by Mr. John Snetzler of Oxford Road on account of Mr. Richard Grubb of London –

In the Great Organ	Pipes
1. An open Diapason of mettal in front & gilt	57
2. An open Diapason of mettal in the inside	57
3. a Stop'd Diapason of Wood & mettal	57
4. a Principal of mettal	57
5. a Twelfth of mettal	57
6. a Fifteenth of mettal	57
7. a Tierce of mettal	57
8. a Sesquialtra of 4 ranks of mettal	228
9. a Cornett of 5 ranks of mettal which is down to C	145
10. a Furniture of 3 ranks of mettal	171
11. a Trumpett of mettal	57
12. a Clarion of mettal	57

1057 Pipes

=========

In the Choir Organ	
1. A Stop'd Diapason of Wood & mettal	57
2. an open Diapason of mettal	57
3. a Principal of mettal	57
4. a Flute of wood & mettal	57
5. a Fifteenth of mettal	57
6. a Cremona of mettal	57
7. a Vox Humana of mettal	57

---

399 Pipes

========

Eccho & Swell Down to G below the middle of the keys	
1. An open Diapason of mettal	34
2. a Stop'd Diapason of mettal	34
3. a Principal of mettal	34
4. a Cornett of 3 ranks of mettal	102
5. a Trumpett of mettal	34
6. a Hautboy of mettal	34

---

272 Pipes

========

The said work will be putt into a neat wainscot case with proper carving to consist of three setts of keys with soundboards, Bellows Rolerboards, [*sic*] the front pipes to be gilt with the best gold, the compass to be from Double Gamut long Eights up to e in alt, will be finished & pack'd up in packing cases and delivered free of all expenses at the keys [i.e., docks] for the sum of Six Hundred and fifty Pounds & to be finished as soon as possible. The Frontispiece to be heighly carved ornamented & finished according to the draught – London the 19th February 1762
signed by John Snetzler

The work to be subjected to the most critical & nice inspection when compleated to the Tryal & approbation of proper Judges – signed by John Snetzler

The organ was delivered to New York and set up in 1764.

*

This letter is an intriguing glimpse into the world of cathedral (and larger parish church) music. Though ostensibly about singers, it includes some surprising statements about and implications for the management of choral and organ music at the time, and about the duties of the organist – especially in playing his 'voluntaries' and accompanying the choir and soloists. It is transcribed, without abridgement, from the original text as published in the *Gentleman's Magazine*, vol. 35, pp. 213–4. The authorship of the letter was kindly confirmed by Simon Heighes.

Rules to be obferved by Cathedral Singers.

RULES *neceffary to be observed by all Cathedral Singers in this Kingdom.*

IN the first place every finger should take particular care to obferve a proper plainefs in singing; for, as too much finery adds no ornament to a beautiful personage, but has a quite contrary effect, fo too much gracing of a mufical compofition, often ends in a total *difgracing*. There feems to be the *cantandi fimplicitas* in the latter, as well as the *fimplicitas munditiæ* in the former*.[1]

With regard to a long grace at the end of any part of an anthem, I think it fhould be very cautioufly avoided, becaufe it breaks in too much upon the ferioufnefs and dignity of church mufick. But if a finger fhould be determined to favour a congregation with a *gratiofo*+,[2] I would advife the organift to play a little short voluntary as foon as the grace is quite finished, in order to qualify the finger to go on with a *quantum fufficit* of breath for the remaining part of the anthem, becaufe there are fo many twiftings and twinings,

---

[1]* There are feveral parts of cathedral mufick which can never be fung and accompanied with too much fimplicity and plainefs. To inftance in one particular, *i.e.* the *Vouchfafe O Lord*, in *Purcell's Te Deum*. If finger and accompanier would do juftice to this ftrain, I would advife them to ufe nothing but the *appogiatura*, and even that with great caution and referve. But inftead of this I have often had the misfortune of hearing the greateft part of it fmother'd (for what elfe can I call it?) with fuch a farrago of fuperfluities, that between finger and player they have almoft made a very tolerable country dance of it.

It very often happens that there is more difficulty in the application than in the formation of a grace. The inventive faculty of a finger may be awake when his judgement is quite faft afleep. This is often the cafe with many inftrumental performers, who, inftead of doing juftice to a *Handel*, a *Corelli*, and a *Geminiani*, are often playing a great number of furprifing tricks, to the no fmall injuftice of the authors.

[2] + *i.e.* Any part of an anthem, where the finger is not relieved by an additional fymphony of the compofer: In this cafe the organift may omit the voluntary, becaufe the fymphony will make up the deficiency, and anfwer the same purpofe. As for the conclufion, the finger is relieved of courfe by the chorus.

fo many inftantaneous ups and downs in a thing of this fort, that the *arteria afpera* is often put into a fort of convulfive motion, and more particularly fo when this faid grace requires a confiderable degree of vocal velocity *fed hoc obiter notandum eft.*

The power of the organift in a full chorus feems to be of a defpotick nature. He is the *primum mobile:* Every finger muft conftantly hearken to the organ. In the nature of things it cannot be otherwife++.[3] You'll fay, perhaps, that the organift may be deficient fometimes with refpect to time: – it is granted; – and fo may the greateft performer: a *Handel* may vary with refpect to time, and be a *Handel* ftill! But fuppofe the organift is not always regular, yet it is the bufinefs of the whole choir to attend to him.[4] In other parts of cathedral mufick, (fuch as a folo and duett) the organift may humour the finger, and the finger the organift, in cafe both of them are well converfant in compliance and good nature. But when I talk of compliance between player and finger it is certainly more practicable in a folo than any other part of church-mufick.

With regard to the leading of a *point* in a chorus,[5] every member fhould exert his voice as much as the nature of his conftitution will admit of. – The too frequent ufe of the fwell is attended with bad confequences, unlefs the voice is extremely good; and where the voice is good (unlefs the finger is well converfant in the *ne plus ultra* of his windpipe) it very often degenerates into a fudden instantaneous bawl or fquall.

The practice of finging the octave above inftead of the octave below, (and fo *vice versa*) has a very unnatural effect. Singers often take too much liberty in this refect, little confidering that although it may be the fame with regard to the laws of compofition, yet there feems to be an obvious difference in nature.

Let me now give a fhort friendly hint or two to the organift.

If the organift would think proper to play one of *Mr Handle's* [sic] fugues, fometimes (not but I propofe this with all due fubmiffion) instead of a conftant voluntary of his own, it is more than probable that fuch an innovation may bring no fingular difgrace upon the character and reputation of an organift. Befides which it may border very near upon compaffion and good nature to give an *innuendo* of this fort, in order to afford fome friendly relief to the inventive faculty of the organift; becaufe it may be very prejudicial and hurtful

---

[3] ++Although the power of the organift, in a full chorus, favours very ftrongly of defpotism, yet in other parts of church-musick it partakes of the nature of a mixed limited monarchy; *i.e.* in harmony he feems monarchical, but not in melody.

[4] It ought to be confidered that the organift has always the moft difficult tafk to engage in. The finger has only his refpective part to attend to, whereas the organift is obliged to obferve the whole of the harmony, for which reafon any little deviation in point of time may happen, even to the moft fkilful performer. But there is another very good reafon to be affigned why the organift is particularly to be attended to in a full chorus, because in cafe of any miftake, it is eafy for a fingle part to come into the whole, but the whole cannot come into a part: Thofe who underftand mufick will eafily perceive what I mean.

[5] *Mr Beard* is the beft finger of a chorus I ever heard. He attends to the organ, and is an excellent directory at any time to the whole of a mufical performance. He is greatly to be admired (in like manner) in a recitative both of the common, and that of the accompanied one. He takes off that tedium or wearinefs which fuch kind of compofition is apt to caufe upon the generality of an audience. But whether in fome few inftances he does not pay greater attention to the common fpeech (I am now fpeaking as to oratorios) than to tuneful pronunciation, is a thing which I fhall not take upon me to determine. By the common recitative I mean mere fpeech, by the accompanied one, tuneful pronunciation.

to the conftitution to have the invention always upon the full ftretch. But if the organift should perfevere in extempore playing, (for the organ is an instrument finely calculated for it) it would be kind of the organift to keep to his fugue; and not only this, but to chufe one of a moderate length; because in this cafe the audience may more probably remember the fugue, and confequently more eafily digeft the voluntary*.[6] But there is one thing relative to the organift which I fhould have mentioned before, which is this, If the organift fhould tranfpose an anthem out of the original key of a compofer (I mean at sight) in order to eafe the voice of a finger, it would be prudent of the finger to thank him, the firft opportunity, for fuch a compliance; becaufe the organift, ftrictly fpeaking, is obliged to tranfpofe out of the original key.

In the winter feafon the organift fhould never prefume to play upon the organ in gloves, unlefs there is a great neceffity for it.

But let me not be thought too prefumptuous if I should give a little advice to the chantor.

If the chantor of every cathedral would read a fhort lecture upon the nature of harmonicks, or make a brief defcant on feveral paffages in church–mufick, fuch a method as this might be of great ufe to church mufick, and at the fame time add confiderable weight and fignificancy to the office of chantor.

The chantor fhould have a correct fcore of all the mufick that is performed in the church; and if a miftake should happen in a fingle part, fuch miftake fhould be conftantly corrected from his fcore.

If the chantor defires a rehearfal of any mufick, all the members muft comply, and more particularly fo if the chantor fhould defire it in a polite, genteel, and friendly manner.

But, after all, I believe it will be readily granted that the beft manner of finging, either with graces or without them, will be of little or no confequence unlefs all the members are in peace and harmony one with another: With unison of found, therefore, it will be always neceffary to join union of brotherly love and affection.

 I am, Sir, &c.   W—M H—S,
a Member of the Cathedral Church of
     Worcefter.

*

---

[6] * It muft be allowed that for compofitions, how well foever executed upon an organ, will always have the appearance of stiffnefs (at least to a difcerning and judicious ear) when compared with thofe that come voluntary from the mind. Extempore playing is certainly the thing, in cafe an organift will take some pains to excel.

Appendix 6   *The Warrant for Snetzler's Denization, 12 April 1770*

[P. R. O., S. P. 44/380 X/K.3885]

George R.
Our Will and Pleasure is that you prepare a Bill for Our Royal Signature to pafs Our Great Seal of Great Britain for the making of Joseph Planta of Great Rufsell Street Bloomsbury, Gent. Abraham Kirkman of Great Poulteney Street in the Parish of St. James within the liberty of Westminster in the County of Middlesex, Harpsichord Maker, Jacob Kirkman the Younger of Broad Street in the Parish of St. James Westminster aforesaid Harpsichord Maker, John Snetzler of Oxford Road in the Parish of St. Mary Le Bone in the County of Middlesex Organ Builder, Michael Schlapfer of Wood Street Spitalfields Weaver, John Steinmetz of the Parish of St. Ann Limehouse in the County of Middlesex Baker, & Nicholas Adams of Bow in the County of Middlesex Victualler, Aliens born, free Denizens of this Our Kingdom of Great Britain, & that they have & enjoy all Rights Privileges & Immunities as other Free Denizens do, And you are to insert therein all such clauses as are usual & necefsary in cases of the Nature And for so doing this shall be your Warrant,
Given at Our Court at St. James's the 12th day of April 1770 in the Tenth year of Our Reign.

To Our Attorney or   } By His Majesty's Command
Solicitor General   }   Rochford

*

Appendix 7 *William Ludlam's letter to the* Gentleman's Magazine, *1772*

As with William Hayes's letter in Appendix 5, a careful reader of William Ludlam's letter (December 1772, vol. 24, pp. 562–5) will find much that betrays the aesthetic ambitions, and more of the actual attainment, of the time.

A fhort account of the feveral forts of Organs *ufed for* Church Service*[7]

ALTHOUGH the organ is an inftrument that varies greatly both in its form and fize, yet thofe defined for church–fervice may be very well reduced to three sorts, according as they have one, two, or three rows of keys.

Thofe with one row of keys are fufficient where the fervice of the church confifts in plain *pfalm–finging* only. In that cafe the pfalm–tune is given out on fome of the fofter ftops, but the congregation is accompanied in finging the pfalm by the full organ throughout. Here, then, no variety is required.

In *fervices* and *anthems*, one or two perfons frequently fing alone, and then the whole choir together; the verfe fingers and the chorus anfwering alternately. In thefe fudden tranfitions from foft to loud, two rows of keys are abfolutely neceffary; one belonging to what is called the leffer organ, the other to the great organ; that fo the player may infantly fhift his hand from the foft to the loud organ. Was there only one row of keys, viz. that belonging to the great organ, it would take up too much time to change the organ by altering all the ftops. Two rows of keys are ftill more neceffary in *oratorios*, where the whole band of inftrumental mufic, together with the loud organ, frequently ftrike in for a few notes only; the organ at other times being foft enough to accompany a fingle voice.

In cathedrals, where all the variety of church mufic is admitted, and where the organ is confidered as a perfect inftrument of itfelf, it is ufually furnifhed with three rows of keys, one of which belongs to the great organ, another to the leffer organ, and the third to the fwell. The pipes belonging to this laft row of keys are made to fwell; increafing in their ftrength gradually from the fofteft breathings to the thunder of the great organ. Befides thefe three rows of keys, fuch large organs are frequently furnifhed with pedals. Thefe are keys to be played on by the feet. There are feldom more than 12 of thefe pedals, which always belong to the deepeft notes in the organ, and when managed with judgement, have a moft folemn and awful effect.

The names of the ftops in the great organ are, Stopped Diapafon, Open Diapafon, Flute (or elfe Nafon), Principal, Twelfth, Fifteenth, Sefquialtera, Cornet, Trumpet. Of thefe the two Diapasons are by far the moft important, being indeed the foundation of all the reft, and are the only ftops (except the trumpet, which is an imitation) that are concert pitch;

---

[7]* A fubfcription for an organ having been fet on foot, in each of the parifhes of St. Martin's, and St. Margaret's in Leicester, this account was originally drawn up at the requeft of the fubfcribers there, but it may be ufeful to others alfo.

all the other ftops being above concert pitch, and their pipes fmall+.[8]

The pipes of the open Diapason are of metal, the larger ones are fet in the front, and gilt. In cathedral organs, which have two fronts, there are two open Diapafons. When the great pipes are fet within, (as some of them muft be, when the front will not hold them all) the organ–makers have a trick of fubftituting two little pipes inftead of one great one. The ufual excufe for this is want of room, efpecially in height: however, this plea cannot be made with any modefty, when the organ ftands in so large a church as St. Margaret's. The ftopped diapafon is of wood, ftopped at the end, whence its name. Modern organ–builders make the upper part of metal, which is louder. Not fo, the celbrated *Father Smith* ++.[9] A caveat fhould be entered againft making any part of this ftop of metal.

What has been faid of the ftopped diapafon may be applied to the flute, which differs from the ftopped diapafon in pitch only, being an octave above it. The nason differs from the flute, only in having the ftopper at the end perforated, which makes it a little louder. Principal is 8 notes; twelfth and fifteenth are 12 and 15 notes above the open diapason, from whence they have their names.

In the fefquialtera, three pipes fpeak at once to each note. Thefe pipes are very fmall, yet together make a moft furprizing noife. Modern builders are fond of the ftop, and make 4 or 5 pipes to every note; knowing full well that they can by this means make a very great noife for a very little money, and that nothing pleafes childifh customers like a great noife, be it ever fo coarfe.

The cornet has likewife many fmall pipes to each note. Thefe are fometimes fet on a board, raifed up to a great height in the cafe, that their found may be the more diftinguisfhed: it is then called a mounted cornet. This ftop goes half way through the keys and no more, it belonging to the treble only.

The trumpet is an imitation of that inftrument, and is ufed as fuch in conjunction with the diapafons. The bafs, in trumpet voluntaries, is played foft on the ftopped diapafon, though fometimes the trumpet breaks out fuddenly in the bafs **.[10] The trumpet, when mixed with the other ftops, gives great fpirit to the full organ.

The price of an organ with one row of keys, in a deal cafe, is fet by one maker at 220 pounds, exclufive of carriage and gilding; by another, at 140 pounds, including the gilding, and (as is fuppofed) the carriage. When it is confidered, that the gilding alone may coft 15l.

---

[8] + The mufic for the diapafons should be flow, folemn, with binding notes
In linked fweetnefs long drawn out,
of which there are fome admirable fpecimens in Stanley's voluntaries, worth the organift's notice, if he has not too little tafte, or too much conceit, to attend to them.

[9]++ So called by way of diftinction from his nephews Gerard and Bernard. [*sic*] He built the organ in the Temple church in London, St. Mary's in Cambridge, &c.

[10]** A remarkable inftance of this is in Stanley's voluntaries, opera fefta. Volun. V. line 6th of the trumpet part; where the trumpet and echo anfwer to each other. In that place, the trumpet bafs on the great organ fhould undoubtedly be ufed, though not particularly directed; and when you come to the holding note on A. the left hand fhould come down to the lower row of keys belonging to the leffer organ, having the ftopped diapafon only drawn. There are many inftances in thefe voluntaries, where the good tafte of the player muft fupply the want of more particular directions for the management of the ftops.

the difference between the two will be little or nothing.[11] Indeed, between makers of credit, there can be no difference worth regarding. They who flatter their cuftomers with felling them an uncommon bargain, have always a fecret way of making themfelves ample amends.

Organs made with two rows of keys, being of the middle fort, differ more from each other than either of the other two forts. An organ between the plaineft parifh organ, and one fit for a cathedral, muft have fomewhat more than the former, yet cannot have all that is in the latter. Such a one fhould have fome of the fofter ftops, in the lower row of keys, and fome of the ftops in the swell of a cathedral organ. Thus it might ferve to accompany a folo finger, as well as the congregation, and might have an agreeable variety when ufed by itfelf for *introits* and *voluntaries*. The following plan was sent a few years ago to the officers of St. Martin's, by a very eminent builder:

The ftops in the great organ, the fame as before mentioned.

The ftops for the upper row of keys, and which are to fupply the office both of the leffer organ, and the fwell in cathedral organs, as follow: Stopped Diapafon, Flute; both thefe to go through the whole compafs of the keys, and their upper part (as far as to F below the tenor C) [*sic*; he corrects this instantly] likewise to the fwell: befides thefe, Open Diapafon, Cornet, and Trumpet in the fwell only, which (as was said) [*sic*] goes down to F below the middle C. The price of the whole, including gilding and fetting up, to be 325 pounds.

It was debated, whether a Principal (throughout) fhould not be added; the additional price for this was to be 15 pounds. The builder faid, it would undoubtedly be an improvement; but, that many organs were without it.

One other plan may be propofed, which is to lay the foundation of the organ of the largeft size, and furnifh it with the mufical part by degrees, as fubfriptions come in. On this plan, the cafe muft be made large enough to contain the pipes for three rows of keys: Provision muft be made at firft for receiving all the machinery to be afterwards added, but no more of this work need be put in, than what belongs to one row of keys only. Such an organ may coft at firft 300 pounds or more, and each ftop of pipes afterwards put in, may be reckoned at 12 pounds, one with another; befides the machinery, which cannot be added piece–meal. The whole machinery for each row of keys muft go in at once. The expediency of chufing such a plan, (confeffedly imperfect at first) must depend on the hopes we may entertain of feeing it compleated hereafter.

Here fome one, perhaps, may have the curiosity to afk what ftops are to be found in organs of the largeft size? Befides thofe before mentioned as compofing the great organ, we often find Teirce [*sic*], Larigot *[12], Clarion, Furniture, and Cymbal.

Teirce is 17, and Larigot 19 notes above the Diapafons; Clarion is a trumpet an octave above concert pitch; Furniture and Cymbal are like the Sefquialtera, with this odious circumftance, that their pipes return over again the fame in each octave; fo that one cannot fay of thefe ftops, that they have either treble or bafs. Such ftops as thefe do indeed greatly increase the noife, but can never improve the harmony of the inftrument. In truth they are not to be found in any of Father Smith's organs. That celebrated builder made sometimes in the great organ what has been called a Block Flute. The pipes of this ftop are the pitch of a fifteenth, but larger bodied. Their tone is clear, fweet, and piercing; refembling that of the fteel bars ufed for the *Carillon* in the oratorio of Saul. One of thefe Block Flutes is

---

[11] The gilding of the front of St. Mary's organ in Cambridge, coft 20 guineas in the year 1765.

[12] * A French name for a flagelet.

in the organ at Trinity College, Cambridge. This ftop feems to be the fame with the *Doublette* of the French.

The leffer organ (of one of thefe very great inftruments) has ufually in it, Stopped Diapafon, Flute, Principal. Fifteenth, Vox Humana, and perhaps fome others. The fwell has the two Diapafons, Principal, Cornet, Trumpet, Crom-horn.[13] We find likewife Baffoon, Hautbois, French-horn, and Dulciana**[14], among the ftops now in vogue. A very abfurd imitation of the kettle-drum is fometimes made by two geat pipes, out of tune to each other; whofe harsh gratings bears fome refemblance to the beating of a very bad drum. The foreigners have likewife what they call *Le Tremblant*. It makes the whole organ figh and fob moft dolefully, and is therefore ufed at funerals. There is one of thefe *Tremblant's* in the organ at the (greater) German chapel in the Savoy; an inftrument that well deferves the notice of the curious for better reafons than this+.[15]

They who defire more particular information may confult the Harmonics of *Mersennus*, (in French 1635, or in Latin 1648) and the *Facteur D'Orgues* of *D. Bedos* among the *Desfcription des Arts et Metiers* lately published at Paris++.[16] -- But to return,

With regard to thofe points which concern organs of every fize, it may be obferved that the organ-builders had formerly a cuftom of leaving out two or three of the deepeft notes in the organ, making what they call *fhort octaves*. Thus they faved themfelves the expence of many large pipes, but robbed the organ of thofe notes which are its greatest glory. They, likewife, made their organs a note or two above concert pitch, by which means all the pipes were reduced in fize. But a man of credit will not do so. If an organ was to be erected in *St. Margaret's* church, its pitch fhould by all means be made to agree with that of the bells; fo that if the organ fhould begin before the fermon bell is ceafed, they need not be at variance. So noble a bell would add to the harmony of the organ*.[17] This would require

---

[13] That is, *crooked horn*.

[14] ** From the Spanifh. What this inftrument was, we learn from *Quixote, Lib.* vi., *Cap.* 26. – *entre Moros – fe ufa – un genero de Dulçaynas que parecen uneftras Çhirimias.*

[15] +When a note or two is held on in the bafs, and full chords are ftruck *ftaccato* in the treble, [*sic*; treble and bass are apparently reversed] the beft organs (even Father Smith's) are apt to fob in this manner, and from the fame cause. No inftrument can be more free from this and every other inequality in the force of the wind, than this organ in the Savoy. It has pedals to the laft 12 notes and their femitones.

Moft foreign organs have two of thefe *Tremblant's; Le Tremblant-fort*, and *Le Tremblant-doux*. It is the latter of these and the *Voix-Humane* together, that imitates in fo remarkable a manner the common ballad-fingers with their ditties, to the great admiration of our travelling gentry.

[16] ++ We are apt to be aftonifhed at what is told of the immenfe fize of the foreign organs, which have always four rows of keys, befides pedals; but when we are informed that thefe keys go no lower than cc, and that the ranks of the larger pipes are not completed to the bottom, the wonder ceafes. In fact, thefe great organs are filled with nothing but a repetition of the fmaller and lefs harmonious ftops, and fome others that are meer whims. Neither have any of thefe foreign organs a fwell. See the defcription of that in the abbey of *Wiengarthen*, by *D. Bedos*. This organ has in it 6666 pipes. The whole number of ftops is 66, among which are the fiddle, the drum, the cuckow, the nightingale, and the roaring of the fea. – *Rifum teneatis?*

[17] * In this church is the nobleft peal of ten bells in England, without exception; whether *tone* or *tune* be confidered.

no expence. The organ-maker has only to take the pitch of the bell, and accommodate his note D to it. 'Tis true he cannot do this and put off a fecond hand organ (of another pitch) for a new one.

Nothing with precision can be faid about the *Cafe*, unlefs the materials, dimenfions, manner of framing, number and nature of ornaments, were fpecified. The tafte of the common organ-builders in this refect is moft wretched, or rather they have no tafte at all. They ufually retain fome mean joiner in their pay, who makes all their cafes in one form; and they never regard what, if it be but of a proper fize for their work. Their credit is from the mufical part within; outside beauty their utterly defpife. A gentleman in this neighbourhood, of diftinguifhed tafte, not chufing to be directed by thefe ignoramus's, had an organ cafe made exactly after the pattern of that in the univerfity church at Cambridge. That, and the other great organ in the chapel of Trinity college there, are, perhaps, the moft elegant patterns in the kingdom; the one of a fingle, the other of a double cafe: yet it muft be acknowledged that a maker cannot go out of his ufual way of working without great lofs. A plain cafe, found workmanfhip without ornaments, at leaft without fuch as are abfurd or ridiculous, is all that can be procured without extraordinary expences.[18]

Leicefter, Dec. 1.   W. L.

*

William Ludlam (1717–1788) was the son of a Leicester doctor; he became a fellow of his college (St John's, Cambridge) in 1744. He was vicar of Norton-by-Galby, Leicestershire, from 1749 (where there was a small organ by Smith) but was also junior dean of his college (1754–7) and Linacre lecturer in physic (1767–9). He was one of the three assessors appointed to report to the 'board of longitude' on John Harrison's chronometer, 1765. He became the (absentee) rector of Cockfield (Suffolk) in 1768, but then 'retired' to Leicester to pursue his interests in practical mechanics and astronomy, and to write his 'Rudiments of Mathematics' (1785) which was for the next generation the standard text-book in Cambridge. The 'short account' given above was but a small part of his published papers and letters to general, scientific and theological journals.

It is not clear which 'gentleman in this neighbourhood' had a case copied from that in the university church (Great St Mary's) in Cambridge. It has been generally thought that the organ set up by Crang and Hancock in St Margaret's church, Leicester, in 1773 was partly made by Smith (see TO 150/63–5), but there is no real evidence for this: Ludlam's comments about pitch above in fact appear to rule out a 'second hand' organ there. The case is now in the Wesleyan chapel in Bishop Street, next to Leicester Town Hall, and indeed it resembles Smith's 'four tower' design. The 'gentleman' may, of course, be Ludlam himself.

---

[18] The old organ at Lynn had on it a figure of King David playing on the harp cut in folid wood, larger than the life: likewife feveral moving figures which beat time, &c. This is an old practice, and alluded to by Dr. Donne:

> *As, in fome organs, puppets dance above,*
> *And bellows pant below, which them do move.*

Some modern organ-builders (perhaps in complaifance to an abfurd canon) fet up the Royal Arms; and we fee the British Lion, with gogle eyes and fhaggy mane, grinning enough to fright all the congregation.

[PROB/11/1135 f.526]

In the Name of God Amen

I, John Snetzler, late of Oxford Street in the Parish of Saint Marylebone in the County of Middlesex an organ builder but at present residing in Bentinck Street in the Parish of Saint James Westminster in the said county of Middlesex being of sound and disposing mind, memory and understanding so make and swear this my last Will and Testament in manner following that is to say

First I will and direct that all such just Debts as I shall owe at the time of my decease and my Funeral Expences be fully paid and discharged

I give and bequeath to my Nephew John Henry Schnetzler Son of my late Brother Isaac One Hundred Pounds reduced three per Cent Bank Annuities over above the share which he will be intitled to of and in the residue of my Estate and Effects under or by virtue of this my Will

I give and bequeath to my Nephew and Godson Benedict Fischer Son of my late sister Barbara One hundred pounds reduced three per cent Bank Annuities over and above the share which he will be intitled to of and in the residue of my Estate and Effects under or by virtue of this my Will

I give unto David Peyerimhoff of Amen Corner London Merchant and James Jones of Stephen street in the parish of Saint Pancras in the said County of Middlesex Organ Builder my Executors hereinafternamed the Sum of Ten pounds each as a small acknowledgement for their trouble in the execution of this my Will

And as to all the rest residue and remainder of my Estate Goods Chattels and Effects whatsoever and wheresoever which I shall die pofsefsed of or be any ways intitled to at the time of my decease I give and bequeath the same unto the said John Henry Schnetzler and Benedict Fischer In trust that the said John Henry Schnetzler and Benedict Fischer or the Survivor of them or the Executors or Administrators of such Survivors shall and do as soon after my decease as conveniently may be divide and distribute the said rest residue and remainder of my estate and effects unto and among my Kindred or Relations according to the Laws and Customs of the Canton of Schaffhausen in Switzerland

And I do hereby will and declare that the Receipt or Receipts of the said John Henry Schnetzler and Benedict Fischer or the Survivor of them or the Executor or Administrators of such Survivor shall be ample and sufficient Discharge and Discharges to my Executors for the same

And I do hereby nominate and appoint the said David Peyerimhoff and James Jones Executors of this my last Will and Testament and hereby revoking and annulling all former and other Will and Wills by me at any time heretofore made I publish and declare this to be my last Will and Testament In Witnefs whereof I have herewith set my hand and seal this Eighteenth day of October in the Year of our Lord One thousand seven hundred and eighty four.

[John Snetzler]

Signed Sealed published and declared by the said
Testator as and for his last Will and Testament in
the presence of us who at his request in his presence
and in the presence of each other have subscribed
our names as Witnefses hereto
        [H. Grojan Attorney Vine Street Piccadilly
        Henry Jeanneret Clerk to Mr Grojan]

This Will was proved at London the twentieth day of October in the year of our Lord one
thousand seven hundred and eighty five before the worshipful George Harris Doctor of
Laws Surrogate of the Right Workshipful Peter Calvert Doctor of Laws Master Keeper or
Commissary of the Prerogative Court of Canterbury lawfully constituted by the oaths of
David Peyerimhoff and James Jones the Executors named in the said Will to whom
Administration was granted of all and singular the Goods Chattels and Credits of the
deceased having been first Sworn duly to Administrators.

*

Appendix 9   John Marsh's Preface, 1791

Having been frequently applied to by young Practitioners on the Organ, to lend the following Pieces in MS. and also to recommend Voluntaries of the same Kind, requiring but a moderate degree of Execution, most of those already published being too difficult for young Performers readily to execute; and those Pieces denominated Easy Voluntaries, being generally too light and trivial a Nature for the Church Service; and having observed that for want of such easy Voluntaries in a proper Style for the Church, Scraps of Harpsichord Lessons, Minuets, marches, &c. are frequently substituted as such. With a view therefore of accommodating young Performers in this respect, I have been induced to publish the following Pieces, and shall at the same time take the opportunity of explaining to the inexperienced Organist, the nature of the Stops of the Organ, with the several Mixtures and Combinations that may be made thereof, to which I shall add a few thoughts on the proper Style of touching the different Stops, for want of understanding which, the Organ is frequently exhibited to a disadvantage it does not deserve, and the effect of good Music is marred, though in other respects properly executed.

A complete Organ has usually Three Sets of Keys, of which, the middle One is for the *Great Organ*, the lowest for the *Choir Organ*, and the uppermost (which seldom extends lowers than F or G below middle C) for the *Swell*.

The principal Stops in the Great Organ, are the *Diapasons*; the *Principal* having been originally so called, as I should apprehend, not by Organ *Players*, but Organ *Builders*, who finding it convenient to make their standard for tuning the other Stops by, (it being a mean between the Diapasons and 15th, Sesquialtera, &c.) might give it that Name. The Diapasons may therefore be considered as the Two Unisons and foundation of the whole Mixture, and must always be drawn, no other Stops being to be used without being joined with them, though they may themselves be used alone.

The OPEN DIAPASON (1) so called from the Pipes being open at the Tops, is the loudest of the Two, but the Bass Pipes being generally slow in speaking, it is usual, as well to assist it in that Respect, as to strengthen it, to join

The STOPT DIAPASON (2) with it, the Pipes of which are generally stopt with wooden Plugs at the Tops, on which Account they are softer toned, and but half the length of those of the Open Diapason.

The PRINCIPAL (3) is tuned an Octave above the Diapasons, and is occasionally joined to them, as well to strengthen, as to render them more brilliant.

The TWELFTH (4) so called from being tuned 12 Notes above the Diapasons (or a 5th to the Principal) must never be drawn without the Three foregoing Stops, and also

The FIFTEENTH (5) with it, which being higher than the Twelfth, the Effect of the Succession of Fifths, (between the Principal and Twelfth, which would be intolerable without the Fifteenth above, is thereby qualified, the Octaves being greatly predominant, whilst at the same Time the Twelfth enriches the Mixture, so that neither of these Two Stops should be drawn without the other.

These Five Stops form a proper Mixture to accompany the Choral parts of the services in Cathedrals in common, and to accompany a small Congregation in the psalms in Parish Churches. — The next Stop to be described is

The SESQUIALTERA (6) which is a Compound Stop, consisting of Three, Four, or Five Pipes, (according to the Size and Scheme of the Organ) to each Note, tuned in 3ds, 5ths, and 8ths, so that every Note is a common Chord; to prevent any mischievous Effect from which, this Stop must never be used without the Five preceding Stops, or at least the Diapasons and Principal, to qualify it. This Mixture is sufficient whenever the *Full Organ* is directed to be used, and to accompany the Choral parts of Services and Anthems in Cathedrals on Sundays, or a common Congregation in the Psalms in a Parish Church. Where however the Church or Congregation is pretty large, the Chorus may be made one Degree louder by drawing

The MIXTURE or FURNITURE (7) which also consists of Two or more ranks of Pipes, but shriller than those of the Sesquialtera, so that it should only be used in addition to that Stop. The next degree of augmentation is made by using

The TRUMPET (8) *instead* of the Furniture. This Stop when it does not render the Organ too powerful for the Voices, always *improves* as well as increases the Chorus, as by being in unison with the Diapasons, it strengthens the foundation, and thereby qualifies the 3ds and 5ths in the Sesquialtera, &c. by rendering them less prominent. — This Mixture should however only be used to accompany Voices in Cathedrals, in the Chorusses of *Verse* Services or Anthems (which should be very full in order to make the greater Contrast to the Verse) and in Gloria Patrias, Hallelujahs, &c. where the drowning of the words is of no great consequence; and in parish Churches, only for a single Verse or two by way of contrast; or where the Congregation and Church are very large; or where some Score of Charity children add their voices to the Chorus, when the deep and powerful bass of the Trumpet serves to qualify the shrillness of the Children's Voices; —the whole therefore forming as grand and as powerful a Chorus as can be made without the help of other Instruments: This may however be further augmented and also improved, (where the magnitude of the Church and Congregation permits) by the addition of the Furntiure also; to which the only increase that can be made, is by adding

The CLARION (9) or Octave Trumpet, which also where the Church and Congregation are very large, *improves* the Chorus by rendering it more brilliant. This Stop however must never be used but in addition to all the foregoing, the force of which altogether, will be too great to accompany Voices even in Gloria Patrias, &c. except on particular festivals or times when the Church is much crowded, or the Voices exceedingly numerous, for which purpose it should be reserved.

So that there may be five different kinds of the full Organ used, viz. The Sesquialtera (with the five preceding Stops). —2d. The Furniture added to the Sesquialtera. —3d. The Trumpet added instead of the Furniture. —4th. The Trumpet and Furniture both added. —And 5th. The Clarion added to the whole.

I have been the more particular in mentioning the gradations, becasue in Scores and Organ parts of Church Music, it being usual to put only in general terms, the Words *Full Organ*, too much is left to the discretion of the Organist, many of whom (especially young people) are apt to be too ambitious of being distinguished above the Voices, thereby making the Organ a Principal instead of an Accompaniment.

There are two other Stops in many Organs, which can only be properly used in the Full Organ, viz. the TIERCE (10) or sharp Third to the Fifteenth, and LARIGOT (11) or Octave Twelfth. These stops I look upon to be put in by Organ Builders, merely to make a shew of Stops to draw, at a small Expense, as they only incumber an organ, and consume wind to little or no purpose. —The only Stop remaining in the Great Organ (in modern Organs) is

The CORNET (12) which is also a compound Stop, having Five Pipes to a Note, tuned something like the Sesquialtera, but as it is only a half, or treble Stop, it ought never to be used in the Full Organ, but only with the Diapasons, in Voluntaries, giving out Psalm Tunes, Symphonies of Anthems, &c.

Before I conclude as to the Great Organ, it may be proper to mention, that when the Trumpet is used as imitative of the real Trumpet, it is then only joined with the Diapasons.

*

The Choir Organ (vulgarly called the Chair Organ), usually consists of the following Stops, viz.

The STOPT DIAPASON, (1) which for want of an Open Diapason to draw with it (the Bass pipes of which are too large and powerful for a Choir Organ) may be joined with

The DULCIANA, (2) which though the Pipes are also open, and in unison with it, is yet much smaller and softer than the Open Diapason; it is however seldom carried down lower than Gamut. This stop (as it's name implies) has a peculiar sweetness of tone, and may be used quite alone.

The PRINCIPAL, (3) with the two preceding Stops, makes the proper Accompaniment in full Services, where the Sides sing alternately, and not together (when the Full Organ should be used) or during the Chanting on week days, to which may also be added (especially if there be no Dulciana)

The FLUTE, (4) of which the Pipes are stopt, and in unison with the Principal, but softer. This is also frequently used alone, (as an imitation of the common Flute or Flageolet) but is more properly joined with the [Stopt] Diapason, which Two stops (with the Dulciana at pleasure) are the proper accompaniment in Solo or Verse parts of Anthems, the Principal being too loud for that purpose, except where the Voices are unsteady, and require to be led.

The TWELFTH (5) and FIFTEENTH (6) may be added to the foregoing Stops to accompany the Chants on a Sunday, and in full Services (except when the two sides sing *together*) when the Congregation is large, or the Singers numerous; amd also in Parish Churches in some of the middle Verses of a plain Psalm tune by way of relief; to which, and for the same Purposes, may occasionally be added

The BASSOON, (7) which is in unison with the Diapason and Dulciana, with which only it must be joined, when used as a fancy Stop in Voluntaries.

Some Organs have a VOX HUMANE, or CREMONA, (or Cromhorn, as it is sometimes called) instead of a Bassoon, which Stops should only be used with the Diapason, (with which they are also in unison) and not in the full Choir Organ, as the Bassoon may; the Bass of the other two being very rough and disagreeable.

*

The only Part of the Organ remaining to be described, is the *Swell*, the usual Stops in which are

The two DIAPASONS, (1, 2) which when used alone produce much the same effect as the Dulciana in the Church organ; they are therefore generally joined at least with

The PRINCIPAL. (3) The most beautiful Stops however in the Swell are

The HAUTBOY, (4) and TRUMPET (5) which being in unison together, may be used either singly or both together, but always with the Diapasons. To the whole of which may be added

The CORNET, (6) which altogether makes what is called the *Full Swell*.

The Swell is frequently used in accompanying Voices instead of the Treble of the Choir Organ, for which it may be sometimes more convenient, as the Sound may be increased or diminished so as to accommodate such Voices as may require such assistance; but it's principal use is in Voluntaries, giving out Psalm Tunes, &c.

Having now described the several Stops of the Organ, it may not be amiss to observe, that the Trumpet, Clarion, Bassoon, Hautboy, Vox Humane, and Cremona, are called Reed Stops, on account of the Wind passing into them through a small Brass Tube (called the Reed) to which is fixed a thin piece of Brass called the Tongue, by the vibrations of which their peculiarity of tone is occasioned. These Stops are the most liable of any to get out of tune, (particularly the Clarion, Vox Humane, and Cremona) of which the Performer should be aware, when he fixes upon his Voluntary, especially in the Country, where the Organs are in general very much neglected.

I shall now subjoin a few directions to the inexperienced Organ Player, as to Voluntary playing and accompanying the Psalms. —In the first place he should totally divest himself of the idea of setting down merely to entertain, or exhibit his Skill to an audience, as at a Concert; instead of which it would be much more to his credit to make *Style* the object of his ambition, rather that Execution, considering at the same time the solemnity of the service, of which Voluntary playing forms, if not an essential, yet an ornamental part. Voluntaries during the time of service, should therefore be grave, but yet with a sufficient degree of Air and Expression in them to excite *Attention* in the audience, which is most likely to be effected by *Contrast*, varying the Stop, and a proper attention to the different Style of touching each. And though in most printed Voluntaries particular directions are given as to the managements of the Stops, yet the judgment of the performers may be sufficiently exercised, or put to the test, in the proper selection of them, of which so great a variety is published; chusing Diapason pieces, or Adagios on the Swell, for Sacrament Sundays, and those of a more brilliant nature than ordinary for Festivals; shortening such as exceed five or such minutes in length, and rejecting all such as are of a thin, light, or trivial nature, particularly many of the Cornet and Flute Pieces in Major Keys, which are fitter for the Harpsichord than the Organ. —But besides the several Voluntaries published as such, many of the Airs and Chorusses from Handel's sacred Oratorios, may, with a little alteration and contrivance, be adapted for that purpose, and to particular seasons. For instance, the Pastoral Symphony in the Messiah (on the Diapasons and Swell) *"He shall feed his flock,"* shortened by leaving out some of the repetitions (the Symphonies on the Diapasons, and Voice part on the Swell) and any of the Chorusses in the first part for the full Organ, will make very suitable Voluntaries at Christmas. Also *"He was despised"* (on the Diapasons and Swell) —*"But thou didst not leave"* (on the Cornet, and Swell, or Choir Organ) —*"I know that my Redeemer liveth"* —*"The Trumpet shall sound,"* with a little alteration (as a Trumpet Voluntary) with the grand Hallelujah, and any of the Chorusses in the 2d or 3d parts, will be very proper for the season of Easter. In like manner, select parts of Handel's Funeral Anthem on the death of Queen Caroline, may be played on solemn occasions, and the Coronation Anthem *"God save the King,"* on the King's birth–day, the accession, or Coronation day. —These kind of Voluntaries, if played with expression, have this advantage, that the particular idea conveyed by the words to which they have usually been sung, are very likely to be excited by the Music alone.

There are also many other requisites to a good performer, which cannot be exactly and explicitly communicated in musical characters, and in which he must be left to his own judgement; for instance, as to what concerns *Accent*, and *Expression*, and what is commonly known or conceived by a good *Touch*; towards which however the following hints may be of use.

First it should be considered that no Music can be expressive that is not *accented*, marked, or enforced at proper intervals, as at the beginning, and sometimes (in common time) in the middle of a Bar. This may be in a great measure effected on the *Swell* of the Organ, by the management of the Pedal, especially in slow Movements, (which are most proper for the Swell) but on the other parts of the Organ, must be done by other means, such as Appoggiaturas, and by occasionally doubling the Bass note at the accented parts, by taking the Octave. For this purpose it is proper in passages where one bass note is repeated in Crotchets or Quavers, for several Bars together, not to strike the Octave below to every note, but only at the beginning of the Bar, and hold it out to the end. Also where a Bass note, and it's Octave, are repeated alternately in Quavers, it is better, on the Organ, to hold the lower Note, and strike the upper one successively in Quavers. —Before I quit the subject of octaves, I must just caution the young performer against the too common practice of taking Octaves in different notes, in succession with the left hand in *quick* passages, as however they may succeed on the Harpsichord or Piano–Forte, they cannot but have a bad effect on the Organ by making the Bass too staccato. —Also it may be observed that where the Clarion is drawn (that being in itself a powerful Octave) the effect of Octaves in the Bass (in quick passages where they cannot conveniently be taken on the Keys) may be produced by playing an octave lower than the Music is written, (if the compass of the Organ will admit of it) the Notes in the lowest Octave having a very grand effect where there is a Clarion, which also renders the lower Bass notes very distinct. To execute however quick passages on this requires a very strong finger.

*

Next to Voluntary playing, a few hints on the manner of giving out, and accompanying the Psalms (which in fact is more material to be attended to) may not be useless to the young Organist.

All Tunes of a lively and joyful nature, may be given out on the Cornet, and those of a plaintive kind on the Diapasons or Swell; and though the modern practice seems to be, to give out the whole on one Stop, yet I must own, I think the old custom of playing alternate lines of plain Psalm Tunes on different Stops (using the Swell for the 2d and 4th lines) has it's use, especially in tunes that are not universally known, as it more easily enables the unlearned to adapt the Tune to the Metre. For the same reason they should be given out quite plain, or with no other graces or embellishments than a good Singer would naturally apply; except at a Close, when a short, neat Cadence on the Swell, may not be improper.

Having already treated of the accompaniment of the Voices, in describing the Stops of the Organ, and different mixtures of them, nothing farther remains to be observed on this subject, as I shall speak of Interludes between the verses in the next Section, under the head of *Extempore* playing, to which they more properly belong.

*

The Organ being, of all Instruments the best calculated (on account of the variety it contains) for Extempore play (the effect of which by skilful Masters is far superior to that of Music precomposed for it) on which subject, as I do not recollect to have ever heard of any practical Treatise, I shall, before I conclude, subjoin a few hints thereon, and on *Style* in general; in order to attain which, it will be first necessary to understand the proper method of touching the different Stops (as the style of playing varies considerably on each); secondly the proper selection of them for Voluntaries, and lastly something of the art of Modulation, without a little knowledge of which, a very small progress can be made in Extempore performance. As to Fancy and Invention I shall say nothing on that head, they being gifts of nature, and not acquired, but of which some small share at least is also necessary.

For the DIAPASONS, the style should be grave, and of the *Sostenuto* kind, gliding from note to note, or chord to chord, with almost always a holding note, either in the Treble, Tenor, or Bass of the Organ. —If the PRINCIPAL be added, the style may be more brilliant, the fingering more *staccato*, and quicker passages may be executed with better effect than on the Diapasons alone. The Bass also being rendered more distinct by the Principal, it is usual (as well as to avoid the shrillness of the upper notes) to keep both hands lower down, than when the Principal is not drawn.

For the TRUMPET, the style should also be grave, and majestic, playing chiefly in the key of C, or D, and keeping nearly to the natural compass of the *real* Trumpet, on which rapid and chromatic passages not being to be executed, they must of course be *improperly* used in an *imitation* of it. Double notes in the manner of two Trumpets may occasionally be used, and a long holding note on the 5th or Key note, with a 2d part moving, has a good effect. The Bass should chiefly by played on the Diapason, Dulciana, Principal, and Flute of the Choir organ, except now and then by way of Contrast, particularly toward a grand Close, when the Trumpet Bass (qualified by the Principal) or Full Organ may be introduced with great effect.

For the CORNET, quick music, in brilliant style, without double notes or Chords, is proper. This Stop, though frequently used in Voluntaries before the first Lesson, is yet, I think, of too light and airy a nature for the Church: I should therefore recommend it's being used but sparingly in Voluntaries, and only in the Minor key, except of Festivals and joyful occasions, for which it may properly be reserved. —The Bass to it may be played on the same set of Keys, provided the left hand is kept below middle C.

The FLUTE may be played in much the same style as the Cornet, except that the Bass may be played on the same Stop, which being an octave one, there may be more execution with the left hand than usual on the Organ. This also being of too light and trifling a nature to be much used in Churches, I think entire Flute pieces should be avoided, and the Flute only used as an echo, or by way of relief to the more noble parts of the Organ.

The DULCIANA may be touched something like the Diapasons, except that it being seldom or never carried throughout the Bass, the left hand should be kept higher up. A tender soothing style, without the least degree of execution (which this stop is too delicately voiced to bear) is proper for it.

The STOPT DIAPASON and PRINCIPAL are together capable of as much Execution as the Flute alone, the same style of play will therefore serve for them. I should indeed almost at all times recommend this mixture instead of the Flute, it being by no means so trivial in effect.

For the CREMONA, or VOX HUMANE (if it be worth using, which is not always the case) the *Cantabile* stile is of course proper, confining the right hand to about two octaves, or more, from about the C below middle C upward, and playing the Bass on the Diapasons. Double notes, in the manner of two voices singing, may have a good effect. —The BASSOON may also be played in much the same stile, except that the Bass being infinitely better than that of the other two, it may be used down to Gamut or lower.

The manner of playing the SWELL requires more judgement than any other part of the Organ, as by a judicious management of the Pedal, the human voice may be much better imitated than by the Vox Humane; the cantabile style is therefore also proper for it, though it is capable of a considerable degree of execution, particularly when the Cornet is drawn. —Double notes and Chords judiciously swelled and diminished have a good effect. —The Bass may generally be played on the Stopt Diapason and Flute of the Choir Organ (with or without the Principal, according to the number of Stops drawn of the Swell) or where the compass of the Swell extends below middle C, both hands may occasionally be employed thereon. —The Swell is frequently used as an echo to the Trumpet, Cornet, &c. —The finest Mixture in which is, that of the Diapasons and Hautboy, with the Trumpet to strengthen it, if required. The Principal should not be drawn, without both the Reed Stops, as the octave will otherwise be too predominant, and destroy the effect of the *Sostenuto* passages. —The CORNET in the Swell shou'd, I think, never be used as such, it being necessarily so very inferior to the great Cornet (which consists of more ranks ofpipes, and has the great Diapasons to qualify it) but only used with the other Stops to make a full Swell, as an echo to the full Organ. it is however frequently used as an echo to the great Cornet, and strictly so, in repeating the two or three last notes of it, it may be proper, but in repeating whole passages after the great Cornet it has but a mean effect.

In making Cadences on the Swell, they, being of an episodical nature, (if I may so express myself) and not essential to the subject (especially in giving out Psalm tunes) should be introduced or prepared *loud*, sustaining the Note at the Pause till the Pedal is gradually raised (or the sound diminished) after which the Cadence should be continued *soft* till the close of it, when the sound should be gradually increased again. By this means the Cadence (or Episode) may be kept (as in a Parenthesis) distinct from the main subject. The holding down the 4th below, the Key note, on the Bass of the Choir Organ, during a Cadence has a good effect, as it confines the Cadence to one Key, and thereby prevents unnatural excursions, and also helps to distinguish it from the original subject. As to the peculiar advantage and effect of the Swell in expressing the *Pianos, Fortes, Crescendos*, and *Diminuendos*; the performer must there be left to his own judgment, as no particular rules can be given in extempore performance. He should however consider that the mere see–sawing the Pedal up and down at random, and without meaning, can have no better effect than what is produced by a peal of Bells ringing on a windy day.

For the FULL ORGAN, Choral Music, Fugues, &c. are most proper. Upon the Treble, rapid passages may be executed, but *Arpeggios* and quick passages of accompniment in the Bass, such as are common in Harpsichord lessons, should be avoided, the Bass of the Organ being too powerful for accompaniment. Where however the Bass is made *Principal*, and the Treble only a kind of Thorough Bass to it, Execution for the left hand may have a fine effect. —Chords held down in the Treble, with the Bass moving in Quavers (in the style of many of Corelli's Basses) have a good effect, but Chords in the Bass should seldom or never be used, though a 5th to the Fundamental or Key Note may occasionally be added. —As to Extempore Fugues (a very common style of Play for the full Organ) though I am far from denying that there have been and are now many, who by dint of study and practice, have attained to great proficiency therein; yet most of those commonly played as such, do not appear to me strictly to deserve that appellation, as I cannot help suspecting them (especially where they are coherent and well worked up) to have been studied before, though they may not have been actually written down; and where that is not the case, the air in the Treble when the Bass takes the subject, is seldom superior to that of common Thorough Bass.

*

After knowing the proper method of touching the different Stops, the next thing to be attended to is the proper selection of them for Voluntaries, of which those before the first lesson should be *generally* introduced with the Diapasons, or Swell, after which the Trumpet, Vox–Humane or Bassoon may be used with intermediate passages (for the sake of variety and contrast) on the Swell or Choir Organ. As the real Trumpet is not capable of modulating into different keys (without which music soon becomes tiresome and insipid) Trumpet pieces should therefore be very short; or else, instead of adopting a style for the Trumpet Stop, not natural to that of the Instrument of which it is a professed imitation, a transition had better be made for that purpose to the Flute, (in a minor key) the Swell or Choir Organ, after which a return may be made to the Trumpet.

The Cornet I have said before should be but sparingly used, especially in the Major key, when however it is introduced, I think it should always be succeeded (if but for a few bars) by the Diapasons or Swell, so as for the Voluntary not finally to conclude with the Cornet.

Nothing however produces a more striking and grand effect than a few touches of the full Organ, after gliding for some time on the Swell or Diapasons, after which a return to the soft parts of the Organ is enjoyed with greater relish than before. The judicious Organist will therefore (when he has a fine Organ, and three sets of keys at command) not make it his constant practice to sit thrumming for five or six minutes upon the Diapasons, or confine himself entirely to the Swell or full Organ; but will, if he exceeds two or three Minutes in his Voluntary, occasionally change the Stop; and not give up one very eminent advantage which the Organ possesses above all other Instruments, viz. that of *Contrast* and *Variety*, which are as much the life and soul of Music, as light and shade are of Painting.

I shall conclude my hints on that head, with a caution to young extempore performers against being led away by their ideas into a rapid hurry–scurry style of playing, which is neither proper for the Organ or the Church. In order to make the audience *feel*, they must have *time* so to do, which cannot be the case in a quick succession of fleeting passages, which make no impression, but leave the mind in the same (if not worse) state than it found it in.

As for those little Voluntaries and Interludes between the Verses of the Psalms, I shall only observe that the shorter they are, and more they coincide with the style of the Psalm tune the better. Of course the Cantabile style is proper, though now and then for variety's sake, a neat flourish, or point taken upon the full Organ may not be improper. But long Interludes, in which two or three sets of keys are alternately used, are impertinent to the subject (and mischievous in effect, as they tend only to discompose the devout Psalm singer, instead of merely giving him breath. Nothing also can be more impertinent than those long Shakes *constantly* between each line, without regarding whether there be a pause in the version [versification] or not, on which account it might not be amiss for the Organist to put the word of the Psalms, as well as the Music, before him (if he conveniently can) or at least, to look them over first.

For the concluding Voluntary, the full Organ is generally, and I think with propriety used; in which the Performer (at least after a few bars in a grave style) may be allowed a little more scope for his Fancy and Finger, than during divine service. When however it immediately succeeds an affecting, pathetic discourse, I think the Organist should endeavour, in some measure, to co–operate with the Preacher, by adapting his style accordingly, for which purpose, some soothing gliding play on the Diapasons may be proper, for some little time at least, till those who may wish not to quit every serious idea, with the Church, may have time to go out, after which a return to the full organ may be made; as nothing tends more to drive people out of that frame of mind they may be brought into by a fine and well delivered Discourse, than a light, trivial Anthem; or a rattling, noisy unmeaning Voluntary.

I shall conclude these remarks with a few thoughts on MODULATION, or the art of varying the harmony, in order to prevent the insipid and monotonous effect of continuing too long in one key. As however this is not intended to be a complete Treatise thereon, but only to convey a few hints, just to set the young or inexperienced performer going; I shall take it for granted that he is already acquainted with the common rules of Thorough Bass (and of course with the difference between the Major and Minor keys or modes, and the proper and natural arrangement of Flats or Sharps to each Key) without a previous knowledge of which, Extempore performance ought not to be attempted.

The most obvious and natural modulations are to and from those keys most nearly related to each other; which are those in which a part of the harmony or common Chord of one Key may be continued in, or belong to another; and which require the smallest alteration of Flats and Sharps.

In order the more clearly to explain the manner in which Keys are related to each other, I shall take C major as the *original* or principal Key, whatever therefore is said of that, will also equally apply to any other original *major* Key. Also when I mention the Keys of F, G, and A minor, &c. I only mean those Keys *particularly* or *exclusively*, when C is the Original; so that F always means the 4th of any original *major* Key, G the 5th, and A minor the 6th (or 3d below) &c.

The Key which is in the first or nearest degree related to that of C, is the Key of A minor, which requires no additional flat or sharp (except in ascending to the Key note) and in which, two of the notes of the common Chord of C, (viz. C and E) may also be held or continued.

The next is the Key of E Minor; to the Harmony (or common Chord) of which, the notes E and G belong, as well as to that of C, but which requires the addition of a Sharp, to the F or 2d.

The Keys of F and G major are in the next degree and both equally related to that of C; the former requiring the addition of a Flat to the 4th, and the latter a Sharp to the 7th of the key; and each of them having one Note in it's harmony in common with that of C; the key note of G being 5th to F is equally related to that Key.

The Keys that are in the next degree related, are those in which, though one or even two of the notes of the Chord of C may be also continued, yet a greater alteration of Flats or Sharps must take place, as in changing the Key of C major into C minor, when though the Key note and 5th both continue unaltered, yet the 3d, 6th, and 7th of the minor key must be flattened, so that to change any major Key into the minor requires the addition of three Flats. —In the *same* degree may be reckoned the Key of G minor; for though it may seem to be not so nearly related, as having the note G only in common with both that Key and C, yet as only two additional Flats are required, that brings them more nearly related again.

Next may be reckoned the modulation from C into the Key of A major, with three Sharps; or into E major with four, both of which Keys are only related to that of C, by means of the Note E.

The *last* Key I shall mention as related to C, by means of a part of the Harmony being common to both, is that of F minor, with four Flats, to which the note C is 5th. —For though a transition may be made from C immediately into E♭ (by continuing the G) or into A♭ (by continuing the C) or into C♯ minor (by continuing the E) yet as in each of these, *both* the notes of their succeeding Chord, except that held or continued must be flattened or sharpened, the transition will be too abrupt, and the effect bad of course.

Though the foregoing are all the Keys that may be said to be *related* to the Key of C, yet it is allowable to pass from one common Chord to another, not related to it, if not too far distant from it, and the transition be easy, as from C into B♭ or D minor, and *vice versa*, but this must be done by a contrary motion of the hand, to avoid the effects of consecutive 5ths and 8ths.

As every change of the Key therefore (except from the major Key to the minor Key of the 3d below, and *vice versa*) requires a different arrangement of the Flats and Sharps, the following Rules may next be learnt.

1st, In modulating from any *Major* Key, into that of the 5th *above*, or into the *minor* Key of the *Note above*, a *Sharp* must be applied to the 4th of the original Key.

2d, In passing from any *Major* Key into that of the 5th *below*, or into the *minor* Key of the *Note above*, a *Flat* must be applied to the 7th of the original Key.

3d, a transition from any *Minor* Key to that of the 5th *below*, or into the Major Key of the 3d below, requires the addition of a *Flat* to the 2d of the original Key.

4th, Changing the Major Key into the Minor, requires the addition of three *Flats*, and *vice versa* three *Sharps*.

5th, Modulating from any Major Key into the Minor Key of the 3d *below*, and *vice versa*, requires *no alteration* of the Flats and Sharps.

These Rules, which are *general*, and will serve for every Key, are all that I think necessary to burden the memory of the Pupil with, as in modulating into the more distant Keys, the best way is to consider the particular arrangement of the Key he iks going into; for instance, should he enter the Key of A major, he will of course know three Sharps to be necessary (as naturally belong to that Key) whatever Key he may modulate from.

It may here be proper to mention to the *young* Performer, that the *addition* of Sharps and *Suppression* of *Flats* and (*vice versa*) produce exactly the same *effect*, so that where I have directed the one to be added, it may be necessary in many Keys to take off the other by means of *Naturals*, as no note already sharp can at once be made flat, and *vice versa*. For instance, the 4th Rule directs three Flats to be added in changing the mode from Major to Minor, which is strictly right in the Key of C, F and B♭ Major, but should the Major Key be E, with four *Sharps*, then the Minor must be formed by taking off the three *last* (in the order they naturally arise) and leaving on only that on the 2nd Key. Also, in changing G with one Sharp into the Minor Key; that Sharp must first be taken off, and then two Flats added.

The Pupil may now try his skill according to the following plan. —Supposing the Key he sets out from to be C major, he may by adding F♯ according to the 1st Rule, pass into that of G, where the first Close may be made, after which he may proceed to that of E minor, without any additional Flat or Sharp, (*Rule 5.*) From hence he may by suppressing the sharp (*Rule 3*) which is tantamount to adding a Flat, pass into A minor, and from thence, by adding B♭ (*Rule 3.*) go into F major, from whence a transition is easily made to the original Key, by dropping the Flat, which is the same as adding a sharp. (*Rule 1.*) He will then have passed through two major and as many minor Keys, besides the Key he begins and ends with; which is as great a variety of modulation as need be, for a single strain, especially if it be not very long. Should he however wish to proceed farther, he may afterwards change the mode from C *major* to C *minor*, by adding three Flats (*Rule 4.*) from whence he may proceed to E♭ major without further alteration, (*Rule 5.*) and from thence to B♭ major, by suppressing a Flat (*Rule 1.*) after which he may modulate into G minor, and from thence (after changing to G major) to the original Key of C major. —After this trial, he may for the sake of perfecting himself in the foregoing Rules, make B♭ (with two Flats) or D (in two Sharps) his original Key, and practice the same modulation, except changing the *former* for the Keys into the *minor* Key (by the 4th *Rule*) B♭ minor requiring five Flats, which is too imperfect as well as difficult a Key for the Organ, wherefore he had better make a finish at the first return to the original Key.

This track is however by no means reccommended as the best, or most natural that might be contrived, as that entirely depends on the fancy of the Performer, who may begin with modulating into the 5th *below*, which though not so common, is yet quite as natural as the 5th above; or at once into the Minor Key, or return to that of the original as often as he pleases.

He may also begin with the Minor Key, or make that his original, and with more propriety than the Major when he means his style to be particularly grave and plaintive. When this is the case, the modulation is usually first into the Major Key of the third above (according to the 5th Rule) after which it may be pursued more or less according to the foregoing track, returning however to the original key at last, which indeed must always be the case, whether such original be either Major or Minor. Also, by passing through several Keys related to each other, (taking care however so to mix and blend the two Modes, as not to use more than two Major or Minor Keys successively) he may at length extend his modulation into those Keys that are remote from the original; though it may not be prudent top venture so far in public till after much practice, lest he should find it difficult to get back again.

It may here also be proper to caution the Performer against entering those Keys which are peculiarly imperfect on the Organ, as into the Major Keys of B♭, F♯, and C♯, and the Minor keys of E♭, B♭, and F, to all which the 3ds are bad, or into A flat Major, to which the 3d and 5th are both very imperfect. On this account it is better to modulate from E with four Sharps into the Key of A instead of that of B♭; and from E♭ into B avoiding the common Chord of A♭ as much as possible, especially upon the full Organ.

Time however and Practice will render these natural and easy Modulations (which are all founded on the harmony of *Common Chord*) quite familiar to the Pupil, who may thereby gain a sufficient insight to the nature of the Modulation in general, to enable him to proceed, by ingenious use of *Discords*, to the more obstruse kinds of Modulation, avoiding Closes, and resolving one Discord into another (by continuing the 7th or 9th) which may be called continued or *incessant* Modulation, but which is sometimes carried too far, as if the performer was merely trying how often he could disappoint the Ear: for though to excel in Modulation be one essential requisite, yet it should be considered that it is *but one*, the several others herein before discussed being also necessary to form a good and *complete Style*. He therefore who would aspire to the character of a capital Extempore player, should endeavour to unite them all; and if to the proper *Touch* of the Organ, (with a competent degree of execution) a judicious *variation of the Stop*, and attention to the *proper Style of each*, with *ingenious* but not unnatural *modulation*, he also adds *Fancy* and *Invention*: he possesses every requisite I can conceive to be necessary to an Organ Player of the first Class.

After all, I should advise the young Practitioner by no means to be satisfied with these or any other Hints, or Treatise, he may meet with on the subject, but to take every opportunity of hearing the best Masters, and Performers of most acknowledged excellence on the Organ, from which more may be learned as to Modulation and Style in general, than from any Treatise whatsoever.

*

Select bibliography

Note: this bibliography does not include references given in endnotes, nor those to individual organs noted in chapters 3 and 5, nor does it include general matters pertaining to modern organ-building.

Adam, R. and J., *The Works in Architecture* (3 vols., London, 1778–1822)

Audsley, G. A., *Organ Stops and their Artistic Registration* (New York, 1921)

Barker, F. and Jackson P., *London, 2000 Years of a City and its People* (Cassell 1974/Macmillan 1983)

Baumann, M., *Schaffhausen Stadt und Landschaft* (Schaffhausen, 1975)

Bédos de Celles, Dom F., *L'Art du Facteur D'Orgues* (4 vols., Paris 1766–78; various modern versions)

Bedwell, G. G., *The Evolution of the Organ* (London, 1907)

Brackett, O., *Thomas Chippendale: A Study of His Life, Work and Influence* (London, 1924)

Brenninger, G., *Der Straibinger Orgelbauer Christoph Egedacher* (Munich, 1976)

Brown, D., 'Identifying Snetzler Chamber Organs', *The Organ Yearbook 5* (1974)

Burney, C., *An Account of the Musical Performances ... in Commemoration of Handel* (London, 1785, reprinted Frits Knuf, 1964)

Cobb, G., *The Old Churches of London* (Batsford, 1941–2)

Cumming, A., *A Sketch of the Properties of the Machine Organ ...* (E. and H. Hodson, London, 1812)

Dawe, D., *Organists of the City of London 1666–1850* (Dawe, 1983)

Freeman, A., *Father Smith ...* (London, 1926; revised edition by John Rowntree, Positif Press, 1977)

Helmholtz, H., *On the Sensation of Tone* (reprinted Dover Publications, 1954)

Hill, A. G., *The Organs and Organ Cases of the Middle Ages and Renaissance* (London, 1883; 2/1891, reprinted Frits Knuf, 1975)

Hubbard, F., *Three Centuries of Harpsichord Making* (New York, 1965)

Lees-Milne, J., *The Age of Adam* (London, 1947)

Peeters, F. and Vente, M. A., *The Organ and its Music in The Netherlands 1500–1800* (Antwerp, 1971)

Rees, A (ed.), *The New Cyclopaedia* (45 vols., London, 1802–1820)

Routh, F., *Early English Organ Music from the Middle Ages to 1837* (London, 1973)

Routley, E., *The Musical Wesleys* (London, 1968)

Williams, C. F. A., *The Story of the Organ* (London, 1903)

Williams, P. F., 'The Organ', *The New Grove Dictionary of Musical Instruments* (Macmillan, 1986; and separate off-print 1988, with Barbara Owen)

Williams, P. F., *A New History of the Organ from the Greeks to the Present Day* (Faber, 1980)

Gazetteer of owners and places

The following lists all known locations and owners of Snetzler's organs. Present or last–known locations are printed in **bold** type; the **bold figures** refer to the 'catalogue' numbers in chapter 3.

Aberdeen Musical Society **15**
Acton Place, Long Melford **20**
All Saints' convent, Oxford 53
Alphamstone, Suffolk, parish church 96
Andover, Hampshire, the parish church **85**
Arbourthorne, St Paul's church **21**
Arlecdon, St Michael's church 27
Armagh cathedral **68**
Ashford, Kent, 'Mersham–le–Hatch' 17
Ashley House, Frodsham, Cheshire **75**
Ashman, E. (Bath) [?] **106**
Assembly Rooms, York **25**
Banbury, Oxfordshire, the Unitarian church **107a**
Barber Institute, Birmingham University 29
Bard, Dr Samuel (New York) **52**
Bard/Johnstone family (New York) **52**
Barford Hill House, Warwickshire **42**
Barrington, Lord (Durham) 105
Bath, Brook Street, St Margaret's chapel 89
Bath, E. Ashman [?] **106**
Bath, Holborne of Menstrie Museum 76
Bath, the Octagon Chapel **76**
Bedford, Duke of [?] **20**
Bedford, Duke of (Woburn?) **32**
Belfast, Clarence Place hall 102
Belfast, Donegall Square, the Methodist church 68
Belfast, St Anne's church **102**
Belfast, the cathedral **102**
Beverley, Yorkshire, the minster 79
Bibby, Bernard **26**
Bird, Revd J. J. S. (Colerne) **89**
Birkbeck, W. J. **47**
Birmingham, Great Barr, R. C. church **60**
Birmingham, St Martin's church 91
Birmingham, St Philip's church 92

*

Technical concordance to chapters 2 and 4

This index is designed to enable specific technical matters, chiefly the individual stops and action parts of Snetzler's organs, to be found where they are discussed in the course of the two chapters chiefly devoted to these topics.

General index of people, places and events

Note: a search of the Gazetteer (pp. 328–335) will more readily find the 'catalogue' entry for a specific organ by Snetzler, listed under all its known locations; technical matters are dealt with in the Technical Concordance (pp. 336-340).

Entries marked with asterisks (*) refer to events in Snetzler's life.